Early
Literacy
Instruction

◆◆◆

Early Literacy Instruction

◆◆◆

Elfrieda H. Hiebert
University of Michigan

Taffy E. Raphael
Michigan State University

Harcourt Brace College Publishers

Fort Worth   Philadelphia   San Diego   New York   Orlando   Austin   San Antonio

Toronto   Montreal   London   Sydney   Tokyo

Publisher Christopher P. Klein
Acquisitions Editor Jo-Anne Weaver
Product Manager Don Grainger
Developmental Editor Tracy Napper
Project Editor Tamara Neff Vardy
Production Manager Cynthia Young
Art Director Carol Kincaid

Requests for permission to make copies of any part of the work should be mailed to: Permissions Department, Harcourt Brace & Company, 6277 Sea Harbor Drive, Orlando, Florida 32887-6777.

Address editorial correspondence to:
Harcourt Brace College Publishers
301 Commerce Street, Suite 3700
Fort Worth, TX 76102

Address orders to:
Harcourt Brace & Company
6277 Sea Harbor Drive
Orlando, FL 32887-6777
1-800-782-4479

Web site address:
http://www.hbcollege.com

Harcourt Brace may provide complimentary instructional aids and supplements or supplement packages to those adopters qualified under our adoption policy. Please contact your sales representative for more information. If as an adopter or potential user you receive supplements you do not need, please return them to your sales representative or send them to:

Attn: Returns Department
Troy Warehouse
465 South Lincoln Drive
Troy, MO 63379

Printed in the United States of America

ISBN: 0-03-044972-3

Library of Congress Catalog Card Number: 96-79967

7 8 9 0 1 2 3 4 5 6   016   9 8 7 6 5 4 3 2 1

This book is dedicated to
Frieda Töws Siegfried
whose courage and commitment
will be remembered always.

Preface

One of the most challenging areas facing literacy educators today is introducing young children to the joys and purposes as well as the underlying skills and strategies related to literacy. In order to encourage lifelong literacy while simultaneously developing basic understandings of letters and sounds, how books work, and ways that literacy exists and can be used in everyday life is one of the more hotly debated topics in our field. *Early Literacy Instruction* is intended for teachers, both preservice and inservice, and teacher educators who wish to expand their knowledge about teaching young children to read and write. We have written the book so that educators with a variety of experiences—from classroom teachers to those working in resource rooms to the family support system—can build and expand their knowledge about early literacy instruction.

The comprehensive scope of the book encompasses standards for early literacy instruction, instructional strategies, alternative assessment procedures, strategies for making program connections, and ways to integrate children's home literacy into the classroom. This engaging, user-friendly text makes the ideas readily accessible to those interested in helping young children learn to read. We begin each chapter with a set of vignettes, which are windows into the thinking, reading, and writing of young children before they engage the text. These vignettes provide real-world examples of children entering print worlds. The vignettes that begin each chapter have been carefully chosen to emphasize key points in the chapter—in effect, the vignettes are the text equivalent of videotapes, brief plays, or photo albums that illustrate the principles and key points within the chapter. Through the vignettes, the instructional ideas come alive.

The vignettes instantiate the second key feature of the book—an overarching set of principles grounded in socio-cultural theory as applied to the literacy education of young children. We detail a coherent theory about what literacy is and how children learn literacy. Each chapter focuses on a specific aspect of how teachers create classrooms that immerse children in theoretically-sound, meaningful literacy through events, lessons, and activities.

We present a balanced perspective of early literacy instruction. We balance information about theory and practice. We balance between and among the language arts, between holistic literacy activity and specific skill development, and we balance between a school-to-home and a home-to-school connection. For both beginning and experienced teachers, we provide specific ideas and tools to support their teaching. These ideas and tools include book lists, assessment tools, sample lesson plans, word lists relevant to different activities, and activities for writing in library and play centers.

This perspective is especially appropriate for classrooms with high concentrations of low-income children, because of its emphasis on reasons for reading and writing as well as on the foundational skills of reading and writing. From the kindergartner, who is eager to read but doesn't recognize any words, to the second grader, who is anxious to read more chapter books in third grade, literacy learning over the early childhood period covers a gamut of skills and understandings. The overviews and chapter summaries make the content of each chapter easy to identify by the reader and provide quick access to specific information included in the chapter.

This book is designed for teachers, parents, and teacher educators who are looking for an engaging and accessible text that focuses on the topic of learning to read. In today's climate, a book that supports readers' theoretical understanding and provides practical knowledge can be extremely valuable. Early literacy instruction is one of the most fundamental goals of schooling—one that sets the stage for our students' lifelong learning and success. We hope that this volume can provide an important contribution to the search for ever-improving ways to meet the needs of our diverse, young learners.

This volume would not have been possible without the help from a number of people, shaping our initial conceptions of the book and supporting the development of the text. We gratefully acknowledge the children and teachers in the Right Start in Reading Project and the Early Literacy Project. We have learned much about learning to read and creating classrooms where children learn to read by being members of these classrooms and of these teacher communities.

The content of this book also benefits immeasurably from the questions our students asked as we used this book in teacher education courses at the University of Colorado, Boulder, the University of Michigan, and Michigan State University. The reviewers of earlier versions of this manuscript—Sheila Cohen, SUNY Cortland; Jill Fitzgerald, University of North Carolina, Chapel Hill; Lea McGee, Boston College; and Bill Teale, the University of Illinois at Chicago—also raised questions and proposed solutions that aided us immensely in achieving our goal of a comprehensive and accessible book for a range of educators. The patience of Karen Skalitzky, Katrina Saltonstall, and Lori Levin, who conducted endless searches for children's books and other resources, meant that our vision of a rich set of examples and resources became a reality.

Without the support of Jo-Anne Weaver at Harcourt Brace, the Harcourt Brace Literacy Series and this book would not have been accomplished. We are confident that Jo-Anne did not anticipate the length of our relationship when we contacted her with the idea of the series, including this book. Tracy

Napper, our developmental editor at Harcourt Brace, has been patient and encouraging, which are dispositions that she had many occasions to abandon but, thankfully, did not. For their vision, good humor, and consistent encouragement, we are truly grateful to Jo-Anne and Tracy.

Finally, for their support in so many ways, we thank Charley Fisher and Jim Gavelek. They can now watch the summer sunsets on Beaver Island without the background of our discussions about "the books". . . at least until the next edition.

EHH/TER
Ann Arbor

Contents

section One

A Perspective for Early Literacy Instruction

chapter 1

Beginning the Process: Understanding the Perspective

On the first day of school, Christopher, a kindergartner, responded to the question of what he was going to learn in school with the comment, "To read! So that I can say the words in case my mom forgets how."

(Boulder *Daily Camera,* August 26, 1987)

In sitting on a plane beside a four-year-old who was holding a copy of "Little Red Riding Hood," a literacy educator commented to the child, "Oh, I see you're reading 'Little Red Riding Hood'." "I'm not reading it," the child stated emphatically. "I'm just looking at the pictures. I'll learn to read when I'm in kindergarten." Later, as the educator saw the child mouthing some of the words, she commented, "I thought you couldn't read." The child replied, "I wasn't reading! I was just remembering." Still later, after observing the child's turning back a page to look more carefully at the text, the educator said, "I caught you. You were too reading." To this the child responded, "Okay! So probably I did read just that one little part!"

(Harste & Burke, 1993, pp. v–vi)

The kindergartner in the first vignette expresses a wish of many young children when they enter school—to learn to read and write. Young children typically are enthralled by books and want to learn to read and write. As the actions and comments of the four-year-old in the second vignette demonstrate, many young children know a great deal about reading and writing, including the ability to read "just that one little part" of familiar books.

As teachers of young children, our task is to build on what children already know about reading and writing and to turn their expectations about becoming readers and writers into reality. We recognize that this does not happen either magically or instantly. Reading and writing are acquired through the hard work of children, their teachers, and their families. The goal of this book is to provide teachers with insights to help them create contexts where their students can thrive as readers and writers.

The building blocks that create the foundation for such contexts are teachers' understandings about how children learn to read and what literacy is. These understandings determine the experiences that teachers initiate and the interactions they have with children. For example, in a kindergarten classroom that values children's existing literacy knowledge, children are invited to bring familiar books to share with their teacher and classmates. Accomplishments with familiar books such as those of the child in the second vignette are acknowledged and referred to frequently as new reading and writing tasks are introduced. If the first day of school finds kindergartners taking home a picture with an accompanying label that they can share with family members, they will soon see themselves as readers. In contrast, the wish of kindergartners such as Christopher in the first vignette may soon be extinguished in classrooms where literacy is equated with matching letters or shapes on worksheets, or engaging in other decontextualized skill activities.

Because teachers' actions in classrooms emanate from underlying views of literacy and literacy acquisition, we devote the first section of this book to developing the foundation for a particular view of literacy and its acquisition—the emergent literacy perspective elaborated by social constructivist theory. The theoretical foundation underlies the remaining two sections of the book: the presentation of instructional experiences, materials, and assessments in Section II and the liaisons to other school and community contexts in Section III.

In this chapter, we contrast two prominent views of literacy and how it is acquired, views that dominate today's classrooms: reading readiness and emergent literacy. However, because we believe a unified view creates a solid and manageable foundation for creating desirable classroom contexts, we elaborate one of the perspectives—emergent literacy—as the basis for our book. This perspective provides a strong conceptual and practical foundation for understanding both how children become literate and the knowledge they must acquire.

Views of Literacy Acquisition

Philosophies about the best way to introduce novices to literacy are as old as literacy itself (Venezky, 1984). In 20th-century America, issues surrounding the instruction of reading have loomed larger than ever, mostly because of the central role that literacy serves individuals and society in a technological age. In the last survey, conducted over a decade ago, well over 165 beginning reading programs were identified (Aukerman, 1984). In each of these programs, assumptions are made about what children need to learn to become literate and how this learning can be fostered most effectively in classrooms. Were we to do an analysis of the assumptions of all of these programs, the majority would indicate a grounding in one of two theories about children's literacy acquisition: (a) the reading readiness view and (b) the emergent literacy view.

The reading readiness and emergent literacy theories present contrasting views on how children become literate, what is learned in becoming literate, and the contexts that support literacy learning. The reading readiness view is best characterized as "bottom-up." Learning begins with the discrete skills of letter naming and facility in matching sounds and letters, moves to word recognition, and, once sufficient skills have accumulated, results in comprehension. In the emergent literacy perspective, literacy processes are seen to be acquired interactively. As children participate in read-aloud and other literacy activities with adults, they comprehend the functions and meanings of literacy. Within these contexts, children are guided by their interest and the support of adults in learning about the features of text. Because these views manifest themselves quite differently in instruction, materials, and tests, the choice of one view or another by teachers should be thoughtful and based on an understanding of what these views imply about the nature of learning and teaching.

Reading Readiness

According to the reading readiness perspective, there is an appropriate mental age at which children can learn to read. The proclivity for reading will blossom when children have reached this particular maturational point. Until children have reached this point, maturationists regard involvement in reading activities as futile or even deleterious. According to this argument, children could acquire faulty strategies or poor dispositions toward reading because of their lack of maturation. When children attain the maturational stage associated with reading, the belief is that children will learn to read with ease regardless of the kind or quality of instruction.

From this perspective, maturation for reading is no different from that for other physical proficiencies, such as walking. Other than time, the only factor that could hasten or slow down children's readiness is intelligence. That is, as a result of his or her intelligence, a child might arrive at the maturational stage for reading sooner or later than his or her chronological peers. Because the maturationists viewed intelligence as genetically predisposed, teachers had little function other than to wait for children to arrive at the appropriate maturational stage for reading. Just as the instructional program is not a factor in determining children's success once they achieve the appropriate mental age, neither will environmental activities hasten children's readiness for reading.

This theory of maturation was advocated by psychologist G. Stanley Hall (1904) at the beginning of the 20th century. Through the writing of Hall's students, Arnold Gesell (1925) most notably, this theory became popular among educators during the 1920s and 1930s. A pressing task became the identification of the ideal age for children to learn to read. A quickly accepted answer was Morphett and Washburne's 1931 finding that the children who performed best in the reading program of the Winnetka, Illinois, schools had a mental age of 6 years, 6 months. Questions were not asked about the particulars of the reading program, even though Winnetka had a reputation for innovative methods. Mental age soon became equated with chronological age, an erroneous assumption about the intelligence-testing tradition from which the mental age metric comes. The official point for reading instruction became midway into first grade, when students' average age is six and a half years.

Once the six-and-a-half-year age was widely accepted as the ideal time for initiating children into reading, educators were faced with a logistical problem. If instruction needed to be delayed to await the maturational process, a set of activities was required for the first half of first grade when children were not yet at the appropriate mental age of 6 years, 6 months. These activities would need to be ones that would not interfere with children's participation and success in reading once they were ready. Consequently, those activities that came to be called "reading readiness" did not involve reading directly. Instead, they related to dimensions that might be prerequisites for reading but which did not involve reading itself, such as visual discrimination and auditory association. Such activities included discriminating among geometric shapes or objects (e.g., different size rabbits or cars), and eventually discriminating among different individual letters or letter strings. Auditory association exercises included asking children to identify pictures of objects that began with the same sound.

By the end of the 1930s, the structure of the reading readiness perspective was in place despite some critical voices of educators who advocated other views (e.g., Gates, 1937). The age of 6 years, 6 months had been identified as the ideal maturational point for learning to read. Reading instruction was preceded by a period of reading readiness activities that did not directly involve books or reading. The reading readiness view continued to be the dominant philosophy held by teachers well into the early 1980s, according to Durkin's (1987) interviews and observations. Hiebert and Papierz (1990) examined kindergarten and first-grade materials of the prominent reading textbook programs that were approved for use in Texas schools from 1987 through 1992. They found a heavy emphasis on reading readiness activities. At the kindergarten level, visual, shape, and color discrimination exercises dominated the workbooks. In the first level of grade-one materials, auditory discrimination activities were most prominent. No program included illustrated literature that teachers might read aloud, nor were there books for children to explore. Instead, children's materials at these beginning levels consisted entirely of workbooks.

In response to the mandates of the 1989 California textbook adoption (California Language Arts/English Framework Committee, 1987), enlarged or big books have been integrated into kindergarten programs (Hoffman, McCarthey, Abbott, Christian, Corman, Curry, Dressman, Elliott, Matherne, & Stahle, 1994; Morrow & Parse, 1990). However, the presence of big books in textbook programs does not signal an end to the readiness tradition.

Teachers' guides often contain recommendations for exercises that emanate from the reading readiness perspective, and workbooks or worksheets related to the books often are patterned after readiness assumptions.

The influence of the reading readiness perspective extends beyond materials or instructional guides. Tests based upon the reading readiness construct dominate the assessments given to young children. In many states and districts, these tests are a primary source of information that kindergarten and first-grade teachers use in recommending whether children should enter school or be retained in kindergarten or first grade if they are perceived to be "unready" (Shepard & Graue, 1992). The numbers recommended for retention based on such information are high in some districts and states (see, e.g., School Readiness Task Force, 1988). Evaluations show, however, that these tests fall far short of the mark in predicting children's success in first grade. In studying the practices of nine school districts, Ellwein, Walsh, Eads, and Miller (1991) found that the reading readiness tests used for decisions about school entry or kindergarten retention were accurate in verifying a child's success in first grade *less than half* the time (i.e., less accurate than a coin toss). However, the majority of districts continued to use the tests as the basis for recommendations to parents and for teachers' decision making. Such examples of reading readiness test use reflect how entrenched the reading readiness perspective has been in early childhood contexts in American schools.

Emergent Literacy

The phrase "emergent literacy" came into currency in the mid-1980s with the publication of Teale and Sulzby's (1986) edited volume. However, the construct the label represents had been present for several decades, with origins dating back even earlier (see, e.g., Dewey, 1938). The emergent literacy perspective has achieved widespread recognition through the research within cognitive psychology and linguistics during the 1960s that raised questions about the reading readiness concept. Further, mandates from large states (e.g., Texas Proclamation, 1990) required beginning reading materials to reflect an emergent literacy perspective, furthering its recognition.

In this section, we describe three expressions of the emergent literacy perspective during the past several decades: (a) learning to read as natural, (b) the Piagetian view of literacy acquisition, and (c) emergent literacy elaborated by a social constructivist perspective. Although the perspectives can be distinguished from one another, all share the essence conveyed by the term "emergent literacy." The "emergent" part of the label means that literacy is seen as developing over an extended period of time. In home and community contexts, young children see written language on signs, labels, and television. Even when adults do not consciously teach children to read and write, children create hypotheses about the uses, meanings, and forms of written language. The use of "literacy"—rather than reading or writing—has an important implication as well. Not only is writing viewed as important in its own right but it interrelates with reading. The term literacy also conveys the grounding of learning in language. As a language process, literacy builds on what children already know—and young children know a great deal about language.

The first manifestation of emergent literacy can be traced to a new theory in linguistics—that young children are predisposed to learn language (Chomsky, 1965). The second view of emergent literacy—as a set of cognitive and linguistic processes—reflects the popularity of Piaget's (1962, 1977) theory that described young children as active cognitive processors. A third view of emergent literacy, based on social-constructivist theory, emphasizes the mechanism of social interaction in children's literacy learning. Most teachers identify one or both of the first two perspectives—learning to read as natural and the cognitive and linguistic processing of literacy acquisition—when asked to describe emergent literacy. We present these two variations before discussing the contributions of the social-constructivist perspective.

Learning to Read as Natural.   The fundamental principle underlying this view of literacy acquisition is that children learn to read and write in the same way that they learn to talk and listen. Children successfully acquire oral language at an early age in the busy contexts of homes and communities such as grocery shopping, getting dressed, and taking a bath. This learning has been described as natural because children become adept at speaking and listening without a single lesson on elements of speech. This perspective built on Chomsky's (1965) theory that all children are born "wired" for the universals of linguistic structure. According to Chomsky, evidence for this innate disposition to learn language comes from the shared systems of semantics, syntax, and phonology across languages, which argue for shared physical and mental characteristics of human beings. Without a language acquisition device, Chomsky reasoned, the task of extracting the rules of these underlying systems would be nearly impossible for young children because of the chaotic nature of daily talk.

This theory of an innate disposition to develop rules about language systems was applied to literacy learning as well. Goodman and Goodman (1979), in their article "Learning to Read Is Natural," which gave this perspective its label, wrote "We see both oral and written language as learned in the same way. In neither case is the user required by the nature of the task to have a high level of conscious awareness of the units and system. In both cases control over language comes through the preoccupation with communicative use" (p. 139).

Drawing heavily on anecdotes of parents and reports of the literacy learning of preschool readers, Goodman and Goodman (1979) characterized participation in daily literacy events as paramount to preschool readers' learning. Amidst the "noise" of home environments, children watched, listened, and asked questions in storybook reading with adults, talked about words on clothes while adults assisted them in dressing, or scribbled messages to other family members. In the process, these children became conventional readers and writers.

Substantiation that young children acquired the rules or conventions of the systems of written language in these natural settings came from linguists such as Read (1971, 1975). After examining the writing of young children, Read described the spellings in these productions as showing evidence of "invented spelling" systems. These young children had developed ways of systematically representing sounds with symbols as they wrote messages. The rules that governed older preschoolers' spellings were closer to the speech-symbol representations that adults use than those of younger preschoolers. But the representations of younger preschoolers showed consistent application of a particular set of rules. The presence and evolution of these invented spelling systems, Read suggested, reflect students' natural development of their knowledge of the written language system.

Early literacy acquisition from the learning-to-read-as-natural perspective occurs when children are immersed in contexts where they can use written language to communicate. When children's home environments have not held sufficient opportunities for them to become proficient readers and writers, the responsibility lies within schools to create such contexts. The learning-to-read-as-natural perspective came to describe the underlying view of literacy acquisition in the whole language movement, a philosophy that has been influential in American literacy instruction over the past decade (Goodman, 1986, 1989). The major roles of teachers in primary-level, whole language classrooms were to make available many meaningful literacy experiences for students and to converse and conference with students (see, e.g., Edelsky, Altwerger, & Flores, 1990; Weaver, Stephens, & Vance, 1990).

The Piagetian View of Emergent Literacy.   The second strand of the emergent literacy perspective drew as heavily from Piaget's (1962, 1977) theory of cognitive development as it did from work on language development. Piaget's influence is reflected in an emphasis on cognitive structures and processes as the source for literacy acquisition (see Clay, 1966, 1972, 1991; Ferreiro & Teboroskey, 1982; Sulzby & Teale, 1986, 1991). Researchers such as Clay, Ferreiro, and Sulzby and Teale did not ignore the underlying linguistic foundation of literacy learning, but they were particularly intrigued by Piaget's concepts, such as assimilation and accommodation, the two primary mechanisms of development, as well as his suggestion of developmental stages.

From this perspective, the writing system becomes an object of knowledge for young children. They construct hypotheses to explain the nature and uses of writing. These constructions are unique, not simply replicas of what adults have attempted to teach them or what they have seen. For example, a child may produce a wavy line and state emphatically that the line says "I love Grandma" even though the child has never seen anyone "read" a wavy line. Because of underlying cognitive structures and processes and the nature of the representational system of writing, the constructions

children of (handwritten margin note)
known stages (handwritten margin note)

of different children share a developmental progression as they make sense of the forms and rules of writing. Although the hypotheses of children are not precisely the same, the issues that puzzle children and the processes that they bring to bear on these issues are similar. Children's hypotheses about written language follow a general progression in their consistency and logic that can be characterized as stages (Teale, 1986). The hypotheses about written language of children at a developmental level will deal with similar dilemmas and illustrate the application of similar cognitive processes.

Children use processes of assimilation or accommodation as they attempt to make sense of writing. *Assimilation* refers to the transformation of new knowledge into the known or familiar (Yussen & Santrock, 1978). When the new knowledge is sufficiently discrepant or the tried and true strategies do not mesh with the new, children may modify their existing modes of thinking to accommodate the new knowledge (Yussen & Santrock, 1978). This accommodation may be slight initially as children attempt to restructure their understanding of the writing system. When the information is discrepant enough and the familiar structures inadequate, children go through an "aha" experience as they realize new rules or ways of constructing rules.

example of a girl assimilating and having trouble (handwritten margin note)

An illustration of assimilation and accommodation of information about the writing system comes from Ferreiro (1986). In her longitudinal project in Mexico, individual interviews between an adult and a child occurred every several months, beginning at two years of age and extending to six years. These interviews centered around such tasks as writing names or familiar words. By age 4 years, 8 months, Mariana—one of Ferreiro's case study children—had learned to write and read her name. In the interview that occurred at this point, Mariana was asked to write *oso* (bear), which she had learned to write at school. She dutifully wrote it—OSO. Then the interviewer asked her if more or fewer letters would be needed to write *hormiguita* (little ant). Mariana promptly answered: "Less! Because it is very small! Only two" (Ferreiro, 1986, p. 46). Her writing of the word *hormiguita* illustrates assimilation in that she used the word she knew which represented a big animal—*oso* (bear)—and produced SO. When Mariana read "Hor-mi" as she pointed to SO, she added the letter "s" to the end (SOS), saying "ga" when she pointed to that letter. When reminded by the interviewer that the word was *hormiguita*, Mariana added yet another letter (SOSE) and read "Hor-mi-gui-ta." At this point, however, she compared her text of "SOSE" with the text of "OSO" for bear. She declared that neither one was right. She realized a conflict that she was unable to resolve at this developmental stage. The changes or accommodations that she had made to her spelling of *hormiguita* were based on the hypothesis that every unit of sound (i.e., a syllable) should be represented by a symbol. When this hypothesis resulted in a representation for *hormiguita* that was substantially longer than *oso,* there was a conflict with Mariana's earlier hypothesis that the physical size of the object and its written representation should correlate. Six months later, Mariana's writing showed that the hypothesis regarding a correlation between the quantitative size of objects and symbols had been dropped. She had changed her view of the writing system to accommodate the idea that particular sounds are consistently represented by particular letters, stopping to correct herself when she made the sound "ri" while pointing to the letter "a" in her name.

As this illustration of Mariana illustrates, children's cognitive processes are in the foreground in this perspective of emergent literacy. Occasions for interacting with adults and other children in literacy activities are not disregarded or viewed as irrelevant. Ferreiro includes descriptions of Mariana's home and preschool literacy experiences in the case study. These activities are not studied, however, for insight into the conversations or events that supported the changes in Mariana's hypotheses. The emphasis within this perspective is on the manner in which children transform information from their environments. In Ferreiro's (1986) words, ". . . social practices as well as social information are not received passively by children. When they try to understand, they necessarily transform the content received. Moreover, in order to register the information, they transform it. This is the deep meaning of the notion of assimilation that Piaget has put at the core of his theory" (p. 16).

Emergent Literacy Elaborated by Social-Constructivist Theory.   Scholars from the learning-to-read-as-natural and the Piagetian perspectives of emergent literacy directed attention to young children's knolwedge about literacy. As the directives for textbook adoptions in major states indicated (California Language Arts/English Framework Committee, 1987; Texas Education Agency, 1990), these emergent literacy views soon became integrated into policies and materials. Such widespread implementation of emergent literacy perspectives raised numerous questions about the translation of this theory into practice. Would children who had not been immersed previously in literate environments become highly literate through natural language activities in classrooms? Were Piagetian stages something that teachers needed to await as a function of children's cognitive growth or were they influenced by instruction?

Almost all of the emergent literacy research on young children's strategies and knowledge had been based on youngsters from middle-class homes or preschools. For example, Read's (1971, 1975) conclusions on the emergence of invented spelling systems had been based on children who attended Montessori preschools in which children are taught early about correspondences between sounds and letters (Montessori, 1964). Children who have had frequent opportunities to apply their sound-letter knowledge with wooden blocks and other materials might be expected to approach the task of spelling words with ease and confidence, as Read's subjects did.

Older preschoolers' invented spellings understandably would be more sophisticated than younger preschoolers', but children's capabilities at invented spelling and other aspects of literacy required constructs beyond linguistic and cognitive processing. Specifically, what were the conversations that directed the cognitive processes of a child such as Mariana to new features of literacy? The social-constructivist (also referred to as sociohistorical) theory of Vygotsky (1962, 1978, 1987), directs attention to the interaction around books in children's homes. With the benefit of Vygotsky's insights into how children learn, we can revisit the studies of young children with extensive emergent literacy to glean from these contexts principles that educators might apply to classrooms for children with limited prior literacy experience.

In particular, Vygotsky's theory directs attention to the role of adults in children's learning of scientific concepts, such as literacy. Literacy is one of the higher-level tools of a culture, according to Vygotsky, not a cognitive process that develops naturally in all humans. Unlike oral language, literacy has not been a part of all cultures. In cultures where literacy was developed, it served functions that allowed a culture to maintain records, to negotiate and interact across distances, and to document the history and commerce of the culture. Literacy systems are distinguished by their consistent, systematic relations, which have been codified within cultures and have become the object of analysis and study (Panofsky, John-Steiner, & Blackwell, 1990). In contrast, although oral language systems are complex, children become facile in oral language without such analysis because it is a spontaneous system acquired through immediate use. Proficiency with one's native language develops before the cognitive structures that support the acquisition of scientific systems have been acquired. Further, oral language is one of the tools that individuals use in acquiring literacy. In Vygotsky's words, everyday concepts stand "between the conceptual system and the world of objects" (Vygotsky, 1987, p. 180). The everyday concepts of oral language are needed to understand the manner in which written language systems represent ideas and objects. Mariana, Ferreiro's (1986) case study child, believed that the size of a written representation and that of an object were correlated. Through oral language, particularly in conversations (including those with the interviewers who kept probing for explanations), Mariana came to understand the true nature of writing.

When we examine studies of young children's literacy acquisition, we find a substantial amount of evidence that parents of children with extensive emergent literacy had conscious aims about their children's learning. These parents can describe at length goals for their children's literacy learning and the activities in which they engage their children (Fitzgerald, Spiegel, & Cunningham, 1991). Parents are aware that children's analysis of written language changes over the preschool years (Heath, 1983) and that this analysis does not occur through didactic instruction. For example, rhyming word games on a car trip are a favorite pastime of these parents and their children (Tobin & Pikulski, 1983). Parents are also strategic in their selection of nursery schools, making choices that share their philosophy about literacy learning (Cochran-Smith, 1984). By contrast, parents of children whose levels of emergent literacy are less developed believe that instruction should be didactic and have not regularly engaged their children in literacy activities, such as read-alouds, and free play with literacy materials, such as chalkboards and books (Fitzgerald et al., 1991).

The manner in which parents talk with their young children, including encouragement for children to ask questions and the willingness of parents to respond to these questions, is the primary means whereby parents translate their goals and wishes for their children's literacy into reality. This social interaction, Vygotsky (1978) argued, is the means whereby adults draw children's attention to the critical elements of literacy. Thus, oral language becomes critical to the acquisition of literacy not only because literacy is a way of codifying the relationships between sound and print but also because oral language is the means that adults and older children use to explain the workings of literacy to young children.

When we revisit the literature about young children's interactions with their parents around books, we find substantial confirmation for Vygotsky's construct of social interaction as the means whereby children come to analyze print (Wells, 1986). Book reading in homes where children learn a substantial amount about literacy prior to school entry are characterized by extended talk about the meanings of books and of words as well as the features of print itself (Flood, 1977; Yaden, Smolkin, & Conlon, 1989). These events are not designed solely as literacy guidance. Rather, as parents ask children to rhyme words from a book and as children ask parents to show them a word in a book, children begin the analysis that leads to reading and writing.

In sum, the social-constructivist theory provides constructs that uncover reasons why some children learn a great deal about literacy prior to school entry and others do not. Although all children are exposed to words on signs and labels, the difference for learning about literacy lies in the interactions that adults have with children around that literacy. Vygotsky's theory focuses on the intent of adults. His theory also highlights such additional mechanisms as the features of tasks and the manner in which interaction with peers complements the guidance of adults. We will elaborate on these constructs in the next chapter. It is clear, however, that the social-constructivist theory allows educators to look beyond the seemingly magical literacy acquisition of children in supportive home and community environments and identify strategies that can be applied in school settings for children without extended prior literacy experiences.

The basis for this book lies in an emergent literacy perspective that has been informed by a social-constructivist perspective. We refer to this elaborated perspective as emergent literacy throughout the remainder of the book. The social-constructivist perspective is critical in describing how children have come to know what they know and how contexts can be created for those children whose literacy experiences occur primarily in schools— the concern of Chapter 2. Educators who were influenced strongly by Piaget and linguists such as Halliday (1977) contributed new views of what children learn in becoming literate—a topic that will be the focus of Chapter 3. However, before we embark on these discussions, we wish to clarify our focus in this book on applying an emergent literacy perspective within school contexts.

Elements of an Emergent Literacy Perspective in Schools

In looking at the *how* and the *what* of literacy learning, the creation of classroom contexts, and extensions to other literacy contexts, we have chosen to emphasize the following: (a) emergent literacy learning in classroom contexts, (b) the literacy learning of at-risk children, and (c) developmental changes from ages 5 through 8.

Classroom Contexts

Advocacy of an emergent literacy perspective for children's literacy acquisition has been common in the pedagogical literature (see, e.g., Harste & Woodward, 1989; Holdaway, 1979; Strickland, 1989), but the emphasis on the learning-to-read-as-natural and Piagetian interpretations of emergent literacy has meant a "hands off" approach in terms of early intervention. If teachers provide rich experiences, children will develop literacy naturally because of either their linguistic disposition or cognitive reasoning abilities. There have been few analyses of what makes literacy acquisition in classrooms unique from literacy acquisition at home and of how classroom learning environments might be created that accommodate these differences. As a result of this lack of attention, Cazden (1991) concluded that numerous questions exist about the nature of literacy learning in classrooms guided by an emergent literacy philosophy. These previous gaps in emergent literacy theory are addressed with the elaboration of emergent literacy by social-constructivist principles.

This volume applies the elaborated emergent literacy perspective to classroom settings. Such an emphasis does not mean that the literacies that children bring to school or the literacies dominant in their homes are ignored. Quite the contrary, the already existing literacies form the foundation on which an emergent literacy program builds. Further, the goal of an emergent literacy program is to enhance children's use of literacy in all contexts, especially those of community and home. But the elaborated view of emergent literacy means that literacy is not viewed solely from the histories of middle-class children, as was the case with earlier manifestations of the emergent literacy perspective. The role of schooling in society and the contexts of classrooms are sufficiently different from the role and contexts of children's homes. Emergent literacy philosophy has much to contribute to the creation of early childhood environments in which children become proficient and enthusiastic readers and writers. This book has been written because, without a recognition of the uniquenesses of classroom settings and without the identification of solutions that account for these uniquenesses, the contributions of the emergent literacy perspective may not be realized.

Children in High-Poverty Schools

In this volume, we are particularly concerned with extending an emergent literacy perspective to classrooms where a high percentage of children live

home literacy activities may rarely or never occur in school settings

in poverty. From the outset, we emphasize that low income cannot and should not be equated with low expectations or low levels of knowledge. There is hardly a home where literacy experiences do not occur (Anderson & Stokes, 1984). Yet, the literacy experiences in some homes can take different forms from the common literacy events of schools. For example, the primary literacy interactions between adult and child in some homes occur around advertisements for toys in a weekly flyer or favorite comics (Pellegrini, Perlmutter, Galda, & Brophy, 1990). But it is a rare kindergarten or first-grade classroom that integrates these experiences. An emergent literacy perspective in which meaningful literacy experiences and the existing literacies of children are recognized is especially appropriate for ensuring the success of children who have often struggled in traditional school programs.

We explicitly make this focus on children in high-poverty schools not because the instruction for this group or any other group is different but precisely because it is the same. Gifted, at risk, low income, high income— all children need to be immersed in reading and writing experiences from the start. In many school contexts, low-income children receive discrete skill instruction—learning letters, letter-sound correspondences, and high-frequency words such as *the* and *of*—before they are given books and allowed to write. In contrast, the children who already know a great deal about literacy are involved in meaningful literacy experiences. This phenomenon has been called the "Matthew effect" (Stanovich, 1986, p. 38) from the biblical referent (Matthew 25:29): "For unto every one that hath shall be given, and he shall have abundance: but from him that hath not shall be taken away even that which he hath." In such a scenario, the rich become richer and the poor become poorer. The emergent literacy perspective is not aimed at privileging any particular group. All children benefit in classrooms where literacy experiences are plentiful and meaningful. Because children who depend on schools to become literate have been the ones most likely to be subjected to a "skill and drill" regimen, we make repeated references throughout the book to the involvement of at-risk children in meaningful literacy experiences. Our purpose in doing this is to ensure that teachers have a firm vision of the extension of the emergent literacy perspective to all children. Our intent is *not* to perpetuate the labeling of children. An emergent literacy perspective is an inclusive one, describing the literacy learning and instruction of all children.

Attending to Needs of Children from Ages Five through Eight

In this book, we are concerned with applying an emergent literacy perspective to children from ages five through eight. This period spans the primary grades, beginning with kindergarten and ending with second grade. During these years, children are initiated into the institution of school, where learning to read is one of the first tasks. In most schools, the primary grades are the only time when children are involved in experiences geared to make them independent readers. If children are not fluent readers by the end of second grade, occasions to acquire that proficiency will be few and far between.

Although the emergent literacy period begins long before school entry and the underlying principles of learning extend beyond this period, the expectations placed on children during this period require careful application of emergent literacy ideas. Educators within early childhood organizations have expressed considerable concern with literacy practices for young children, questioning which practices are developmentally appropriate (Bredekamp, 1987; Bredekamp & Rosegrant, 1992). Read-aloud activities are included in lists of developmentally appropriate, child-centered practice, but few other examples of literacy events are provided. Examples of developmentally inappropriate practices inevitably highlight such techniques as auditory discrimination worksheets or letter-naming lessons (Hyson, Hirsch-Paske, & Rescorla, 1990). At the same time, unfortunately, analyses of early childhood contexts indicate that drill and practice activities characterize the literacy experiences for a growing number of young children (Gallagher & Sigel, 1987; Knapp, Shields, & Turnbull, 1992). When true to the notions of emergent literacy, the experience of literacy acquisition in the early years of schooling does not involve drill and practice exercises. When an emergent literacy perspective is applied to school settings, literacy learning during the primary grades can be an appropriate and enjoyable experience for young children.

Although the general principles of the emergent literacy perspective apply to preschool contexts as well, their expression in school contexts should be unique. Interested readers can find descriptions of developmentally appropriate preschool literacy programs in such books as that of Schickedanz (1986). The primary-grade period is sufficiently diverse and complex to merit exclusive attention. Within a particular grade level, the differences across students can be immense and need to be recognized within an instructional program. So, too, the differences in children across the primary grades are great. The five-year-old who begins his or her day of school apprehensively and the second grader anxious to move to third grade differ substantially in knowledge about literacy. The emergent literacy program within a classroom at any grade level recognizes differences across children just as the emergent literacy program across the primary grades varies in emphases.

Summary

Success in reading and writing is a goal that is shared by all—teachers, parents, and children themselves. But views on the means of achieving that goal have been the source of considerable debate. These views emanate from one of two different philosophies on how children learn and what literacy is: reading readiness and emergent literacy. From the reading readiness perspective, reading learning begins when children have reached a developmental maturity level. Their first task is to master skills related to the smallest parts of written language, specifically letter naming and matching sounds with letters. These skills become the basis for the next set of skills, and so on, cumulating in proficient reading or writing.

From the emergent literacy perspective, young children know about and participate in the functions of literacy long before they can identify or discriminate between letters or letter-sound correspondences. Participation in such literacy events as loud reading of favorite books with adults or scribbling on paper and chalkboards provides the incentive and knowledge base for acquiring the forms of conventional literacy, such as recognizing words. To date, the emergent literacy perspective has been informed largely by linguistic and cognitive perspectives, leading to emphases on either learning to read as natural or the influence of cognitive thought structures on literacy learning. The social-constructivist perspective enriches emergent literacy theory with its attention to the means whereby children's literacy learning is supported through particular social interactions and events. By elaborating upon the special roles of teachers and peers, the social-constructivist perspective can be helpful for designing school contexts for children whose literacy learning occurs primarily in schools. This book applies this elaborated emergent literacy perspective to the primary grades, particularly in schools where many children have had few prior literacy experiences.

The next two chapters extend this elaborated emergent literacy perspective. In Chapter 2, attention is drawn to *how* children become literate and, in Chapter 3, to *what* children learn in becoming literate.

How Do Young Children
Become Literate?

——————————— VIGNETTE 2.1: ———————————

At the writing center, Deborah Rowe, a participant-observer in a preschool classroom, and several children are making a "Get Well" book for one of the teachers who is in the hospital. Deborah's message is, "Dear Carol, We hope you get well SOON ! ! !" As she writes the last word, she reads the letters out loud: "S O O N, exclamation point, exclamation point, exclamation point. Because I want her to get well soon!" Kira, one of the children at the center, first asks, "And this is extamotion point. How come?" and a little later, "And this is extamo . . . mo . . . motion point cause you want her to get better real, real fast . . . really fast!" On each occasion, Deborah replies, "An exclamation point makes people know that you really mean it and that you are excited about it. You want her to get well soon! Not just soon, but soon! Right?" Later, Hana, who has listened to these interactions, begins a page for Carol and fills the bottom with upside-down exclamation points. She shows her finished page to Susie, another teacher, saying, "Carol's really gonna like this one. There's a question mark—" "Exclamation point," Susie says. "—exclamation point because I really want her to get well quicker!"

(Rowe, 1989, p. 339)

——————————— VIGNETTE 2.2: ———————————

Corey is a second grader in a classroom where writing is encouraged as a means for communicating. When the teacher presents a lesson on a new form of writing—persuasive writing—Corey knows exactly to whom and about what he wishes to write:

> Dear Mrs. Vargas why won't you
> let us talk in the cafatearia? We
> have a right to! after all you talk
> in the longe any way.

(Temple, Nathan, Burris, & Temple, 1988, p. 201)

—————————— VIGNETTE 2.3: ——————————

Over several days, Anne Hemmeter, a kindergarten teacher in San Antonio, Texas, has taught children the nursery rhyme, Hickory Dickory Dock. In these events, a poster-sized version of the rhyme has been present and Ms. Hemmeter has tracked the print for students as the rhyme is chanted. This chart has now been placed in the library corner where it is available for children to use. Jerry and Jacob have chosen the library center as their free play center on this particular day. As they pretend to read the chart, they sweep their hands across the page as they have seen the teacher do, although not with the one-to-one correspondence between the oral and written versions. The text states, "Hickory, dickory, dock. The mouse ran up the clock, The clock struck one, The mouse ran down. Hickory, dickory, dock." Jacob says, "I'll try one. Hickory, Hickory, Dock, Tick Tock. The mouse ran up the clock. The clock struck one, the mouse ran down." Jerry follows Jacob with: "Hickory, Hickory, Dock. The mouse ran up the clock. Tick Tock."

(Hemmeter, 1991, p. 13)

In each of these vignettes, children are engaged in literacy acts. Corey's spelling of "ca-fat-ear-ia," Kira's "extamotion point," and a mouse left stranded at the top of the clock in Jerry's rendition of a classic rhyme are all unique expressions of literacy. As we will discuss in Chapter 3, these expressions of literacy are important milestones on the way to becoming literate. Through experiences such as those illustrated by these vignettes, children become literate.

Vignette 2.1 shows how oral language permeates interactions that are part of writing messages. As adults talk about the features of writing, the attention of Kira, Hana, and their peers is drawn to a new symbol—the exclamation point. Further, children express their interpretations of this new feature of written language, uncovering misconceptions the adults hear and then clarify through additional comments.

Vignette 2.2 demonstrates the manner in which literacy tasks that fulfill a genuine purpose for young children push them to apply literacy skills and strategies. When Corey is given the chance to write a persuasive message, he chooses to write about a problem that bothers him. His message is well structured and to the point. His need to communicate is strong enough that he attempts to spell words that might be intimidating for many second graders—cafeteria and lounge.

Contexts with teachers and with peers serve different but complementary purposes in children's literacy learning as illustrated by Jerry's and Jacob's experiences in Vignette 2.3. Both the content of the read-aloud and the strategy of tracking print that Ms. Hemmeter has modeled are used in Jerry's and Jacob's pretend readings with their peers. Teachers introduce new knowledge and strategies that children apply and transform in learning situations with one another.

The processes of literacy learning we highlight through these vignettes have their roots in the interdisciplinary theories that we identified in Chapter 1 as the foundation of the emergent literacy perspective. These theories, especially that of Vygotsky (1978), substantiate the importance of three processes as the means through which children acquire literacy:

- literacy learning occurs through meaningful use of reading and writing,
- literacy learning is embedded in oral language, and
- literacy learning occurs in multiple contexts with teachers and with peers.

In this chapter, we discuss each of these important processes, processes that serve as principles for guiding teachers' creation of emergent literacy classrooms.

Literacy Learning Occurs through Meaningful Use of Reading and Writing

Languages are used for human beings to communicate with one another to accomplish the tasks of the culture or, as Searle (1969) has described it, "to get things done." This principle of meaningfulness is as fundamental to written language as it is to oral language. Human beings write messages to persuade others to take particular actions, to document business transactions, and to share joys and sorrows. Written records allow human interactions to span great distances of space and time. For example, through writing, mandates from a government can be distributed to far-flung municipalities. Individuals in one generation can document their experiences for another generation.

These processes in which human beings can engage because of literacy—reflecting upon and traversing time and distance—led Vygotsky (1978) to characterize reading and writing as tools of higher-level psychological processing. By higher-order tools, Vygotsky referred to the use of reading and writing as ways of acting and reflecting upon one's experiences. Describing the ways in which literacy allows human beings to process information in new ways, Bruner (1991) states that literacy is the "first step in the empowerment of mind, albeit a crucial one . . . literacy not only provides access to the culture's written record, it also shapes the way in which mind is used" (p. vii). Literacy, then, involves a higher-level set of psychological processes both in the manner in which it is acquired and in the functions in which it allows human beings to accomplish those processes.

All cultures have not developed reading and writing, nor do all members of a literate culture use literacy at the same levels. While some individuals in a technological society survive without literacy, human beings require facility with the higher-level tools of literacy to participate in the culture as full-fledged members. There are individuals who can technically read and write but who do not use literacy as a source for accessing the literary and scientific knowledge of the culture and for integrating and transforming this knowledge in their lives. These individuals, Heath (1991) argues, are not truly literate. Writing and reading for individuals who are truly literate are not ends in themselves but are means or tools for accomplishing various acts and goals that would otherwise be impossible.

This view of literacy as higher-order tools of a culture is critical in understanding its acquisition by children. Unlike oral language—which adults use with children from the moment of their birth—written language is used to differing degrees by the adults in children's environments. Further, skills in reading and writing are not required for young children's nurturing and growth. While children must speak and listen to accomplish goals such as being fed and receiving attention from significant others in their environments, they do not need to read and write to accomplish vital functions. The expectation is that individuals will have acuity with the higher-level tools of the society, especially literacy, when they come of age. While adults in children's homes and communities disclose the existence of literacy to children and, sometimes, uncover the underlying processes to them, school has been designated as the context where children become facile with the higher-level tools of the culture, such as literacy and mathematical and scientific systems. The mandate of the school relates to literacy as defined by Heath (1991) and Bruner (1991). Technical mastery is expected but so too is acquisition of the knowledge of the culture, such as its literatures, histories, and philosophies. This definition of literacy also includes proficiency at interpreting the knowledge of the culture in terms of contemporary experiences.

To begin on the lifelong journey that the tools of reading and writing permit, young children need to participate with literacy in meaningful ways. Book-reading with adults is a primary way for young children to interact with literacy, but there are other ways in which they can begin to read and write as well. Halliday (1977) identified the functions that oral language served for his young son, functions which can also describe young children's early reading and writing efforts in their classrooms and homes as the examples in Table 2.1 suggest.

In these illustrations of literacy use, two features are particularly prominent. First, the productive side of literacy, or writing messages to others, captures children's interest as much as, or even more than, the receptive side of literacy, reading the messages of others. Through signs, journals, and letters, children can communicate messages. Observations of young children verify that the production of writing holds at least as much, if not more, interest for them as does their participation in reading (Durkin, 1966; Read, 1975). Similar to the production of talk, writing a message allows children to test hypotheses that are not entirely possible with reading. Writing produces something concrete for young children as a physical representation that communicates a message of importance. While reading, too, requires hypothesis testing and experimentation, children either respond to the text or they do not. In contrast, with a written message, young children can apply

TABLE 2.1   Functions of Oral Language

Function	Description	Examples from Young Children's Use of Written Language
instrumental	"I want" (meeting child's material needs)	Sign-up sheets in a classroom for milk count
regulatory	"Do as I tell you" (child gets others to do what he/she wants them to do)	Signs put up by children such as: DO.NAT.KM.IN.ANE.MOR.JST.LETL.KES (Do not come in any more. Just little kids.) (Newkirk, 1989)
interactional	"Me and you" (child interacts with someone else)	Reading or writing a note to a friend who has moved away
personal	"Here I come" (child expresses his/her uniqueness and self-awareness)	Writing in a personal journal or rereading a favorite book
heuristic	"Tell me why?" (child explores the environment)	Reading a book such as *The reason for a flower* (Heller, 1983); recording information about the growth of a plant
imaginative	"Let's pretend" (child creates his/her own environment)	Reading a book such as *Hey, Al* (Yorinks, 1986); writing a fanciful story
informative	"I've got something to tell you" (child conveys information)	Writing a report about dinosaurs after reading or listening to several books about dinosaurs

Adapted from Halliday (1977), p. 37.

partial knowledge in a manner that can be understood by adults. Most adults can decipher readily what the young child meant by "KM," "ANE," and "LETL" in the message displayed in Table 2.1.

Despite the value for children of creating messages, involvement in writing is often delayed until children can read or, at the very least, is given much less attention than reading acquisition. While the productive side of oral language is the source of joy and celebration as toddlers' first words are recorded and shared with family members, young children's initial attempts in written language are often viewed with fear and trepidation by parents and teachers. Reversals of letters are inspected apprehensively; unique spellings are quickly corrected lest a faulty spelling pattern be ingrained (Gentry & Gillet, 1992; Wilde, 1992).

As the examples in Table 2.1 show, the acquisition of reading and writing should go hand in hand. In recognition of the interest that children show in producing messages and the importance of this production in literacy acquisition, in an emergent literacy classroom writing and reading share equal billing. Corey's message was written in a classroom where children are encouraged to share their messages whatever their current grasp of spelling. Many occasions that support children's conventional writing are part of the emergent literacy classroom as well, but the function of writing to communicate meaningful messages is always at the heart.

Second, children can participate in these functions as they are acquiring the correct forms. In Vignette 2.1, Hana's message with the upside-down exclamation points is intended to communicate to Carol, her teacher, that she wants her to get well very quickly. Jerry and Jacob are aware that a consistent message is associated with the marks on the chart. Children begin to integrate information about the forms of literacy as they use literacy to communicate. As children work to communicate for a particular purpose, information from their teacher makes sense. A common way of describing this phenomenon is that "form follows function" (Hymes, 1974). That is, once children understand the purposes that literacy serves for them, they become intent on mastering the mechanics and code themselves so that they can use these tools on their own.

Using literacy in meaningful ways is central to an emergent literacy classroom. Because the functions of literacy are so ingrained in our ways of life, it may be difficult for adults to fathom how children may be unaware of literacy's functions. Consequently, adults may shortchange attention to literacy's functions as they emphasize learning about its forms (e.g., associations between sounds and letters). Using literacy in meaningful ways within emergent literacy classrooms provides the context in which attention to information about form makes sense. While young children do not need to use literacy in the same way that they need to use oral language, literacy can serve many, meaningful functions for young children in emergent literacy classrooms.

Literacy Learning Is Embedded in Oral Language

The relationship between oral and written language acquisition, as often is the case with any intimate association, is complex. In Chapter 1, we distinguished between the manners in which oral language and written language are acquired. We noted that written language, as a scientific system, is learned differently from oral language. While acquisition of a spontaneous system such as oral language seems to occur "naturally" as part of daily events, the acquisition of a scientific system such as written language depends on the learner's oral language facility for analyzing the system (Panofsky et al., 1990; Vygotsky, 1978). Oral language provides the vehicle by which children's attention is drawn to literacy, including its features, functions, and processes. Through oral language, children come to hear and see the uses of literacy as stories are read aloud. Through oral language, adults tell young children about the processes of literacy use and they describe and ask young children about the features of written language.

In Vignette 2.1, Deborah Rowe models well an adult's role in introducing children to a feature of written language. As the teacher writes, she describes aloud what she is doing and why she is doing it: placing an exclamation point at the end of the sentence because she wants to communicate the urgency and strength of her message. Kira and Hana hear Deborah's description of this interesting new written symbol. Their interest is piqued and they quickly add exclamation points to their messages. As Kira and Hana put the exclamation point in their messages, they talk about their understanding of the exclamation point. They are not quite fluent with the vocabulary yet—Kira calls the symbol an "extamotion point" and Hana refers to it as a question mark. An observant adult rephrases the child's comment with the conventional label and reiterates the function of the exclamation point. This interaction illustrates how through oral language:

(a) adults identify, explain, and draw children's attention to forms and functions of literacy, frequently by asking children questions;

(b) children state their interpretations aloud to themselves, their peers, and adults and they ask adults questions for further information or clarification; and

(c) adults give children feedback about their interpretations of literacy, clarify their confusions, elaborate on explanations, and provide models of the conventional uses and forms.

Without such talk, the processes and features of literacy can remain mysterious and hidden to young children even in contexts where words appear on commercials, signs, and labels. For example, when told that a parent is reading the newspaper, children may be mystified about what reading actually is. When children participate in nightly bedtime reading, the act of reading is noisy, active, and, above all else, visible. However, when a parent reads the newspaper, none of these features is present. Paris and his colleagues (Paris, Lipson, & Wixson, 1983) write about the importance of "making thinking public." This awareness of our own thinking has been called *metacognition,* a term cognitive scientists coined in the 1970s (Flavell, 1970, 1979).

Book readings provide one valuable context in which adults have children's undivided attention and can involve them in metacognitive discussions about language and concepts (Snow, 1983; Snow & Ninio, 1986). For adults who might not otherwise be aware of the nature and forms that these metacognitive conversations about literacy can take, Miles (1995) offers the book, *Hey, I'm Reading.* This book suggests points of departure for adults in initiating conversations that enhance young children's metacognitive awareness about literacy. Each type of metacognitive knowledge is presented in this book with numerous examples that simultaneously uncover an aspect of literacy and direct the attention of adults and children to similar aspects of literacy in their environments. Two types of metacognitive knowledge about

a complex system like literacy have been identified as particularly important: declarative knowledge or knowing "that" and procedural knowledge or
knowing "how" (Paris, Wasik, & Turner, 1991).

Declarative knowledge refers to knowledge about what the task of literacy entails. Declarative knowledge does not assume a child's ability to actually engage in reading and writing. Rather, it means knowing that reading
and writing exist and understanding their fundamental functions. *Hey! I'm
Reading* begins with descriptions of what it is that young children already
know about reading in the following way: "You know that what you read is
writing. You see writing wherever you go: on trucks and on T-shirts, on build-
ings, and on boxes" (Miles, 1995, pp. 2–3). Miles then describes reading as
"figuring out what the writing means" (op. cit., p. 3). Teachers support children's literacy awareness by asking many questions about environmental
print such as cafeteria signs, signs on restroom doors, the principal's name-
plate, and the names on classroom doors. A chart with pictures of common
objects with print—wrappers from popular fast-food restaurants, labels from
cola containers—can encourage children to explore their environments for
familiar objects with writing. The availability of enlarged or big books also
makes it possible for teachers to track or point to the text as they read to
children, informing them of the source of the message that they are reading.
In short, by highlighting print in this way, adults make visible what reading
is about and how it functions in our society.

Procedural knowledge includes the repertoire of possible behaviors or
strategies that readers and writers use to meet their goals. Miles presents six
different ways of participating in reading:

- getting help from pictures
- remembering
- sounding out the letters
- expecting what comes next
- writing, and
- making sense.

Miles's explanation for the strategy of getting help from pictures is: "Most
new readers are good at looking at pictures. What you see in a picture can
help you figure out the words that go with it" (op. cit., p. 14). Miles provides
examples of words on cans, crayons, book titles, and finally, a picture from a
book with a caption of conversation that can be associated with the scene
represented in the picture.

Consistent discussions that point out the processes of reading can occur
from the first day of kindergarten. As children locate their names on the
daily attendance chart, the teacher can discuss with children the similarities
in their names. Those children whose names begin with the same initial
letters can be encouraged to read their peers' names. This type of task can
be aided with teachers' comments such as, "If your name is Sylvia, you may
be able to figure out Sam's name because it starts just the same." Children
can also be encouraged to find words on the chart of environmental objects

that start with the same letter as their names. Sylvia and Sam can find *stop* and *Sesame Street,* while Matthew and Mikayla can locate *milk* and *M & Ms.* Such classroom conversations where short explanations are given about what is involved in using literacy and where adults elicit and answer children's questions about literacy are the pathways to literacy acquisition.

Literacy Learning Occurs in Multiple Contexts with Teachers and Peers

Multiple contexts in which children can engage in language and literacy use with both peers and their teacher are critical to their literacy development. These different social relationships lead to different ways of talking about and using literacy. One model we have found useful for depicting these social relationships is the Vygotsky Space (Gavelek & Raphael, 1996; Harré, 1986). The Vygotsky Space reflects different spaces, or quadrants, formed by crossing two important dimensions of social relationships that are critical to cognitive development: (a) the public-private and (b) the social-individual. The public-private dimension refers to the degree to which the cognitive activities can be observed. It may be hard to think about public cognitive activities, because cognitive activities are defined in terms of mental activity. But it is possible to observe students' cognitive activities within settings such as whole-class and small-group discussions. Cognitive activity at the private end of the continuum can only be inferred through students' written texts (e.g., journal entries) or through their public talk. The social-individual dimension refers to the participation of others in the literacy interaction with the child. At times, the child may be part of a literacy event with the whole class, while at other times, he or she may be reading and writing alone.

The two dimensions intersect as illustrated in the matrix in Figure 2.1 (Gavelek & Raphael, 1996, p. 186). In interactions that fall into the "social and public" quadrant of the matrix (i.e., the area numbered I in Figure 2.1), children can observe and participate as teachers model conventional forms of literacy. For example, the "Hickory Dickory Dock" read-aloud by Ms. Hemmeter in Vignette 2.3 illustrates such an interaction, as does Rowe's modeling of the use of an exclamation point in her get-well letter to Carol in Vignette 2.1.

In more private interactions but ones that retain a social character or those interactions that fall into the second quadrant, children test their knowledge about literacy. Jerry's and Jacob's pretend readings of the chart show how the literacy actions of the teacher are appropriated by children in a manner that reflects their social—or community—engagement in literacy. Their pattern of interaction mimics that modeled by their teacher. Their activity reflects the second quadrant of the Vygotsky Space, the social-private area. The teacher can observe that Jerry's attempt to engage in the read-aloud is parallel to what she had modeled. He and Jacob are engaged in this relatively private activity as they work on their own in the library center.

FIGURE 2.1   The Vygotsky Space

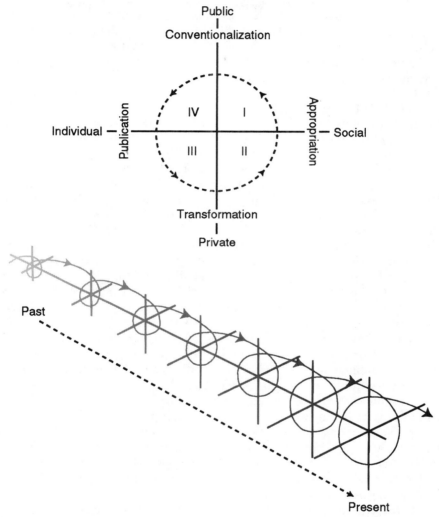

From J.R. Gavelek & T.E. Raphael (1996). Changing talk about text: New roles for teachers and students. *Language Arts, 73*, p. 186. © 1996 by the National Council of Teachers of English. Reprinted with permission.

It is clear that they have "appropriated" what they have seen, though it is also clear that Jerry is not yet "conventionally" literate. Jerry will need to participate in private, individual events (i.e., area III in Figure 2.1) as he works to transform what he has seen and heard into more conventional forms of literacy.

Evidence of transformation and activity within the private-individual space captured in quadrant III is illustrated by Corey's persuasive letter from Vignette 2.2. He has learned about a persuasive writing format and he has learned about letter/sound correspondences. He is transforming this knowledge to meet his own goal—persuading his teacher to allow children to talk in the cafeteria. While the actual cognitive activity that would have occurred in quadrant III was not observable, the "publication" of his letter allows his teacher to infer his transformation of learned literacy strategies and forms.

In the social and public interactions that are represented by the area marked IV in Figure 2.1, individuals have opportunities to receive feedback from other members of the literacy community. They learn that other strategies or interpretations might be made. Further, some of their individual ways of using literacy may become part of the conventional knowledge of the classroom. In Kristin Grattan's first-grade classroom (Grattan, in press), her students asked to take turns leading a morning sharing-time event called Morning Message typically led by the teacher. Eventually, students' leading the discussion became the conventional way of running the activity in Kristin's classroom.

Notice how both Corey's persuasive letter and students' leadership during Morning Message reflect learning over time. This temporal dimension is an important part of the Vygotsky Space, illustrated in the bottom part of Figure 2.1. This figure depicts the notion that any learning is built upon the history of interactions among a range of individuals and across a range of circumstances. The further back one traces the learning, the more fuzzy or blurred the interactions and influences become, but these historical interactions are still critical. For example, Corey's production of a persuasive essay was unlikely to have occurred simply because his teacher introduced persuasive writing. Prior to that, she had spent a large part of the school year emphasizing that writing is used to communicate. Further, Corey had interactions that led him to believe that his opinions mattered. He also had learned something about equity (implied by his comment that, "you talk in the longe any way"). In short, Corey's participation in interactions that were public and social, and his opportunities to appropriate and transform what he had learned through those interactions, contributed over time to his competence in generating a persuasive letter.

In these different types of interactions, teachers and peers serve unique functions. These roles are complementary and equally important in children's learning. To further explain the roles of teachers and peers in children's literacy acquisition, Vygotsky (1978) described a construct that is unique to each. The construct that explains teachers' interactions is scaffolding, while play explicates peer interaction.

The Role of Teachers

The vignettes that introduced the chapter demonstrate the multiple roles of teachers in children's literacy learning. As Deborah Rowe did in Vignette 2.1, teachers explain features and functions of written language, such as the purpose and form of exclamation points. Susie, another teacher in the classroom featured in Vignette 2.1, corrects Hana's use of the term *question mark* when referring to exclamation points. In doing so, she demonstrates how teachers give children feedback when children may be confused or have an incomplete understanding. As Corey's teacher did in Vignette 2.2, teachers create occasions for children to use reading and writing in engaging and meaningful ways. As Anne Hemmeter did in Vignette 2.3, teachers give lessons where they model strategies of reading such as tracking print. A common thread can be seen across all of these roles: Teachers are active participants in their students' learning. Unlike a peer who collaborates with a child, the teacher knows the strategies and knowledge that comprise reading and writing. Unlike a peer who plays with a child, a teacher can encourage a child's performance at his or her optimal levels of development because of the adult's ability to take the child's perspective.

Such interactions where an adult guides children to higher levels of processing have been called "scaffolding" (Wood, Bruner, & Ross, 1976). The metaphor of the scaffold is particularly appropriate in describing the nature of teaching. Similar to construction crews that erect a scaffold to build or repair a building, teachers provide a temporary structure to assist children's learning. Teachers hope their modeling, questions, and guidance culminate in children's proficiency, thus leading to the reduction and removal of the scaffolding. The purpose of their interactions is to assist children in developing strategies and the ability to generalize their knowledge. Once the scaffolding has served its function, it is moved to another set of strategies or domain of knowledge. Teachers continue to have a role for an extended period of time in children's literacy learning but the literacy strategies and knowledge that are the focus of scaffolding would be expected to shift noticeably across a school year and across the emergent literacy period.

Central to Vygotsky's view of the teachers' function in children's learning is the zone of proximal development (ZPD). The ZPD refers to the distance between children's "actual" and "potential" levels of development (Vygotsky, 1978). When children independently solve a problem, they function at their *actual* level of development. By observing Jerry in Vignette 2.3, his teacher could see he has yet to establish a one-to-one correspondence between spoken and written words. However, when Jerry participates in a group with Ms. Hemmeter, he is able to follow the words as his teacher points to them. Through the support provided by an adult or a more capable peer, children can perform at their *potential* level of development. With support, Jerry is coming to an understanding of the one-to-one correspondence between oral and written language. In contexts without the scaffolding of an adult, however, he shows that he is aware of the presence of the relationship but he is not yet distinguishing individual words in writing.

This discussion shows that successful scaffolding requires teachers to integrate information from several sources. First is knowledge about the domain of literacy and its manifestations at various points in children's development. Conventional literacy is not acquired in one step. Rather, it is preceded by learning numerous forms of literacy, including recognition of familiar words in the physical environment (e.g., "Stop") and consistent memory of phrases from familiar stories (e.g., "Little Red Riding Hood").

Second, to scaffold students' learning experiences, teachers need to know where their students are along the continuum of knowledge acquisition. When teachers are aware of favorite words that particular students know instantly, they use these words as the basis for introducing new material. When teachers have identified books their kindergartners have memorized, these are integrated into library corners and into reading lessons. Finally, scaffolding involves knowledge about ways that move children to new levels of understanding, such as questioning, explaining, and modeling.

The Role of Peers

According to Vygotsky (1978), the interaction between peers can best be described as play. While older children's play often occurs in organized games with formal rules, young children use play to understand their worlds. An instance of such play can be seen in Vignette 2.3 as Jerry and Jacob give their renditions of "Hickory Dickory Dock." They are pretending that they are reading. This example of play in an emergent literacy classroom has the two elements that Vygotsky (1978) identified as valuable about play: (a) its representational quality and (b) its rule-based nature.

The pretend book reading is representational in that Jerry's and Jacob's referent is an actual event rather than an imaginary situation. Young children's interest in play lies in recapturing events that they have observed or in which they've participated. Jerry and Jacob chose to spend their free time in the library corner. Using the big book that they had seen and heard with their teacher, they gave their own renditions of the text. Such play is a reconstruction of something that has actually happened rather than a novel creation of an imagined situation.

The rule-based nature of children's play is another factor in the learning that play contexts facilitate. As children reproduce events from their lives in play, much of their interaction with one another has to do with the implementation and negotiation of the underlying rules. Not all words are appropriate for the text that Jerry and Jacob read, only words they remember from shared book events with the teacher. In these behaviors, Jerry and Jacob are showing their efforts to understand the rules of literacy.

While adults commonly perceive play as a chaotic free-for-all, close study of children at play shows that their efforts more typically resemble those of Jerry and Jacob in its rule-governed character (Christie, 1991; Pellegrini & Galda, 1993). According to Vygotsky (1978), these efforts to interpret the rules of events in the world around them are another means whereby children perform at the upper levels of the ZPD. Had Jerry been asked to spend this time at his desk quietly completing a worksheet on letter-sound correspondences, his emerging attempts at reading familiar texts would not have manifested themselves. Thus we say that the play context allowed Jerry to perform at his potential rather than his actual level of development.

Vygotsky's perspective toward play has implications for emergent literacy classrooms in at least two ways. The first is integrating contexts that support children's interactions with one another. These opportunities exist in the form of library, writing, and play centers, as the example from Anne Hemmeter's classroom shows. These centers allow children to recreate the interactions that they have participated in with their teachers and family members. While play centers that elicit real-life contexts are frequently associated with nursery schools, the benefits of such contexts to children's literacy acquisition can be seen in observing an interaction in a play center that has the charts, signs, writing materials, and clothing of a veterinarian's office. The literacy participation that these materials supported is evident in the observations of one occasion in this kindergarten class. Joshua has assumed the role of the veterinarian and another classmate that of a client who has brought in a sick dog—a stuffed animal. As he prepares to write in the patient's folder, Joshua states: "You know what? I'm going to write his name in dog language. How do you spell RUFF?" (Morrow & Rand, 1991, p. 400).

A second implication of the construct of play has to do with a stance that underlies the emergent literacy classroom. Specifically, this stance means flexibility toward the form of children's products and the talk that surrounds the creation of these products. Observers of emergent literacy classrooms have noted that some young children will respond with idiosyncratic forms of reading and writing only when adults give them permission to "pretend" (Ferreiro & Teberosky, 1982). In conventional terms, this stance might be described as supporting young students' risk taking.

An atmosphere of risk taking characterized the classroom where Corey produced his persuasive letter. Without such a context, Corey would have spent much of the writing period waiting for the teacher's attention so that he could write cafeteria and lounge correctly. He may have decided not to write this message at all. An environment that acknowledges and supports children's need to be inventive and playful with written language provides frequent occasions to write journal entries, to read along in books that have rhymes, and to create signs for various centers in the classroom.

These interactions with peers, as with teachers, support multiple aspects of children's literacy development. The cycle of interactions that are represented in Figure 2.1 occurs over and over again in literacy learning. Students do not move through the cycle in one swoop to become literate ever after. Even as adults, our mastery of a new domain depends on multiple interactions that introduce us to new information and that allow us to transform and appropriate the information for our own settings. We will return to this view of learning as an explanation for our growth as teachers in the final chapter of this book.

Summary

In this chapter, we described the three principles that characterize how children become literate. First and foremost, literacy is acquired through using writing and reading for purposes that are meaningful to children. At the point when young children read the illustrations rather than the text in books, they can participate in a variety of functions, such as writing or dictating signs or writing a card to a grandparent or to a friend who has moved away.

The second process that characterizes literacy acquisition is its immersion in oral language. Oral language is the means whereby children's attention is directed to the features and functions of written language. Young children hear stories read aloud. Words on labels and signs are described to them in talk. Through question-and-answer routines that adults usually introduce but which children extend, attention is drawn to the critical features of written language.

Third, literacy learning benefits from participation with both adults and peers. The four quadrants in the Vygotsky Space that are formed by the intersection of the two dimensions of public-private and social-individual illustrate the roles of teachers and peers. For example, in the public-social context that is led typically by the teacher, children are introduced to new information. In the private-social contexts with peers, children negotiate meanings and ideas about literacy. The scaffolding of teachers enables children to perform at their potential levels of development. Peer relationships allow for playfulness, encouraging children to reconstruct and experiment. To create the literacy acts where children interact meaningfully with one another and to scaffold learning experiences appropriately for their students, teachers also need to understand *what* it is that children learn in becoming literate—the topic of the next chapter.

chapter 3

What Do Young Readers and Writers Learn in Becoming Literate?

Brett, a four-year-old: "I don't know how to read. I don't know how to write numbers either. I need some help, some practice." When the interviewer asked Brett if there was anything that he could read, he said: "I can just read easy things like Exit, Stop, Mom and Dad." Melanie, a five-year-old: "I know how to read my own books, but I don't know how to read this."

(Hiebert, 1979)

These are the responses that a group of children at the beginning of first grade gave to these lines of text in an illustrated book, *Would you like to fly?* (Williams, 1990):

> Would you like to fly in a seaplane?
> Would you like to fly in a jet?

Ben: [pointing to the word like]
       /l - l - l / I don't want to read this.
Brenda: That's an airplane.
       Another airplane.
Adam: He's ready to fly.
       He goes up in the air now.
Wesley: you in a
       you in a
Kyle: Would you like to fly in a sea-airplane?
       Would you like to fly in a jet?

(from Hiebert, Colt, Catto, & Gury, 1991)

At the beginning of grade one, children were asked to write about something they like to do. Here is what they wrote and what they said when asked to read what they had written:

Travis:	(scribble)	I went up in the mountains.
Mandie:	I MOMIRTS	I love Mom. I like to play at recess.
Juan:	I HAD Fe A Me F H	I had fun at my friend's house.
Albert:	I HaF FON WeN I Woke Hom Weth my SeSr AND Hr FrN.	I have fun when I walk home with my sister and her friend.

(from Hiebert et al., 1991)

In these three vignettes, young children share their literacy expertise. While Brett's and Melanie's expertise (Vignette 3.1) looks different from that of adults, they demonstrate clear expectations and views about what counts as literacy. Such views vary considerably across beginning first graders, as we see in the children's responses to reading and writing in Vignettes 3.2 and 3.3. Some children—like Brenda and Adam—are aware that books communicate meaning, and they use the illustrations to give their "reading" of the text's story. Others—like Wesley and Kyle—read more conventionally. The children's writing displayed in Vignette 3.3 is further evidence of the varying forms that exist during early literacy learning. From Travis's scribbles to Albert's extended sentence, children create messages about important people and times—playing with friends and siblings, a trip to the mountains. Mandie and Juan represent words in their messages using at least one symbol per word, while Albert reveals his awareness that sounds are represented in syllables of words. While the range in these beginning first graders' literacy is considerable, the processes that are represented in this body of responses are all crucial to becoming literate.

In this chapter, we examine critical processes that characterize early literacy. The progression from the eager kindergartner who expressed his wish to read in Vignette 1.1 and Kyle's rendition of *Would you like to fly?* (Williams, 1990) in Vignette 3.2 may seem almost magical. While the movement to proficient reading and writing will always retain a touch of magic for even veteran primary-level teachers, it represents hard work on the part of children and their families, as well as knowledge and design on the part of their primary-level teachers. What distinguishes beginning literacy teachers from those who work with older children is their knowledge of the processes involved in literacy acquisition and of the manner in which particular processes can be facilitated through experiences and instruction.

A Description of the Processes

The multiplicity and complexity of literacy processes can be daunting to teachers. Which processes are critical? Which are tangential? How do these processes fit together? Which processes should be emphasized at particular points in time? The processes that support young children's movement to proficient reading and writing can be clustered into the three categories in Table 3.1.

At the core of reading and writing are the comprehending and composing processes. "Calling out" written words or copying a written text are not *acts* of reading and writing. When readers can interpret the meaning of a written message and when writers can produce a written message that others can comprehend, they are reading and writing. We have labeled the acts of comprehending and composing as the central processes of literacy.

Comprehending and composing written language involve facility in using the unique manifestations of the four written language systems: graphophonic, syntactic, semantic, and pragmatic (Goodman, Watson, & Burke, 1987). Becoming adept at handling these relationships may differ within the acts of reading and writing. We provide an overview of the four systems, because the processes necessary for comprehending and composing are specific to these systems.

We begin with the graphophonic system because it is unique to the written form of a language. This system involves the relationships between the sounds of oral language (phonemes) and their corresponding written symbols (graphemes). Phonemes are the smallest units of sounds within a language.

TABLE 3.1   Processes of Literacy Learning and Their Components

Process	Component

Central	Comprehending
	  • Personal Response
	  • Critical Response
	Composing
	  • Communicative Intent
	  • Conventions

Necessary	Word Recognition
	  • Contextual Supports
	  • Meaningful Chunks or Morphemes
	  • High-Frequency Words
	  • Letter-Sound Patterns in Words
	Spelling
	  • Invented Spelling
	  • Conventional Spelling Strategies
	Literary Elements
	  • Genres
	  • Language Play

Interim	Concepts of Print Phonemic Awareness Letter Naming

For example, the word *cat* consists of three phonemes: /k/, /a/, /t/. Graphemes are the written systems used to represent a sound in a language. In the previous example, each phoneme is represented by a single grapheme. In some cases, however, a phoneme may be represented by more than one grapheme as in the word *free* where two graphemes—e, e—represent a phoneme.

In English, particular clusters of sounds occur consistently and are represented by particular clusters of letters. Examples of consistent and common letter-sound patterns are *at* and *am.* For example, in *Green Eggs and Ham,* Dr. Seuss (1960) used the *am* pattern in the name of the character "Sam-I-am," who continually offers "green eggs and ham." While the pattern *am* also functions as a word (not the case with all consistent sound-letter patterns), words that share this sound-letter cluster do not convey the same meaning. The tenacious Sam-I-am wins over his antagonist by presenting the green eggs and ham in a variety of venues, all of which occur in couplets that end with a common letter-sound pattern: *box-fox, house-mouse, there-anywhere, rain-train, goat-boat.* Dr. Seuss was uncovering for young readers the consistencies of the sound-letter patterns within the graphophonic system. When children use information about sound-letter correspondences to figure out unknown words, they are drawing on the body of knowledge known as phonics.

Both readers and writers need to associate written symbols with particular sounds. In reading, the sounds that are associated with particular symbols may vary across regions within a country and across countries of English speakers. But, regardless of pronunciations when reading, the spellings of written words remain the same.

The syntactic system of a language refers to the set of relationships among words that generate sentences and paragraphs, also called the "grammar" of a language. Languages differ in their grammars. For example, adjectives follow the noun rather than precede it in some languages. Within a given language, however, the syntactic system is the same in its oral and written expressions. English is a positional language, which means that the order of words in a sentence or phrase influences meaning. Consider the following four sentences:

1. I saw the cattle grazing in the field.
2. I saw the cattle while I was grazing in the field.
3. I saw the cattle that were grazing in the field.
4. I saw the cattle that were grazing field the in.

Most readers will describe the first and the third sentences as conveying essentially the same meaning (Schank, 1973). The inclusion of the second pronoun in the second sentence changes the meaning substantially, while the reordering of the last phrase in the fourth sentence produces a nonsensical statement.

For young children who can recognize some words, their intuitive sense of the grammar can be used to predict the meaning of unfamiliar words. Take the case of the first grader who encounters two new words in this sentence from the picturebook, *Coco Can't Wait* (Gomi, 1979):

> Coco lives on top of the --------, in the house with the purple ----.

By drawing on his or her knowledge of what "sounds right" in oral English, this child can narrow down the choices to a particular category of words—nouns. While not formally able (or needing) to define a noun, the child will make predictions from this category of words.

If the child predicts that the word was *mountain,* this reader was also using the third cueing system of *semantics.* If the child had only been using syntactic clues, predictions would have been nouns but not necessarily something that has a top and on which a person or animal can live. While the text indicates that it is a hill on which Coco lives, the child's prediction of "mountain" indicates that he or she is using knowledge about the world to make meaning of the unknown word. The semantic system, then, pertains to the meanings of language.

Syntactic and semantic cues are almost always used together. The syntax creates particular constraints on choices but the collective meaning of the words that are familiar for the reader narrows down the choices even more (Durkin, 1993). This collective meaning is used by readers to draw on their conceptual and experiential backgrounds to select words of particular grammatical categories that make sense in that context. For example, adult readers quickly grasp that the word "wind" has different grammatical functions, meanings, and pronunciations in the sentences: "The wind blew" and "He had forgotten to wind the clock." Words have particular meanings as a function of the context in which they are used. Further, words also hold particular meanings for readers as a function of their prior world experiences. For example, children who are reading a predictable book entitled *If I Had a Pig* (Inkpen, 1988) may differ in their previous experiences with snow, influencing their ease in figuring out a compound word that the author has coined—"snowpig."

The willingness of children to make predictions about words can be influenced by aspects of the fourth system of language—pragmatics. The pragmatic system refers to the use of language in particular contexts. For example, children's views of the expectations and norms of the classroom literacy context can influence their willingness to make predictions about words (Mosenthal & Na, 1980). For particular children, reading orally for the whole class may create stress, especially if they know that their peers will call out the "correct" word for any transformation to the text (Allington, 1983a). Consequently, children may be less willing to apply strategies to unknown words. Mosenthal and Na (1980) confirmed differences in children's reading responses in an informal or low-risk task and a formal or high-risk task. In the high-risk task, children knew they were being evaluated and that their performances would determine future classroom placement, while the low-risk task was a small group interaction with no grade or consequence. Children's responses to the text were richer in the low-risk setting than in the high-risk setting, particularly for children who were still developing as readers.

The pragmatic system pertains to features of texts as well as features of tasks and classroom contexts. Children who have heard many folk tales will be very comfortable with a story that begins "Once upon a time." As writers, they may eagerly put pencil to paper and use a similar structure. However, if they approach an informational book on leaves such as *Red Leaf, Yellow Leaf* (Ehlert, 1991) or on animal families such as *Whose Baby* (Yabuuchi, 1981) with the expectation that a plot will result in fanciful characters living happily ever after, they will be confused. Or, children who have been given a heavy diet of predictable books may come to expect that they can memorize the text patterns, an expectation that falls short when they encounter books such as *Eat Up, Gemma* (Hayes, 1988), *Cookies* (Lobel, 1972), or any one of the thousands of picturebooks that do not have a predictable structure. How readers make meaning of texts and the meanings that they communicate as writers are influenced by their knowledge of how written language is used in different texts and contexts.

There are similarities and uniquenesses in how these four language systems are used in reading and writing but children need to coordinate all four systems to comprehend and compose. Both comprehending and composing require the integration of the syntactic and semantic systems. Further, both comprehending and composing require attention to the pragmatic, or the contexts of texts. This awareness becomes critical as writers compose their ideas. What structures are most helpful for describing the care of a dog? What structures work best to describe a favorite time with one's pet dog? As writers, children need to make choices such as these; as readers, their comprehension is aided when they are aware of the choices that authors have made. For example, a strange word such as the sound "Sppppssst!" made by a cat might be more expected in a story with elements of playfulness than in one intended solely to communicate information.

Comprehending an already existing message differs from composing a unique message in that readers respond to an existing text, while writers create a text on the blank page or screen. However, the underlying system is the same across both reading and writing. To comprehend written text, individuals need to be facile in recognizing elements of the graphophonic system, while to compose written text, individuals need to be facile in producing the graphophonic system. In reading, this necessary process is called word recognition and, in writing, spelling.

When readers and writers are guided in using their existing knowledge and polishing new strategies to use these four systems, they are able to make use of the "cues"—signs or prompts—of written language (Goodman, 1973). To become facile with these signs or prompts, readers and writers need guidance in the *necessary* processes of literacy that support the *central* processes of comprehending and composing. There are also *interim* processes such as letter naming and phonemic awareness that are needed to become facile in the necessary processes. Once readers and writers are adept in the necessary processes, these interim processes are no longer a focus of literacy instruction. In the next sections, we describe the central, necessary, and interim processes related to literacy acquisition.

The Central Processes

The purpose of reading is to comprehend a written message. Similarly, the essence of writing is to communicate a message. The written language system can be "read" and "written" in a technical sense without comprehending and composing. An individual can "read" a text by meticulously applying the letter-sound rules of English. An individual can transcribe a message without knowing what any of the symbols mean, as was the case with scribes who carefully copied documents in the Middle Ages. However, neither of these constitutes acts of reading or writing. Individuals are readers when they are able to understand the message of the text, making connections between the spoken and written systems. Similarly, individuals are writers when they can use the written language system to communicate a message.

To become independent readers and writers, individuals must be adept at the technical aspects of making associations between sounds and letters. It is in the arena of technical knowledge that young children are challenged, not in the fundamental stances of comprehending and composing. They approach books and writing events as occasions for meaning. Keeping this fundamental disposition alive during the time when children are learning the technical aspects of literacy is a primary challenge for emergent literacy teachers. The emergent literacy perspective with its elaborations from social-constructivist thinking can guide teachers in juggling the basic stance of young children that books and their own messages are intended to communicate, and the need for young children to acquire fluency with the symbol system to become independent readers and writers. The basic stance toward literacy should continually emphasize the central processes of comprehending.

Comprehending

Children typically respond enthusiastically to stories that they have heard read aloud. After hearing *Madeline,* children want to tell about their scars and injuries. Children also want to ask questions after they've heard a story read aloud. "Why did the peddler carry his hats on his head?" may arise after a reading of *Caps for Sale* (Slobodkina, 1940). Whether reading *Madeline* or *Hamlet,* two stances represent the essence of comprehension—personal and critical interpretations.

Personal Responses.　At the most basic level, comprehending involves a reader's personal response. Personal response to literature asks children to engage in such activities as sharing personal experiences and feelings, putting themselves in the situation described in the text, or comparing themselves to the characters. Sulzby (1985) has found that children attempt to respond and create meaning from stories, even before they are able to read conventionally. She identified a range of responses to books among young children, which can be found in Table 3.2.

Responses of the types that Sulzby identified can be found among the transcripts of first graders' readings of texts in Vignette 3.2. Both Brenda and Adam rely on the pictures in the text. Adam uses the pictures to tell a story, while Brenda labels the pictures as she identifies a pictured seaplane as "an airplane" and then the jet as "another airplane." Wesley initially refused to attempt to read the text but, with encouragement from an adult, could iden-

TABLE 3.2   Responses to Books[1]

Response Type	Description	Example
1. Refusal	Little or no explanation characterizes this low-level refusal to read.	"I don't want to."
2. Picture-Governed, No Story a. Labeling and Commenting	Illustrations are labeled or described, sometimes as if the action were occurring at that instant.	2a. *Text*[2]: "The trouble with elephants is . . . they spill the bathwater when they get in. . . ." *Child:* "There's a little girl. There's an elephant."
b. Following Action		2b. *Text*[3]: "One day Coco wanted to see Grandma very much." *Child:* "She's running. The grandmother is running too. Now she jumps on the bus. She's standing to see. She is jumping on a bus."
3. Picture-Governed Story a. Oral Language-like b. Written Language-like	While children continue to rely on the illustrations, they attempt to tell a story. When children are familiar with the book—especially those with predictable structures, they may paraphrase parts of the written text, speaking in a rhythmic manner.	3a. *Text*[4]: "Snail is on the bench. Snail listens." *Child:* "Ready, set, said the coach. Go and bat." 3b. *Text*[5]: "You can ride on a train. You can ride on a bus." *Child:* "We can ride a train. We can ride a bus."

TABLE 3.2	Responses to Books *(continued)*	
Response Type	**Description**	**Example**

4. Print-Governed
  a. Refusal based on print awareness
  b. Applies few words
  c. More extensive recognition of words but still not reading all of text
	Responses indicate awareness of text features, ranging from refusal to read because of print awareness to attempting some words but not self-correcting nonsense words or omissions.	4a. "I know how to write letters but I don't know these words."
		4b. *Text* [3]: "Coco lives on top of the hill, in the house with the purple roof."
		Child says "on" and "the," while pointing to those words.
		4c. *Text* [6]: "A Duckling came out of the shell. I am out! he said."
		Child: "A Duck cried out of the shell. I am! had sad."

5. Independent Reading		

[1]Adapted from Sulzby (1985), p. 464.
[2]From *The Trouble with Elephants* (Riddell, 1988).
[3]From *Coco Can't Wait!* (Gomi, 1979).
[4]From *Hooray for Snail* (Stadler, 1984).
[5]From *You Can Ride* (Koss, 1996), pp. 6–7.
[6]From *Chick and Duckling* (Suteyev, 1972).

tify consistently a handful of words. Unlike Wesley, Ben refused to read the book and, even with probing, was unable to identify letters on the page. Kyle gives a conventional reading of this text, making a meaningful substitution for an unusual word—seaplane.

These responses illustrate a range of meaningful stances that young children have toward text. Regardless of how children have been introduced to literacy, however, there comes a time when the task of "figuring out the words" dominates and children may say, as Wesley did initially, that they cannot read. The task that challenges emergent literacy teachers is to keep children's personal responses to text alive during this phase. One of the primary ways to do this is to extend personal responses to texts during read-aloud events. For example, a point for pausing during a read-aloud of *The Pet Show* (Keats, 1972) occurs as the pets that the children will bring to school are described in the book: "Matt said he would bring ants. 'I'm gonna bring my mouse,' bragged Roberto. 'What are you going to bring?'" (p. 4). Children might share their personal experiences with pets. As children begin to read their own texts—even when the texts consist of a handful of words such as *Have You Seen My Cat?* (Carle, 1973)—

devoting time for children to engage in and share their personal responses is fundamental.

Critical Responses.   Teachers should also encourage children's questions about the content of books, building upon the questions as a source for critically thinking about text. Critical responses involve children's attempts to make predictions or ask questions about the text, clarify vocabulary or interpretations, summarize or organize ideas from the text, analyze characters, and make connections to other texts (Palincsar & Brown, 1984).

The manner in which teachers encourage these processes of predicting, clarifying, summarizing, analyzing, and connecting can be seen in the following excerpt from an emergent literacy classroom. The teacher is reading *Ben's Trumpet* (Isadora, 1979), a story about a boy who loves jazz and wishes to be a trumpeter. Words from the text are provided in italics, while comments of the teacher and students appear in regular type:

Teacher:	*On his way home from school, he goes by the Zig Zag Club.* Zig Zag Club—that's what that sign says, and there's Ben practicing his trumpet.
Student:	He's not really.
Teacher:	Is there a trumpet in his hands?
Class:	No.
Teacher:	So, what's he doing?
Student:	He's using his hand . . . and his imagination.
Teacher:	*The next day, after school, Ben stops and listens to the musicians practicing a red hot piece. He starts blasting away at his trumpet. Some kids in front of the candy store watch him. "Hey, what ya doing?" they yell. Ben stops and turns around. "What ya think ya doing?" they ask again. "I'm playing my trumpet," Ben answers. "Man, you're crazy. You got no trumpet." They laugh and laugh.* Does he have a trumpet?
Students:	No.
Teacher:	He's using his imagination. So maybe these children who are making fun of him aren't using their imagination.
Student:	Maybe they don't believe in imagination.
Teacher:	Maybe.
Student:	Maybe he has a real one.

(McGill-Franzen & Lanford, 1994, p. 268)

In all likelihood, most of the children were not familiar with a jazz club or the instrument that Ben was imitating. However, the teacher encourages children to use a concept that was discussed frequently in this emergent literacy classroom—one's imagination—in relation to the experiences of a character in the text. The teacher is using the known, or children's prior knowledge, to examine a concept—imagination—as well as to learn about other contexts and individuals. Becoming a critical reader of text requires the melding of these two processes: (a) using one's knowledge about the world in interpreting and understanding new texts and (b) using a text to gain new insights about the world.

With regard to the first process, children's knowledge about the world enters into successful reading and writing in that knowledge about the world underlies literacy that is reflective, interpretive, and personal. Activating prior knowledge from one context to another and from one text to another characterizes readers who use literacy thoughtfully and reflectively.

Knowledge of the world comes from reading as well. An example from a book designated as an easy reader illustrates the manner in which knowledge of the world is required for a meaningful interpretation. The book *Hooray for Snail* (Stadler, 1984) begins in the following manner: "Snail is on the bench. Snail listens. Snail gets the bat." To understand Snail's dilemma, a child needs some basic understanding about baseball and the speed of snails. Further, the book only makes sense if the reader realizes not only that the characters are anthropomorphized, but also that the plot turns fanciful as Snail hits a ball that flies to the moon. Thus, while the words used in this book are ones within emergent readers' vocabulary, the book itself presents an opportunity for the teacher to teach students about world knowledge (e.g., baseball, snails) and literary style (e.g., anthropomorphizing animals, realistic fiction versus fantasy).

Composing

Young children approach the task of writing a message in the same way that they approach the task of reading a book—with communicative intent. Even if young children cannot form letters, the descriptions that they give to their messages involve communicative intent. All of the productions in Vignette 3.3 are evidence of this disposition toward meaningfulness, including Travis's "reading" of his scribbles. The messages tell about important events in children's lives—favorite times such as recess, walking home from school, being at a friend's house, going to the mountains—and describe central figures in their lives—parents, siblings, and friends.

Physical production (handwriting or facility with a keyboard) and spelling are often equated with composing. Yet, the central process underlying all aspects of writing is the communication of meaning. To communicate a message, however, also requires development in the conventions of writing. These two dimensions of composing—communicative intent and conventions of writing—form the core of the emergent literacy program.

Communicative Intent.   When children are given freedom to explore literacy, they communicate through scribbles, drawings, "mock letters" (see Travis's in Vignette 3.3), strings of letters, and invented spelling. DeFord's (1980) list of the types of writing found in the compositions of young children appears in Table 3.3. Unlike reading stages, writing stages are less consistent. That is, children may use their graphophonic knowledge in one setting (e.g., writing at least a letter of their first name), but communicate in other messages through drawing. Also, unlike the labeling or storytelling phases of reading, all children do not progress through the scribbling phase (i.e., "mock letters") that is evident in Travis's response.

Young children's initial efforts at engaging in the act of writing resemble those of proficient writers more closely than do their efforts at reading. A child who has even a little proficiency at encoding can produce a message that others will recognize as a message. For example, even without Mandie's reading of her text in Vignette 3.2, an adult reader can establish that her message has to do with her mother. Albert's message can be gleaned in its entirety, even though he has substituted the word "woke" for the word "walk." The context of the text enables proficient readers to make sense of his message. As youngsters become more facile with language conventions, their messages become easier to decode.

Conventions.   In the first stages of writing, parents and teachers are the recipients of the messages. Not unlike the initial stage of language development where adult family members and friends give meaning to children's

TABLE 3.3	Forms of Writing
Category	Subcategories
Writing-like Responses	1. Scribbling 2. Differentiation between drawing and writing 3. Concepts of linearity, uniformity, linear complexity, symmetry, placement, left-to-right motion, top-to-bottom directionality, development of letters and letter-like shapes
Attempts to Apply Sound-Letter Correspondences	4. Combination of letters, possibly with spaces, indicating understanding of units (letters, words, sentences), but may not show letter-sound correspondence 5. Writing known isolated words—developing sound-letter correspondence
Focus on Messages	6. Writing simple sentences with use of inventive spellings 7. Combining two or more sentences to express complete thoughts
Conventional Messages	8. Control of punctuation—periods, capitalization, use of upper- and lowercase letters 9. Forms of discourse—stories, informational material, letters

[1]Adapted from DeFord (1980), p. 162.

oral productions, adults give meaning to children's writing. Interactions with adults are fundamental to children's written literacy engagement. Without these interactions around meaning, children may learn the conventions and usage of writing but may not view themselves as writers. Hagerty, Hiebert, and Owens (1989) found that second graders in classrooms where children wrote frequently and for a variety of reasons perceived their literacy involvement positively and eagerly, while their peers in classrooms where writing occurred as grammar exercises were less positive. Similarly, when teachers place less emphasis on first-grade students' spelling and mechanics, the students write considerably more than in classrooms where teachers require correct spelling (Clarke, 1988).

Peers, as well as adults beyond the immediate context, may have a more difficult time understanding young children's communications, thus making clear the importance of movement to conventional writing. In addition, students need to be involved in writing within a variety of genres, not simply messages to their teacher or other adults within their classroom as illustrated in Vignette 3.3. Thus, two aspects of language conventions form a critical basis for instruction: knowledge about the appropriate spelling, punctuation, and structure of language; and knowledge of the range of genres within which ideas can be conveyed.

An instructional program that builds on children's willingness and eagerness to communicate their experiences and interests does not have to go through a period where children are stymied by the task of moving to conventionality. Young children may create messages within a variety of genres with only partial knowledge of the conventional use of language. As children's audience and purposes in writing expand to include their peers and beyond, they increasingly attend to these conventions. At this point, lessons and activities should encourage children's application of the conventions they are learning to use.

Necessary Processes

Each of the *central* processes of literacy is built on a set of *necessary* processes. In the case of comprehending, the set of processes is word recognition and, for composing, the parallel set consists of spelling processes. Both recognizing and spelling words involve multiple strategies; neither is a unitary skill to be acquired in a constrained period of time. A third set of necessary processes is common to comprehending and composing—understanding the literary elements of texts.

Recognizing Words

Meaningful reading depends on the automatic recognition of words. If readers need to figure out a significant portion of the words in a text, their attention will not be focused on text comprehension (Lesgold, Resnick, & Hammond,

too much decoding → comprehension

1985). Central goals of an emergent literacy program include children's acquiring a set of strategies for figuring out words in meaningful ways and applying these strategies so that words are recognized automatically.

The various strategies of word recognition can be clustered into four basic groups: (a) common graphophonic patterns, (b) high-frequency or common words used in sentences (e.g., *the, a, or*) (c) meaning chunks of words, and (d) contextual supports through meanings of sentences, texts, and illustrations. Each of these strategies relates to one or more of the cueing systems of written language. The use of common graphophonic patterns guides children in using the graphophonic cues. The high-frequency words that are used as the "glue" of English grammar relate to the syntactic system. Guidance in the meaning chunks of words such as root words and endings (e.g., stop, stops, stopping, stopped, stoplight) encourages children to use the semantic cueing system. Finally, learning about and applying these strategies to engaging and meaningful text allows children to use the cues provided by the pragmatic system. We begin with the final strategy—the use of contextual supports—because the other strategies are useful insofar as they are applied and coordinated with the contexts of texts.

Contextual Supports.   As the description of the cueing systems showed, readers have four contexts or systems that they can use when they encounter unfamiliar words in a text. Use of all four systems is highly interdependent, whatever the level of a reader. At the beginning stages, however, syntactic and semantic cues can only be used when children have at least some facility in the third or graphophonic system. That is, until children can recognize a core group of words in the sentences of a text, they cannot use the syntactic and semantic cues provided by the grammar and meanings of sentences. When all written words are unfamiliar to readers as is the case with young children at the early stages of the process, they rely on the pragmatic system: the illustrations of a book and their previous experiences with books and storytelling to read the text. The readings of Brenda and Adam that are presented in Vignette 3.2 illustrate such use of the pragmatic system to make meaning of text. Fortunately for children's literacy learning, their ability to use the pragmatic system or *general context* of texts can be the basis for acquiring a core group of words (Lipson & Wixson, 1991). Once children can recognize some core words, they can use the cues from the *local contexts* provided by the syntax and semantics of phrases, sentences, and paragraphs to figure out unknown words (Lipson & Wixson, 1991).

Here we give a preview of the manner in which young children's ability to use the general context can be the foundation upon which word recognition strategies are built. When kindergartners or first graders see the book in Figure 3.1, their knowledge base, sometimes called a "schema" (Anderson & Pearson, 1984), about air travel will be activated. This hypothesis is confirmed if the teacher states that the title of the book is *You Can Ride* (Koss, 1996). The sight of a small child flying a plane will also trigger the idea that

FIGURE 3.1   Example of a Predictable Text

You can ride on a wagon.
2   3

You can ride on a dragon.
4

You can ride on a plane.
5

You can ride on a train.
6

You can ride on a bus.
7

But come back to us!
8

From *You Can Ride* by Amy Koss, illustrated by Darius Detwiler, © 1996 Silver Burdett Ginn Inc. Used with permission.

this is not a "real" story, leading children to expect that some of the characters or events in the remainder of the book may be fanciful. If the first page of text has an illustration of a child in a wagon, children will activate another schema—the category of things that can be ridden. When the next episode shows the book's character riding a dragon, some children may recognize the rhyming structure of the text. By the time that the teacher has read the second iteration of "You can ride on a . . .", many children will understand that the book has a predictable structure and will join the teacher in reading along the next several lines. This predictable structure, however, changes in the concluding page of the book. However, by pausing before stating the final word *us*, the teacher can encourage children to use the rhyming pattern. By focusing on words in predictable books such as *dragon, wagon,* and *ride* that are meaningful to children and by steadily directing children's attention to the high-frequency words such as *can* and *you,* children begin to consistently recognize a core group of words. We will describe predictable books and the instructional procedures that guide children in recognizing words later in this chapter and in other chapters in this book. The underlying motivation for these materials and activities in emergent literacy classrooms is to build on young children's extensive knowledge about the world around them and about stories and their interest in the engaging illustrations and the rhythmical patterns of books.

As children acquire fluency with a group of words, strategies related to syntax and semantics become relevant. These two systems are almost always used simultaneously. When readers encounter an unknown word such as the italicized word in the phrase "on *top* of the hill," their sense of grammar restricts their choices to only certain words—nouns. But just any noun will not do. The meaning of the recognized words in the phrase confines the choices even more. The following examples show the range of facility with syntactic and semantic cues among first graders at the same point in the school year:

Text:	"Coco lives on top of the hill, in the house with the purple roof." (Gomi, 1979).
Alex:	"Coco lives on top of the hill, in a house with her people."
Toby:	"Coco lives on top of the hill, in the house on the purple road."
Becca:	"Coco lives on top of the hill, in her house with a purple roof."
Carlos:	"Coco lives in on top of the hill, in a house with the purple roof."

Alex is intent on establishing meaning. When he encounters new words— "purple" and "roof"—he chooses to ignore the word "roof" so that his substitution of *people* for *purple* makes sense. Toby, who was uncertain about the word *roof,* substitutes another word that begins similarly—*road*. A purple road is conceivable but is not supported by the illustrations that accompany the text. As is typical of children at the very early stages of reading, Toby chose not to retrace his steps.

As children's facility with other word recognition strategies increases, transformations such as Toby's and Alexander's are likely to be corrected to ensure meaning and to account for the words on the page. In the case of Becca's transformation of *the* to *her* and *the* to *a,* the meaning is acceptable. Since Coco is female, the expression "her house" is appropriate. As Carlos reads ahead after saying *in* for *on,* he quickly realizes that "in top" does not make sense. While his substitution came from the same grammatical class, the meaning was not acceptable. He engages in a *self-correction* where he retraces his steps and gives a response that makes sense in the context.

But facility with the graphophonic system does not preclude transformations by readers. When children are highly engaged in what they are reading, they may say "daddy" for "father." Children who speak dialects of English may transform a phrase in a text to comply with the underlying rules of their dialect, changing "He is going" to "He be going" (Goodman, 1973).

The next three word recognition strategies—meaningful chunks of words, high-frequency words, and letter-sound patterns—all relate to the cues provided by the graphophonic system or the word level of English. For children to develop as readers, however, these strategies are useful insofar as children can use them in the context of interesting text. Carlos's self-correction illustrates a reader's monitoring of the meaning that occurs when all of the word recognition strategies are used simultaneously. For children such as Alex who eliminated words or Toby who was oblivious to nuances in meaning, guidance in coordinating information from the four cueing systems is necessary. Clay (1985) has identified "cross-checking" as a strategy that can be useful for beginning readers. Cross-checking refers to "checking cues against one another" (Clay, 1985, p. 73). Teachers' comments that support children in becoming adept at cross-checking include: "Check to see if what you read looks right and sounds right to you" (Clay, 1985, p. 73). Toby's teacher might also have encouraged him to cross-check by saying, "It could be *road* but look at the letter *f* at the end of the word" (Clay, 1985, p. 73).

Meaningful Chunks of Words.   *Morphemes* are the smallest meaning units of language (Lindfors, 1980). There are two types of morphemes or meaning units in English: free or base morphemes and bound morphemes. Free morphemes communicate the essential meaning. These units can stand alone. Take the word *play.* The smallest unit of that word that communicates meaning is *play.* This morpheme appears with bound morphemes such as -ing, -s, -ed, and -ful. Bound morphemes never appear alone but, when attached to a free morpheme, as in *plays, playing, played, playful,* refine its meaning.

The examples of bound morphemes with the word *play* demonstrate their two types: inflectional endings and derivational endings or affixes. These types of morphemes are present in almost any book that beginning readers will see. For example, the use of inflectional endings can be seen in the following sentence in Else Holmelund Minark's (1960) *Little Bear's Friend:*

> They **walked** along **eating cookies** and **talking,** and soon they **came** to the river.   (Minark, 1960, p. 21, boldfaced type added)

There are three types of inflectional endings in this sentence: (a) plural—cookies, (b) past tense—came, walked; (c) continuous—eating, talking. A fourth category—possessive—is in the title: Bear's. If Little Bear had described his friend, Emily, as his "best" friend, the fifth type of inflectional ending that designates "comparative" would have been present (i.e., best, better). The sixth type of inflectional ending is the word "hugs" in the sentence "Emily hugs Little Bear"—the third person singular form of a verb.

The functions of words are also refined through a second group of morphemes, derivational, that pertain to suffixes and prefixes. Two sentences from a popular children's book entitled *Fortunately* (Charlip, 1964) illustrate the nature of this group of morphemes:

> Fortunately there was a parachute in the airplane.
> Unfortunately there was a hole in the parachute.   (Charlip, 1964)

The word "fortunately" has two suffixes, "ate" and ly," that are added to the noun "fortune." The word "unfortunately" in the second sentence illustrates yet another modification through the addition of the prefix "un."

These two sentences from *Fortunately* demonstrate one additional way in which morphemes are combined and changed to convey different meanings: compound words. The word "airplane" has been formed by combining two base or free morphemes. The word "parachute" is also a compound word but using Latin origins which are not as well known as the components of airplane. "Para" means to "prepare" and "chute" means "to fall." As both examples of compound words show, the addition of two morphemes is not simply the sum of the parts. The meaning of compound words usually retains a connection to the component words but is typically not a literal translation. A "firehouse" is not a house on fire. Neither is a "housecat" a cat which is a house (Fromkin & Rodman, 1974).

We are not suggesting that young children should be taught any of the distinctions about morphemes that we have described. As teachers, however, such distinctions are important ones to understand in guiding instruction and in choosing books. In the past, each form of a word has been treated as another "stimulus" for children to learn. Yet young children are quite facile with many morphemic forms of language by the time they enter school (Chomsky, 1972). Encouraging children to understand that they can also read *plays, played,* and *playing* when they have learned the word *play* builds on the syntactic and semantic cueing systems that we described earlier. Children should be introduced early to the ways in which a word is refined in the morphemic system through extensive modeling and exposure to these "families" of words that share meanings and often vary only slightly in their form. All too frequently, the attention of educators has been diverted to the debate over the relative role of phonics in beginning reading instruction. Consequently, the cues provided by the semantic system of English have not been used fully by beginning readers.

High-Frequency Words.   High-frequency or common words are the "glue" words of written language. In the last sentence, there were four of these words—*or, are, the,* and *of.* Books can be written without many high-frequency words, but to do so requires using a structure that is primarily one of labeling, such as the concept books that parents frequently read to toddlers. Further, young children often write labels and lists that do not require high-frequency words. But high-frequency words become important if children are to move beyond the labeling and listing stage. The list of the 100 most frequent words in written English that appears in Table 3.4 (Carroll, Davies, & Richman, 1971) illustrates the nature of this group of words.

TABLE 3.4	100 Most Frequent Words in Written English		
the	or	out	its
of	by	them	who
and	one	then	now
a	had	she	people
to	not	many	my
in	but	some	made
is	what	so	over
you	all	these	did
that	were	would	down
it	when	other	only
he	we	into	way
for	there	has	find
was	can	more	use
on	an	her	may
are	your	two	water
as	which	like	long
with	their	him	little
his	said	see	very
they	if	time	after
at	do	could	words
be	will	no	called
this	each	make	just
from	about	than	where
I	how	first	most
have	up	been	know

From J.B. Carroll, P. Davies, B. Richman (1971). *Word frequency book.* Boston: Houghton Mifflin.

As can be seen in studying the words in Table 3.4, the high-frequency words that occur over and over again in sentences are primarily the prepositions, conjunctions, pronouns, and articles that form the structure of sentences rather than the nouns, verbs, adjectives, and adverbs that convey the ideas. The abstractness of these words is one of the features that makes them so difficult for young children to learn. Even for adults, the task of providing clear definitions of words such as "the" and "and" is not easy. It should not be surprising, then, that young children state emphatically that these are not "real words" (Adams, 1990).

The functions that these words serve are often many, leading to multiple meanings of words. For example, *The American Heritage Dictionary* (1992) gives 12 different meanings for the word *can.* Adding to the complexity of high-frequency words is the presence of numerous homophones—words that sound the same but are spelled differently. For example, the fifth word on the list in Table 3.4—*to*—is such a word as are numerous others (e.g., *or, would, no, here*).

High-frequency words are important in children's development as facile readers. In the text that third through eighth graders read, the 100 words in Table 3.4 and 9 additional words account for about 50% of the words (Adams, 1990). In the past, instruction in these words dominated children's beginning reading experiences. Only when they had mastered the core group of words (usually defined in terms of the 200 or so most frequent words), could they move on to highly meaningful words. For many children, especially those with limited prior literacy experiences, the hurdle of memorizing high-frequency words was a formidable one.

Because these words are often ambiguous and abstract, children will need a substantial amount of guidance in attending to and recognizing them instantaneously. When children's reading development is examined in home and preschool settings, the first words that children recognize instantaneously are words that are personally highly meaningful. When preschoolers' favorite words—chosen daily over nine months—were examined, 98% of the words were nouns, and half of these were proper nouns, names of favorite people ("Uncle Dan" for one child), favorite things ("Magic Markers" for another child), and favorite places or events ("Disney World" for a child about to go on a vacation) (Hiebert, 1983). Where do these words come from? Ashton-Warner (1963) described the earliest words as "organic" words—words that live for children.

Teachers can guide children in developing a core group of words by showing them the words that they recognize, including those from the physical environment. These words may include ones such as *stop,* shown on the common shape of a stop sign (Hiebert, 1978), as well as names of fast-food restaurants. Children's names—their own and their classmates'—are an additional source. Yet another source for this core group of words are books that are made up of highly meaningful words—nouns, verbs, sometimes adjectives and adverbs. Numerous books that consist of labels of objects or actions have been published recently with content for primary-level children, rather than the toddlers who are often the audience of labeling books. Some of these books contain rhymes such as *What Rhymes with Snake?* (Brown, 1994). Many alphabet books fall into this category. Artists such as Donald Crews are masterful in drawing on environmental print (e.g., *School Bus*), while photographers such as Tana Hoban portray critical concepts such as opposites with photographs and captions, as in *Push Pull Empty Full* (Hoban, 1972). Because these books can assist children in learning a core group of words, we have included a list of them in Table 3.5. The purpose of these books, as with other sources of highly meaningful words such as print from stop and yield signs and children's own organic words, is for children to associate words that they use and understand in oral language with written words. Once children have a corpus of 20 or so words, teachers can begin showing children how to create sentences by adding words from the category of high-frequency words in Table 3.4.

Consistent Letter-Sound Patterns in Words. Focusing on consistent graphophonic relationships within words is another skill that children need to gain to become independent readers and writers. While there is an exception to almost every rule about English letter-sound correspondences, English is

TABLE 3.5	Label Books
Author and Title	**Concept**
Brown, Rick. *What Rhymes with Snake?*	rhyming words (e.g., cow, sow)
Crews, Donald. *School Bus*	trip on a school bus
Crews, Donald. *Truck*	loading and travel of a trailer truck
Florian, Douglas. *Nature Walk*	sights and sounds on a hike
Hennessey, B. J. *School Days*	members and activities of a classroom
Hoban, Tana. *Push Pull Empty Full*	opposites
Kalan, Robert. *Rain.* Illus. Donald Crews	weather
MacDonald, Suse. *Alphabetics*	alphabet letters that evolve into objects (a=ark)
Maurer, Donna. *Annie, Bea, and Chi Chi Dolores: A School Day Alphabet.* Illus. Denys Cazet	alphabet of school activities (a=all aboard)
McMillan, Bruce. *What the Class Pet Saw*	contents of a school
Miller, Margaret. *Whose Shoe?*	matching shoes and their owners

alphabetic. A picture or ideograph such as a Chinese character is not suddenly inserted in English, and there are patterns that will never occur as a word (e.g., "SBXA").

The term "phonics" refers to the body of knowledge about the English letter-sound correspondences. The intent of phonics instruction is for readers to use this knowledge *to figure out the pronunciation of words with which they are unfamiliar in written form* (Anderson, Hiebert, Scott, & Wilkinson, 1985; Durkin, 1993). The words in the last sentence are highlighted to emphasize that phonics instruction involves children's use of English letter-sound correspondences to pronounce unknown words in text and, in so doing, recognize these words as part of their lexicon. The aim of phonics instruction is not for children to recite rules about these relationships. Nor is the intent that young children learn the rules so that they can decipher strings of letters with letter-sound correspondences that could appear in English but do not, such as *jat* or *vam*.

The tool of phonics is an important one in that many of the words that children encounter early in their reading are ones that they use in oral language and that have consistent letter-sound patterns. Without this tool, children are left guessing and using trial-and-error procedures. The continual controversy around the use of phonics with beginning readers pertains to the number of letter-sound relationships children are expected to know. There are several hundred rules for the relationships between letters and sounds in English (Venezky, 1967). Although some of the programs of the 1970s attempted to do so, it is relatively futile and not worthwhile to try teaching all the rules to children. However, children do benefit from knowledge of the most common patterns. When children have been guided in common patterns, they begin to look for patterns that they have not been taught (Juel & Roper-Schneider, 1985). That is precisely the stance that teachers need to generate: the sense that the sounds and letters relate to one another in systematic ways.

Unlike words, individual syllables are physically distinguishable in speech. For example, a listener can detect two separate units representing each of the two syllables *yel* and *low* when the word *yellow* is spoken aloud. Syllabic awareness has been described as the link between children's interest in rhythmical and rhyming patterns in oral language and the focus on individual sounds or phonemes that is required to figure out unknown words (Adams, 1990). Consistent with this theory, young children more easily perceive the part of the syllable with the vowel and the consonants that follow it such as *at* in *cat* than they can perceive a string of individual phonemes such as /a//t/. This part of the syllable that consists of the vowel and the consonants that follow it is called the *rime*. In the word *cat*, the "c" is described as the *onset*, that part of the syllable that precedes the vowel. In some contexts, rimes are also referred to as phonograms or as word families. According to a dictionary definition, the word "rime" is an equivalent to "rhyme" historically (American Heritage Dictionary, 1992). In our discussions, we will use "rime" to refer to the consistent patterns formed by vowels and consonants, such as *am* in

[handwritten margin note: more easily than rime than phoneme]

ham, Sam, and *am* or *ain* in *train, plain, rain, main, Spain.* The word
"rhyme" will be used to refer to poem or verse where words with rimes occur
at the ends of lines. For example, in *Green Eggs and Ham,* Dr. Seuss (1960)
used the rime *am* to form the rhyming verse:

> I do not like them,
> Sam-I-am.
> I do not like
> green eggs and ham   (p. 12).

The ease with which rimes can be perceived is good news for word recognition because many of the basic rimes form one-syllable words that appear
often in young children's books. Further, a small set of these rimes accounts
for a large number of words. According to Wylie and Durrell (1970), 37 rimes
account for 500 words that occur frequently in the texts for primary-level
students. These 37 rimes are clustered according to their vowel pattern in
Table 3.6. There are many additional rimes within each of the categories in
Table 3.6 but the major categories of vowel patterns are included. As an
example of the additional rimes within a category, consider the instances of
the "V-C" pattern. According to Fries (1963), all of the following rimes occur
in single- or multi-syllable words:

ab, ad, ag, am, **an, ap,** as, **at,** ax
ib, id, ig, im, **in, ip,** is, it, ix
eb, ed, eg, em, en, ep, et, ex
ob, od, og, om, on, **op,** ot, ox
ub, ud, **ug,** um, un, up, ut, ux   (pp. 171–173)

V-C
vowel consonant

The boldfaced patterns also appear in Table 3.6. The number of instances of
patterns in this category illustrates that the rimes in Table 3.6 comprise only
a fraction of the rimes. The six V-C rimes in Table 3.6 represent 14% of the
rimes within this category. From this, we can conclude that the V-C rime is
one that occurs frequently enough to warrant attention in a beginning literacy program.

Among the more puzzling rimes for some children will be the vowel
dipthong in which a new sound is created by the combination of vowels. One
rime of this type appears in Table 3.6—*aw.* There are a number of others
with which teachers should be familiar as they work with beginning readers:
oo (cool, cook), ew (crew), au (auto), ou (out), ow (owl), oi (oil), and *y
(oyster).*

One consistent pattern that does not appear in Table 3.6 is the single
vowel at the end of a syllable as in *so, no, go, ho, yo.* This pattern will be
easier for beginning readers to grasp than the vowel dipthong in that the
sound associated with the vowel is similar to the letter name.

In addition to the vowel patterns, attention to particular clusters of consonants that are represented in the "Illustrative Words" in Table 3.6 can also
assist children. The words that share the rime "ake" in Table 3.6 include two
types of consonant groupings: (a) consonant blends as in *Blake, brake,*

TABLE 3.6   Characteristics of the "37 Rimes in 500 Primary-Level Words"

Vowel Pattern	Frequently Occurring Rimes[1]	Illustrative Words[2]
"Short" vowel • Basic pattern: V[3]-C[4]	• an, ap, at, in, ip, op, ug	• can, Dan, fan, Jan, man, Nan, pan, ran, tan, van, bran, clan, Fran, plan, scan, span, Stan
• Extended pattern: V-C-C	• ack, ank, ash, ell, est, ick, ill, ing, ink, ock, uck, ump, unk	• back, hack, Jack, lack, Mack, pack, rack, quack, sack, tack, black, clack, crack, knack, slack, smack, snack, stack, track, shack, whack
"Long" vowel • V-C-e (silent e)	• ake, ale, ame, ate, ice, ide, ine, oke	• bake, cake, fake, Jake, lake, make, rake, sake, wake, Blake, brake, drake, snake, shake
• V-V-C	• ail, ain, ay, eat	• bail, fail, Gail, hail, jail, mail, nail, pail, rail, sail, tail, vail, wail, snail, trail
• V+ght	• ight	• fight, light, might, night, right, sight, blight, bright, fright, plight, slight
"R-controlled" vowel • V-r	• ir, or	• fir, sir, stir, girl, twirl, swirl, whirl
• V-r-e	• ore	• bore, core, gore, more, pore, sore, tore, wore, store, chore
Dipthongs (two vowels or vowel/consonant that create a single, unique sound)	• aw	• caw, haw, jaw, law, raw, saw, claw, draw, flaw, straw, thaw

[1]Rimes are the 37 that Wylie and Durrell (1970) identified as accounting for 500 words that occur frequently in text for primary-level children.
[2]Illustrative words are for the first rime of each type.
[3]V is an abbreviation for vowel.
[4]C is an abbreviation for consonant.

drake, snake, and (b) consonant digraphs as in *shake.* In a blend, each consonant retains its unique sounds. Consonant digraphs, like vowel dipthongs, are pairings that provide a single sound that is different from that associated with either letter. Directing children's attention to the unique sound that occurs when particular consonants are paired can be helpful. As well as the consonant digraph *sh* as represented in *shake,* several other consonant digraphs can be located in Table 3.6: *ch* in *chore* (as well as *ch* in *chill*), and *th* in *thaw* (as well as *th* in *the*). Three additional consonant digraphs are: *ph (phone), -ng (sing), -gh (rough).*

In considering which information about the letter-sound system to highlight, teachers will want to put a priority on those patterns that give children the greatest leverage. For example, some of the V-C rimes occur in only a word or two and/or appear rarely in books or conversations (*gat, neb*). Further, there is no evidence that each pattern should get equal billing in an emergent literacy program or that all patterns should be taught. Within the research literature, there have been few examinations of how much exposure to rimes children with low levels of conventional literacy require to understand the alphabetic principle. At the same time, there is no evidence that going through all of the patterns will bring children to this understanding.

Guiding children to a working knowledge of the groups of patterns in Table 3.6 will be useful as long as this knowledge is viewed as a means rather than an end of learning. Playfulness with these patterns will likely go much farther than attending to each of the patterns individually. The metacognitive stance that we discussed in Chapter 2 where children reflect on what they have learned and establish what is the same and different about words that they are learning will also be useful. Encouraging children to collect words, including multisyllabic words, that fit particular patterns can assist in this process. Presenting these words on kiosks or word walls (Cunningham, 1995) has proven an effective context for supporting this metacognitive stance toward letter-sound patterns.

With experience in hearing and seeing words with consistent patterns, children can be guided in extending their knowledge to new words. Comparing and contrasting the patterns in unknown words with those in known words is described as the analogy strategy (Cunningham, 1979; Goswami & Mead, 1992). After recognizing *at* in *cat,* children are guided in extending their knowledge to *fat* and *sat.* The use of the analogy strategy in young readers can be enhanced if the books that children are given allow them to apply their knowledge (Juel & Roper-Schneider, 1985). Such books need not contain tedious text such as the "Dad had to fan Nan. Dad had to fan Dan." of past eras' reading textbooks (Rasmussen & Goldberg, 1964). Stories must flow naturally and not be stilted, while giving opportunity for application of knowledge about word patterns. The line "'Let's dig, dig, dig!' said the little pigs" (Kirk, 1996) illustrates the natural flow of language while preserving the potential for students to apply their emerging knowledge of letter-sound patterns. As children progress in their reading, they will learn to draw on already-known patterns in multisyllabic words. Students learn to expect that word patterns give cues to pronunciation which they can use to connect to their knowledge of word meanings derived from background knowledge and contextual supports.

Spelling Words

Traditional spelling instruction has often been associated with didactic methods, where children are presented with new words on Monday and tested on Friday. They spend the intervening days using a variety of techniques to memorize the words for Friday's test. Over the past several decades, the lenses of cognitive psychologists and linguists have shifted perspectives on spelling instruction. In particular, linguists such as Read (1975) described children's attempts to spell as evidence of their knowledge of the relationships between speech and print, efforts known as "invented spelling." While this idea has been interpreted by some educators to imply an entire philosophy about learning to spell, we suggest that invented spelling represents a necessary start on the road to proficient spelling. While children may be limited in their accuracy when asked to invent their own spellings, they require many opportunities to test their hypotheses about sound-to-letter relationships. Thus there are two aspects to understanding early primary grade spelling processes: (a) the construct of invented spelling and (b) the strategies of conventional spelling.

Invented Spelling.   Invented spelling refers to the forms of children's spellings when they are encouraged to represent their knowledge about sound-letter relationships in whatever form they can as they create meaningful messages. The examples in Vignette 3.3 show the range of spellings in children's compositions in the fall of grade one. According to Read (1975), the spelling patterns of a particular child at a particular time or of a group of children who represent a range of developmental levels are neither random nor haphazard. Children's spelling productions manifest consistent rules. For a particular child at a particular point in time, similar rules will be used to spell different words. In Vignette 3.3, Juan always represents a word with one of its key letters, sometimes two. The exception to this rule is the spelling of an entire word that Juan has learned, "HAD." Mandie spells two words, "I" and "MOM," and uses letters she associates with the other important word in her message: "RTS" for recess.

Read (1975) described these productions of young children as "inventing" the spelling system. According to Read and other observers (e.g., Gentry, 1982) of young children's compositions, consistent patterns can be seen in children's spellings over time. Primary patterns that characterize young children's spellings are summarized in Table 3.7. The patterns detailed in Table 3.7 apply to children's spelling efforts at the point where they have moved to representing letters (see Table 3.3, the fourth of DeFord's writing categories). Of the first graders whose compositions appear in Vignette 3.3, all but Travis are using one of the prominent spelling strategies.

TABLE 3.7 Strategies in Children's Spelling

Prominent Strategy	Description	Example
Prephonemic	Letters are used to write words but the sound-symbol relationships are unrelated to target word.	"C" for "hat"
Early phonemic	Some phonemes are represented by letters, typically most salient phoneme(s) in a word.	"DR" for "Dear"
Phonetic	Attempts are made to represent most sounds in words, often letter name that most closely resembles sound.	"wns" for "once"
Simple Associations	Simple vowels and consonants are represented correctly but complex patterns are not.	"bid" for "bird"
Strategic Extensions	With complex vowels and consonants, attempts reflect complex English patterns, although not the conventions of English.	"bote" for "boat"
Conventional		

These strategies represent an elaboration of stages originally proposed in J.R. Gentry (1982): An analysis of developmental spelling in *GNYS AT WRK. The Reading Teacher, 36,* 192–199.

Mandie's and Juan's spellings are typical of early phonemic strategy use. Both children attempt to represent most words with at least one letter. Mandie's and Juan's compositions illustrate, however, that there are processes at work other than those that are strictly associated with knowledge of sound-letter correspondences. Children also memorize spellings, indicated by Mandie's production of "MOM" and Juan's spelling of "HAD." The use of the phonetic strategy can be seen in Albert's composition, where he represents most of the sounds he hears.

Conventional Spelling Strategies. While the typical schemes of invented spelling (see, e.g., Gentry, 1982) cluster children's spelling together once they have attained some conventional proficiencies, there are substantial differences in children's proficiencies and in the strategies that they use. The task is exacerbated by the idiosyncrasies of English spelling, which means that rule application for one word may not apply to another similarly pronounced word, whether idiosyncratic to the child's dialect or part of the mainstream pronunciations. Table 3.7 includes strategies that distinguish children's progress toward conventional spelling.

Many children are quite effective using a basic association strategy but are reluctant to attempt strategic extensions. These children expect each sound to have a corresponding letter-sound in English spelling. Unfortunately, this is an erroneous generalization to make about all English spellings. Without the willingness to take risks—and to err—children will have difficulty becoming good spellers. Because spelling is not a direct derivative of phonological knowledge, the sounds in the spoken word must be analyzed and corresponding knowledge about how these sounds are represented must be invoked before the associated spelling is produced. Difficulty in either phonemic analysis, knowledge of spelling patterns, or both inhibits good spelling.

Spelling patterns are sufficiently complex to make the task a difficult one. There is considerably more uncertainty in sound-to-spelling than in spelling-to-sound translations. For example, the letter f quite reliably symbolizes the phoneme /f/. In contrast, the phoneme /f/ can be spelled as f, ff, ph, or gh (Adams, 1990). Adams (1990) reports a study in which the sound-to-spelling patterns in the one- and two-syllable words that six- to nine-year-olds commonly write were analyzed. Within this core group of words that primary-level children write, there were 166 different sound-to-spelling relationships represented. Because it is difficult, if not impossible, for emergent writers to learn all of these patterns, it is not surprising to find that those who attend to the patterns of letters within words, rather than individual sound-letter correspondences, are the more proficient spellers. Once children apply strategic extensions, they may find another strategy, examining the spelling to see if it "looks right," to be valuable. Checking the appearance of a word's spelling involves the use of visual imagery. Drawing on their knowledge of spelling patterns and the implicit recognition of words they may have encountered (i.e., they "look right") are all important information sources for emergent spellers.

Awareness of Literary Elements

When we introduced the fourth system of language, the pragmatic, we noted that written language assumes different forms. Sentences are organized into paragraphs and paragraphs are related to one another to form particular text structures. These structures help us, as readers, to anticipate the kind of information authors include in their texts and the form through which they present the information. For example, when we begin to read a novel, we assume that early in the text, the author will introduce and begin to develop the story's primary characters and setting. In contrast, if we were to choose an informational text, such as a book on the role of herbs in healing common health problems, we would expect to see descriptions of herbs that are used for different purposes and possibly explanations of how and why they work. Stories and informational text illustrate variation across a critical literary element: the text's structure. We use the term *literary elements* in this section to encompass such traditional features as point of view, use of figurative language, and specific structural aspects (e.g., character, setting, plot, conflict), as well as specific characteristics of books for young readers, such as predictable word patterns and other forms of language play.

Literary elements have usually been more central to the curriculum in the middle grades and above, remaining in the background in early childhood classrooms. However, we believe that two elements are worthy of early introduction—genre and language play—because they can positively influence children's literary acquisition and dispositions toward text.

Genres.   The term *genre* refers to the type of text structure or style that writers use to organize their texts. Three genres are common to young children: stories or narrative text, informational or expository text, and predictable or rhyming text.

Narrative texts or *stories* tend to be structured around a set of characters who face a particular conflict. The narrative takes place within a defined setting, and the flow of the tale usually follows from the introduction of the conflict or problem that the characters attempt to resolve. Narrative texts may be fictional such as Bunting's (1994) *Smoky Night,* which also relates information about historical events: The story is a fictional account of interactions between neighbors during the riots in Los Angeles in 1992. Narrative texts take a variety of forms. Folk tales, myths, fables, rhymes and poems, historical fiction, modern fantasy, autobiography/biography, and modern fiction are among the most common.

Informational books are, of course, books that provide information about concepts, events, people, and so forth. Just as narrative texts take various forms, expository texts have a range of forms, usually referred to in terms of the text structure: explanation, comparison/contrast, problem/solution, description, and so forth (see Armbruster & Anderson, 1984; Meyer, 1975). Early introduction of informational, or nonfiction, books to young children helps them become accustomed to the different ways in which informational texts are written relative to the more common narrative texts they frequently encounter. The uses of informational books are demonstrated in a kindergarten class where children were asking whether dinosaurs can jump (Richgels, 1995, p. 248). After a vote on the question, the following exchange occurred:

> **Teacher:** Some of you said "Yes" and some of you said "No." What could we do, what could we do to find out more information about that? What could we do?
>
> **C:** Look in a book!

Children in this classroom clearly understood that texts can take different forms, and providing information is one of their key purposes. By using informational texts to uncover specific information, teachers can model using a book's table of contents and index, exploring pictures for information, reading sections of text out of sequence, and other strategies unique to texts of this type.

Predictable books are common ones children see in schools. These books can draw on a variety of content—information as well as events associated with stories. The use of a pattern defines a predictable book. Nursery rhymes (see Jerry's and Jacob's responses in Chapter 2) illustrate this repetitive form of text. Some predictable books use an enumerative structure where various aspects of a class or category are listed. For example, in Shaw's (1947) *It Looked Like Spilt Milk,* the text is predictable due to the repetitions of the children's perceptions of a cloud. Some books use a predictable pattern that encourages labeling. The popular book *Brown Bear, Brown Bear, What Do You See?* (Martin, 1967) illustrates this pattern. Other books use a more sophisticated topic and more complex pattern, such as the sequence of steps in making something. Westcott's (1987) *Peanut Butter and Jelly* is illustrative of this type, beginning with the words, "First you take the dough and knead it, knead it." The text moves through the sequence of making bread and jelly, ending with, "Then you take the sandwich and eat it, eat it. Peanut butter, peanut butter, Jelly, jelly." There are also many "stories" among predictable text. For example, Wildsmith's (1982) *Cat on the Mat* tells a story using a repetitive pattern.

Understanding the ways in which these genres function can be especially helpful to children at the beginning stages of reading. For example, one of the primary ways in which children can apply their emerging word recognition strategies is through reading predictable texts with a repeated phrase. However, children need to be aware of this text structure for its predictability to prove useful. Text structure awareness is as, if not more, essential to children as writers. To communicate their message, they must make choices about genres.

Language Play.   Language play is prominent in books for young children. It consists of various techniques, including the rhymes and repetitive elements that we have already discussed. Other techniques used to play with language and generate story interest involve unusual names of characters or odd twists and turns in the storyline. In the earliest books for young readers, these humorous uses of language and of storylines are often fairly obvious to young children. A quick question or two by the teacher will be sufficient for most children to see the humor and understand the meaning.

One important form of language play that may be less expected or evident to young children is onomatopoeia, the creation of a word by imitation of a sound associated with its referent. This technique is used frequently in children's books and adds much humor and interest to reading for young children as they learn to associate letters and sounds. Dr. Seuss was a master at inventing words and unique sounds such as the "zyzzer-zazzer-zuzz" for the letter Z in his *ABC* book. However, this technique may cause confusion for young children because successful application of phonics knowledge may end up, correctly, in identifying a set of sounds that create a "pseudoword," not an actual word in the language.

For example, as the turtle in *I Wish I Could Fly* (Maris, 1987) attempts the specialties of other animals, his efforts are summarized with words that represent his clumsy attempts: CRASH! BANG! WALLOP! CRUNCH! When these sounds are familiar and exaggerated, the story becomes humorous. Without guidance, however, some children will treat these as words that may not make sense but must be "read correctly." We have watched a child who was struggling with basic concepts of print read *Cat on the Mat* rhythmically until she reached the sound "Sssppstt!" of the cat. At that point, she stopped and hesitated, rather than try to read the pseudoword. For occasions such as this, children can benefit from discussing authors' "language play." As the little girl plays outside in *Rain Talk* (Serfozo, 1990), the rain goes, "Plip-PlipPlipPlipPlipPlip." Children may benefit from talk about other sounds of the rain and how these might be written. Indeed, such talk highlights language play using rimes and onsets, discussed as part of children's automaticity with patterns of written language.

These necessary processes form an important basis for children's ongoing literacy acquisition. They are as critical to successful literacy use as are central processes. In the next section, we examine those processes that help young learners develop both necessary and central literacy processes.

Interim Processes

Interim, or temporary, processes aid in acquiring the necessary processes of recognizing and spelling words. The three interim processes include concepts about print, phonemic awareness, and letter naming. These three processes are important as children grapple with the alphabetic principle, the underlying rule-based system that connects oral with written language. Once children have made the transition to conventional word recognition and spelling, these interim processes need no longer be an instructional focus.

Concepts about Print

Gough and Hillinger (1980) refer to readers' understandings of written language functions and forms as "cryptanalytic intent," making the parallel between reading acquisition and deciphering a coded or cryptic message. This analogy may assist teachers in thinking about the task that confronts students who have had few prior experiences with reading and writing. Like sleuths attempting to decode a secret message, young children need to decipher the code of written language. Through interactions with adults in their environments, children learn the clues that allow them to decipher the written language system. Two categories of information are critical in establishing what written language is and the functions it serves: (a) print carries a message and (b) print has conventions and units (Juel, 1996).

Print Carries a Message.   Knowing where adults get the information to read and to write can be confusing to young children. When preschoolers were asked to identify the part of a book that their teachers and parents read to them, many three- and four-year-olds selected illustrations (Hiebert, 1979).

By age five, most children could identify the print as the source of the message. For children whose experiences with print have been primarily in environmental contexts, print may be confused with the logo, the distinctive type, or the colors on signs or labels (Masonheimer, Drum, & Ehri, 1984). Until children come to realize that the lines and shapes that people refer to in books and the environment represent the meanings that they use in oral language, they will struggle in literacy instruction. Young children can be taught to name or write letters but, without an understanding of the hows and whys of written language, they do not learn to read faster or better (Samuels, 1972).

Print Conventions and Concepts.   Once children understand that the squiggles represent meaning, they need to understand the conventions and units of this system. The rules underlying the system of a written language are arbitrary. For example, while choices regarding directionality differ across written languages, in English, directionality is from left to right and top to bottom. As teachers and parents point to print in enlarged books, children come to understand the directionality of written language.

Other concepts refer to the units of importance in written language and the relationship between oral and written language (e.g., word, letter, sentence, text or book, sounds, alphabet). The concept of "word" is critically important to acquire. In speech, words run together (e.g., Howyadoing?). In contrast, when writing or when reading printed text, children must understand where words begin and end. It is hard to connect the first letter in "monster" to the sound /m/ if the child is confused about where the word "monster" is on a page. Emerging readers and writers come to understand that the strings of letters between the spaces are the same units that they use in their speech.

Phonemic Awareness

Phonemes are the "smaller-than-syllable sounds that correspond roughly to individual letters" (Adams, 1990, p. 40). For example, the sound of /b/ in the word *bat* illustrates a phoneme. Researchers have related the ability to manipulate sounds or phonemic awareness to children's reading development (Bradley & Bryant, 1983; Juel, Griffith, & Gough, 1986; Juel, 1991; Perfetti, Beck, Bell, & Hughes, 1987). Why might this be? In oral language where words are run together, children need to focus on the *sense* of words, rather than their *sounds*. In fact, if people were consciously aware of each phoneme in an oral message, listening comprehension would become impossible. But, in learning to read and write, awareness of distinct sounds and their representation in written forms is essential. When children cannot distinguish between sounds in oral language, they will have a difficult time making links between sounds and letters. For example, to use the vowel-consonant pattern of *at* to figure out words such as *bat* and *fat* once the word *cat* has been learned, children need to be able to delete the initial phoneme and replace it with new phonemes. To form the spoken word */bat/* when viewing b and at, children also need to integrate or blend the onset with the rime.

Such aspects of phonemic awareness are necessary for children to successfully apply their knowledge of phonics, one of the word recognition strategies that we described earlier. However, phonemic awareness is not an interchangeable label for phonics. Phonemic awareness involves the ability to focus on and manipulate discrete sounds, while phonics involves the connection between a written symbol and a sound (Lipson & Wixson, 1991). In conventional phonics instruction, children may be asked to delete, blend, and segment sounds of words without specific guidance. For example, asking children to identify from a list of words one that begins the same as the word "fish" assumes children are able to isolate the initial sound in fish, then associate it with another at hand. In fact, this task requires children's facility with both blending and deleting phonemes, two aspects of phonemic awareness that have been identified consistently by researchers as important to literacy acquisition.

Children who have played rhyming games in their homes or preschools often have a strong sense of phonemic awareness (Tobin & Pikulski, 1983). When children have not had such opportunities, experiences need to be integrated into the emergent literacy classroom. Typically, such programs engage children in a variety of games and activities involving nursery rhymes, rhymed stories and rhyme production, segmentation of sentences into individual words, investigations of word length, clapping and dancing to syllabic rhythms and solving puzzles, and finally, isolation and identification, first of initial phonemes, and then of word-final and internal phonemes. The most successful methods have used nursery rhymes (Lundberg, Frost, & Petersen, 1988) which involve rhyme and alliteration, such as "Hickory Dickory Dock," presented in Vignette 2.3. Such language play is helpful, and most effective when coupled with the meaning-making activities we have described earlier. Through these activities, young learners come to understand how our written symbol system works and why it is valuable to have access to this code.

In this section, we emphasized the phonemic awareness that is required to distinguish the sounds of spoken language. The use of this knowledge in beginning reading and writing needs to be coupled with knowledge about the written symbols to allow the application of phonics. To make this connection, children also require knowledge of letters—the interim process to which we turn next.

Letter Naming

Think about learning to tell apart items that are distinguished by subtle changes in orientation. That is the task that confronts young children in learning to recognize the alphabet. The quartet of b, d, p, and q immediately comes to mind as the most complicated to remember. Yet, there are other confusing pairs such as f and t; s and z; h and n. Without the association of letters with sounds in familiar spoken words and as parts of recognizable words, the letters individually have no meaning. The letter B on a wall is as ornamental to young children as a cupola on a Victorian house. In addition, there are two forms of these letters—uppercase and lowercase—and two types of scripts—manuscript and cursive. Add to this mix the host of orthographies that are used in printing books and signs, where particular letters can differ considerably in their appearance. Unlike other aspects of the physical world where children are taught to give the general name—for example, chair—to numerous different objects, the letter-naming task requires children to give different names to meaningless squiggles that look very similar.

Young children are often praised by adults for attending to letters, and may be eager to please adults by attending to this aspect of their world. Many children come to school able to recite the letter names, especially as part of the alphabet song. But it is only when letters become associated with children's names and those of family members that the task becomes a meaningful one for them. The critical task for beginning reading is more than simply letter recitation. In the 1970s, the U.S. Office of Education studies (Bond & Dykstra, 1967) showed that letter naming was the best predictor of reading success, which led several researchers to initiate projects where children were taught to name the letters. They found that letter-naming drills alone, without immersing children in literacy tasks, did not increase children's success in becoming literate (Samuels, 1972). Letter naming is part of a host of other things that children are learning. Mason (1980) described a broad array of concepts of and experiences with print that paralleled children's acquisition of letter naming. In homes, letter naming occurs as part of book reading as well as tasks such as playing with magnetic letters to make names of favorite people.

In their work with initially low-performing first-grade children, Hiebert and her colleagues (Hiebert, Colt, Catto, & Gury, 1992) found that the majority of the children (87%) were facile in naming uppercase letter names but much less so in naming lowercase letters (29%). Letter naming was closely tied to phonemic awareness, and phonemic awareness predicted children's fluency in reading at the end of the year. By midyear, all but one child was able to name lowercase letters proficiently. The researchers examined how children came to learn letters and, more importantly, to associate these letters with sounds. They identified three dimensions of instruction that supported children's learning: (a) pairing letters in contrastive pairs, (b) assuming a metacognitive stance, and (c) embedding letter naming in meaningful print use.

The order of letter introduction was given considerable thought. The order was derived from the phonological features of the sounds and the graphic distinctiveness of the letters. While an extended discussion of speech theory is not possible here (see Perkins, 1971), several examples illustrate the underlying distinctions. Feel the shape of your mouth as you begin saying the words mad and dad. Now do the same with the words pat and bat. What makes sounds distinctive involves the place where the sound comes from and the manner in which the sound is made. The sounds /m/ and /d/ are different from one another in the place where the sound is produced: /m/ is produced with both lips, while /d/ is produced through contact with the "alveolar ridge." These two sounds also differ in the manner in which the sounds are made. The sound of /m/ is nasal in that air is directed through the nose while the sound of /d/ involves creating pressure in the air tract and releasing it. The letters that are associated with these two sounds also differ significantly from one another: the "m" consisting of curves and the "d" using a partial circle and a high, straight line. By contrast, the place and manner of making the sounds of /p/ and /b/ are similar. Both sounds are made by both lips and involve pressure in the air tract. They differ only in that the /b/ is voiced and the /p/ is unvoiced. Further, their graphic forms are minimally different.

We have clustered pairs of letters together in a manner that provides maximum contrasts for children in the phonological and graphic characteristics of sounds and letters:

h-c

m-d

l-g (g as in get)

s-p

t-v

b-r

n-w

j-k

f-n

When letter-sound correspondences are presented in pairs, children can make distinctions that are not possible with single letters and sounds. The letters and sounds that occur less frequently and usually at the ends of words—z and x—can be integrated when appropriate, as can the occasional but interesting combination of "qu."

The metacognitive stance that was described in Chapter 2 means that the uniquenesses and likenesses of letter-sound correspondences are the object of conversations. In an analysis of teachers' manuals a decade ago (and we suspect this would be the case today), each letter was treated as if no letters had been previously taught or learned (Hiebert & Papierz, 1990). When the learning of each letter is treated as an isolated event, children are confused about the relationships of letters to one another as well as to the larger task of reading. By emphasizing the uniquenesses of letters as they are contrasted to other letters, children are encouraged to take a metacognitive stance in learning about letters and their correspondences to sounds.

Finally, to become fluent and adept with letter-sound correspondences, children need to be exposed to many books and, even more importantly, to daily occasions where they can write. Gury (1994) found that, through shared book reading events in kindergarten with heterogeneous groups of children, children's letter-naming abilities rose and their phonemic awareness increased as well.

Orchestrating the Processes

Early views of literacy acquisition within the reading readiness tradition took a passive stance—young children would become facile in literacy when they were ready. In contrast, within the emergent literacy tradition, becoming prepared is an active process inseparable from ongoing literacy acquisition. Children learn to read as a result of extensive involvement in literacy activities. According to Vygotsky (1978), "the only 'good learning' is that which is in advance of development" (p. 89). Learning experiences should point to the processes and knowledge of the next stage of learning. If, for example, a young child knows the letters in his or her name, adults draw the child's attention to these letters in new words and even exaggerate the pronunciation of words with this letter-sound correspondence. "Jessica, this word in the book starts exactly like your name—j-j-j-j-just."

The initial mastery of particular knowledge provides the "basis for subsequent development of a variety of highly complex internal processes in children's thinking" (Vygotsky, 1978, p. 90). Without particular notions about literacy, young children will not read well, which results in failure to acquire other areas of competence. While we do not believe in a specific detailed sequence of instruction, we do believe that concepts build upon one another. If particular aspects of knowledge are not established, children will be at a disadvantage. The progression is not a neatly sequenced hierarchy but, as children write extensively, participate in frequent read-along and read-aloud events, engage in rhyming games with the content of predictable books and nursery rhymes, and receive guidance on particular features of written language, they move toward conventional literacy.

Attention needs to be paid to all of these processes in the initial stages of literacy acquisition because the simultaneous use of various different systems in comprehending and composing is the essence of literacy use. A term that describes the simultaneous manner in which processes need to be orchestrated or coordinated is *automaticity* (LaBerge & Samuels, 1974). Automaticity refers to the ability to identify or spell words rapidly so that the literacy user's resources can be directed to comprehending and composing. Accuracy in using the systems of written language in reading or writing is not sufficient for comprehending or composing. If accuracy alone is achieved, a reader or writer may spend so much time focusing on individual words that the overall message is lost.

Teachers can support the development of automaticity through the texts that they select and the opportunities that they create for writing. Whatever the level at which children are reading or writing, they require opportunities to consolidate their strategies. When children can apply their strategies successfully in reading or writing a text, they experience *fluent* reading or writing (Allington, 1983b). For example, in an oral reading of *Cat on the Mat* (Wildsmith, 1982), the reading of entire sentences such as "The goat sat on the mat" might be modeled by the teacher. A repeated reading of the text models for children the manner in which meaningful phrases are read rather than word-by-word reading. For children to acquire fluent application of strategies, emergent literacy contexts need to include frequent events where fluent reading of text is modeled and where students can apply their emerging strategies with easily accessible text.

In Table 3.8, we have presented some of the points along the way that characterize this learning that is occurring simultaneously on a number of different fronts. When teachers are scaffolding children's learning, these markers or indicators of growth in literacy strategies are the basis for creating new experiences. Take, for example, the child who is applying knowledge of simple vowel-consonant rimes to the words "pink," "pig," and "at" and recognizes the words "I" and "me" in the sentence "I saw a pink pig looking at me" from the book *I Went Walking* (Williams, 1989). According to Table

---

TABLE 3.8   A Progression of "Growing" Strategies from Novice to Facile Reading

Level	Emerging Strategies
Novice	• Handles books from front to back, left to right • Associates illustrations with the meaning of text • Tracks print as it is read
	• Uses knowledge of initial consonants in verifying prediction from illustration (cross-checking) • Predicts phrases and/or sentences from the pattern of the text • Recognizes differences in high-frequency words with teacher scaffolding (e.g., realizes that article is "the" rather than "a") • Recognizes presence of basic word patterns (e.g., V-C rimes) with teacher scaffolding
	• Applies knowledge of basic word patterns (e.g., "at," "an") independently in figuring out unknown words • Recognizes 5–10 high-frequency words independently and consistently • Integrates knowledge of topic and uses illustrations to support application of word pattern and high-frequency word knowledge
	• Increases knowledge of word patterns to more complex rimes (e.g., V-V-C and V-C-e) • Recognizes 20–25 high-frequency words
Facile	• Extends knowledge of word patterns to two-syllable words and words with complex rimes (i.e., vowel digraphs and variant patterns) • Recognizes core group of 50 or more high-frequency words automatically

3.8, this child would be functioning about halfway between novice and facile reading. This child's teacher would be intent on encouraging the child's exposure to word patterns with more complex rimes and high-frequency words. Following Vygotsky's (1978) view that learning leads development, these markers, or indicators of growth in literacy strategies, are used to set the stage for this child's extended learning. Such a perspective differs radically from the behaviorist view where children were not introduced to new material until they had mastered a particular body of knowledge. The emergent literacy perspective encourages both exposure to new books, strategies, and knowledge about literacy as well as focus on a core set of critical features and strategies.

Summary

In this chapter, we clustered the critical processes that make up early literacy into three groups: central, necessary, and interim processes. The acts of comprehending and composing are at the center of literacy. At the most basic level, comprehending involves readers' personal responses—sharing personal experiences and feelings, putting themselves in the situation described in the text, or comparing themselves to the characters. Critical responses also need to be developed where children study the content of books relative to their prior experiences, the author's purposes, and their experiences with previously read books. Young children approach the task of writing a message in the same way that they approach the task of reading a book—with communicative intent. Even if young children cannot form letters, the descriptions that they give to their messages involve communicative intent. To successfully communicate with a range of audiences also requires proficiency with different structures and conventions of writing.

Each of these central processes of comprehending and composing is built on a set of necessary processes. In the case of comprehending, the set of processes is word recognition and, for composing, the parallel set is processes of spelling. A third set of necessary processes is common to comprehending and composing—understanding the structure and literary elements of texts.

Meaningful reading depends on the automatic recognition of words. The various strategies of word recognition can be clustered into four basic groups: (a) common graphophonic patterns, (b) high-frequency words used in sentences (e.g., *the, a, or*) (c) meaning chunks of words, and (d) contextual supports through meanings of sentences, texts, and illustrations.

Early primary-grade spelling processes involve (a) invented spelling and (b) the strategies of conventional spelling. Invented spelling refers to the forms of children's spellings when they are encouraged to represent their knowledge about sound-letter relationships in whatever form they can as they create meaningful messages. While the typical schemes of invented spelling cluster children's spelling together once they have attained some conventional proficiencies, there are substantial differences in children's proficiencies and in the strategies that they use to spell words conventionally.

With regard to the necessary process of awareness of literary elements that is part of both comprehending and composing, the two elements of genre and language play influence young children's literary acquisition and dispositions toward text. *Genre* refers to the type of text structure or style that writers use to organize their texts, specifically stories or narrative text, informational or expository text, and predictable or rhyming text. Language play refers to such techniques as rhymes and repetitive elements.

Finally, we described interim or temporary processes that aid in acquiring the necessary processes of recognizing and spelling words, including concepts about print, phonemic awareness, and letter naming.

Many questions have been raised about the order in which the necessary and interim processes are gained. Development of literacy knowledge occurs on a number of different fronts simultaneously. Consequently, the best advice that teachers can heed is that of Vygotsky who viewed learning as leading development, meaning that children are introduced to new contexts, materials, and concepts about literacy even before they have mastered all of the previous strategies or skills. In the next section of the book, we illustrate the manner in which teachers create classrooms where such experiences occur. Children's literacy processes are enhanced through oral language interactions, the books that children read and that are read to them, the writing that children do themselves, the contexts in which literacy events, activities, and lessons occur, and the way in which assessments are conducted.

Creating the Early Literacy Classroom

chapter 4

The Oral Language Patterns of Early Literacy Classrooms

─────────────── VIGNETTE 4.1: ───────────────

A first-grade class has just finished hearing a teacher read-aloud about Big Max, a detective who has been hired by a king to find a lost elephant. The phrase "crocodile tears" has come up in the story.

T: When they talk about crocodile tears, what could that mean?
C: Fooling tears.
T: Fooling tears.
C: [Unclear]
T: I wonder if you think this would be true, boys and girls. If Mark or Eric or Genia or Jim or any of you ever have crocodile tears?
C: No. Yes.
T: Raise your hand and tell me if you think so. David.
C: When you're faking.
T: When you're faking. What do you mean by that?
C: Well, I'll tell you. When you're faking it means that you're not really sorry . . .
T: Can you think of a child who might fake in other things?

(Mishler, 1972, p. 276)

─────────────── VIGNETTE 4.2: ───────────────

A group of kindergartners are working on their compositions at a writing center.

James: How do you make a 'd'?
Kevin: Want me to make you a 'd'? [Writes one on scratch paper]
James: Uh—I'll do it. [Copies the 'd' onto his own paper]
         Duh—duh—'w'—'w.' [Writes 'M' as he says 'w'.]
Kevin: That ain't no 'w'—that ain't no 'w'—uhuh-uhuh.
Monica: Mr. W is right there. [Points to wall chart]
Latoya: How do you make a 'w'?
Monica: It's like this [Loud, indistinguishable argument about 'w']
Monica: It's like this, James, this is how a 'w' goes.

(Allen & Carr, 1989, pp. 45–46)

The conversations in these vignettes illustrate the types of talk possible in classrooms between teachers and children and among children. Through talk, teachers direct children's attention to interpretations of text such as the meaning of the metaphor "crocodile tears." Through talk, children negotiate with one another as they establish what distinguishes the important features of writing, such as the role of direction in creating a "w" or an "m."

In this chapter, we focus on oral language patterns that are crucial to children's learning in an emergent literacy classroom. We begin by examining the way in which the three principles of literacy learning, described in Chapter 2, provide a lens for our focus on oral language in the classroom. We then explore the elements of oral language patterns in terms of issues of control, control over topics and control over turns, and the different roles teachers assume in encouraging classroom talk about literacy. We end the chapter with a discussion of peer interactions in emergent literacy classrooms. Together, these topics provide a window into and a rationale behind the ways in which teachers create meaningful contexts for students to use literacy.

Oral Language Within the Early Literacy Perspective

In Chapter 2, we identified three principles that describe the literacy learning of young children:

- Literacy learning occurs through meaningful use of reading and writing.
- Literacy learning is embedded in oral language.
- Literacy learning occurs in multiple contexts with teachers and peers.

In introducing each of the chapter topics in this section on instruction and in the next section of the book on connections to communities beyond the emergent literacy classroom, we will discuss the chapter topic as it relates to these three principles.

Literacy Learning Occurs Through Meaningful Use

For young children, meaningful participation in reading and writing is at the center of learning. Making signs for special areas of the classroom (e.g., the name of the class gerbil), listening to books read aloud, and labeling a picture are acts of literacy that have meaning to young children. By contrast, when reading and writing occur as primarily solitary events of copying letters and filling out worksheets, children's interest is not piqued. In the latter context, any talk that occurs is largely about procedures for completing the exercises correctly. When read-alouds of literature and writing by children are at the heart of an early literacy program, there is much to talk about. There is talk about the content of books, such as "What are crocodile tears?" There is also talk about features of print, such as what distinguishes "w" from "m" or how to spell "rhinoceros" or "orchestra."

This talk about the meanings of text and what it means to read and write provides the vehicle for children's first participation in literacy. According to Vygotsky (1981), a higher psychological process such as literacy has its origins in social interactions where literacy use is modeled. With peers and by themselves, children subsequently transform what they have seen or heard for their own uses. When these peer and individual uses of literacy serve a real need for children, the artifacts or interpretations of these literacy acts are shared with others. For example, children make their own version of a predictable book based on *Jasper's Beanstalk* (Butterworth & Inkpen, 1993) about their activities on each day of the week. This sharing, in turn, elicits new questions and comments from adults or older children, leading children to regroup or confirm their ideas about literacy. What precipitated the learning was the meaningful use of literacy.

Literacy Learning Is Embedded in Oral Language

Oral language patterns are the means whereby young children access literacy. By access, we mean that children's first literacy events in school are primarily oral in nature, such as when teachers read books aloud or record on charts the stories generated by the class. As teachers talk about the content and features of print in these literacy acts, children come to understand the processes, functions, and features of written language. Through talk, the secrets of literacy are revealed.

The adeptness of teachers in involving children in talk about literacy has particular consequences for those children for whom a mismatch exists between the *language patterns* of home and school. *Language patterns* refer to the kinds of questions that adults ask children, the types of responses that adults elicit from children, and the norms for responding. The term "language patterns" does not refer to differences between children's native languages and the language of school. In this chapter, we describe ways in which bridges can be built between the language patterns of home and school to ensure children's successful literacy learning. Issues related to teaching second languages to children with native languages other than English are treated comprehensively in such volumes as those of Au (1993) and Freeman and Freeman (1994).

In some middle-class homes, as children near school entry, the exchanges between preschoolers and parents are increasingly like the talk structures of book-reading events (Heath, 1982). While young preschoolers are permitted to dominate the story-reading episode by telling a version of the story themselves or labeling the pictures in the book, older preschoolers are expected to respond to questions or to hold their questions until a page has been read. Following a read-aloud of *Tom's Cat* (Voake, 1986)—a predictable book in which a child confuses noises of different family members with those of his missing cat—a parent's suggestion to "Name what everyone in the family was doing" illustrates a question that asks a child to take on the stance that he or she soon will be asked to take in school.

Other children may face a significant mismatch between home and school language patterns. Without teachers' awareness and recognition of children's unfamiliarity with school language patterns, some children may stop participating in literacy events (Heath, 1983; Michaels, 1981; Wells, 1986). For example, researchers working with native Hawaiian children (e.g., Au & Mason, 1981; Tharp & Gallimore, 1988) describe a common home interaction pattern called "talk-story." This is a traditional form of interaction in Hawaiian communities where turn-taking is shared and all participants contribute to constructing a response. It is dramatically different from the turn-taking patterns found in schools where the teacher asks a question and children bid for a response turn by raising their hands, speaking only when called upon by their teacher.

When the native Hawaiian children participated in a reading lesson, they drew upon familiar interaction patterns, which some teachers interpreted as interrupting. When such children are reprimanded frequently, they may move to the fringe of the story circle. Such children may become uninvolved in literacy because their interaction patterns are not acceptable in school, not because they are incapable of learning to read. The Kamehameha Early Education Project (KEEP), a program for native Hawaiian children (Au, 1993), demonstrated the shift in children's literacy participation when talk-story elements were integrated into discussions. The focus shifted from the form of children's answers to their interpretations and personal responses to stories.

Given the success of talk-story, teachers and researchers working in a school on a Navajo reservation encouraged teachers to use the talk-story pattern with their young Navajo students (Vogt, Jordan, & Tharp, 1987). This experiment in teaching methods helped illustrate why there are no universal interaction patterns to be applied across all settings. Navajo students' home interaction patterns are characterized by giving speakers "space," by considering the whole story before responding. Thus, unlike the Hawaiian students, the Navajo students found the talk-story pattern to be awkward and perhaps rude. Further, unlike the Hawaiian students, the Navajo students preferred to discuss the complete story first, rather than focus on individual events and then put the events together (see Au, 1979). While it is inappropriate to stereotype entire cultures because of the great variability within a given culture, it is, nonetheless, reasonable to be aware of relatively widespread and characteristic patterns of interacting if we wish to encourage connections between home and school interaction patterns. The principle of embedding literacy in oral language implies a need for teachers to be sensitive to the interaction patterns that are familiar to their students, and to support their interactions as part of literacy acts.

Literacy Learning Occurs in Multiple Contexts

The two conversations that introduced this chapter illustrate the varying roles that teachers and peers assume during classroom talk. Adults draw children's attention to aspects of written language of which children may be unaware. At the same time, peers serve a critical function because interactions among children provide opportunities to work out understandings or engage in exploratory talk (Barnes, 1976, 1995). Talk with peers is characterized by frequent hypotheses that use phrases such as "could have" and "probably." Such experiences help students transform and make these ways of talking and related ways of thinking their own. Through student-to-student talk, with related rights and responsibilities, peers engage in literate behaviors even before they may have complete control over literate skills, and they accomplish something together that they may be unlikely to achieve alone.

The three principles emphasize teachers' choices in designing conversations and how their choices can influence children's access to literacy learning. Often, these choices have not been articulated. Our aim in this chapter is to increase teachers' awareness and knowledge of the relationship between language patterns and children's literacy learning. In the next section, the elements in oral language exchanges that are under the control of teachers are discussed, followed by a discussion of the interaction patterns created in classrooms based on these understandings.

Elements of Oral Language Patterns

Oral language patterns are so ingrained in classroom cultures that teachers may be unaware of their presence or effects. For example, few—if any—primary-level teachers would choose to record planned oral language patterns within their lesson plan books. Yet, constructs in oral language interaction can be consciously applied to accomplish different purposes in classrooms. From studying conversations, sociolinguists have identified elements that determine the course and outcomes of a conversation (e.g., Coulthard, 1977; Philips, 1972): designation of topics, rules of turn-taking, response, and timing of response. The manner in which topics and turns are designated in conversations particularly influences students' learning opportunities. The two vignettes that introduced the chapter illustrated talk among the two groups in classrooms—teachers talking with children and children talking with one another. The types of conversations that can occur in teacher-led and in peer-peer talk are infinite, differing as a function of how topics and turns are designated.

Designating Topics and Subthemes of Topics

Vignette 4.1 illustrates an adult's choice of topic and control over turn-taking, both quite common in teacher-led interactions. This teacher's goal for reading aloud was to build children's interest and knowledge through the book's reading and discussion. As the conversation continues, the teacher invites children to share their own experiences, anxious that the children show their understanding of crocodile tears by relating a personal experience. Note that this shift in the direction of the topic from the content of the story to the children's own personal experiences is, like the topic itself, under the teacher's control.

In contrast, when students interact among themselves, topics have quite different origins. In Vignette 4.2, James's need to form the letter "w" initiates a lively conversation among the children at the writing center. His reason for raising the topic differs from typical teacher questions—James has an immediate need to form the letter "w" in his composition. These children's conversation is directed at solving an immediate problem. If we had a transcript of the entire conversation during that day's writing session, we would expect shifts in topics. For example, a child might comment on what he or she is writing about, followed by comments of other children. Such a conversation occurs in the following illustration of children working on "I am" books in a first-grade classroom's writing center. Lamar is illustrating an adventure in the water under the sentence "I am a swimmer."

> **Lamar:** Do you know what these lines are? [pointing to his own drawing] They're the waves. They're pushing me this way.
> **James:** Look at these waves. [pointing to his own drawing]
> **Lamar:** And then the water gets higher. [drawing his waves higher]
> **James:** Mine's gonna get higher too. My water's higher than you.
> **Lamar:** Shoot. Mine is higher than yours.
>
> (Dyson, 1993, pp. 159–160)

Through oral dialogue, Lamar and James elaborate and extend their stories in a manner beyond their current independent writing abilities. When talk among children is part of classroom writing contexts, children can try their ideas out, receive feedback on their ideas, and experiment with elaborated plots and dialogue.

The Control of Turns

The control of turns—who gets to contribute to the conversation and when—is a function of power to an even greater extent than topic identification in conversations. At social events such as dinner parties, adults share an understanding of common norms of turn-taking: listening intently to an individual, entering the conversation when the speaker pauses sufficiently, and sharing speaking opportunities. In other settings, such as a faculty meeting or a classroom, the norms of conversation differ from those typical of social events. Instead of equally shared opportunity to guide the conversation, the power to allocate turns resides with the discussion leader. In most classroom contexts, the leader is the teacher. The children's role is to listen and to speak at the invitation of the teacher. If a child overextends what a teacher regards to be an appropriate turn, the teacher has the power to end the turn. If one child interrupts another child or several children respond simultaneously to the teacher's invitation to take a turn, as occurs in Vignette 4.1, the teacher makes the classroom rules for turn-taking explicit, stating "Raise your hand" or, perhaps, "One person at a time." When children do not respond immediately to the teacher's invitation to take a turn, the teacher has the prerogative to make the invitation specific to a child or several children as the teacher does in Vignette 4.1 with her comment, "If Mark or Eric or Genia or Jim or any of you ever have crocodile tears?"

The Content and Timing of Responses

The final two elements of conversations—the content of the response and timing of responses—are at the teacher's discretion as he or she guides the turn-taking in most teacher-led groups. The ways in which teachers use these two elements influence the quality of thinking in which children can engage during classroom discussions.

The choices that teachers make in the tone and the content of their response to children's turns are critical in determining ongoing levels of student participation in conversations. One set of responses is aimed at clarifying, verifying through repetition, or building on the contributions of children; a second set of responses casts a negative light on children's contributions by evaluating, dismissing, or asking the same question without revision, thereby signaling to the group that the first child's response was incorrect and that others in the class can now show their superior grasp of content to the errant youngster (Mason, Peterman, Powell, & Kerr, 1989). The teacher in Vignette 4.1 displays responses of the first type when she confirms a student's definition of crocodile tears by repeating the child's definition of "fooling tears." When the teacher next asks a question, she does not dispute this definition but asks children for verification. Another question type used by this teacher requires children to clarify and elaborate their thinking, as in "What do you mean by that?" Finally, this teacher asks children to extend their knowledge to other contexts when she asks, "Can you think of a child who might fake in other things?"

This teacher scaffolds children's responses so as to extend their thinking. While she controls the conversational turn-taking, her responses are used in a manner that encourages her children to reflect. When children share what they are thinking with their peers, they are shown respect for their contributions and these become a source for furthering the entire group's thinking as the teacher repeats children's comments and builds questions upon previous comments.

Few transcripts—such as those from which Vignette 4.1 was derived—include information on the amount of time that passed between teacher's requests for contributions, children's comments, and teacher's responses. Yet, the amount of time that the leader of a discussion allows to elapse between turns is an important influence on the value of the discussion for children's thinking. A considerable body of literature has been generated around the construct of "wait time"—the amount of time that teachers allow to lapse before calling on children for a response (Fisher & Berliner, 1985). In many classroom conversations, children barely have time to catch their breath before the teacher begins calling on children to volunteer. If teachers wait even several *seconds,* children are much more likely to engage in reflection and to produce more cogent answers (Rowe, 1986).

The turn allocation in typical teacher-led interactions is in sharp contrast to the turn-taking in the kindergartners' conversations in Vignette 4.2. At one point in the conversation, the children compete for turns with such intensity that neither observer nor transcriber of the conversation is able to establish the content of the conversation. In the conversation between James and Lamar, the children compete with one another for control of the conversation.

There are also times, however, when even young children can apply rules with one another, not unlike the teacher-led conversation. Such an example comes from the first-grade classroom of which Lamar and James were a part. The class has completed an experiment in which doll clothes were washed and hung outside to dry. Small groups had been formed to discuss how the clothes would get dry on a gray, cool day. Vera has been assigned the role of group leader, with Jameel, Anita, Edward, and Sonya in the group.

Jameel:	Um see the air goes inside the thing [the clothes] and then it pushes the water out and then it's dry.
Sonya:	The heat.
Jameel:	It's too cold out there. So it's gotta be the wind, go inside it, push the water out. [Several turns of conversation occur in which Edward and Anita state their agreement that it is heat, followed by Jameel who reiterates his point of view with the comment that heat and wind are the same thing. He concludes, then, that everyone really is "going with" or agreeing with him. Sonya responds by stating that it is heat, not wind.]
Jameel:	I object. She's [Sonya] going with me. He's [Edward] going with me.
Sonya:	What are you talking about?
Jameel:	Because heat and wind are the same thing, but heat is hot and wind is cold. So they both can push, and then it's the same thing.
Vera:	Jameel. Jameel. Jameel. And don't talk when someone else is talking, please.
	[Vera says she's going with heat.]
Jameel:	So you're going with me. It's final.

(Dyson, 1993, p. 139)

Vera's admonition to Jameel, "And don't talk when someone else is talking, please" indicates Vera's solid grasp of the conversational norms equated with classroom life. These children, however, are genuinely engaged in expressing their points of view about the outcomes of the experiment. This level of conversation reflected considerable teacher planning and many experiences in conversations such as this one over the school year. In the next section, we will explore the manner in which productive conversations like this student-led group develop in classrooms. Participating in interesting, meaningful, and high-quality conversations is a skill acquired by teachers and their students.

Designing Productive Classroom Talk

Our description of the emergent literacy perspective details how talk is both a means whereby children learn about literacy and an outcome of literacy learning as children express their interpretations of texts and literacy events. In accounts of classrooms, patterns of classroom talk have been identified that are less than effective in encouraging children's literacy learning (Mehan, 1979; Sinclair & Coulthard, 1975). Typically, the students' role is to sit quietly until bidden by the teacher to produce an answer to which the teacher responds with an evaluative comment that confirms or negates the content. This talk pattern of *I*nitiation by the teacher, followed by a *R*esponse from one or more students, and concluded by an *E*valuative comment from the teacher has been called the IRE pattern (Cazden, 1988; Mehan, 1982).

When people interact with one another, particular patterns of interaction can be identified as socially accepted modes of communication, often referred to as "scripts" (Bakhtin, 1986). We described a "dinner party script," the "IRE classroom script," and the "talk-story script" in earlier sections. These examples help illustrate that scripts, in and of themselves, are not inherently good or bad. The problem with the IRE pattern is that it is often the only script for classroom talk. Since particular forms of oral interaction facilitate particular ways of thinking about literacy and engaging in literate acts, the reliance on a single script leads to limitations in thought and literacy use. Teachers' goals should include becoming facile with an array of classroom talk structures. Then, teachers can choose particular patterns for particular purposes from their repertoire of talk structures. To develop an extended repertoire of talk structures requires an understanding of the fundamental ingredients of oral language patterns—control of topics, turn-taking rules, and content and timing of responses—and the ways in which these can be varied to foster particular processes in students.

Through observations of classrooms, talk structures have been identified that produce various learning opportunities. Teachers are participants in some of these interactions; in others, they are not direct participants but, as models and guides, they contribute to peer interactions.

Participation Structures with Teachers

In their observations of classrooms, Raphael and Goatley (1994) identified three talk structures that teachers used to accomplish different goals: facilitation, guided participation, and explicit instruction. The choice among teachers is not to select one particular form of interaction and use that form as a signature. Rather, each type of interaction serves particular purposes in literacy learning and all three meld to create a comprehensive emergent literacy program.

Teachers as Facilitators of Interaction.   Teachers use a facilitative structure when the goal of a classroom context is for children to share interpretations of what they have read, compositions that they have written, or knowledge that they have gained from experiences. Such occasions are frequent in emergent literacy classrooms, including the sharing that occurs after a period when children have read from books that they have chosen, presentation of compositions by classroom authors during a time called "the author's chair" (Graves & Hansen, 1983), or Show and Tell, when children share treasured objects and experiences.

In contexts such as author's chair or Show and Tell, turns likely will be allocated by children as they select classmates to comment on their composition or contribution to Show and Tell. The presence of the teacher in facilitating the child's leadership in pursuing a topic or in allocating turns can be the source for modeling, especially during a child's first experiences in the role of author or contributor to Show and Tell. An example of a facilitative role by the teacher can be seen in the following excerpt from Show and Tell in a kindergarten classroom:

Mindy:	When I was in day camp we made these um candles.
Teacher:	You made them?
Mindy:	And uh I-I tried it with different colors with both of them but one just came out this one just came out blue and I don't know what this color is.
Teacher:	That's neat-o. Tell the kids how you do it from the very start. Pretend we don't know a thing about candles. OK? What did you do first? What did you use? Flour?

(Michaels, 1981, p. 431)

In this short interaction, the teacher uses several techniques to encourage Mindy to elaborate on her chosen topic of candlemaking. Initially, the teacher reiterates the child's statement to encourage her to continue, saying, "You made them?" After Mindy stops once more, the teacher uses two techniques to encourage Mindy to elaborate further. First, she makes a positive evaluation by commenting "That's neat-o" and, second, she prompts Mindy's further elaboration by setting up a structure for the description of the process of making candles. In the face of Mindy's reticence, the teacher's scaffolding becomes more and more explicit.

An example from the same teacher in the same classroom context of Show and Tell but with a different child demonstrates how a child's contribution can be thwarted rather than facilitated, even when the context is aimed at students' sharing their own topics.

Teacher:	Deena, I want you to share some one thing that's very important. One thing from where you are . . . is that where you are . . . is that where you were . . .

Deena:	No.
Teacher:	OK.
Deena:[1]	Um . . . In the summer . . . I mean w-when um I go back to school I come back to school in September I'ma have a new coat and I already got it and it's um got a lot of brown in it and when, um and I got it yesterday and when I saw it my um my mother was was going somewhere when my when I saw it on the couch and I showed my sister and I was readin' somethin' out on on the bag and my big sister said . . . my big sister said Deena you have to keep that away from Keisha 'cause that's my baby sister and I said no . . . and I said the plastic bag . . . because . . . um . . . when . . . um . . . sh-when the um . . . she was um with me . . . my cousin and her . . .
Teacher:	Wait a minute you stick with your coat now. I said you could tell one thing . . . that's fair.
Deena:	This was about my c—
Teacher:	OK, all right, go on.

(Michaels, 1981, p. 435)

Even before Deena begins, the teacher attempts to control Deena's contribution. While, unlike Mindy, Deena is eager to elaborate on her chosen topic, the teacher interrupts Deena to tell her to limit her topic. When the observer of this session later interviewed Deena, Deena was able to convey several anecdotes around the coat-related topic. Her cousin entered into the story because Deena had to keep his messy hands away from the coat. Her younger sister (Keisha) was relevant because of fear that the plastic bag on the coat might injure her. To the teacher, however, these links were not apparent. Consequently, she had initiated rules like "sticking to one topic" (which she attempts to reinforce with Deena) and picking "important" things for sharing. Unlike the interaction with Mindy, the teacher does not ask Deena thematically relevant questions that might connect the subthemes together for the audience but, in essence, asks Deena to quit.

These two excerpts illustrate the potential for limiting some children's access to classroom contexts, for reasons we discussed earlier. Some students may have difficulty participating in classroom events because of the mismatch between the talk structures of their homes and those of the teacher (Michaels, 1981). When the talk structures of the teacher and student matched, as they did with Mindy, the teacher knew precisely how to facilitate Mindy's Show and Tell contribution. But when students' talk structure differed from that of the teacher, as was the case with Deena, the teacher's feedback served to impose presentation norms rather than facilitate topic discussion. Questions to assist students such as Deena to make links are appropriate but require that teachers become familiar with talk structures that characterize their students' communities and homes.

---

[1]Deena's contribution to Show and Tell is a verbatim quote from the transcript in Michaels (1981).

Teachers as Participation Guides.   There are many occasions in classrooms where teachers must build on children's existing understandings or lead children in elaborating on their responses and interpretations. In contexts such as these, the teacher assumes the role of a guide. She asks children to extend and clarify comments and draws the group's attention to commonalities and differences across the contributors' comments. A prominent event of this type is the read-aloud where teachers read to students, and the responses of children to the text provide the focus of a conversation. The interaction in Vignette 4.1 in which the teacher guided children in understanding a figure of speech—crocodile tears—is an instance of guided participation during a read-aloud event. The teacher elicits children's understandings and uses these as the basis for creating children's shared understanding of the term.

In guided participation, teachers may vary the amount and nature of their scaffolding as a function of the instructional goal and also as a function of children's expertise in responding to and elaborating upon one another's responses. While teachers invoke children's responses and children may introduce new subthemes of the topic, the selection of the topic is guided by the teacher. In some interactions where teachers have consciously worked on introducing new interaction patterns—such as the talk-story format of the KEEP classrooms—children may follow one another in taking a turn at contributing to the conversation. More commonly, however, teachers direct turns as illustrated by the teacher in Vignette 4.1, who invites particular children to contribute and, when multiple children are responding, advises children, "Raise your hand and tell me if you think so."

Martinez and Teale (1993) observed kindergarten teachers' read-alouds to determine the degree to which guided participation structures were present. These observations occurred in classrooms in the same district where teachers read aloud from the same set of books: *Alexander and the Wind-up Mouse* (Lionni, 1969), *Harry and the Terrible Whatzit* (Gackenbach, 1977), *Ira Sleeps Over* (Waber, 1972), and *Strega Nona* (dePaola, 1975). By studying interactions around the same books, these researchers were hopeful that they could clarify the features of talk structures that encouraged young children to think about and express their thoughts about books.

A first finding was that the amount of talk that occurred around these books varied substantially from one kindergarten classroom to another. At one end of the continuum was a classroom where storybook sessions averaged 23 minutes, while at the other end was a classroom where sessions with the same books averaged 13 minutes. A second finding was that the sparsity of talk indicated by short read-aloud episodes related to substantially less thought-provoking conversations. Differences were found in the ways in which teachers supported children's sharing of their interpretations and subsequent revisions of these interpretations if parts of the book had been misconstrued. The following two classroom discussions, one from each end of the spectrum, illustrate these differences.

In one classroom, the teacher read a segment from *Alexander and the Wind-up Mouse:* "'The moon is round, the pebble found,' said the lizard.

'Who or what do you wish to be?'" At this point, the teacher stops reading and initiates the following exchange:

Teacher: What is Alexander going to wish for?
Class: [in unison] Wind-up mouse.
Teacher: Think he's going to wish to be a wind-up mouse?
Class: [in unison] No.
Teacher: After what happened to Willy?
Class: [in unison] No.

(Martinez & Teale, 1993, p. 185)

In another classroom, this discussion followed a read-aloud of *Harry and the Terrible Whatzit:*

Teacher: Why is the Whatzit sad?
Child: Because the boy been mean.
Teacher: Okay. Joel.
Joel: Because the boy was hitting him.
Teacher: Okay. Now if you were getting smaller and smaller, and you kept getting smaller, what would you be afraid might happen? If you keep getting smaller and smaller, what will happen? Brian.
Brian: He might think he would step on him.
Teacher: Okay, he might be afraid he's going to get stepped on. Alex.
Alex: You'll disappear.
Teacher: That's right. He might be afraid he's going to disappear. And why did he tell the boy he was getting smaller?
Child: He's not afraid of him anymore.
Teacher: That's right. Whenever the boy's not afraid of him, it makes him get smaller. Look at him now.

(Martinez & Teale, 1993, pp. 184–185)

In both of these dialogues, there are misconceptions among students who have listened to the story read aloud. In both cases, the teacher is interested in redirecting children's interpretations. In the first illustration, the teacher's questions require monosyllabic answers until children give the right response. These children know the interaction script well enough to recognize that their answer is incorrect when the teacher repeats the question. The only thinking that is involved in this episode is "giving the teacher the answer s/he wants to hear." The teacher does not probe the children to understand their thinking behind their initial response that Alexander would wish to be a wind-up mouse, nor do children need to think through why Willy's fate would lead to Alexander's wish not to be a wind-up mouse.

The children who have listened to *Harry and the Terrible Whatzit* in the second illustration have misinterpreted an event in the passage just as their peers in the first illustration had misunderstood Alexander's views on being a wind-up mouse. In the second classroom, however, the teacher does two things that characterize the guided participation structure. First, the teacher attends to the misperception by asking several children to explain the Whatzit's emotion. When several children respond incorrectly, the teacher changes her tack and personalizes the dilemma for children by asking, "If you keep getting smaller and smaller, what will happen?" Second, she provides an ongoing summary of the contributions that lead to the author's intended interpretation. In this scenario, children are asked to reflect on the events and their effect on characters.

Just as teachers using the facilitation participation structure are responsible for ensuring that the conversation continues to be a productive one, teachers have the same role within the guided participation structure. But unlike the facilitation structures where the purpose is for children to talk about their own topics, the aim of guided participation is the creation and elaboration of shared understandings of topics and events that arise in children's own writing, the writings of other authors, and events in and beyond the classroom. To achieve these shared understandings of experiences and texts, teachers take a more active role in guiding the conversation than is the case with the facilitation participation structure. Even here, however, teachers' responses to children's comments and the manner in which turns are allocated vary considerably from the "interrogative" questioning mode that has often been equated with classroom talk. Instead, talk within the guided participation structure is characterized by students' and teachers' summaries of one another's comments and by reference to what has been read. Because of this, the nature of discussion and, subsequently, the level of children's thinking can be challenging and stimulating.

Teachers as Explicit Instructors.   Occasions also exist in classrooms where teachers have a fairly explicit aim relative to the knowledge or skills that children are to acquire. These occasions range from focuses on safety procedures to directions for particular literacy-supporting activities. For example, a lesson on strategies for assisting a peer with an unknown word might involve a detailed presentation on how one responds to someone's effort to figure out a word (Rhodes & Nathenson-Mejia, 1992).

Occasions when teachers are explicit in their descriptions and presentations form yet another part of the repertoire of an effective teacher. Yet, an explicit talk structure should not be equated with the IRE talk structure. A skillful teacher using an explicit talk structure to support children's grasp of particular strategies employs a range of response patterns. As previously discussed, responses in which teachers repeat, ask for clarification, and extend children's comments generate a level of student involvement and learning quite different from responses that are critical or negatively evaluative. The manner in which teachers wait for children's contributions and probe children's thinking also contributes to the efficacy of the explicit instruction mode of talk (Eeds & Wells, 1989; Villuame, Worden, Williams, Hopkins, & Rosenblatt, 1994).

Peer Interaction

Teachers influence students' conversations indirectly through the opportunities they create for peers to engage in interactions among themselves. Such contexts include cooperative learning, students' literary circles, learning centers, group projects, and so forth. In each of these cases, students are expected to work without direct teacher support to achieve particular goals (e.g., completing a report, discussing a book, creating a product).

The technique of cooperative learning, where children share the responsibilities of a task in a small group, has been described and encouraged extensively (e.g., Ashman & Elkins, 1990; Brown & Palincsar, 1989; Sharan, 1990; Wynn, 1993). Learning to participate in and lead the interaction in a group of peers is important as a skill in its own right, as well as for what children are able to accomplish within such groups. But there is more to talk among students in classrooms than the talk in cooperative groups. How students talk with one another when working on independent tasks is recognized as an important part of the emergent literacy classroom. Within an emergent literacy perspective, the talk among peers that often is viewed as surreptitious and secretive in many classrooms is recognized as serving a function in children's learning, no less important than the talk with teachers. We consider, first, productive informal interactions in classrooms and, next, the nature of small-group interactions.

Informal Interaction

Even when teachers discourage talk among students in a classroom, peers develop active communication systems, what Hubbard referred to as "underground literacy" in her observations of an upper elementary classroom (Hubbard, 1989). Similarly, in an emergent literacy classroom with many native Hawaiian children—before efforts were made to match their home and school talk structures—children would assist one another when teachers' backs were turned (Vogt et al., 1987). Once this "underground" talk has been legitimized, children have been observed requesting and providing assistance, commenting on activities or words in books, and reflecting on peers' activities.

Previous examples in this chapter such as the discussion between James and his peers in Vignette 4.2 demonstrate children's efforts to make written language their own. This talk is not idle chatter. Rather, it provides a means for children to experiment and test their hypotheses about written language. These students had been in classrooms where they were frequently part of teacher-led interactions in which productive talk structures were modeled and facilitated. Contrast the quality of interaction in the two examples that follow with those previously noted such as the conversation in Vignette 4.2 or the dialogue in which Lamar and James engage as they write.

Scenario 1:

> **Ann:**   Judi, what's in this . . . ?
> **Judi:**   You gotta read the directions by yourself.

Scenario 2:

> **Tammy:**   Stuck on another word.
> **Mitch:**   Well, you help her, Al.
> **Al:**   No.
> **Tammy:**   Yep.
> **Al:**   What word? Ask Mary, I gotta do this. Mary knows it, she already gots her whole thing done.
> **Tammy:**   You did too.
> **Mitch:**   Yeah Al.
> **Tammy:**   Here Al, what's the word.
> **Al:**   Don't you know it? Cave.

(Wilkinson & Dollaghan, 1981, p. 273)

Students' refusals to interact about the assignment content (Scenario 1) and the strategy for figuring out a word (Scenario 2) are quite different from the interactions described in Vignette 4.2 when James asks for assistance in figuring out letters. In the interaction between Ann and Judi and the discussion around Tammy's difficulty with a word, children attend to rules of interaction rather than to the content at hand. The interaction between Lamar and James, too, could be described as an attempt to display authority, as Al does in the second scenario. But in the case of Lamar and James, this process resulted in an embellished version of a story, while in the case of Al, the result is an argument about process.

The children from Wilkinson and Dollaghan's project worked at tables where they were permitted to talk. However, the modeling and guidance that they had received from their teacher for interacting with peers had been minimal. When students have been part of many teacher-led conversations where strategies are emphasized for figuring out new words, students will carry over similar guidance to peers in informal work situations. Rather than "telling" the word—as Tammy expects—or asking for a more capable reader to provide the directions—as Ann expects—children learn to guide one another in identifying and applying strategies to figure out both words and directions.

In addition to directly modeling how to interact in small groups, teachers influence student-led participation structures by their ability to monitor and provide support to groups as they interact. In Ann and Tammy's classroom, the teacher worked with one group at the front of the room while other students participated in small groups in the rest of the classroom. The teacher rarely left the group with which she was working. The teachers in James's and in Lamar's classrooms were well aware of the benefits of stating clear expectations for the outcomes of independent work time, and of their students' needs for feedback and monitoring *in the midst of the task,* rather than hours (or days) later. While neither of these teachers usurped the students' leadership and participation in the small group settings, by observing them in the context of centers and other independent work contexts and stepping in during "teachable moments," the teachers were able to support and encourage students' continued growth in these settings. Productive interactions and independent writing and reading in informal work contexts benefit from a teacher's periodic monitoring.

Interaction in Small Groups

In a variety of venues, teachers have been encouraged to have their students work in cooperative groups. As we saw earlier in the interaction among Jameel and his peers, young children can interact with one another productively, though the cognitive processes which are shared or modeled may not be at the level of somewhat older students. Jameel is the only one of the children who explains the reasoning behind his choice, when he says, "So they both can push, and then it's the same thing." Even with this somewhat elaborated reasoning, Jameel is unable to convince his peers. Sonya's explanation of "The heat" gives little insight into her reasoning. When Vera, Edward, and Anita give their view, they, too, do not elaborate on why they believe that heat is the primary mechanism and not wind.

Interaction among young children, especially kindergartners and first graders, poses issues different from those associated with cooperative learning in middle schools. Younger children have much less experience working in goal-directed small groups, and they frequently have less prior knowledge on which they can draw. It is naive to suggest that cooperative activities effective for upper-grade students may simply be put in place for young children without an awareness of the types of support structures that young children may need to work profitably in a cooperative group. In the case of the heat-wind debate between Jameel and his peers, the teacher has laid a solid foundation to establish prior knowledge through a large-group interaction where considerable talk occurred as the experiment was begun. Second, she made sure that the task was clear, to make it more likely that the interaction would be fairly productive, giving the group a specific mandate: "Discuss how the clothes would get dry on a gray, cool day." Third, the teacher designated a leader, Vera. Jameel is a central figure in the classroom (Dyson, 1993) who works hard to assert himself. Note, however, how Vera claims her role as group leader by asserting the rules for turn-taking: "And don't talk when someone else is talking, please."

In the"heat-wind" example, the group has been formed for a specific purpose and a short duration. The use of groups that remain together for a longer duration has been a central part of literature-based pedagogy. Raphael and colleagues (McMahon & Raphael, in press; Raphael & McMahon, 1994; Raphael, Goatley, McMahon, & Woodman, 1995) have described these discussion groups as "Book Clubs," a group of individuals who meet to share responses to and interpretations of books. In a similar vein, Eeds and Wells

(1989) have initiated groups with the intention of having "grand conversations" within groups. In both instances, the initial projects were with middle-grade students. More recently, these efforts have been extended to emergent literacy classrooms (McGee, 1992). In the case of Book Clubs (Grattan, in press), teachers monitor the interaction among groups using a "fishbowl" format. Small student-led discussion groups (i.e., book clubs) take turns sitting at a table in the center of the room, surrounded by their observing peers. They lead their own discussion, but the teacher is able to support the interactions if needed. Further, because of the fishbowl format, exemplary practices can be highlighted fairly close to when they appear, and confusions can be clarified rather quickly. In grand conversations (McGee, 1992), the teacher is a more integral member of the group. We focus on student-led interactions, rather than the teacher-led guided participation structure of grand conversations.

Even with older students, productive small-group interactions depend on the nature of the task, guidance on interaction norms, and preparation by students for the small group session (Raphael et al., 1995). When students have completed response journals and summaries, such as character sketches in preparation for the Book Club session, they have time to engage thoughtfully with their texts prior to interacting with peers. Not surprisingly, the quality of interaction in sessions improves appreciably with such reflective opportunities.

Students also benefit from tutelage on the norms of participating and leading a group. O'Flahavan (1989) has demonstrated the nature of this tutoring and the structure that a group session requires in order for younger children's book response sessions to be productive. Productive talk structures in peer groups required sessions where teachers led students in "talk about talk." Guidelines for peer interaction were identified and kept visible during the peer-led groups. With support from the teacher in question-asking and in guidelines for interaction, most groups were able to engage in productive talk. The level of exchange that can occur among second-grade students in a peer-led group is illustrated in this interaction from one of O'Flahavan's groups:

C8:   You don't go up there and say, 'Be my friend,' like that.
C4:   No, I say that when you get in there, you go up to somebody and just say it, and not, I be smart enough about it to go up to them and say it.
C8:   Like—
C4:   I just can't like this—
C8:   You—
C4:   I just can't go up to one of them and say something and say: 'Be my friend,' or something like that.
C8:   I know.
C1:   That's my point. That's my point. It takes time. It takes time. It takes time.

C4:   I know it takes time but that's just it.

C1:   You got to get used to those people and you get lonely, you could just go up there and ask them.

C4:   If I get used to them I ask 'em then.

C1:   Let's use an example. If you're shy and you're in first grade—were you shy?

C4:   I told you I was.

C1:   And did you make friends with those kids?

C4:   A long time ago, I mean it took a long time, not the first day I came.

C1:   See, I said it takes time.

(O'Flahavan, 1989, p. 264)

Children in this group show they can explain their views. In this particular scenario, children relate their experiences to those of the character in the story that they have read prior to the session. Even when other views are stated, children persist in clarifying and elaborating upon their perspectives. The contribution of the phrase, "Let's use an example," by one of the participants stems from a technique that had been modeled and discussed in large-group settings as productive for small-group discussions. These students are a year older than the students who were part of the "heat-wind" debate, which may explain their ability to share their reasoning to a greater extent. But age is only part of the explanation in that the conversations of older students can be cryptic and trivial. Conversations such as this one occur when students have been part of facilitative and guided participations with their teachers and when they have been part of discussions and lessons on the content and forms of peer-led conversations.

Summary

Classroom talk is a rich and exciting site for students' intellectual development. As we have discussed in this chapter, the opportunities for talk within an emergent literacy classroom are not only widespread, they are crucial to students' literacy development. Through talk, students learn to negotiate ideas, to clarify confusions and elaborate on their initial thoughts, to debate and question, to solve problems, and to both create and respond to print. Teachers have a range of ways in which they can structure and promote classroom talk, from teacher-directed talk designed to teach specific strategies, skills, and knowledge to student-led discussions that challenge young children to take responsibility for their own participation in learning. Teachers armed with this knowledge can create classrooms that take advantage of the wide range of participation structures, using structures that facilitate the achievement of particular literacy goals, as well as promote students' general development as individuals and citizens.

chapter 5

The Texts of Early Literacy Classrooms: Texts Children Read

──────── VIGNETTE 5.1: ────────

In a second-grade classroom, the following conversation transpired during a shared book experience:

Teacher: I'd like for you to choose an Old Favorite big book today.
Students: *Madeline.*
Teacher: What do you like best about the story?
Student: I like the rhyming.
Student: She was surprised with a scar on her stomach.
[Some students share stories about their own scars.]
Student: I know which is Madeline [looking at cover]. She's the smallest one. They are holding her hand. I like the part where they come into Madeline's room with solemn faces.
[Teacher and students discuss what is meant by solemn.]
Student: I like the way the pictures all point up!

(Reutzel, Hollingsworth, & Eldredge, 1994, p. 48)

──────── VIGNETTE 5.2: ────────

When kindergartners were asked to select a favorite book from the classroom collection, Doug selected *The Carrot Seed* (Krauss, 1945). When asked to read the book, he gave a storylike rendition in an oral reading style with slowed cadence and stress. Doug's rendition for the repetitive response of "I'm afraid it won't come up" by different family members to the child in the story illustrates the form of his reading:

And his mom said to him, "That will never grow. Needs water." So one day he watered it. Then his dad said, "Nothing's gonna gro—ow." And his brother came and said, "Nothing's gonna grow."

(Sulzby, 1985, p. 469)

These vignettes demonstrate the various expressions of written language, or texts as we will refer to them, in early literacy classrooms. As in Vignette 5.1, literary classics such as *Madeline* are read in shared book events with the teacher. The world of text in the early literacy classroom also includes text that children can read on their own. A predictable book such as *The Carrot Seed* allows children to participate as readers in a variety of ways, as is evident in Doug's adaptations of the pattern in Vignette 5.2.

Written Texts Within an Early Literacy Perspective

The role of text as young children learn to read is grounded in the three principles of literacy learning underlying the early literacy perspective: providing meaningful use of literacy, building upon a strong base in oral language, and occurring in multiple contexts with teachers and peers.

Literacy Learning Occurs Through Meaningful Use

As we saw in Chapter 2, there are many ways in which young children can be involved in using text meaningfully. When children read signs and labels to perform a task, they use text in the form of *environmental print.* Environmental print is critical for children's development of an initial corpus of recognizable words. Yet, often, environmental print, as a source for developing word recognition, can be ignored or underused in primary-level classrooms.

Just as emergent literacy teachers emphasize environmental print as a meaningful use of literacy in the classroom, they also want to move beyond such basic functional use of print to the higher-level literacy use associated with literature. The meaningfulness that comes from books for young children is grounded in a variety of purposes. Some purposes are pragmatic, such as the functions we described in Table 2.1. Some meaningful purposes arise through social interaction with others, such as the intimacy and camaraderie of a shared experience with adults and other children (e.g., shared reading of a big book, shared creation of a group experience story or a morning message). Some purposes that make reading meaningful are associated with the book content: learning information on favorite topics such as dinosaurs or birds, learning about problems and resolutions for common and unusual experiences.

Some meaningfulness comes from playing with language and humor within books. However, while children's love for playfulness can be the basis for reading funny text that rhymes and has strange and wonderful illustrations as Dr. Seuss showed so well, a heavy diet of nonsensical text epitomized in "The fat bat sat on the hat. The fat gnat sat on the vat." has not proven palatable to either teachers or children. To sustain children's motivation and interest in learning to read, texts need to be both intellectually stimulating and aesthetically pleasing. But, finding text that is both meaningful and that allows children to be successful when their independent reading skills are still limited has challenged educators for generations. Recent solutions to this problem focus on involving children with texts that are meaningful and interesting, while containing text and word patterns that beginning readers can understand. These solutions emanate directly from the principles of literacy learning as embedded in oral language and as occurring across multiple contexts with adults and children.

Literacy Learning Is Embedded in Oral Language

Before children have the skills to read alone or with one another, their reading occurs through oral language as an adult reads aloud. Often these read-alouds occur as shared readings in which a large version of a book—a big book—is visible to children. When text structures within the big books involve units that are repeated (e.g., repeating the phrase "What do I see" in Bill Martin's popular, 1967 book *Brown Bear, Brown Bear, What Do You See?*), children can use their aural memories to remember the repeated text, and rely on their teacher's guiding hand to associate that message with the print. Through this experience of repeating memorized words as the teacher points to the print, children come to associate oral and written words.

Doug's rendition in Vignette 5.2 is the result of such repeated read-along experiences with *The Carrot Seed*. Through these repeated read-along opportunities, children begin to focus on particular words, usually words of high meaning such as *carrot*. Occasions when children interact independently with these books at the library or writing center encourage increasing familiarity with these words until children have a group of words that they can recognize in other texts (i.e., their "corpus" of recognized words in print).

Oral language is also the means whereby young children express their interpretations of the books that are part of reading experiences with their teacher. This is evident in the children's interactions described in Vignette 5.1 around the meaning of *solemn*. It was also evident during the discussion of crocodile tears in Vignette 4.1. Oral language becomes the medium for children to experiment with their current construction of what it means to read, as Doug does in Vignette 5.2. Through oral language, young children try out their current constructions of the message on the page. This oral expression creates the instructional opportunity for adults to guide their reading and provide other models and interpretations.

Literacy Learning Occurs in Multiple Contexts

In our discussion of the second principle, it was clear that read-alouds and read-alongs are important contexts for students' literacy learning. However, teachers also scaffold children's peer and independent interactions with text through their selections or recommendations of books. Features of text—length, words, illustrations, and so forth—differ substantially from book to book. Some of these differences are immediately obvious as one leafs through a book. Even a child who is not yet a conventional reader can discern differences such as the presence or number of pictures and the length of the book. But what about differences between *Cat in the Hat* and *Brown Bear, Brown*

Bear, What Do You See? Or between *Madeline*, part of the shared reading in Vignette 5.1, and *The Carrot Seed* that Doug, the five-year-old in Vignette 5.2, identified as his favorite? Are all of these books equally appropriate for beginning reading instruction?

Some features of text provide various scaffolds (e.g., picture/text relationships) for the beginning reader, although initially, a shared reading event with the teacher may be necessary for children to make use of these scaffolds. As children steadily acquire knowledge about literacy, they begin to use these scaffolds on their own. We devote a considerable portion of this chapter to identifying the manner in which particular features of text influence young readers' success in comprehending a book. Teachers' book selections for instructional lessons and independent activities are crucial for students' development as independent readers. We organize the remainder of the chapter in terms of two types of text: (a) texts that teachers read to students and (b) texts that children read, both with the teacher and on their own.

Texts That Teachers Read to Children

Whatever the age of students, teachers read aloud literature—or "trade books," a term publishers use to distinguish literature from textbooks—to broaden their students' interactions with topics, genres, and authors. For young children who are able to read many picturebooks independently, the texts that teachers read aloud are complex picturebooks such as Van Allsburg's (1983) *Wreck of the Zephyr* or Coerr's (1993) *Sadako*. A key goal of the read-aloud is to extend children's involvement with books, with the teacher rereading old favorites as well as new titles on topics and genres that challenge children's thinking.

The diversity and richness of children's literature make the task of selecting books both pleasurable and daunting. Further, there are few restrictions or guidelines from districts or states or from prepackaged programs on teachers' choices of read-aloud books. In fact, teachers choose from an endless assortment of trade books. There are classic books, such as *Make Way for Ducklings* (McCloskey, 1941) or *Madeline,* enjoyed by children across generations, and each year, many trade books are added to an already resplendent collection. Some of these books, like *Smoky Night* (Bunting, 1994), have become instant favorites. Others may not endure the test of time but are part of the array from which teachers can choose. Sifting the wheat from the chaff in children's books is an ongoing part of teaching—a process that is to be savored and enjoyed by teachers because of the many superior children's books that are available.

Teachers will find long lists of recommendations and award winners for just about any kind of children's book. There are times when good literature helps us relax, laugh, or escape the hectic pace of a school day. There are times when good literature challenges our thinking, introduces us to new people, places, and times. There are times when good literature serves to inform or intrigue us, capturing our curiosity or pushing our imagination. Given the power of literature, it is important for teachers to be aware of the range of purposes a single book can serve, as well as the particular purposes that a book might serve (Cullinan & Galda, 1994). In Chapter 3, we discussed the literacy goals that underlie emergent literacy classrooms. The literacy goal most central to literature selection in these classrooms relates to the central process of comprehending the content communicated within the trade books. Two dimensions of the content of trade books bear consideration: (a) themes and (b) cultural values.

We first elaborate on these two dimensions, then review resources that can guide book selection to support the goals of the emergent literacy classroom. Our discussion of themes and cultural values, however, requires a group of books as referents; thus we focus our discussion on books from the award winner lists displayed in Tables 5.1 and 5.2.

Table 5.1 consists of the beginning independent reading and younger readers (ages 5–8) portions of the 1994 Children's Choices. This annual list of books, established by the International Reading Association and Children's Book Council in 1974, selects winners from several hundred books. Regional review teams work with teachers and students who read and vote on the books. Those with the highest votes are designated as Children's Choices.

Teachers' Choices, included in Table 5.2, represent a similar effort of tallying teachers' responses to a large set of books. Teachers are asked to identify books they view as exceptional in curriculum use, reflecting high literary quality, and that may not be discovered or appreciated by children without introduction by a knowledgeable adult.

The other two lists of award winners in Table 5.2 represent the most prestigious awards given to picturebooks by panels of librarians and other experts. Since 1938, the American Library Association has awarded the Caldecott Medal to the illustrator of the most distinguished picturebook for children published in the United States in the year preceding the award. Although the illustrator of a book receives this award, the stories of these books are often high in literary quality. Another list of award winners that appears in Table 5.2 consists of the recipients of the Coretta Scott King Illustrator Awards, given annually to an illustrator of African-American descent.

The Themes of Literature

Whether a book tells a story, communicates a rhyme, or conveys information, its content pertains to a theme. And, unwittingly or intentionally, the illustrations and text of a book convey values. Trade book themes can be considered in relation to children's developmental interests, classroom community goals, and interdisciplinary themes.

Developmental Themes.   Developmental themes are ones that interest children at particular points of development. The selections on the Children's

TABLE 5.1   Classification of Selections From Children's Choice[1] (Young Readers' List), 1994

Genre/Topic	Selection
Beginning Independent Reading	Curtis, Jamie Lee. *When I Was Little: A Four-Year-Old's Memoir of Her Youth.* Illus. Laura Cornell Gwynne, Fred. *Easy to See Why* Siracusa, Catherine. *The Giant Zucchini* Russo, Marisabina. *Trade-in Mother*
Predictable/Rhyming	Carle, Eric. *Today Is Monday* Compton, Kenn & Joanne. *Granny Greenteeth and the Noise in the Night.* Illus. Kenn Compton Emberley, Ed. *Go Away, Big Green Monster!* Numeroff, Laura. *Dogs Don't Wear Sneakers.* Illus. Joe Mathieu Pinczes, Elinor J. *One Hundred Hungry Ants.* Illus. Bonnie MacKain

Realistic Fiction
  Common Family Situations:
    Travel
    Sibling rivalry
 	
  New Situations:
    School
 	
    City child at farm
  Uncommon Situations:
    Lost in the woods
 	
    Searching for a home
 	
    Natural disasters
    Being different
	
	Brown, Marc. *Arthur's Family Vacation*
	Martin, Jane Read & Marx, Patricia. *Now Everybody Really Hates Me.* Illus. Roz Chast
	
	Kline, Suzy. *Song Lee in Room 2B.* Illus. Frank Remkiewicz
	Petersen, P.J. *The Sub.* Illus. Meredith Johnson
	Ericsson, Jennifer. *No Milk!* Illus. Ora Eitan
	
	Kinsey-Warnock, Natalie. *The Bear That Heard Crying.* Illus. Ted Rand
	Jennings, Linda. *The Dog Who Found Christmas.* Illus. Catherine Walters
	Stover, Jill. *Alamo Across Texas*
	Versey, Amanda. *Hector's New Sneakers*
	Shannon, Margaret. *Elvira*

Fantasy
  Animals/Monsters Come
    to Life
	Berian, Kathryn Hook. *Andrew's Amazing Monsters.* Illus. Maxie Chambliss
	Camp, Lindsay. *Dinosaurs at the Supermarket.* Illus. Clare Skilbeck
	Dubanevich, Arlene. *Calico Cows*
	Greenblat, Rodney A. *Slombo the Gross*
	McPhail, David. *Pigs Aplenty, Pigs Galore!*
	Mahy, Margaret. *The Three-Legged Cat.* Illus. Jonathan Allen
	Roddie, Shen. *Mrs. Wolf.* Illus. Korky Paul

[1]From Children's Choices for 1994. *The Reading Teacher, 48,* pp. 147–155.

TABLE 5.1   Classification of Selections From Children's Choice (Young Readers' List), 1994 *(continued)*

Genre/Topic	Selection
Children Changing the Environment	Arnold, Tedd. *Green Wilma* Buehner, Caralyn. *A Job for Wittilda.* Illus. Mark Buehner Hearn, Diane Dawson. *Dad's Dinosaur Day* Holleyman, Sonia. *Mona the Brilliant* Leemis, Ralph. *Smart Dog.* Illus. Chris Demarest Potter, Katherine. *My Mother the Cat* Schanzer, Rosalyn. *Ezra in Pursuit: The Great Maze Chase* Serfozo, Mary. *Benjamin Bigfoot.* Illus. Joseph A. Smith
Humor	York, Carol Beach. *Pudmuddles.* Illus. Lisa Thiesing

Folklore
   Traditional European-
      American Tales, changed
	Auch, Mary Jane. *Peeping Beauty*
	Perlman, Janet. *Cinderella Penguin*
	Trivizas, Eugene. *The Three Little Wolves & the Big Bad Pig.* Illus. Helen Oxenbury
	Vozar, David. *Yo, Hungry Wolf!* Illus. Betsy Lewin

Retellings of Tales European origins	Langley, Jonathan. *Goldilocks and the Three Bears* Slater, Teddy. *Walt Disney's Mickey and the Beanstalk.* Illus. Phil Wilson Rounds, Glen. *Three Billy Goats Gruff*
African origins	Rosen, Michael. *How Giraffe Got Such a Long Neck.* Illus. John Clementson
New Tales	Marshall, James. *Rats on the Range and Other Stories*
Nonfiction	Hewett, Joan. *Tiger, Tiger, Growing Up.* Photo. Richard Hewett Jeunesse, Gallimard, et al. *Castles: A First Discovery Book.* Illus. C. & D. Millet Jeunesse, Gallimard, et al. *Whales: A First Discovery Book.* Illus. Ute Fuhr & Raoul Sautai Michel, François. *Water.* Illus. Yves Larvor
Fiction/Nonfiction Mix	Myers, Laurie. *Earthquake in the Third Grade.* Illus. Karen Ritz Reiser, Lynn. *Tomorrow on Rocky Pond*

TABLE 5.2 Recent Award Winners: Teachers' Choice (1994), Caldecott (1986–1995), Coretta Scott King Illustrator (1986–1995)

Award	Year	Titles
Teachers' Choice[1]	1994	Appelt, Kathi. *Elephants Aloft.* Illus. Keith Baker Coerr, Eleanor. *Sadako.* Illus. Ed Young Dunphy, Madeleine. *Here Is the Arctic Winter.* Illus. Alan James Robinson Say, Allen. *Grandfather's Journey* Siebert, Diane. *Plane Song.* Illus. Vincent Nasta Simon, Seymour. *Autumn Across America* Soto, Gary. *Too Many Tamales.* Illus. Ed Martinez Stock, Catherine. *Where Are You Going, Manyoni?* Uchida, Yoshiko. *The Bracelet.* Illus. Joanna Yardley
Caldecott Medal Winner	1986	*The Polar Express* (Chris Van Allsburg)
	1987	*Hey, Al* (Richard Egielski; Illus. Arthur Yorinks)
	1988	*Owl Moon* (John Schoenherr; Illus. Jane Yolen)
	1989	*Song and Dance Man* (Stephen Gammell; Illus. Karen Ackerman)
	1990	*Lon Po Po: A Red Riding Hood Story From China* (Ed Young)
	1991	*Black and White* (David Macaulay)
	1992	*Tuesday* (David Wiesner)
	1993	*Mirette on the High Wire* (Emily Arnold McCully)
	1994	*Grandfather's Journey* (Allen Say)
	1995	*Smoky Night* (Eve Bunting; Illus. David Diaz)
Coretta Scott King Illustrator	1986	*The Patchwork Quilt* (Valerie Flournoy; Illus. Jerry Pinkney)
	1987	*Half a Moon and One Whole Star* (Crescent Dragonwagon; Illus. Jerry Pinkney)
	1988	*Mufaro's Beautiful Daughters: An African Tale* (John Steptoe)
	1989	*Mirandy and Brother Wind* (Patricia McKissack; Illus. Jerry Pinkney)
	1990	*Nathaniel Talking* (Eloise Greenfield; Illus. Jan Spivey Gilchrist)
	1991	*Aida* (told by Leontyne Price; Illus. Leo and Diane Dillon)
	1992	*Tar Beach* (Faith Ringgold)
	1993	*The Origin of Life on Earth: An African Myth* (Katherine Atkins Wilson; Illus. David A. Anderson)
	1994	*Soul Looks Back in Wonder* (Maya Angelou et al.; Illus. Tom Feelings)
	1995	*The Creation* (James Weldon Johnson; Illus. James Ransome)

[1]From Teachers' Choices for 1994, *The Reading Teacher, 48,* pp. 239–241.

Choice list (Table 5.1) indicate themes that interest children during the emergent literacy years. One prominent theme relates to central issues in human beings' experiences, such as: (a) the relationship with nature (*Earthquake in the Third Grade*), (b) family relationships (*Trade-in Mother*), and (c) one's own history (*When I Was Little: A Four-Year-Old's Memoir of Her Youth*). Many of these themes are treated, however, in anthropomorphized form with animals dealing with the crises of the search for a new home, a natural disaster, or a family vacation gone awry. Note that themes of human conflict and dilemmas are of interest to young children when the primary characters are animals rather than children like themselves.

Another universal theme to which young children resonate relates to control over their environment. In the spirit of Roald Dahl, an author with a popular following among middle-grade students, many books deal with the theme of children's control over or desire to change their environment. In *Dad's Dinosaur Day,* dad becomes a dinosaur who can play with the child and is not the inaccessible parent who goes to work.

Themes depicted in traditional fairy tales are popular in their updated versions. *Yo, Hungry Wolf!* and *The Three Little Wolves and the Big Bad Pig* feature the pig as the antagonist, illustrating twists on the traditional fairy tale. Similarly, some authors create retellings of traditional tales using popular media characters such as Mickey Mouse, featured in *Walt Disney's Mickey and the Beanstalk.*

Finally, some developmental themes are told through stories about a particular character. Just as many of us are eager to read the next John Grisham tale, young children have favorite authors who write about favorite characters. The series represented by *Arthur's Family Vacation* is illustrative of such stories. Children delight in learning about Arthur's exploits with his family, adventures that may approximate their own experiences or may provide insights into new ways of thinking about and solving problems. While not in the same category of great literature as award winners like *Lon Po Po* or *Grandfather's Journey,* such books are important components of the emergent literacy classroom library, strong additions to a library of award-winning texts.

Classroom Community Themes. These themes relate to occasions that are part of classroom life such as newcomers to the class, the transition from summer vacation to school, absences from school by teacher or students, and birthdays of class members. Many of the books on the lists of award winners relate to these themes. For example, transitions to school from the summer can be recognized by reading *Where Are You Going, Manyoni?* which tells the story of a girl's journey to school. Exploring different holiday traditions can begin with Soto's *Too Many Tamales,* a story of a Hispanic-American family's celebration of Christmas. Other community events may occur far away, but be brought to students' lives through television. Books such as *Smoky Night,* the 1995 Caldecott winner, can help students reflect on human disasters. Eve Bunting conceived of this book's theme as fires burned in Los Angeles in 1992.

Interdisciplinary Themes.   Literature should be integrated across the curriculum. Past award winners such as *Owl Moon* and *The Patchwork Quilt* illustrate connections to science and social studies content. *Owl Moon* tells about learning to observe nature under the light of the moon. *The Patchwork Quilt* conveys the values and treasures that a child receives from her grandmother as they make a quilt.

There are entire volumes written on the role of children's literature in interdisciplinary instruction (e.g., Pappas, Kiefer, & Levstik, 1990; Weaver, Chaston, & Peterson, 1993). The themes that extend across subject areas should deal with the "big ideas" of cultures, or *megathemes* as Valencia (1995) has called them. Some examples of these large themes are development and growth, transitions, creation and imagination, ingenuity and survival, interdependence, humor, and adventures—ordinary and not so ordinary. The intent is for teachers within schools and districts to talk with one another about manifestations of these themes at various points across students' school years. As these themes appear, children can make connections across books that they have read and build on what they have already learned.

Because high-quality literature lends itself to a range of readings (i.e., interpretations, focuses), teachers have substantial leeway in choosing books to study to address particular themes. What teachers want to do, however, is to be certain that the themes that they choose do not shortchange the content. In their survey of themes for integrated units, Lipson, Valencia, Wixson, and Peters (1993) found that far too many themes chosen by teachers to organize their instructional units were trivial in nature. For example, while "apples" or "the circus" are popular choices, they do not constitute themes. By reconfiguring such topics as part of larger, underlying themes, more can be done with the literature to create meaningful literacy events that are likely to have long-term influences on students' learning and thinking. For example, the topic of "apples" could be part of a theme related to "Living things grow and change" or "Living things are part of a cycle of life." A book such as *Autumn Across America* (on the Teachers' Choices 1994 list) graphically and beautifully conveys ideas about harvest and, for children in non-apple-growing areas, encourages connections across communities.

Cultural Values

Any piece of literature communicates values and principles, while teachers and community members are the arbiters of values. We have two aims in discussing cultural values in teachers' selection of literature. First, the implicit and explicit values in a piece of literature should be understood in selecting literature; and, second, the literature selections themselves should both recognize and represent the diversity of cultures in our society.

Implicit and Explicit Values.   A culture's literature communicates the principles that it prizes. For example, a book such as *Mirette on the High Wire* (McCully, 1992) communicates values of courage and friendship. Even in a fractured fairy tale such as *The Three Little Wolves and the Big Bad Pig,* the cultural value of ingenuity in the face of adversity is apparent. In introducing the notion of implicit and explicit values, we are not advocating a particular set of values or viewing literature as a source for "traditional values" in the fashion of Bennett (1994). Rather, we do so to emphasize that values are inherent in the literature read to and by children and that, as teachers, it is important to be aware of the values the texts convey. In the two illustrations that follow, the implicit and explicit values in literature are highlighted to show how choice of literature may: (a) facilitate or inhibit children's ability to relate to storyline and characters and (b) promote or debunk stereotypes.

Depending on their experiences with literature, children may come to view texts as simply windows into the strange and unfamiliar, rather than as both windows into other lives and mirrors that encourage readers to reflect on their own lives (Cullinan & Galda, 1994). Ladson-Billings (1994) describes her experiences as an African-American child in the 1950s reading about Dick and Jane and the lack of connection to her world. Not only were the physical appearances of these characters different from those of Ladson-Billings and her classmates but the characters lived in communities and did activities quite unlike any that she and her classmates knew.

For children in today's classes, the range of cultural groups and contexts that are represented in the recent explosion of children's books should give students with diverse cultures and experiences characters and stories with which they can identify. Books such as *Smoky Night* depict African-American, Asian-American, and Hispanic-American groups living in the same community and working hard to resolve differences. *The Patchwork Quilt* represents the connections across the generations of an African-American family, while *Grandfather's Journey* conveys the roots of an Asian-American family in Japan and in the United States. Such books provide many characters and storylines with which children can identify.

Depending on the literature selected for children, teachers may implicitly reinforce particular stereotypes within the culture. An analysis of the textbook series that had been used in every classroom in California during the 1970s demonstrated the rigid stereotyping of characters' roles and lives (Women on Words & Images, 1975). In one story in the second-grade textbook, a pigeon flies into the garage. Mother is helpless in the face of this dilemma, waving her apron at the pigeon. The young girl, Janet is also unable to help solve the dilemma. Only Mark, a young boy, is able to get the pigeon out of the garage. Such stereotyping is easily avoided given the wide range of literature available in today's classrooms. In the lists that appear in Tables 5.1 and 5.2, for example, female characters appear in books such as *Mona the Brilliant* and *Mirette on the High Wire,* who provide models of adventurous individuals, while male characters in books such as *Benjamin Bigfoot* and *Hector's New Sneakers* show that individuals, regardless of gender, can express their vulnerabilities.

These examples illustrate the presence of values within the literature that students read and hear, as well as the power of literature to challenge students' thinking about things that a culture values. Our task is not to designate the values that should be part of the curriculum but to emphasize the need for considering the values, often implicit, in books.

Cultural Diversity.   In addition to making the values in the books an explicit aspect of literature selection, the diversity represented within the literature should be an important factor. The representation of cultures in the literature that teachers read to students communicates an important message to children. Consider once again the notion of literature as a mirror reflecting who we are, what we value, and how we interact within our worlds, and literature as a window revealing unfamiliar and perhaps distant peoples, places, and times. Cultures' representation in literature selected for children should represent both goals. Ladson-Billings's (1994) comment about her lack of recognition of herself and her life in the stories she read as a child reflects a diet too heavy in literature as a window. This can happen from lack of attention to the diversity of our students (i.e., assuming that literature about children reflects all of their lives), drawing too heavily on traditional mainstream, middle-class settings and characters. In fact, in most of today's classrooms, any single book read by or to children is likely to serve as a mirror for some students, while for others, it serves as a window.

The ways in which cultural groups are represented by themes and illustration can be seen in the award winners. When children's favorites are the only basis for a read-aloud curriculum or when the canons of classics govern selection, diversity of themes within cultural groups can be overlooked (Applebee, 1991). In the lists of award-winning books, we can see that when chosen by adults, diversity is quite highly represented. Six of the ten Caldecotts represent the stories of diverse cultures. Among the nine Teachers' Choice selections, six tell the stories of cultures other than those of European-Americans. The other three are informational in character and presumably cut across different cultures. Further, the representation involves authentic stories of the cultures. For example, *Too Many Tamales* is realistic fiction conveying an event that could well occur in any culture, but it plays out in one that is uniquely Hispanic-American. As a Hispanic-American family makes tamales as part of their Christmas preparation, Maria, who has tried on her mother's wedding ring, discovers that it is missing only when all of the tamales have been made.

While cultural representation is rich in the selections made by teachers and librarians, a similar range of representation cannot be seen in the books that were popular with children. Only one book had a primary character and problem dealing with cultural uniqueness—*Song Lee in Room 2B*—and one book consisted of folk tales from a historical tradition other than European—*How Giraffe Got Such a Long Neck*. Presumably, children were presented with a range of selections, including books representing various cultural groups. Does this mean that children, regardless of cultural heritage, shared an interest in particular kinds of books? Or does this feature of children's choices represent their developmental interests in rhyming text, fanciful characters, and happy endings? While questions such as these cannot be answered without more information on regional choices and the composition of classes that participate in the selection of books, this feature does emphasize the need for teachers to share a variety of books with children.

We have suggested the importance of considering both the values reflected in young children's literature as well as the diversity of cultural groups. Ultimately, however, the basis for selecting books that further the goals of an emergent literacy curriculum needs to be the curriculum itself. While award winners or titles recommended by professional organizations or experts can be expected to have particular characteristics, the theme and values within a book need to be examined against the curriculum of particular classrooms.

Resources for Finding Children's Literature

Given the plethora of literature available today for use in reading aloud, instruction, and encouraging students' independent reading, it is important for teachers to have access to sources of information about the books. We drew on four lists of award-winning books for children in our previous section. However, despite the value of these four lists, our discussion conveyed their limitations as well. In this section, we examine resources that teachers can draw upon, from lists of award winners to reviews in professional journals and recommendations from professional organizations.

Award-Winning Books.   Approximately 125 awards for children's books are listed in *Children's Books: Awards and Prizes* (Children's Book Council, 1992), but primary-level teachers should be aware that many of these awards are given to books for intermediate-level students. As a group, the four award winners that are listed in Tables 5.1 and 5.2 are the most comprehensive for emergent literacy classrooms. Teachers can stay current with the annual winners of these awards quite easily. The Children's Choices appear in the October issue of *The Reading Teacher,* an instructional journal published by the International Reading Association. Teachers' Choices are published in the same journal's November issue annually. Announcements of the Caldecott Awards and Coretta Scott King Illustrator Awards are made in newspapers annually. Further, local bookstores (including the franchises of national bookstores) often feature these award winners and will provide copies of the Caldecott and King award lists upon request.

Recommendations by the Profession.   The voice of professional educators can be heard in book reviews written for journals, in book lists provided by districts, and in recommended books published by specific organizations. Further, lists included in professional books reflect both critical reviews and personal recommendations of individual authors (e.g., Jim Trelease's *Read-Aloud Handbook* [1989] and Cullinan & Galda's *Literature and the Child,* Third edition [1994]). As the Internet grows in listings and in use, the number of lists of recommended books can be expected to increase even more than the many that already exist. The critical task for teachers will be to make wise choices in selecting from this overload of information. Wise choices will stem from: (a) teachers' curricular and instructional needs, (b) the interests and needs of their particular children, and (c) consideration of the intended uses and selection criteria of the professionals who created the list.

Reputable sources also include professional journals such as *The Reading Teacher* and *Language Arts,* which regularly carry columns of book reviews. A list that illustrates the ones created by professional educators is displayed in Table 5.3, which also highlights an area in which all of the

TABLE 5.3	Bibliography of Nonfiction Read-Alouds
Topic	**Titles**
Animals: Communications, Habitats, Habits, and Characteristics	Clayton, Gordon. *Foal* Machotka, H. *Outstanding Outsides* Patent, D.H. *What Good Is a Tail?* Illus. W. Munoz Peters, Sharon. *Animals at Night.* Illus. Paul Harvey Robinson, Fay. *Real Bears and Alligators.* Illus. Ann Iosa
The Natural World	Hausherr, R. *What Food Is This?* Heller, Ruth. *The Reason for a Flower* Kitchen, Bert. *When Hunger Calls* Wandelmaier, Roy. *Stars.* Illus. Irene Trivas Wexler, Jerome. *Flowers Fruits Seeds*
Ocean Life	Cousteau Society. *Dolphins* Grenner, B., and Chardiet, B. *Where's That Fish?* Illus. C. Schwartz Zoehfeld, K.W. *What Lives in a Shell?*
People and Their Habitats and Food	Harrison, T. *Children of the Yukon* Kuklin, Susan. *How My Family Lives in America* Markle, S. *Outside and Inside You* McConkey, L. *Sea and Cedar: How the Northwest Coast Indians Lived.* Illus. D. Tait Miller, Margaret. *My Five Senses* Morris, Ann. *Bread, Bread, Bread.* Photo. Ken Heyman Morris, Ann. *On the Go.* Photo. Ken Heyman
Geography	Bash, B. *Desert Giant: The World of the Saguaro Cactus* Hartman, Gail. *As the Crow Flies: A First Book of Maps.* Illus. Harvey Stevenson
Weather and Seasons	Hirschi, Ron. *Summer.* Photo. Thomas Mangelsen Kramer, S. *Avalanche.* Photo. P. Cone Kramer, S. *Lightning.* Photo. W. Faidley Peters, L.W. *The Sun, the Wind and the Rain.* Illus. Ted Rand

award winners have been deficient—informational books. The list began with recommendations in a *Reading Teacher* article (Doiron, 1994). A column in *The Reading Teacher* (Fried, Hershey, Koblitz, Stiles, Stotts, Unanue, Woodman, & Pierce, 1995) expanded the list. We then added some personal favorites from the recent wave of new informational books for young children.

For teachers who wish to keep current on recent publications of books, the *Horn Book Magazine* is a bimonthly publication that provides reviews of books as they appear. Two times a year, a cumulative index of all reviews of books published during that time period is provided in the *Horn Book Guide.*

In summary, resources can be extremely helpful in identifying a range of relevant books for reading aloud to students as they listen, or as they read along. From professional literature to word-of-mouth recommendations of personal favorites, these resources provide an important means for teachers to stay informed and up-to-date on children's literature.

Texts That Children Read

Selecting books so beginning readers can experience success while simultaneously developing strategies that lead to independent reading is a task that has challenged educators for generations. In the past, beginning reading programs were known by their allegiance to a single criterion (e.g., high-frequency words or phonetically regular words or high literary quality). Today, the literacy field recognizes the importance of children's early exposure to a wide range of print, with literature selected on the basis of multiple criteria. In this section, we examine the three dominant criteria that have formed the basis for selecting books for beginning readers in American classrooms, in terms of single-criterion and multiple-criteria programs. We then consider a criterion that has often been downplayed or overlooked in selecting an early reading instructional approach: the number of books that are part of the beginning reading program.

Texts Selected Using a Single Criterion

Perhaps no greater debate has existed in the history of literacy education than the one focused on the best texts to use for teaching young children to read. Three primary criteria for selecting texts have dominated the field; these criteria are texts featuring high-frequency words, phonetically regular words, or high literary quality. For most of our history as a reading profession, the debate has been over which criteria should dominate.

For much of the 20th century, most American schoolchildren have learned to read with texts that featured high-frequency words. Use of such texts came under harsh criticism by advocates of texts that feature phonetically regular words. The argument was essentially between whether students initially best learned to read by acquiring a broad sight word vocabulary (i.e., by frequent exposure to common words) or by acquiring knowledge of sound/

symbol correspondence. Texts written to feature high-frequency words and those written to feature phonetically regular words differ significantly from one another in their target words but, because stories are selected for the presence of particular words rather than for the message, both approaches have relied on creating special books for beginning readers. Both these approaches have come under serious criticism in the past decade as questions were raised about literary quality in the literature used to teach young children to read. Thus, recent trends have led to choosing texts for their literary merit. The shift to high literary quality as the criterion for selecting books has meant a focus on the text as a whole. Further, using this as the criterion for text selection has meant that existing library or trade books have become the source for beginning reading materials.

Despite vast differences in emphases across these three stances, their application to reading programs has been exclusionary. If literary quality is the criterion that dominates, the other characteristics of text fall by the wayside. Similarly, when high-frequency words dominated as the guide for beginning reading materials, the literary quality of books and the presence of phonetically regular words were of secondary concern. We examine each of these criteria in turn, then explore what we believe is a rational approach to early reading instruction: the use of multiple criteria in selecting books for teaching beginning readers.

High-Frequency Words.   High-frequency or sight words are those that occur most often in written English (see Table 3.4 for a sample list). High-frequency words as the basis for reading textbooks came into prominence in the 1930s with the addition of William S. Gray to the Scott-Foresman reading series (Elson & Gray, 1930). Gray was prominent among the behavioral psychologists who promised a "new science of teaching" (Smith, 1934/1965). These psychologists believed that behaviorist learning principles (Thorndike, 1903) could be applied to creating texts from which all children of normal intelligence would learn to read. The principles dictated that students practice repeatedly on specific sets of target words to ensure a connection between the stimulus (i.e., the written word) and the response (i.e., the oral reading of the word).

The stories in the Scott-Foresman textbooks in which Gray applied these behaviorist principles centered around Dick and Jane and their menagerie of pets and family members. Other publishers using a similar philosophy created textbook series with different casts of characters. These programs of basic materials in a sequence for the elementary grades came to be called "basal" reading programs. The nature of text for first graders was similar across these programs because of the underlying "science" that children needed to see particular high-frequency words repeatedly in stories with familiar content. The first page of a story entitled *Tiny* (Rider, 1986) illustrates this genre:

> We can go now.
> I can not go.
> I have to get Tiny.
> I will help you.   (p. 19)

On this page and the six that follow it, 19 distinct words are combined in a variety of ways to form a 133-word passage. Except for the name of the protagonist, Tiny, the words are ones that appear frequently in written English: here, come, will, not, to, you, I, have, get, do, help, we, can, it, go, in, now, want. The children who are chasing Tiny are never identified by name, although pictures of their faces appear in front of each line to convey a dialogue (and making it unnecessary to include the repetitive "said Janet" or "Mark said"). The barn into which Tiny escapes is referred to as "here." This mid-1980s version of a passage in a popular textbook series differs little from the Dick and Jane text that characterized the 1940s and 1950s basal textbook series.

Gray's assumptions and those of psychologists who kept this tradition alive into the late 1980s were faulty on a number of counts. First, anyone who has ever had to spend days at school reading text such as "We can go now. I can not go" or any teacher who has ever had to listen to one class after another of first graders struggle through this text will give the resounding message that text that rigidly follows this criterion does not generate motivation for either learning to read or teaching children to read.

A second problem associated with this text is the abstractness and complexity of high-frequency words, as we discussed in Chapter 3. As is evident in the example of *Tiny,* no exceptions were made to the high-frequency criterion. For young children, the exclusion of *any* high-meaning words increased the complexity of learning to read substantially.

Third, as Chall's (1967/1982) analyses highlighted, children were not encouraged to learn about the regular sound-letter correspondences in English. For example, phonetically regular words such as *pig* and *hog* were not integrated into the *Tiny* passage even though those words describe Tiny's species. Nor do the children chase Tiny around the *pen.* Including any of these words—pig, hog, pen—might have supported a disposition among beginning readers to develop the knowledge of rimes we described in Chapter 3 as being an important part of beginning readers' repertoire of knowledge. When children's early instructional experiences are with texts like *Tiny,* they fail to grasp common sound-letter patterns (Juel & Roper-Schneider, 1985).

While psychologists in the early 20th century were correct to assume that automaticity with a group of words is important to independent reading, as we saw in Chapter 3, automaticity with a core group of words is only one of several important strategies. However, the emphasis on high-frequency words became even more entrenched in American reading instruction as these words became a primary criterion for readability formulas (Davison & Kantor, 1982; Klare, 1984). Together with sentence length, the number of high-frequency words was used as part of the readability formulas that established the text difficulty level of texts. To be "easier" according to a readability formula, and thus appropriate for use in a basal reading series, sentences needed to be short and vocabulary needed to be on a high-frequency word list. To meet the requirements of the readability formulas, texts were often changed to feature high-frequency words over more vivid terms used in the original texts. For example, *The Secret Hiding Place* (Bennett, 1960, p. 1) contained the phrase, "lily pads and corn" in its original form. It was rewritten and retitled *The Little Hippo* (Eller, Hester et al., 1980, p. 46) to appear in a beginning basal reader, and the phrase was replaced with the word *food*. Though behaviorist psychology is no longer the driving philosophy underlying text selection, readability formulas continue to influence the passages on the tests prominent in most American school systems, in turn raising the importance of high-frequency words used in instruction.

Phonetically Regular Text.   Phonetically regular words are those that are predictable based on the underlying rules of letter-sound correspondences in the English language. Proposals that texts should be selected on the basis of phonetically regular words periodically challenged the high-frequency criterion (e.g., Flesch, 1957). At times there has been considerable clamor by advocates of this perspective. However, the percentage of American classrooms in which these materials have been used has never been great (Chall & Squire, 1991). Programs developed with this criterion in mind followed the same underlying behaviorist principles as programs featuring high-frequency words. A sequence of words representing particular rimes appeared repeatedly. These words needed to form stories of familiar characters and events that children could read successfully, allowing for reinforcement.

A selection from a textbook series that emphasized phonetically regular words begins in this manner: "Dad ran to the fan. Dad had to fan Nan. Dad had to fan Dan." (Rasmussen & Goldberg, 1964, p. 16). This text from *The Bad Fan* came from the beginning of a reading program when the first vowel-consonant rimes—those with the short vowel *a* as in "ad" and "an"—were taught. Once the "at" rime had been introduced, Nan, Dad, and Dan might have adventures that involve a "fat rat." At this point in the program, the problems of the stories could not include Mom because vowel-consonant rimes with "o" had not been introduced. Nor would Dad be expected to "fix" the fan because the "ix" rime occurred later in the program.

An obvious problem with this type of text is its nonsensical nature. The task of reading *The Bad Fan* resembles a tongue twister more than reading meaningful and engaging text. An inventive writer like Dr. Seuss was able to take the constraints imposed by this philosophy and create text that was appealing. But, as he described later, "I remember thinking that I might be able to dash off *The Cat in the Hat* in two or three weeks. Actually, it took over a year" (Commire, 1982, p. 114). If learning to read requires interactions with many books, the creation of several hundred masterpieces with such regular text will be an unlikely financial venture for many publishers of school materials.

While phonetically regular reading textbooks have never dominated early reading instruction in the United States, there has been a lingering belief among teachers, parents, and critics of American education that this perspective might solve many children's reading difficulties. Research findings partially substantiate this perspective. Some regularity in word patterns in books children read during early stages of reading instruction appears to assist their becoming independent readers more quickly than do books based solely on high-frequency words (Juel & Roper-Schneider, 1985). A tie-in between instruction in letter-sound correspondences and the materials that children read is particularly important. Chall (1982) analyzed American textbook programs published over a decade after her report showing the importance of phonics for beginning readers, *Learning to Read: The Great Debate* (Chall, 1967), was published. She found that phonics instruction had been integrated into the teachers' manuals and workbooks, while children's texts continued to feature high-frequency words. When Juel and Roper-Schneider (1985) studied children's reading acquisition in programs that followed this pattern of phonics instruction without follow-up of phonics patterns in books, they found that children did not integrate the use of word patterns in their independent recognition repertoire.

While it has not been feasible to create phonetically perfect text, the assumption that the instruction on word patterns should be linked to the words children are reading in their texts merits attention. Predictable books found in many primary-level classrooms illustrate that engaging books can be written with rhyming words to encourage application of letter-sound knowledge and that involve children with high-frequency words. Many of these predictable books also fit the criterion that we explore next—high literary quality.

Literary Quality of Text.   It was only in the early 1990s that the dominance of high-frequency words as the criterion for selecting books for beginning readers came to an end, replaced by the criterion of high literary quality. By focusing on high literary quality, educators believed that children would be involved with engaging language and ideas that were both motivating and more like the language they heard in their day-to-day lives.

California (California Language Arts/English Framework Committee, 1987) and Texas (Texas Education Agency, 1990), large states that influence textbook creation by their state adoption policies, required high-quality literature as a primary criterion for their review process. Not surprisingly, textbooks now consist of selections from trade books. The shift can be seen by examining the 1991 edition of the textbook that had included the story of *Tiny* in the 1986 edition. Recall that in 1986, the text had featured high-frequency words. In 1991, at approximately the same place where *Tiny* had appeared, the textbook included a different story about a pig. The text was Mike Inkpen's (1988) *If I Had a Pig*. Note the difference in the words featured and the flow of the story, as illustrated in the first three pages of text: "If I had a pig . . . I would tell him . . . a joke" (Inkpen, 1988, pp. 4–6). The boy then describes fanciful activities that he and his pet might do—make a house, paint pictures, have fights, give each other piggybacks, bake a cake, race, make snowpigs, and finally, "tell him a story and take him to bed." In contrast to *Tiny, If I Had a Pig* is rich with vocabulary, using such words as "wrinkled," "joke," "snowpig," and "Boo."

If first-grade teachers follow the publisher's recommendations for introducing material, children will read this passage during the first trimester of first grade. Teachers are encouraged to use a shared reading experience where children read along, using the predictable pattern of the text ("If I had a pig, I would _____") as a structure for reading. The instructional guidance provides little focus on the high-frequency words (e.g., "if," "I," "had," "a"). Of the 95 words in the story, 57 are unique (i.e., appear only once), one of every two words. On which words do beginning readers focus? With so many words bombarding beginning readers, words that are not high-interest or picturable words are unlikely to be ones to which young children will attend.

Answers to the question of what beginning readers are learning are few, but available reports indicate that those children who do not already have a substantial foundation in emergent literacy at the beginning of grade one struggle when literary quality is the sole or primary criterion for selecting passages. At the end of first grade, about 70% of the children in literature-based classrooms are not able to read trade books even simpler than *If I Had a Pig* (Hiebert, Liu, Levin, Huxley, & Chung, 1995). There are just too many unknown words with complex features for those children who are not already competent readers to learn.

The shift in beginning reading materials has been dramatic and rapid, as illustrated by *Tiny* and *If I Had a Pig.* While there is always a danger of a pendulum swing back to texts such as *Tiny* or *The Bad Fan,* a more reasonable response is to consider how the characteristics of high-frequency, phonetically regular, and high-interest can be integrated along with other critical characteristics.

Texts Selected for Multiple Criteria

Because learning to read is a complex process, educators have moved away from looking at single features of books to examining multiple aspects of books. In this section, we develop this perspective of book selection using multiple elements that we label "text accessibility." This perspective draws on previous research, particularly that of Juel and Roper-Schneider (1985) and of Hiebert and her colleagues (1995), to focus on five features that influence the text accessibility for beginning readers. We evaluate these features in relation to readers at the *early* stages of reading acquisition. Unlike readability formulas that were used in the past to select texts for children from grades one through high school, one size does not fit all when it comes to selecting materials from the vantage point of text accessibility—even in first grade. The descriptions that follow are aimed at the selection of text when children are gaining the strategies we described in Chapter 3.

Three of the elements of text accessibility pertain to the story or selection as a whole: (1) predictability, (2) contextual support, and (3) word density. The other two elements relate to characteristics of individual or distinct words in the text: (4) proportion of decodable words, and (5) proportion of core high-frequency words. Thus we consider five text accessibility features that influence the central and necessary reading strategies we described in Chapter 3. Table 5.4 details the components and the evaluation criteria for the five features.

TABLE 5.4	Critical Features in Beginning Reading Materials	
Characteristic	**Components**	**Evaluation Criteria**
Characteristics of Texts		
Predictability	Size of Predictable Unit	• Small predictable unit (3–5 words) • Sizable unit (6–10 words) • Large unit (11–15 or more words) • No predictable unit
	Proportion of Text Accounted for by Predictable Unit	• Very high: 3/4 or more • High: 1/2 to 2/3 • Moderate: 1/4 to 1/3 • Low: Less than 1/4
Contextual Support	Familiarity of Concepts	• Very familiar (concepts/topics) • Familiar • Somewhat familiar • Not common
	Usefulness of Illustrations in Identifying Key Words	• Very useful • Useful • Somewhat useful • Not useful
Word Density	Number of Distinct Words	• Count of distinct or different words
	Ratio of Distinct to All Words	• Number of all words is divided by number of distinct words
Characteristics of Distinct Words		
Decodability		Of the distinct words in the text, the proportion of words with a vowel-consonant rime is: • Very High: 3 of 5 • High: 2 of 5 • Average: 1 of 5 • Low: less than 1 of 5
High Frequency		Of the distinct words in the text, the proportion of words that are the 50 most frequent English words is: • Very High: 3 of 5 • High: 2 of 5 • Moderate: 1 of 5 • Low: less than 1 of 5

Predictability.   When a phrase or a sentence is repeated in a passage, several readings of the passage with an adult allow beginning readers to recognize the phrase or sentence. To illustrate this and other features of text accessibility, we refer to the book, *Six Go By* (Dobeck, 1996), the text and illustrations of which can be found in Figure 5.1.

As *Six Go By* illustrates, a pattern is repeated in all but the last sentence. Such texts are known as "predictable" or "patterned." This genre has been available for generations in traditional tales such as *This Is the House That Jack Built* (e.g., Peppe, 1970; Underhill, 1987) or classic books such as Margaret Wise Brown's *Goodnight Moon* (1947). But only recently have educators understood the critical role of this type of text in beginning literacy

---

FIGURE 5.1   **Six Go By**

Six Go By by Maryann Dobeck, illustrated by Rosario Valderrama. Part of the *Ready Readers* Series. © 1995 by *Modern Curriculum Press*, Simon & Schuster Elementary. Used by permission.

programs. In *Brown Bear, Brown Bear, What Do You See?*, Bill Martin, with the aid of Eric Carle's illustrations, showed how to create contemporary predictable text. Read-along experiences with predictable books, Martin and Brogan (1971) proposed, allowed children to participate as readers from the start.

In the wake of the popularity of *Brown Bear . . .*, many outstanding writers and illustrators have produced a host of predictable books, some of which are presented in Table 5.5. The descriptions in Table 5.5 show that the ways

---

TABLE 5.5 Predictable Books: Categories and Examples

Books with a Repetitive Pattern in Which a Particular Phrase or Sentence Is Repeated as Part of the Structure of the Story

Prototype: My Friends
> *A child describes a variety of actions and the animal or individual from whom this action was learned. Each episode takes the form of "I learned to ————— from my friend the ————— ."*

Campbell, Rod. *Dear Zoo*
Gomi, Taro. *My Friends*
Grejniec, Michael. *What Do You Like?*
Hennessy, B.G. *Jake Baked the Cake.* Illus. M. Morgan
Kafka, Sherry. *I Need a Friend.* Illus. Meryl Henderson
Lewin, Hugh. *Jafta.* Illus. Lisa Kopper
Waddle, Martin. *Squeak-a-Lot.* Illus. Virginia Miller
Wood, Audrey. *Quick as a Cricket.* Illus. Don Wood

Books with a Repetitive Pattern That Makes Comparisons or Contrasts

Prototype: My Mom Travels a Lot
> *A young child alternates between describing good and bad things about her mother traveling a lot. Example: "The good thing about it is we get to go to the airport. The bad thing about it is there's only one nighttime kiss."*

Bauer, C.F. *My Mom Travels a Lot.* Illus. N.W. Parker
Cuyler, M. *That's Good! That's Bad!* Illus. D. Catrow
Charlip, Remy. *Fortunately*
Shaw, Charles. *It Looked Like Spilt Milk*

Books Where the Repetitive Pattern Involves a Question-Answer Format

Prototype: Whose Mouse Are You?
> *A question (e.g., Whose mouse are you?) and answer (e.g., Nobody's mouse) exchange is followed to form a story (Whose Mouse Are You?) or to enumerate the features of a group, such as the animals on a farm in Spots, Feathers, and Curly Tails.*

Kraus, Robert. *Whose Mouse Are You?* Illus. Jose Aruego
Martin, Bill. *Brown Bear, Brown Bear, What Do You See?*
Tafuri, Nancy. *Spots, Feathers, and Curly Tails*

TABLE 5.5   *(continued)*

Books with a Repetitive-Cumulative Pattern in Which a Word, Phrase, or Sentence Is Repeated in Each Succeeding Episode, Adding a New Word, Phrase, or Sentence to the Sequence with Each Episode

Prototype: The Napping House

> *The scene begins with a napping house where everyone is sleeping. Each episode adds another component—a cozy bed, a snoring granny, a dreaming child, a dozing dog, a snoozing cat, a slumbering mouse, and, finally, a wakeful flea that begins a chain reaction by biting the mouse, that subsequently scares the cat, etc., until "no one now is sleeping." In another example,* Hattie and the Fox, *the cumulative pattern (a hen seeing various features of a creature) is broken up with a rhythmic refrain: "Good grief!" said the goose. "Well, well!" said the pig. "Who cares?" said the sheep. "So what?" said the horse. "What's next?" said the cow.*

Bonne, Rose. *I Know an Old Lady*
Fox, Mem. *Hattie and the Fox*
Mazer, A. *Yellow Button.* Illus. Judy Pedersen
Peppe, R. *The House That Jack Built*
Robart, Rose. *The Cake That Mack Ate.* Illus. Maryann Kovalski
Wood, Audrey. *The Napping House.* Illus. Don Wood

Books with Rhyming Patterns, Many of Which Have Rhyme Combined with Repetition and Cumulative Repetition

Prototype: Who Is Tapping at My Window?

> *The responses of animals to the query "Who is tapping at my window?" are presented in couplets that rhyme: "It's not I," said the cat. "It's not I," said the rat. A growing subset of these books consists of words or phrases that label events or experiences and that rhyme. In Florian's* Nature Walk, *for example, a group takes a walk through woods with the description in couplets that rhyme, such as "On the trail. Cottontail."*

Brown, Margaret Wise. *Goodnight Moon*
Cameron, Polly. *"I Can't" Said the Ant*
Deming, A.G. *Who Is Tapping at My Window?* Illus. M. Wellington
Ehlert, Lois. *Feathers for Lunch*
Florian, Douglas. *Nature Walk*
Krauss, Ruth. *Bears.* Illus. P. Roward

Books with Patterns Based on Familiar Sequences (Cardinal and Ordinal Numbers, Alphabet, Months of Year, Days of Week, Seasons, Colors)

Prototype: Jasper's Beanstalk

> *Each day of the week finds Jasper tending his bean plant. Unlike many "days of the week" sequences, this book goes beyond a single week with the concluding event occurring "a long, long, long time later (on a Thursday, I think)."*

Butterworth, Nick, and Inkpen, Mike. *Jasper's Beanstalk*
Carle, Eric. *The Very Hungry Caterpillar*
Doubilet, A. *Under the Sea from A to Z*
Ward, Cindy. *Cookie's Week.* Illus. Tomie dePaola
Wolff, Ashley. *A Year of Birds*

of making texts predictable are numerous and complex. As new books appear each year, we can see how inventive authors find novel ways to create predictable texts, varying structure, content, and size of the repeated unit. Certainly, teachers need to be aware of the categories in Table 5.5 as they guide children's read-alongs. Yet, the way in which different predictable structures influence beginning readers has yet to be determined. For example, is a cumulative pattern more difficult to remember than a pattern that relies on a refrain? Two factors seem to be especially important in children's reading acquisition with predictable text: (a) the size of the repeated unit and (b) the proportion of the text accounted for by the repeated unit.

Unit *size* refers to the number of words that are repeated in the book. In *Six Go By,* the repeated unit size is three words: six, go, by. Two of these words—*go, by*—are part of every sentence while the third word, *six,* is part of all but the last two sentences. The size of this predictable unit is relatively small, as it is in *Cat on the Mat* (Wildsmith, 1982), in which the phrase "on the mat" is part of every sentence but the last.

In contrast, the size of the repeated unit is large in *This Is the Cake That Mack Ate,* in which a phrase is added to the repeated unit with each episode. "This is the cake that Mack ate" is followed by "This is the egg that went into the cake that Mack ate." This becomes "This is the hen that laid the egg that went into the cake that Mack ate." Even when children are memorizing the text, a large set of words can be hard to hold in memory. In Vignette 5.2, six words in the repeated sentence of *The Carrot Seed* were difficult for Doug to remember. Doug conveys the gist of the phrase with his "Nothing's gonna grow," but the unit in the text—"I'm afraid it won't come up"—is large enough that he is not focusing on any of the individual words. In contrast, a short phrase of three words in *Six Go By* may be remembered and used by children even after the teacher reads the title a single time.

A second feature that contributes to predictability is the proportion of the text that is devoted to the predictable unit. When every sentence but the last has the predictable pattern as is the case in *Six Go By,* children are more likely to read along or attempt to read the book by themselves. As children's reading proficiency increases, teachers will want to steadily pull away the scaffolding of the predictable text. The alternative is not to move back to tedious text such as *Tiny.* Books such as *Snail's Home Run* contain a manageable amount of text for beginning readers but do not rely on a predictable pattern.

Contextual Support.   At the beginning stages, books in which identification of key words is supported by clear illustrations can be useful. Children can use their knowledge of the world around them to identify key words in the text. On this dimension, books move from familiar objects and actions to more unusual and less concrete vocabulary. There are two dimensions to contextual support: the familiarity of concepts and the match between illustrations and text.

The first relates to concept familiarity. In *Six Go By,* the objects are common—balloons and hats. The event that is occurring in the book is also quite familiar to young children. "Surprise!" on the last page refers to a birthday party for a child. In contrast to the familiar objects and the relatively familiar occasion of a birthday party, children may enjoy *Zin! Zin! Zin! A Violin,* a recent Caldecott Honor book. Most children, even those who daily hear music on the radio and see bands on television, will not be acquainted with the different instruments that are presented in this book as a symphony orchestra is assembled. A considerable amount of explaining will be required on the part of the teacher about the instruments in a symphony orchestra. Even an extended discussion may not be sufficient for children to remember the various instruments, no matter how accurately the instruments are represented in the accompanying pictures or photos.

A second manner in which books can provide children with contextual support comes from the pictures. Pictures are particularly useful at the earliest stages of reading. In *Six Go By,* the words that are not repeated in sentence after sentence, such as *balloons and hats,* are clearly pictured. Even when illustrations elicit different labels from children such as "caps" for "hats," children have made a hypothesis about a word that fits the context. These hypotheses can then be matched by examining more closely the letter-sound correspondence of the hypothesized word and the written word. Opportunities such as these encourage children to integrate their word recognition strategies, a process that Clay (1985) has described as cross-checking.

The familiarity of content interacts with the usefulness of the illustrations. While young children typically are interested in animals and know the names of many animals, animals such as a wren and a cony (a rabbit, typically European) in a popular predictable book entitled *Who Is Tapping at My Window?* (Deming, 1988) may be unknown to many children. In cases where the concepts are unfamiliar, children's reading has to be halted while the teacher discusses the meaning of the concepts. While discussions are central to the emergent literacy curriculum, teachers should be aware of the difficulty that children will have in applying cross-checking strategies in cases such as these. Another important point to remember when studying the contextual supports in books for beginning readers is that this strategy usually supports the reading of nouns. While some verbs can be understood from pictures, clear and colorful illustrations will not assist children in reading most high-function words such as "of" and "is."

Word Density.   Children at the very earliest stages of reading can be stymied in their willingness to attempt the reading of a book because of the length of a book or their perceptions of the presence of "too many words" (Hiebert et al., 1995). As children begin to interact with books, however, the critical feature is the ratio of *distinct* or different words to the total number of words in a book. Every time beginning readers encounter a different word in a book, they need to draw on their emerging repertoire of word recognition strategies. If there are many different words in a book, children are likely to struggle.

The example *Six Go By* contains 10 distinct words: six, go, by, balloons, hats, boxes, clowns, candles, we, surprise. The total number of words in the entire text is 27. Thus the ratio of distinct words (10) to all words (27) is 1:2.7, or, for easier reference, rounded to 1:3. Teachers' awareness that children will encounter about 10 different words makes it possible to consider how they might use the book and the amount and kind of support their students might need (e.g., Can students read this independently at the beginning of the year?). The support that readers get from the predictability of the text and the contextual support of the topic and illustrations will influence teachers' selections. This simple ratio, however, is telling when we consider that the ratio of distinct to all words in beginning reading textbooks changed from 1:7 in *Tiny* to 1:2 in *If I Had a Pig.* When the total number of words is held constant, the latter book will be much more challenging to beginning readers than the former. We emphasize once again that this element cannot be viewed alone. For example, texts such as *Tiny* failed to support children in using the contextual supports of text. The point, simply, is that teachers need to select books according to their aims of instruction and the needs and strengths of their students.

Children's success with an entire text is a function of the number of words they find to be unique and their need to draw on word recognition strategies. When the load of new words is dense in a text, beginning readers' entire success may depend on their ability to use contextual supports or text predictability. Since independent reading is a goal of the primary grades, eventually the scaffolds of contextual support and predictable texts are withdrawn. Thus, even at the early stages, books should provide opportunities for children to apply and use word recognition strategies that are required when illustrations are abstract and text structures follow those of narrative and expository texts. The word-level skills required for beginning readers to successfully read a book can be understood by establishing the decodability and commonality of the distinct words.

Decodability of Distinct Words.   When at least some of the distinct words in a book contain common word patterns or rimes, children have the opportunity to apply their emerging knowledge of letter-sound correspondences. The choice of the phrase "at least some" in the preceding sentence is important. Selecting books that have some distinct words with common rimes is quite different from selecting books where words have almost perfect letter-sound associations such as *The Bad Fan.* When books contain only words with a prescribed set of patterns—as does *The Bad Fan*—children are neither generalizing their knowledge of word patterns nor developing a tolerance for the variability of written English. However, consistency in the patterns of some of the words in the books that children read initially can be helpful. Because facility with vowel-consonant rimes characterizes those children who move into the "rapid word recognition stage" (Martin, 1997), books that have a reasonable number of words with vowel-consonant rimes should be part of early reading instruction.

A critical question is, "What is a reasonable number of words with such patterns in a book?" Answers to this question, as with other aspects of literature-based reading materials, will continue to be developed as teachers and researchers observe children's learning with these materials. At the present time, our information is based on the characteristics of books that have been used successfully with children at the earliest stages of reading. A very popular book at the very beginning stages of reading instruction, *Cat on the Mat,* has three of eight distinct words that fit this pattern: cat, mat, dog. In *Six Go By,* three of the 10 distinct words have vowel-consonant rimes: six, boxes, hats.

In Table 5.4, general guidelines for decodability of distinct words are given for teachers in conducting an "eyeball" analysis of books for beginning readers. As can be seen here, more than one word of every five distinct words has a vowel-consonant rime. When the number is around three out of every five distinct words, the text often represents an attempt to play with a particular pattern. In cases such as these, decisions need to be made as to whether the presence of these word patterns does generate playfulness with language in the sense that Dr. Seuss modeled or whether the text has become didactic in the mode of *The Bad Fan.*

Frequency of Distinct Words.   Because of their abstractness and ambiguity, learning to automatically recognize high-frequency words presents a challenge to beginning readers. Concentrating only on high-frequency words to the exclusion of interesting, highly meaningful words is inappropriate, as was apparent in the text based on this single criterion—*Tiny.* At the same time, disregarding these words makes it difficult for beginning readers to gain fluency with a core group of words. How should these words figure into the selection of books for beginning readers?

By definition, high-frequency words occur often in texts, including those for beginning readers. For example, all but one of the five words in the title of *If I Had a Pig*—if, I, had, a—are high-frequency words. Two of the ten distinct words in *Six Go By*—by, we—appear on the list of 50 most frequent words (Table 3.4). Three of the five words in the title of *Cat on the Mat* are among the most frequent words. These illustrations show that specially written texts (e.g., *Tiny*) are not necessary to expose children to high-frequency words. Highly frequent words can be expected to occur often in beginning readers' books. In Table 5.4, we detail guidelines that teachers might use in emphasizing a particular group of high-frequency words in their book selection. When we examined a group of books that had been proposed for beginning readers, we found that about one of every five distinct words in these books appeared in the list of 50 most frequent words.

Once a teacher identifies a group of high-frequency words to emphasize, those words become the focus during conversations about the words in books and during instructional activities. For example, following several readings of a book, children can write its high-frequency words on individual slips of paper, then match those with the words in the book. Teachers' choices as to which and how many high-frequency words to highlight, their consistency in emphasizing these words, and their provision of follow-up writing activities with the words will influence strongly children's automaticity with high-frequency words. When teachers highlight high-frequency words consistently, the texts that children read do not have to overexaggerate high-frequency words, as occurs in books such as *Tiny.*

Features of Current Text Selections for Beginning Readers

To illustrate how teachers might apply these criteria, we selected a sample of books that are used currently in many classrooms in the United States for beginning reading instruction. We have come a long way from books relating the ongoing saga of Dick, Jane, their pets, and their friends, told in stilted and ambiguous language. Two types of books are now used in beginning reading programs: "little books" and trade books.

Little Books.   The phrase "little books" has come to refer to books that have been published for beginning readers. Unlike earlier texts based simply on high-frequency or phonetically regular words, these books have been modeled after books of literary quality and engagement such as *Brown Bear, Brown Bear, What Do You See?* The label "little books" comes from the descriptions that beginning readers themselves have given the books—these books usually are small in size (less than the standard size of literature anthologies and most trade books) and short in length, usually 8 or 16 pages rather than the 28 or more of a trade book. The concept stems from the 1970s, when outstanding writers such as Else Minarik and Arnold Lobel wrote books that became classics—*Little Bear* (1957) and *Frog and Toad* (1976), initially written as part of commercial reading programs for parents rather than schools. Dr. Seuss got in the act as well with *Hop on Pop* and *Green Eggs and Ham.* These books used the high-frequency vocabularies that were popular in school textbooks at the time. Similar series of little books, many with predictable text structures, have been published recently. These little books are presented in "leveled" programs with books grouped in terms of progressive stages of difficulty. Because American publishers began producing little book programs only in the last few years, we have analyzed exemplars from each of five levels of an Australian beginning reading program: *Jack-in-the-Box* (Butler, 1989), *We Make Music* (Connery, 1989), *The Grump* (Pascoe, 1989), *Dad Didn't Mind* (Naden, 1989), and *Morning Star* (Johnson, 1990). A summary of the features of these five books appears in Table 5.6.

Trade Books.   The term "trade books" refers to books chosen from the library books that were described in our earlier section, "Texts That Teachers Read to Children." There are three ways trade books are chosen for beginning reading instruction: (a) teachers select their own books, (b) teachers select books according to a published list of exemplars or suggestions, and

TABLE 5.6 Summary of Text Accessibility Features of Beginning Reading Materials

Book	Level	Predictability		Contextual Support		Word Density		Decodability of Words	High-Frequency Words
		Size of Unit	Proportion of Text	Familiarity of Concepts	Usefulness of Illustrations	Distinct Words	Ratio: Distinct to All		
Little Books									
Jack-in-the-Box	1	small	high	very familiar	very useful	10	1:4	very high	very high
We Make Music	2	small	very high	very familiar	useful	12	1:4	very high	high
The Grump	3	small	low	somewhat familiar	not useful	38	1:2	very high	high
Dad Didn't Mind	4	sizable	high	familiar	useful	74	1:2	average	average
Morning Star	5	large	moderate	not familiar	not useful	170	1:2	low	average
Trade Books: Reading Recovery Exemplars[1]									
Cat on the Mat	1	small	very high	very familiar	very useful	10	1:4	very high	very high
Chick & Duckling	2	sizable	very high	familiar	somewhat	29	1:4	average	average
Across the Stream	3	none	none	somewhat	somewhat	43	1:2	high	very high
Cake . . . Mack Ate	4	large	very high	somewhat	somewhat	29	1:7	high	average
Very . . . Caterpillar	5	none	none	familiar	somewhat	115	1:2	low	low
Trade Books: Textbook Program									
Monster & Baby	1	small	moderate	familiar	useful	24	1:3	average	high
Have . . . Crocodile?	2	large	very high	somewhat	very useful	22	1:7	low	moderate
If I Had a Pig	3	small	moderate	familiar	useful	55	1:2	average	high
Klippity Klop	4	sizable	high	not familiar	not useful	57	1:2	low	moderate
Jimmy Lee Did It	5	none	none	somewhat	not useful	168	1:2	low	low

[1]These five stages involve the clustering of levels, as proposed by Peterson (1991).

(c) publishers select trade books. When teachers create their beginning reading program, they usually combine both little books and trade books, and combine their own favorite trade books with ones chosen by a publisher. Recently, some American publishers have begun presenting programs that combine little books and trade books.

Because teachers' trade book selections come from resources such as lists of recommended books, we illustrate the characteristics of trade books with one of the only available lists that designates text difficulty for beginning readers—the Reading Recovery (RR) list (Peterson, 1991). The RR program has delineated 20 levels at Grade 1, clustered into five stages of four levels. To illustrate each of the RR levels, Peterson (1991) used familiar trade books. Using easily available and well-known books, rather than less familiar and less available little books, to illustrate levels of difficulty creates a model that teachers can apply to other available books. We selected one book from the middle of each of the five stages, which led to the following selections: *Cat on the Mat* (Wildsmith, 1982), *Chick and Duckling* (Suteyev, 1972), *Across the Stream* (Ginsburg, 1982), *The Cake That Mack Ate* (Robart, 1986), and *The Very Hungry Caterpillar* (Carle, 1983). The characteristics of these books are also summarized in Table 5.6.

As we described in the section on using a single criterion for texts, the publishers of basal reading programs have moved from high-frequency words to literary quality of text as the basis for beginning reading materials. But, while the books now contain stories of high literary quality, the structure from the earlier basal readers has been retained: (a) three shorter books (formerly the preprimers) and (b) two longer books (formerly the primer and the first-grade reader). Because each of the five books is a compilation of trade books, these core books are often referred to as an anthology. The stories in each book are divided into two themes, creating a total of ten themes. Within each theme, there are approximately three full pieces of literature and several short pieces, such as poems. Other materials are provided such as additional trade books but, typically, these are not included in the "basic" program that districts or states purchase. For our analysis of text accessibility, we chose examples from the first basal textbook program to consist entirely of trade book selections. The five titles that follow represent the middle trade book from each of the five first-grade anthologies: *Monster and the Baby* (Mueller, 1985), *Have You Seen the Crocodile?* (West, 1986), *If I Had a Pig* (Inkpen, 1988), *Klippity Klop* (Emberley, 1974), and *Jimmy Lee Did It* (Cummings, 1985). Again, the features of these books are summarized in Table 5.6.

Features of Books. We have presented the summary in Table 5.6 to illustrate how teachers can determine the accessibility of specific books for instruction of and independent reading by particular students. We need to emphasize that the sets of materials should not be evaluated as "right" or "wrong" in their characteristics.

First, we as educators know all too little about the interaction between text features and beginning reading development. The use of multiple criteria in selecting books that support or enhance particular strategies of beginning readers is too recent to provide a definitive sequence. For example, many questions remain about the role of predictability in children's reading (Johnson, 1995). How quickly should the scaffold provided by a small unit of predictable text be removed? As the patterns in Table 5.6 show, this question is answered differently in each of the three programs. The little book program provides children with highly predictable text through level 4 when the size of the predictable text increases. The text remains fairly predictable, however, through the fifth level. In the Reading Recovery exemplars, the predictability of text moves from highly predictable in stage 1 to none in stage 3 but then moves back to predictable text in stage 4. Still another pattern is evident in the textbook program of trade books. In this program, none of the texts is highly predictable in the sense of a small number of words accounting for a high portion of the text. Patterns such as these, when manifest across the books of a program, mean different learning opportunities for children.

A second reason that the summary on Table 5.6 should be used for illustrative rather than evaluative purposes relates to the number of examples. The summary in Table 5.6 accounts for only a small portion of the books in any of the three sets of materials. If we had picked different books to represent a level from any program, different characteristics might have surfaced. For example, some books at the very earliest stages would be expected to have highly predictable patterns; others might have a handful of words that allow children to apply their strategies related to high-frequency and highly decodable words. Thus, text may not be uniform at the same point in time within a program because of the different instructional goals that are appropriate at the same point in a child's reading acquisition.

Text accessibility is a complex construct, requiring teachers to be clear about their instructional goals. What we have done in this chapter is to provide a means for teachers to "eyeball" features that are known to influence the accessibility of a text for children who are at the initial stages of movement to conventional reading. With a view of the characteristics of particular texts, teachers can choose books that support the strategies of particular readers. They also can make wise decisions about which books to use in introducing beginning readers to new strategies.

To illustrate how teachers might use information of the type presented in Table 5.6, we will examine the first texts of each set of materials—*Jack-in-the-Box, Cat on the Mat,* and *Monster and the Baby*—in relation to specific children. What choices might Pam Chrisman (a pseudonym for one of the teachers in the Right Start project) make about these books in relation to the students whose reading efforts at the beginning of grade one were presented in Vignette 3.2? You'll remember that Ben refused to attempt the text. Brenda labeled the illustrations in the book. Adam told a story based on the illustrations. Wesley was able to identify several high-frequency words consistently—*you, in,* and *a*. A fifth child, Kyle, was able to read conventionally a short predictable text similar to *We Make Music*.

Jack-in-the-Box and *Cat on the Mat* present fairly similar supports and require similar strategies for beginning readers to read these books meaningfully. A small set of mostly high-frequency words or easily decodable and picturable words—*in, the, box, is, a* in *Jack-in-the-Box*; *the, cat, sat, on, mat* in *Cat on the Mat*—account for a large part of the texts. The concepts are familiar and the illustrations are highly useful in assisting children in figuring out unknown words. For Ben, Brenda, and Adam, the presence of a handful of similar words on different pages in these books would support them in tracking print to correspond with the oral reading of the teacher or peers and in understanding the usefulness of the topic and illustrations in figuring out words. For Wesley, these books would be good ones to use for guided reading where he attempts to use his knowledge of a handful of high-frequency words with the supports provided by the illustrations and the topic. *Cat on the Mat* would also be an excellent book to encourage Wesley's application of emerging decoding strategies with common vowel-consonant rimes such as "at." For Kyle, these two books would be good for independent reading.

Monster and the Baby presents more challenges and fewer supports for this group of beginning readers than either of the stage one books for the little books or Reading Recovery materials. *Monster and the Baby* contains more than twice the number of distinct words than either *Jack-in-the-Box* or *Cat on the Mat*. Its predictable unit accounts for only a modest amount of the text and the illustrations are not highly useful in figuring out many of the distinct words. Further, children's emerging decoding strategies could be applied to only a handful of the distinct words, and knowledge of core high-frequency words, as Wesley has, would be useful with only some of the distinct words.

In thinking about how to use *Monster and the Baby* with the range of readers represented in the group in Vignette 3.2, a teacher such as Pam Chrisman would likely find this trade book useful for instruction of students like Kyle who have sufficient independent word identification strategies to deal with more complex text. For Wesley who can recognize a handful of high-frequency words, *Monster and the Baby* is probably too demanding to use as a book for trying out decoding strategies (which will work only intermittently because of the small number of words with common vowel-consonant patterns) or for using contextual supports to figure out new words (which will work only intermittently because the illustrations do not provide clues for many distinct words). For Ben, Brenda, and Adam, during the first part of the school year at least, this book would be appropriate as a read-aloud but would be challenging as a source of support for tracking print and using contextual supports. Because the text is not highly predictable, its use for establishing one-to-one correspondence between oral and written language would be limited. As Ben, Brenda, Adam, and Wesley acquire fluency with more vowel-consonant rimes and more high-frequency words, *Monster and the Baby* may be an appropriate book for instruction and follow-up independent reading.

These applications of the text accessibility features make one thing clear: Teachers need to consider the features of texts in relation to the existing strategies and the instructional needs of their students. The features of books currently presented for children at the very earliest stages of reading are sufficiently different to lead teachers to be cautious about claims of sequences that work for all students. When teachers are aware of the supports and challenges that particular books provide for particular students, students' existing strategies can be applied and new strategies can be guided. At no time in history have there been as many exciting books for beginning readers. Combined with young children's eagerness to learn to read and their interest in the world around them, the myriad of engaging books makes the task of book selection a rewarding one for teachers and children.

The Forgotten Criterion: Number of Books. As we have seen in this chapter, educators have focused for years on establishing guidelines for the selection of beginning reading materials. However, despite the importance of this debate, it has resulted in ignoring a critically important factor in children's overall literacy development—the number of books with which children need to interact. Researchers have documented the importance of children's extensive early exposure to a wide range of books (e.g., Wells, 1986). Some children have heard hundreds of books read aloud by their parents and preschool teachers before they attempt to read themselves (Adams, 1990). Others have heard only a fraction. Yet, most beginning reading programs have elected to concentrate on a small set of stories. Even with the change to high literary quality as the criterion, the perspective on the number of stories has remained the same. The trade books in Table 5.6 listed for the textbook program are five of the approximately 30 stories in the program. Traditionally, these 30 selections provide a different story for each of the approximately 30–32 weeks that make up a school year. Having one story per week harkens back to the behaviorist perspective when stories were ordered and children were expected to learn the words in these stories in sequence.

Beginning reading programs with such a limited number of books may be appropriate when students have interacted with many books at home and continue to do so. But for those children whose experiences with books occur primarily in schools, the assumption that exposure to a small set of books will be sufficient to develop the necessary strategies for independent reading explains at least some of their struggle to learn to read. Answers to the question "How many books should there be in a beginning reading program?" should vary by classrooms and children. While a single answer is not possible, several guidelines can be followed.

First, an emergent literacy classroom should be filled with books that cover a range of features to support the range of reading strategies that can be expected in any classroom. Books should pertain to many different topics and genres—books about whales, rocks, and lightning, classics that have been part of read-alouds, such as *Madeline,* and books of poems and plays. These books should be available to serve various functions in children's school lives. There are books that children read during free periods. There are books that they use as references in gathering information about a topic or question. There are also books that are aimed at supporting children's acquisition of necessary word recognition strategies.

Second, in choosing the books to support literacy acquisition, the principles that began this chapter should be kept in mind. In particular, children learn through multiple interactions and over an extended period of time.

Third, these books need to assist children in applying the central and necessary reading strategies in progressively more challenging ways. We do not mean that books should be used in a "lock-step" fashion restricting children from interacting with new books until they have acquired particular knowledge or strategies. They should not be expected to recycle through the same books until they "get it right." Yet, books should become progressively more difficult and, at any given level of difficulty, children should have access to multiple titles.

Fourth, the number of books that are part of instructional interactions should be extensive. In the early intervention program in which Hiebert participated (Hiebert et al., 1992), children are involved with at least one different little book a day as part of the small-group instruction. They also take a little book of their choice home every evening. On vacations, this number increases to match the number of days that children are not in school. In addition, children read teacher-selected trade books and choose trade books for free reading in their classrooms. As a result of these many interactions with many different books, the percentages of children who are learning to read in these schools have increased. Opportunities to interact with a hundred or more little books at school and at home have been the primary change in these classrooms.

We caution, however, that a rule such as "one book a day" could create havoc if applied to every child in an emergent literacy program. There will be some children reading chapter books of lengths that would be expected to take several days to read. Problems also can arise when such a guideline is extended across an elementary school. Little books serve particular functions for young children. As children grow older, little books should be replaced with other types of text, such as magazine articles that support interests that represent children's developmental levels (Davinroy & Hiebert, 1994).

Summary

The role of text in young children's reading acquisition is grounded in the three principles of literacy learning within the emergent literacy perspective. As we saw in Chapter 4, the talk that surrounds the reading of text extends children's oral language and provides the source for children's interpretations of the meanings and forms of texts. The stories, information, and rhymes of texts communicate meaning for and generate interest in children.

The need for this meaningful use to occur across multiple contexts directs attention to two kinds of texts: those that teachers read to children and those that children read on their own.

Whatever the age of students, teachers read aloud literature to broaden their students' interactions with topics, genres, and authors. To further these goals, two dimensions of the content of trade books direct teachers' choices of books: themes and the cultural values. Trade book themes can be considered in relation to children's developmental interests, community goals, and interdisciplinary units. Cultural values relate to the implicit and explicit values in a piece of literature and the need for selections to recognize and represent the diversity of cultures in our society. The plethora of literature available today makes it critical that teachers have access to sources of information about the books, including lists of award winners and the recommendations of fellow professionals.

Selecting books so beginning readers can experience success while simultaneously developing strategies that lead to independent reading is a task that has challenged educators for generations. In the past, beginning reading programs were known by their allegiance to a single criterion: high-frequency words or phonetically regular words or high literary quality. Today, the literacy field recognizes the importance of children's early exposure to literature selected on the basis of multiple criteria. Five criteria influence the ability of young readers to access a text: (1) predictability, (2) contextual support, (3) word density, (4) proportion of decodable words, and (5) proportion of core high-frequency words.

When we look for these features in books currently offered as programs for beginning readers in the form of little books, lists of exemplary trade books, or published anthologies of trade books, we find that books vary considerably in inclusion and progression of these features. A "perfect" sequence of trade books or little books cannot be expected; rather, books need to be selected in relation to the existing strategies of particular readers and the strategies that are the focus of instruction. In this process of book selection, teachers should not forget a critical, but often overlooked, aspect of book selection—children's need to interact with hundreds of books in the process of becoming literate.

This section on instruction began with a discussion of how oral language patterns of classrooms provide the means whereby children make meaning of the content and the forms of text. In this chapter, we have examined another ingredient in the foundation of proficient reading and writing—the selection of texts that are read to children and the texts that children read themselves. In the next chapter, a third element of the foundation of reading and writing is presented—the texts that children write.

chapter 6

The Texts of Early Literacy Classrooms: Texts Children Write

Children in a first-grade literacy program write in their personal journals several times a week. On one particular day, here are the entries from a group of three children:

mi fame is go int to dise lan and go ind to watrlan [My family is going to
    Disneyland and going to Waterland.]
I LiK t Pie wi Tls. [I like to play with space toys.]
I got naa Kls. [I got new clothes.]

(Hiebert et al., 1991)

In an urban primary school where writing was central to the literacy curriculum, Eugenie wrote many compositions that drew on interactions with peers, her own experiences, and stories that had been read. She composed the following after repeated class readings of books such as Dr. Seuss's (1957) *The Cat in the Hat:*

The cat sat on the hat.
Cat, don't sit on the hat!

(Dyson, 1993, p. 168)

Tess is part of an emergent literacy program in special education classrooms where thematic units provide a means of integrating language arts. In the theme on animals, Tess chose to write about dogs, a topic on which she is an expert because she has a dog. Her report for the classroom newspaper on caring for dogs follows:

If you have a dog you must feed it tree time a day. because it could be hungry. then you must take it out side to wake it. if your dog get sick you must take it to the vetrinarian. and let the doctor gave his some medicine to maek sure he is good as new. then you can take his home that day. dog

like to ran. you should be nice to your dog because if your not nice to your
dog he might bit you. some kids go by dog that bit. you should be careful.
  —Tess

(Englert, Raphael, & Mariage, 1994, p. 55)

Children's messages arise from diverse and plentiful sources. The "stuff"
of children's lives—new clothes, favorite toys, trips to the mountains, amuse-
ment parks, and grandparents' homes—looms large in their writing. As the
messages in Vignette 6.1 show, young children write eagerly when they have
occasions to share their personal narratives.

Stories from children's lives as well as those from classroom read-aloud
events and children's own reading become the source for another type of
writing—writing stories and predictable texts as illustrated by Eugenie's in
Vignette 6.2. Further, these interests and experiences can be the source for
a third form of writing—informational writing. Tess's paragraph on the care
of dogs in Vignette 6.3 comes from her experiences as a dog owner. Conversations in an emergent literacy classroom were needed, however, for Tess to
see herself as an expert. Tess also needed to learn how to organize what she
knew about caring for a dog. Like Eugenie with her rhyming text based on
The Cat in the Hat, Tess's informational paragraph was the result of numerous occasions for writing and conversations about writing.

The content of narrative and informational texts written by children
draws heavily on their personal experiences. However, the texts children
generate use genres similar to the texts they read and hear—stories, rhymes,
and informational texts. Creating such texts depends on participation in
classrooms where occasions for writing are a frequent and valued part of
each school day. An emergent literacy perspective recognizes early forms of
writing as legitimate and necessary expressions, and places writing at the
center of children's school experiences. In this chapter we begin by examining the principles of an emergent literacy perspective as they relate to children's written productions. We then discuss children's productions: first in
terms of narrative, then informational texts.

Written Texts within an Early Literacy Perspective

We can understand the nature of the texts that children write when we consider the three principles of an emergent literacy perspective: Literacy learning occurs through meaningful use of reading and writing, literacy learning
is embedded within oral language, and literacy learning occurs in multiple
contexts with teachers and peers.

Literacy Learning Occurs through Meaningful Use of Reading and Writing

Producing messages holds great interest for young children. To give an accurate rendition of others' messages, children need to have access to the code.

But their own messages can be communicated with the very beginnings of their literacy skills. In Vignette 6.1, the word "clothes" can be understood by most adults from the spelling "KLS," at least within the particular context. Examples such as this one illustrate how successful young children can be engaging in a variety of functions in writing even before they have mastered the forms of writing.

When we described, in Chapter 2, the functions of written language (see Table 2.1), we noted that most of the functions can be served more readily for young children through their written productions than through reading. In emergent literacy classrooms, children can use writing to accomplish language's instrumental function, meeting specific needs within the classroom such as signing up for lunch or taking milk count for the day. They can "regulate" classroom behaviors by creating signs such as the "Only Three in the Loft" rule that a group of kindergartners enforced (Taylor, Blum, & Logsdon, 1986). There are many literacy acts that allow children to be active participants in their classrooms: writing notes to classmates via a classroom postal center (Greene, 1985) (the interactional function), sharing important thoughts in a journal (the personal function), recording the weather from day to day (heuristic function), pretending to be a character in a story at the time when dinosaurs roamed the earth (imaginative function), and conveying to others the daily care of a dog (informative function).

At its core, writing in the emergent literacy classroom can be authentic and meaningful for children because so many of the topics on which they write come from personal experiences. The focus on meaningfulness also means that the genres to which children are introduced in lessons and read-aloud events give them vehicles for expressing the range of their experiences. As seen in Vignette 6.3, Tess created an informational text using an explanation structure. Without the occasion and encouragement for sharing information on which Tess was an expert—the care of dogs—she might not have begun to write informational pieces of this type.

Literacy Learning Is Embedded in Oral Language

As with other aspects of literacy, children construct their understandings of the content and the forms of their messages through the talk that surrounds shared writing events.

For many children, especially those whose experiences with writing have been infrequent prior to school entry, the talk in the shared writing events introduces them to the power and purposes of writing. They also learn that their comments and information can be put into writing as teachers write down their contributions to a shared class message or to a class book. In the process of writing down children's oral compositions, adults likely will translate some of the oral message. As adults talk about these changes, children learn that written language is not merely a transcript of speech. For example, when teachers write down children's messages on the blackboard or on chart paper to start the school day, children learn that written language is typically more precise and succinct than the oral language of most conversations.

Children's written compositions also need to be viewed as the product of conversations that children have with their peers and their teacher. Considerable talk surrounds young children's writing efforts. Children's comments are sometimes not directed toward any one in particular, yet become the source of conversation among nearby peers who are listening. According to Dyson (1993), much of young children's composition resides in the group's shared social construction. While writing is not the same as oral language, it is inseparable from oral language and oral language is inseparable from the context in which the writing occurs. We turn next to the manner in which peers and adults serve different roles in children's writing.

Literacy Learning Occurs in Multiple Contexts with Teachers and Peers

Peers are particularly important as co-constructors of children's messages. When children write at centers or in clusters of desks, they engage in talk on which peers comment. Numerous illustrations of these conversations and the contributions that peers make to both the content and the execution of a child's message have appeared throughout this book. Chapter 4 included a conversation between Lamar and James in which their talk considerably embellished these two authors' texts and illustrations. Dyson (1993), an observer of that conversation and numerous others like it in an urban school's emergent literacy classrooms, has shown how the written texts are often pale representations of the overall compositions that have been created through children's conversations as they write.

Dickinson (1986) also provided many examples of how children negotiate the style and stances within their stories when they write together, as in the following conversation (p. 375):

Melissa: Don't write 'our.' You know why?
Juanita: Why?
Melissa: Because this is a story.
Juanita: Oh.

While Melissa attempts to convince Juanita that the two of them are writing a story about *other* characters, Juanita sticks to her idea that the text is a personal narrative, about the two of them, as the following excerpt between the two children shows:

Melissa: I said 'girls' not 'bears.'
Juanita: Are we writing about bears or girls?
Melissa: Girls! See? 'Once upon a time two little *girls*' I wrote.
Juanita: Well forget it. I'm writing about us then.

(op. cit., p. 375)

In essence, Juanita is taking the stance that if the story is about girls, it can be, and is, about Melissa and herself. If the story is to be about other characters, they would need to be more distant from themselves (e.g., bears).

Together, the girls negotiate through conversation, not simply through writing, the shape of their story.

Just as teachers model reading through shared reading events (e.g., reading enlarged books), teachers model writing processes and forms for children through shared writing events. These shared events assume many forms. Children may each contribute an episode to a whole-class predictable book (Pinnell & McCarrier, 1994). A class may create a group story, with individual children contributing particular portions of the composition. Regardless of the shared writing contexts, a critical issue surrounding the role of adults in children's writing lies in the degree to which teachers serve as transcribers of children's compositions or as collaborators within the writing process.

In the 1970s and early 1980s, the language experience approach used children's talk "written down" as the text for beginning reading instruction. Teachers served as scribes recording children's oral compositions, modifying them only when absolutely necessary (with debates around what counts as an "absolutely necessary" condition). The point in language experience was for teachers to record the students' oral voices so that the children would be familiar with the text of the written language and thus be able to use familiar words to learn to read.

In shared writing events designed to develop students' sense of authorship and to actively engage them in creating public texts, the role of teachers is somewhat different, and more active. Teachers use the shared writing events as occasions to model forms and functions of both stories and informational texts. On occasions when children's writing goes to a broader community, adults or competent peers (such as older students) can interact with children to clarify parts of messages that others may not be able to decipher (e.g., adding words or labels to pictures, writing the conventional spellings somewhere on the children's pages). Adults are viewed as collaborators rather than as the final judges and arbiters of children's writing (Sulzby, Teale, & Kamberelis, 1989). In such a role, teachers can encourage students to create both narrative and expository texts, to share stories, and to convey information. In the next sections, we describe the types of texts students create within each of these two broad text categories.

Narrative Texts

In the 1970s, cognitive scientists studied the underlying structure of narrative texts to determine features that defined individuals' sense of story. In one line of research, Stein and colleagues (e.g., Stein & Glenn, 1979; Stein & Trabasso, 1982) asked readers of different ages to retell a range of stories. From these retellings, they identified the components of simple stories as: setting, initiating event, internal response, attempt, consequence, and reaction. Components of stories are evident in young children's oral productions when asked by an interviewer to tell a story (Brown & Smiley, 1977). Even for those children who have not heard many stories read aloud, their inclination to tell stories is not surprising. Young children experience many "story-like" texts, including those on television, in cartoons, and in movies. Children who have been immersed in movies such as *Pocahontas* and *Babe* are familiar with storytelling.

While children's oral compositions can be extensive, their written compositions at the same point in time are quite concise, while meaningful. However, their oral language surrounding the composition tends to be extensive, as illustrated by Lamar's composition that we described in Chapter 4. The source of these early messages is often children's personal experience. We examine three types of stories that appear in young children's texts: personal narratives, predictable texts, and true narratives. The examples of these different types of stories come from first graders soon after they began school in the fall. At the end of an interview, they were asked to write a story (Hiebert et al., 1991). Those children who were reluctant to write were prompted with suggestions, such as "Write about something you like to do."

Personal Narratives

Just as reading stories gives children insight into the inner and social worlds of other people, writing narratives allows children to share their inner and social worlds with others, to reflect and explore aspects of these worlds for themselves, and to construct new interpretations of their worlds. Drawing on the work of Bakhtin (1990), Dyson (1993) describes composing by children in an urban primary school, especially their stories, as a link to "composing a place for oneself in the social world" (p. 229).

When narrative is viewed as a means for exploring and reflecting on the complexities and vagaries of life, it should not be surprising to find that children begin with stories about themselves. New babies in the immediate or extended family, trips to stores or to see grandparents across town—the characters, settings, and events of children's lives become the content of their first narratives or *personal narratives*. Regular occasions for writing personal narratives in journals have become popular in many classrooms but, even without the incentive of journals, many of young children's compositions will be personal narratives. When asked to write a story, the majority of first graders wrote compositions of the personal narrative genre:

> I like to play with Matt and we dig Tongos and we hadf fun dig Tongos.
> [I like to play with Matt and we dig tunnels and we have fun digging tunnels.]

> thes is a trou storey
> wen I Was Playing BasBall
> I het a homrun.
> [This is a true story. When I was playing baseball I hit a home run!]

> I am gate decs I mack Pee PL fiL DeT R wen Thae r Fing dad.
> [I am great because I make people feel better when they are feeling bad.]

These three personal narratives illustrate Dyson's (1993) thesis that children use composing as a means of establishing or reflecting on their place in their social worlds. While children do not include all of the elements that characterize stories in these personal narratives, they are composing to express important events (e.g., hitting a home run) and to identify special attributes that they value, such as making people feel better. They also are describing times that they view positively, such as getting new clothes or digging tunnels with one's best friend.

As children get older, obstacles in a personal situation and their actions in relation to these obstacles are described increasingly in personal narratives, or the events are thinly disguised as the problems of fictional story characters. In contrast, young children's personal narratives cut to the chase by focusing on the successful outcome or the source of their happiness and rarely state the dilemmas or the events that lead to the resolution.

In classrooms where children were free to choose their topics for writing and teachers believed that they should not impose on children's choices, the compositions in children's portfolios were almost entirely personal narratives through second grade (Hagerty et al., 1989). Among the 20 titles in one child's writing portfolio for second grade, most included the word "I" or "my" with his pets, trips, and favorite television shows and movies providing the content.

Predictable Texts

There is a strong link between the books read by and to young children and the structures and content of their compositions (Bereiter & Scardamalia, 1984; Tierney & Shanahan, 1991). With the increasing prominence of predictable texts in beginning reading instruction, there are more predictable texts in young children's compositions (though personal narratives continue to be the dominant genre when children do free writing). The following predictable text was among first graders' fall responses to Hiebert et al.'s (1991) request for them to "write a story":

> Ones ther was A Spider thet Cood not find its Mom then he Ment a lizerd and Sed Are you my mom and He sed No then He Saw a Shad and it Ws mom [Child's reading of the text: Once there was a spider that could not find its mom. Then he met a lizard and said, "Are you my mom?" And he said, "No." Then he saw a shadow and it was his mom.]

This child has condensed the form and made it his own but the influence of P. D. Eastman's (1960) *Are You My Mother?* is quite evident, as we might expect if texts children listen to and those they read themselves influence their writing.

Another type of text structure in young children's books enumerates or lists categories of an event (Meyer, 1975). This is illustrated in the text of *Six Go By* (Dobeck, 1996), which is presented in its entirety in Chapter 5. Each episode of the book pertains to another component of a birthday party—balloons, hats, boxes, clowns, candles, and guests. Young writers can manage the enumerative structure quite easily, possibly because they are exposed to such lists from a very young age. They see adults writing a list before going to the grocery store. They may have created their own lists in anticipation of Santa's arrival. List-writing has been described as one of the first forms of writing in which young children engage (Newkirk, 1989). An example of a list without the structure of an evident story was provided by one of the first graders in Hiebert et al.'s (1991) sample of compositions:

> a flRR
> a ross
> a car
> a hssh
> a tap dhanr
> [a flower, a rose, a car, a house, a tap dancer].

Like the initial words that they speak and the words that they initially recognize in writing, a list of important or interesting words dispenses with the need for high-frequency words. A kindergartner created the following list of items she wished to take on her vacation (Durkin, 1993, p. 78):

> gams
> crds
> crlring Books
> Books
> PaPer
> crans
> Pens
> Traks
> Dolls
> PaPer Dolls
> [games, cards, coloring books, books, paper, crayons, pens, trucks, dolls, paper dolls].

Teachers can encourage children to write lists as a means for organizing predictable books, to begin to frame informational writing, and to assist them in creating narratives. For example, in some predictable books, one segment or page of a text tells a complete story. When a class creates a book with such a text structure, each child's contribution can be self-contained, allowing individual children to experience the pleasure of creating a "story." One predictable book that has such a form is Mercer Mayer's (1975) *Just for You*. Each page communicates a good intention that the narrator had "just for you," followed by the catastrophe that made it impossible to do the good deed. One episode is: "I wanted to mow the lawn just for you, but I was too little." (Mayer, 1975, p. 5). In a first-grade class where each child contributed a "just for you" episode to a class book, the following two contributions illustrate children's ability to use the predictable pattern to create a self-contained episode:

> This morning I wanted to put away the flowers just for you but the cat tipped over the vase and I got all wet.
> I wanted to buy a collar for the cat just for you but the collar was too much money.

Martinez, Cheyney, McBroom, Hemmeter, and Teale (1989) describe a similar activity in a kindergarten class that was part of the Kindergarten Emergent Literacy Project (KELP). After hearing the book *It Looked Like Spilt Milk* (Shaw, 1947), each child contributed to a book for Halloween entitled *It Looked Like a Skeleton,* following the pattern, "It looked like _____/ But it wasn't _____." The objects children identified included witches, jack-o-lanterns, trick or treaters, and so on, with the whole class collaborating on the last sentence: "It was just a cloud in the sky on Halloween" (p. 109).

When children have had many opportunities to participate in writing group books and to hear and read many predictable books, it is not surprising to find an entry such as the following one in a child's journal (Hiebert et al., 1991):

> I have a cat it go to bed
> I have a dog it go to bed
> I have a sno man it melt

"True" Narratives

We distinguish "true" narratives from personal narratives students write to highlight the concept of creating a story, not simply relating an event in their own lives. Not surprisingly, children's first narratives are similar to their personal narratives, except that now someone other than themselves appears as the central character. Or, when children cast themselves as central characters, the events are imaginary ones. The structure of these early narratives often uses the same descriptive form of personal narratives, as the following examples from the sample of first graders (Hiebert et al., 1991) show:

> Frade coGr ript sabades had of and thar was blad
> [Freddy Krueger ripped somebody's head off and there was blood.]
>
> faSn
> nud da a Gia Kam to the Sate
> He dnd the Soite is name Bkm KegKun
> He ad a fnd is fud ne is Mad Kool out fa Mads
> [Friends
> One day a gorilla came to the States.
> He destroyed the city. His name became King Kong.
> He had a friend. His friend's name was Mad Man. Look out for Mad Man.]
>
> Us f w a vuree prit uunokon he uv The Quv uunokor no wn wnit
> to hur RCB She uv SO Prit shE uv av Olld av The si
> she sud I will roll flld foof
> [Once there was a very pretty unicorn. She was the queen of unicorns. No one wanted to hurt her because she was so pretty. She was as old as the sky. She said I will rule this land forever.]

These compositions differ in the degree to which children elaborate on particular elements but they are similar in the way they have problem summaries and resolutions but no problem or resolution development. While the unicorn character is described more fully than either King Kong or Freddy Kreuger, the problem in the story is not developed into a discernible course of action. In the Freddy Kreuger story, an event that is presumably a problem—the ripping off of somebody's head—is stated and the consequence of this event—much blood—is stated. However, the composition remains a summary rather than a story.

While young children tend to summarize events rather than to create problems and solutions in their writing, most children can identify the critical components of stories. Even without scaffolding from their teachers, many children can capture the essence of a story quite succinctly, as the following examples from a first grader and a kindergartner, respectively, show:

> The alive Cabbage patch kid
> I have a Cabbage ptch kid that came a live one day. one Firday night when I was going to bed, my doll got my ball and rolled it to my bed. And made me jump. then my pajama's jumped up. I said iiiii. Then I had to put that doll in a cage.
>
> [First Grader] (Hiebert et al., 1991)

> | | |
> |---|---|
> | TARWANSWASA LiTL GRLe | There once was a little girl |
> | AND She WOT lDAFREND | and she wanted a friend. |
> | OAN DAY A LiTL BOY KAME Bi | One day a little boy came by. |
> | Hi IWOtA FRED | Hi, I want a friend. |
> | UALI WOTIDAFENDTO | Well, I wanted a friend too. |
> | UAL LESSBEFENDSOKY | Well, let's be friends, okay? |
>
> (Sulzby et al., 1989, p. 71)

Children benefit from lessons where their teachers guide their story development. An excellent example of a teacher's support in facilitating children's narratives can be seen in a videotape of Dawn Harris Martine's classroom in Harlem, New York (Martine, 1991). When Dawn studied children's stories, she noticed that many were missing critical elements of stories—"the conflict in the story, the solution, the characters, and the setting" (Martine, 1991, p. 21). She begins by reading to the children a trade book that uses a true narrative structure, *Darkness and the Butterfly* (Grifalconi, 1987). Dawn then introduces children to story grammar terms, which she has displayed on a wall chart. The class next writes a story together, intentionally using the structure of *Darkness and the Butterfly*. The class wrote the following story:

> A long, long time ago a little girl named Rudee lived in a village in Africa. One night she had a bad dream when she went to bed. She screamed and her mother came and said, "What's the matter?" and she said, "I keep having a dream about a monster that keeps following me." Mother said, "That's just your imagination because the trees are blowing so close to the house." The father didn't believe her. He said, "You go to sleep so late that the Dream Man gives all of the good dreams first, so only the bad dreams are left." The mother

said, "Rudee, maybe if you could go to sleep very early, maybe the Dream Man would give you a good dream." So Rudee started going to bed at 8 o'clock, and Rudee started having good dreams, like her mother having a baby girl. And she wished real hard and her wish came true. Her mother had a baby. They named her Jody and they lived happily ever after.

Children used the content of Grifalconi's tale but made it more contemporary by placing a favorite television character from a sitcom at the center of their story. Their choice of featuring a television character is common. As children move to true narratives, teachers should not be surprised to find that students' story characters and dilemmas relate to television and movie action heroes. Children are influenced not only by the books they hear and read, but by the films and television programs that they frequently watch.

Informational Texts

Narratives are the dominant form of text that children hear during their bedtime reading events (Heath, 1983), but, interestingly, much adult writing that children observe is non-narrative. Because children's writing is influenced by what they hear and see, it is not surprising that many children write messages that are informational in both content and structure, especially lists, letters, and signs. Newkirk (1989) analyzed primary-level children's writing portfolios over a school year and found that many of their compositions were attempts to record or generate information. He saw lists, such as enumerating the group members (e.g., "My Family") or specific items (e.g., "My Santa List").

The importance of writing to share information with others goes beyond young children's familiarity with functional writing such as listing and labeling. Informational writing involves children in expressing their interest and knowledge about the physical world. Children's questions illustrate their fascination with the world around them. What do butterflies do when it rains? Why does the water in a lake have different colors? Children are equally fascinated with the parts of the physical world that human beings have built, such as skyscrapers, malls, cars, trucks, pianos, and banjos. They are concerned about more devastating effects humans have had on nature, such as polluted water and air.

The content of Vignette 6.3 illustrates the manner in which children's knowledge and interest form a primary source for informational writing. As children become fluent with the structures and styles of informational writing, they extend their knowledge bases through observation, interviewing, and reading books, magazines, and newspapers.

Informational Compositions Based on Personal Knowledge

Children communicate what they believe and feel through their personal narratives. Similarly, personal informational writing is grounded in children's own experiences and knowledge of the world. The difference lies in the organization and perspective toward the topic. A personal narrative about a dog can be found in Matthew's composition:

> I like my dog because she is nice. And she is brown. And when we are done lawn mowing the yard she rolls in the grass.   (Hiebert et al., 1991)

Rather than telling a story about playing with a dog as Matthew does, Tess in Vignette 6.3 uses an enumerative structure to describe elements of caring for a dog. Tess's description of the care that a pet owner should provide to a dog differs in content and structure from Matthew's personal narrative of playing with his dog.

Narrative and informational writing are closely interwoven. For example, to write the story about unicorns, the child described earlier in this chapter drew on previous experiences with myths and fables to get that information. Narrative is full of information and informational text often takes on narrative style. Jamal, the child who was the advocate of "wind and heat" in the science discussion that we cited in Chapter 4, integrates information that he has gained from discussions in science class into a song that he created (from Dyson, 1993, p. 146):

> I love rockets and ships, too.
> I love space
> Do you, too?
> I love space
> because it's fun
> I love space cause you bounce around
> It's just like in Chucky Cheese
> I just love to, bounce around,
> Ban bah bah bah bah bah bounce around.

While we value and encourage children's drawing upon information as they create stories, poems, and songs, we also believe it is important to encourage students to create informational text, to experience the act of writing to communicate information. "True" informational text, which we describe in the next section, is distinct from stories but it exists in earlier forms in emergent literacy classrooms. Personal informational writing can occur through: (a) letters and notes, and (b) one or more paragraphs on a particular topic.

Letters and Notes.   There are letters in children's books such as *The Jolly Postman* (Ahlberg, 1991), while other books deal with dilemmas associated with writing and reading letters. But letter reading is not as prominent a genre in reading as it is in children's early writing. Three of the functions of language in Halliday's (1977) language functions presented in Table 2.1 are best facilitated through letter writing—interactional language, of course, is key: I want to tell you what I've been doing. What have you been doing?

> "Dere mom I love you. You arre nise. Do you love me? I love my atier fanily."
> [Child's rendition: Dear Mom, I love you. You are nice. Do you love me? I love my entire family.]

Two other functions can be better served by letter writing than by narratives, informational text, or rhymes: instrumental language (please come to our class presentation) and heuristic language (I would like to know why you liked *Frog and Toad* so much. Would I like to read it?).

The letter that Corey sent to Mrs. Vargas in Vignette 2.2 demonstrates another function that writing can serve for children—making requests. In a first-grade classroom where the teacher encouraged note writing, as Mrs. Vargas did with her second graders, Shawn wrote his own note explaining his late appearance in school one day:

> I HR NOW THICS Foor MOM IN THE CLOCK WT OFF ON ROG TIM Y WY I M LAT
> SIN SHAN
> I [am] here now. [I had to do] things for mom. And the clock went off on the wrong time. [That's] why I am late. Signed Shawn   (Newkirk, 1989, p. 22)

As well as writing predictable books such as *It Looked Like a Skeleton,* children in KELP classrooms (Martinez et al., 1989; Sulzby et al., 1989) had many occasions for informational writing, especially invitations for events such as storybook reading days, the Thanksgiving feast, and so on. Children were responsible for producing their own invitation, even if at the scribble or the drawing stages of writing. Teachers provided a copy of the individual's name to whom a child was sending the invitation. Children copied the name and then produced the invitation using their current system of communication (i.e., scribbling, drawing, invented spelling, or some combination). Finally, children read their invitations to an adult who wrote down the message if it was indecipherable, and the invitation was sent.

The heuristic function can also be served well by letter writing as has become apparent in projects where children communicate the strengths and weaknesses of books to one another (Hagerty et al., 1989):

> Dear Brian,
> I read the gingerbread man it's a little different than what she told and my favorite part is when the fox eats him. I think he was smart to trick the little fast, fast gingerbread man. He looked good and I wish I was the fox.
>   Love, Bart

> Dear Elane,
> I han't readed your book. And I'll tiry to get my book for you. I foud out that ants eat houny [honey] from ants that spend thre life haging up side down. Did you know that insexs have olus [eyes] on the sid of thry bude [their bodies]? Flies wate ther food than suke [suck] it up.
>   Love, Marisa

The teachers in whose classrooms these letters were written modeled letter writing. In Bart's and Marisa's classrooms, an exchange of letters between the classroom teacher and the district's language arts specialist was displayed on posters placed strategically around the classroom. These letters provided models for the kind of information that can assist another reader in choosing to read a book.

One or More Paragraphs on a Topic.   Often, children's initial forays into informational writing come in the middle grades when they are asked to write "reports." However, emergent literacy classrooms can provide a strong basis for later informational report writing, through a range of age-appropriate writing activities. These activities include: (a) writing brief informational essays drawing on children's already developing expertise (e.g., about taking care of dogs, space travel, dinosaurs), (b) writing autobiographies, informational texts about their own lives, and (c) writing reports based on interviews or observations.

Tess's article on caring for dogs illustrates the way in which children's personal knowledge was used as a source for informational writing in the Early Literacy Project (ELP), a project that extended emergent literacy strategies to special education settings (Englert et al., 1994). In these classrooms, children came to see that their interests and their experiences could be the source for their writing and that they could share their knowledge with peers and family members. Children were described as "experts" on particular topics. Tess was an expert in caring for a dog, information that became the newspaper article in Vignette 6.3. Another child, David, had quite a distinction in that he owned a python. While David had been a hesitant and disinterested writer at the beginning of the school year, his involvement as a writer changed quite markedly when he was encouraged to use his knowledge of snakes as the source for his writing. The composition that follows indicates that this stance of "expert," based on one's unique blend of interest and prior experiences, resonated well with David:

> I am expet at snaks. Snaks are different colors. A snank is very strong. and Some has scales. Some snak are poison. Snaks are cold Blooded animals. There are all sorts of Snaks. Some snak squeeze There prey and some snak infect pisen. I have a snak my self. it is a python. his name is milio and he does not Bit. Becuse he has no teth. he only has teth in the bake of his moth. and Python squeeze ist prey to kill it. then it eats is Prey.   (Englert et al., 1994, p. 26)

Englert et al.'s project is one of the few that we could locate where emergent writers were encouraged to think of themselves as "experts" on topics and to use this expert knowledge in writing informational text. The literature is full of examples of where additional probing and modeling could lead to elaboration of personal knowledge. Beardsley & Marecek-Zeman (1987) provide an illustration where a teacher encourages a reluctant writer, Aaron, to write about a construction from large hollow blocks that he and his friends had made on the playground. When the teacher showed Aaron a Polaroid of the event, he wrote:

> I BLT WND VADR ANDREW WES DRIVG WE GINT SPASP.
> [We built the Wind Vader. Andrew was driving. We all built a giant space ship.]   (p. 163)

This scenario is one where the teacher could have easily guided Aaron to share his expertise about space travel and space vehicles. By asking questions about steps in constructing the vehicle and descriptions about other space vehicles Aaron had built, the teacher could have encouraged Aaron to see himself as an expert. Aaron's reluctance to write may also have lessened as he was exposed to other ways of writing.

A second form of informational writing that draws from children's expertise is autobiography. Children's interest in their own experiences can be used to encourage elaborated writing as they create their own autobiographies. In the following example from Durkin (1993), a kindergarten student with an impressive command of letter-sound correspondences created an autobiography describing important events from her preschool years. As informational text, it provides insights into her own background and it validates her importance as an individual.

> When I was a baby and I was toking and I side mommy and daddy and the uther wrde I side was no. I gowe teeth. my mom tote me to coler. and my dad tote me hode my radle and my tose. my gramol tote me to ride my triskl. and I growe up to be big and I growe up and up in tle I was in knagrdne and I can't wat in tle I'm in frst gade.
> [When I was a baby and I was talking and I said mommy and daddy and the other word I said was no. I grew teeth. My mom taught me to color. And my dad taught me to hold my rattle and my toys. My grandma taught me to ride my tricycle. And I grow up to be big and I grow up and up until I was in kindergarten and I can't wait until I'm in first grade.]   (Durkin, 1993, p. 81)

A third source of information from which young children can develop informational texts stems from their observations of the world around them. Martinez et al. (1989) describe the interviews kindergartners conducted in classes that are part of KELP. Children interview workers in the school about their jobs. When children participate in such information gathering, they learn important aspects of creating informational text, from asking relevant questions to summarizing information. Similarly, in another kindergarten classroom, students recorded observations of the sounds, sights, and tastes of making popcorn. They created a group informational text to summarize their observations:

> The Popcorn
> Russ said, It was hard.
> Christa said, "It was orange."
> Jade and Kari said, "It was slick and smooth."
> Aubin said, "We put it in the popper."
> Justin said, "It went poppity, poppity, pop!"
> David said, "It changed to white."
> Rodney said, "We tasted it, and it was good."   (Hiebert et al., 1991)

These examples convey the importance as well as the feasibility of making informational text writing a part of the emergent literacy program. As children become more facile with the concept of informational writing, they can be encouraged to extend their competence by beginning to draw on multiple information sources to create a single text.

Informational Text Based on Multiple Sources

The personal information writing of the Early Literacy Project (Englert et al., 1994) and the group summary of observations are reminiscent of the "I-Search" papers that have become popular with middle-grade writers (Hoffman, 1992). In these research papers, individuals use their reading, observational, prior experience, and interview abilities to gather information on a topic of interest. For children of the technology age, videotapes and clips from the Internet form one important information source. Written materials such as books, magazine articles, and newspaper accounts provide other useful information. Managing information from several sources can be a challenging task for emergent writers. In the Early Literacy Project classrooms (Englert et al., 1994), integrating information from different sources with one's existing information was modeled initially through a whole class composition. In the following example, a group of early elementary students in a special education resource room worked together to create a class report about turtles, in preparation for the individual research on an animal of their choice.

First, the teacher asked questions of her students to establish class members' existing knowledge about turtles. They generated the "brainstorm list" displayed in Figure 6.1. The organizational map in Figure 6.2 was generated with the information from the brainstorm list and the questions that the teacher and students had raised while developing that list. They then listed potential information sources for unanswered questions. These sources included: (a) consulting books at home and at school, (b) consulting reference books such as the encyclopedia, and (c) interviewing family members.

Children chose particular questions to answer and sources that might help them answer their questions. The teacher then modeled how to keep a record of target words or ideas that answered particular questions by having the group read a short article on turtles from a *Weekly Reader*. Children compared and contrasted a set of words that they had chosen to summarize the key ideas.

Children then pursued answers to their individual questions about turtles, using the sources they hoped would help them. After a few days of investigation, the children came back together as a whole group to share answers from their individual searches. With children's summaries in hand, the teacher discussed how to organize their information, to group their ideas within similar topics, to make it easy for their readers to learn from their texts. They used a simple map, illustrated in Figure 6.2, to group their ideas into categories (what turtles do, what they eat, what they look like, etc.), and then used this map to decide on the order in which each category would be discussed in their written text. They created a draft of their information on turtles using a large piece of chart paper that all could see, the teacher recording the students' suggested sentences. This draft was the source of subsequent rereading and editing. The final composition of the process appears in Figure 6.3.

FIGURE 6.1   Brainstorm for Turtle Story

BRAINSTORM LIST

Turtles put their heads in
   their shells

swim

walk

snap

eat worms

be pets

walk slow

eat flies

lay eggs (hard shell)

snapping turtles

poison turtles

different colors

box turtles

lay on grass

stick their tongue out?

can look at people

hard shells

have claws

can dig

webbed

people can touch them

except snapping turtle

camouflage

From C.S. Englert, T.E. Raphael, & T.V. Mariage (1994). Developing a school-based discourse for literacy learning: A principled search for understanding. *Learning Disability Quarterly, 17*, p. 10. © Council for Learning Disabilities. Reprinted with permission.

The chart was put on long-term display in the writing center while the children developed their individual reports on animals. Whatever the focus of a writing session—planning and organizing ideas, gathering information, writing a draft, or rereading and refining the draft, the teacher gathered the children as a group prior to and following the session to discuss plans and problems.

FIGURE 6.2   Organization Map for Turtle Story

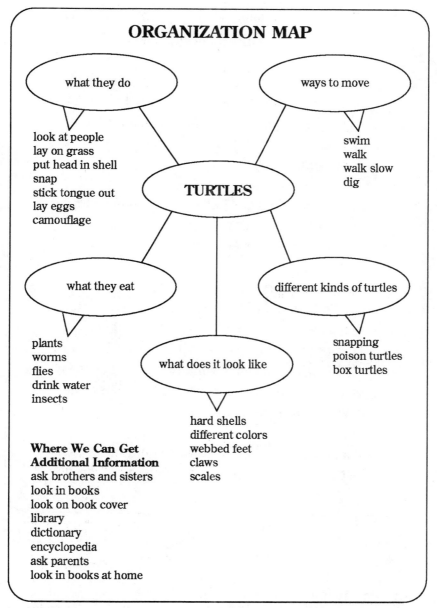

From C.S. Englert, T.E. Raphael, & T.V. Mariage (1994). Developing a school-based discourse for literacy learning: A principled search for understanding. *Learning Disability Quarterly, 17,* p. 11. © Council for Learning Disabilities. Reprinted with permission.

FIGURE 6.3   Published Turtle Story

Turtle Story

Turtle shells are hard. Turtles are different colors. They have webbed feet. They have claws to dig in the ground. They have spots on their body. They can have scales under their body, on their face and feet.

Turtles eat plants. They eat waterbugs and worms. They eat flies. They drink water. Turtles eat insects even ones people can't see.

Turtles swim in the water. They walk very slow. They pull their feet in and float in the water.

Turtles look at people and just stare. We saw a turtle in class and that's what he did. Turtles lay eggs in the grass and cover them up. They use camouflage to hide from enemies.

Turtles can't get up if they are on their backs. A turtle can go into his shell when he is scared.

From C.S. Englert, T.E. Raphael, & T.V. Mariage (1994). Developing a school-based discourse for literacy learning: A principled search for understanding. *Learning Disability Quarterly, 17,* p. 13. © Council for Learning Disabilities. Reprinted with permission.

With opportunities to write about their own expert topics and with participation in group writing events such as writing about turtles, young children can become writers who integrate information from other sources into their own writing. Newkirk (1989) provides two examples of reports by primary-level children, written by a first grader and a second grader, respectively (from Newkirk, 1989, pp. 129–130).

Report 1: Planets
this is plutowe. It is the frthest planit away fam the sun. They thought
it was nata [Neptune] mon but it wasn.
This is natoon. It is the sakint fwst [second farthest] planet away from the sun.
This is satrne it has 10 mos [moons] and it has most rens [rings] in the
solarsistm [solar system]

Report 2: Sharks
    i like birds, cats, dogs, cubs, and some bears. some water animals are
nice to me I like them and I think they are very, very cute. Sharks are fish, if
you didn't know that now you know that. The whale shark is very harmless to
people. A shark does not have any bones. Baby sharks are called pups. The
largest fish in the world is the whale shark. It can weigh more than an elephant.
It's very long. White sharks are the most dangerous sharks of all. When
scientists want to learn more about sharks they get close to them.

The second grader's composition on sharks illustrates well the manner in
which personal information can become the basis for a child's writing, and
be integrated with information from other sources.

Summary

When children are given the opportunity and encouragement, they will write
texts with structures that are similar to the texts they read—stories, rhymes,
and informational texts. Children's written productions are immersed in oral
language and are understood and enhanced through interactions with peers
and adults. The stories or narratives that children first write begin with the
events in their immediate lives. Predictable texts can be a source for children's early writing both because of the popularity of predictable texts in
their reading and because these predictable structures can be emulated by
children. With experience that includes instructional conversations with
teachers, children move to true narratives where the resolution of problems
is made explicit.

Young children's interest in their physical worlds makes the inclusion of
informational text a priority in an emergent literacy classroom. The point of
initiation, as with narrative writing, consists of the topics on which children
are experts such as the care of their pets and the games they play with
friends. With many occasions to write, which include sending letters and
notes to important people in their lives, children will soon turn to other
sources—books, interviews, and observations—to add information and detail to their informational writing.

In the last two chapters, we have described the texts that children read
and write. Throughout these discussions, we have referred to the scaffolding
that teachers provide in the form of conversations or instruction and contexts that they create for students to use texts with one another and by
themselves. The next chapter provides a framework for implementing these
different contexts.

chapter 7

The Learning Contexts of Early Literacy Classrooms: Events, Lessons, and Activities

In inner-city kindergartens, teachers worked on infusing classroom routines such as attendance-taking with literacy. At the beginning of the year, children signed in by matching their name cards to the names under their pictures on the attendance chart. Later, children put their names directly under their pictures without the model. Still later in the year, children signed in by writing their names under the chart for their chosen center of the day.

(Taylor et al., 1986)

In a first-grade classroom using the Early Intervention in Reading (EIR) model, the teacher works daily with a small group of students for a 15- to 20-minute session. This particular session begins with repeated reading of *Who Took the Farmer's Hat?* (Nodset, 1963). The highlights of the book have been written by the teacher on the chart before the session and the students next read this summary version independently. A game where children clap as they read the summary version of the story is next. This activity and the next one that requires children to blend sounds such as /h/ and /at/ as in hat (a key word in the story) are aimed at fostering children's phonemic awareness.

(Taylor, Strait, & Medo, 1994)

In the veterinarian play center in a kindergarten classroom, Preston, who has the role of the veterinarian, examines a pet teddy bear. After taking the bear's temperature and blood pressure, he records the numbers. The bear is given a shot with the reassurance, "I'm sorry, I hope I didn't hurt you." Preston then writes out a prescription in scribble writing, reading it to the bear and its owner: "Now this says that you make sure you take 100 of these pills every hour until you're better."

(Morrow & Rand, 1991, p. 400)

Checking attendance can become tedious for teachers as children fidget and wait for school to begin. But in classrooms such as the one described in Vignette 7.1, attendance-taking becomes a literacy event in which children practice and apply their literacy knowledge. Through consistent lessons with a teacher, the children described in Vignette 7.2 defied statistics suggesting that because of their level of preparedness on entering school, they would be struggling to learn reading and writing skills in first grade. Instead, through daily small-group, teacher-directed lessons emphasizing repeated readings of books and studying words, many of these children acquired conventional literacy. As Preston and his peers used the materials in the veterinarian play center described in Vignette 7.3, they had firsthand experiences using literacy in ways they had seen adults use literacy within doctors' offices or veterinary clinics.

The attendance event, the lesson with repeated reading, and the imaginative literacy activity of the veterinarian play center are all examples of learning contexts in emergent literacy classrooms. In learning contexts, the principles of learning from Chapter 2, the learning goals from Chapter 3, the talk structures from Chapter 4, and the texts of Chapters 5 and 6 converge. In the contexts of events, lessons, and activities, children learn and teachers teach.

Any teacher must make numerous choices when integrating all the ingredients of an emergent literacy perspective to create meaningful learning contexts. In this chapter, we present a framework designed to aid emergent literacy teachers' decision making. Our framework, which is presented in Table 7.1, describes three types of learning contexts—events, lessons, and activities—each of which is reflected in one of the three vignettes that opened this chapter. There are *events,* such as taking attendance, described in Vignette 7.1; *lessons,* such as the teacher-led guidance in repeated reading in Vignette 7.2; and *activities,* such as those encouraged in the play center described in Vignette 7.3. Each type of learning context supports particular forms of learning and, when combined within a single emergent literacy classroom, they create a comprehensive set of learning experiences for young children. In this chapter, we introduce the framework with a discussion of the three principles of learning that underlie an emergent literacy perspective. We then describe in depth the characteristics and the functions of events, lessons, and activities.

Learning Principles Underlying the Framework of Learning Contexts

Recall the three principles that undergird an emergent literacy perspective: (1) literacy learning occurs through meaningful use of reading and writing, (2) literacy learning is embedded in oral language, and (3) literacy learning occurs in multiple contexts with teachers and with peers. These three principles determined which learning contexts were part of our framework. First,

TABLE 7.1   A Framework of Classroom Contexts

Context	Description	Examples
Event	• Literacy is used in the service of classroom community functions and other subject areas. Literacy use is central in an event as a means of interacting but instruction of new literacy strategies or knowledge is not the intent of the event.	• Daily events such as attendance-taking, milk and lunch count, games, songs (Taylor et al., 1986; Richgels, 1995) • Content areas such as social studies, science, and health where books are read for information and reports and summaries are written (Magnusson & Palincsar, 1995) • Morning Message (Crowell et al., 1986) • Read-aloud of books (Hoffman et al., 1993)
Lesson	• Teachers guide children in acquiring facility with the strategies of independent reading and writing.	• Small, teacher-led groups where children have similar literacy needs (Hiebert et al., 1992; Taylor et al., 1994) • Small, teacher-led groups with changing and flexible membership (Radencich, McKay, & Paratore, 1995) • Whole-class shared reading (Reutzel et al., 1994)
Activity	• Occasions are provided for reading and writing both alone and with other children.	• Library center (Martinez & Teale, 1988; Fractor et al., 1993) • Writing center (Allen & Carr, 1989) • Play center (Morrow & Rand, 1991) • Peer-led discussions or book clubs (Grattan, in press)

because of the emphasis on variety and meaningfulness, it is important to think of the three learning contexts—events, lessons, and activities—as complementing one another, each contributing in significant ways to a child's literacy development. Second, because each context is considered valuable for children's literacy development, the contexts should not be in competition with one another, but rather, be distributed equitably across the school experience. We now examine each of these principles in terms of the development of the framework of learning contexts.

Literacy Learning Occurs through Meaningful Use

Throughout the three contexts and across all the roles that teachers and students might assume, one continuing thread is that the opportunities within the contexts are meaningful ones for engaging in reading and writing. *Events* are characterized by children's engagement in authentic uses of literacy within school. For example, children's attendance-taking requires that students be able to match letters, names, and, in Vignette 7.1, pictures. This literacy use is not an end in and of itself, but, rather, it helps the child achieve a particular goal—knowing who is present and who is absent in school.

In *lessons,* children engage in literature that is interesting to them, but the focus is on helping students understand particular features of written language. For example, after several readings of *Who Took the Farmer's Hat?,* the students in Vignette 7.2 are asked to focus on a word in the text, *hat.* Their teacher asks them to find all the instances of *hat,* then to write the word on their acetate slates. After doing this, their teacher asks them to change a letter to create the word, *fat.*

In *activities,* children are immersed in the functions of literacy. The veterinary play center in which Preston and his peers participated in Vignette 7.3 created meaningful opportunities for them to use literacy to meet particular goals. However, in contrast to the *event,* the attention to features of written language are reduced. Thus, Preston could create his prescription, inventing both the content as well as using scribble-writing to convey the meaning. The emphasis on the activity is to provide students with opportunities to mimic the literacy use of mature readers and writers, opportunities that the students create and find meaningful for their own purposes and goals.

Literacy Learning Is Embedded in Oral Language

Across events, lessons, and activities, the oral language used to describe and interpret literacy varies considerably. In *events,* the topic is specified by the teacher (e.g., taking attendance), but the children are less constrained in their turn-taking than they may be in lessons. In *lessons,* teachers engage students in considerable description of the literacy strategies and processes they are using and studying. For example, in the book *Who Took the Farmer's Hat?,* the children might discuss the cross-checking strategy that they used to confirm that one of the animals the farmer encounters was a fly rather than a bug or an insect. Because the illustration is somewhat ambiguous in its depiction, children would be encouraged to talk about the manner in which they checked the letters in the word to determine whether the word was *fly, bug,* or *insect.* In *activities,* students have the opportunity to engage in talk about literacy as they negotiate with one another. For example, in the play center when Preston was interested in writing out a prescription, but was unable to spell any of the required words, peers could talk with him about his other options (e.g., scribble-writing). In short, the oral language used to describe and interpret literacy varies across these three contexts in ways that are important for children's literacy development.

Literacy Learning Occurs in Multiple Contexts

Each of the three learning contexts invites different levels of involvement by teachers and peers. Within *events,* children apply literacy abilities and knowledge under the watchful eye of the teacher, as the class uses literacy for sharing information or for enjoyment. The teacher's role is to facilitate children's use of literacy within the event. For example, in Vignette 7.1, the teacher asks students to participate in classroom routines such as taking morning attendance. In doing so, children are involved in matching letters and names, using literacy, literally within the context of a routine classroom event.

In contrast, within *lessons,* teachers have multiple occasions for guidance and instruction. They focus on teaching particular strategies and processes that they know characterize proficient reading and writing. Teachers scaffold their students' participation in these contexts so that they are using strategies and processes they may not be able to use when working independently. The teacher in Vignette 7.2 ensures that students can read *Who Took the Farmer's Hat?* because of her support through the repeated reading as well as through the summary on the chart.

Within *activities,* students participate with peers in the absence of their teachers' direct involvement. In such contexts, students have opportunities to experiment, construct, and negotiate in play contexts or in academic settings such as the writing center. Their roles vary from those in lessons and events because they must assume more responsibility for their own and their peers' progress. Preston, the child in Vignette 7.3 who created the prescription for the pet teddy bear, illustrates the opportunities for literacy use as peers interact with one another.

Across events, lessons, and activities, teachers' and students' roles vary in distinct ways with different opportunities for them to control the topics and turns of the experiences, different criteria for what counts as appropriate literacy use (e.g., conventional or temporary spelling), and different levels of responsibility for negotiating the outcomes of the experiences.

The three contexts—events, lessons, and activities—are crucial to creating emergent literacy classrooms that support students' growth in oral and written language. They are based on the three principles of learning that guide teachers' decisions in creating such classrooms. In the next section of this chapter, we explore each of these contexts in depth. For each learning context that would be part of an emergent literacy classroom, we consider how teachers: (a) plan the context, (b) implement the context, and (c) extend the context to other literacy events. To illustrate each context, we present an example of the context, then describe how it was implemented in a classroom. We then consider ways in which the teacher extended the literacy knowledge from this context to others within her classroom and across the school day(s).

Framing the Classroom Contexts: Literacy Events

Literacy events are occasions when literacy is used in the service of the classroom community and other subject areas. While literacy use is central in these events as a means of interacting and learning, instruction of literacy strategies or knowledge is not the focus. A "mini-lesson"—a short lesson of several minutes—may occur at some point during the event as the teacher recognizes a teachable moment when a particular dimension of literacy should be highlighted or a confusion about literacy clarified (Harste, Short, & Burke, 1988). However, these short episodes of literacy instruction are secondary to a community function such as learning about kites and wind in a science lesson or establishing who is absent on a particular day.

There are many literacy events in the life of classrooms. Vignette 7.1 illustrates the engagement in literacy of kindergartners when they assumed responsibility for attendance-taking. We have chosen the Morning Message to describe in depth. Unlike the read-aloud event, literacy as part of daily classroom life, or literacy in subject areas, this event may be less common in classrooms. Yet the Morning Message is rich with potential in its ability to assist children in making the transition from home to school, while at the same time allowing teachers to model writing processes.

Exemplar of a Literacy Event: The Morning Message

The Morning Message involves contributions by children and teachers to a news bulletin that the teacher or a class member writes on a chart, the board, or an overhead transparency. The brief event, 7 to 10 minutes, typically occurs at the beginning of the school day. The teacher or class leader initiates the event by asking children for important news from their communities, homes, or classroom. As teachers transcribe students' contributions, they interact with the children about the content, literacy features such as spellings of words, and mechanics and usage of sentences and paragraphs.

Identifying the Literacy in Classroom Events. The development of the Morning Message, created by teachers who revisited the traditional primary grade Show and Tell event (Crowell, Kawakami, & Wong, 1986), illustrates how a classroom event was identified, then modified to highlight literacy-related abilities. These teachers thought Show and Tell had the potential to serve as a bridge between children's homes and the classroom. However, experience had taught them that Show and Tell could be time-consuming and tedious because children had few models for presenting their information. Morning Message, creating a written news bulletin at the start of the school day, provided a context in which students could be guided in summarizing information, and different forms of writing could be modeled. As these teachers implemented this new context, they made choices about the frequency with which Morning Message would occur and the length of time that would be devoted to the event, daily or several times a week. Because the value of an event may wear off as children's attention spans wane, we suggest more frequent occurrences with a shorter duration per event rather than fewer occurrences but of longer duration.

During Morning Message, teachers can comment on various aspects of written language as they or students write the message on a board or overhead. However, because of the rich potential of literacy use within the event, it is helpful to plan the various aspects of literacy to highlight. Creating a mini-lesson on every aspect of literacy that arises during the Morning Message would detract from the purpose of the event. The two classrooms whose Morning Messages are presented next had particular routines as part of the Morning Message. One such routine involved increasing responsibility by children for the spelling of news items over the school year: moving from responding to teacher requests for initial consonants to students writing their own messages. A second routine involved reading and rereading the completed message. In addition to simply identifying Morning Message as a classroom event, children in these classrooms had come to expect and value it as a venue for sharing important news and orienting themselves to the school day.

Highlighting Particular Strategies within the Event.   We draw on an example of the nature of and interactions within Morning Message from Ms. Sakamoto's first-grade classroom, one of the Kamehameha Early Education Program classrooms we described in Chapter 1 (see also, Crowell et al., 1986). On this particular day, Ms. Sakamoto has the children focus on the events of the class day because (as the following message shows) the day is a busy one. On many days, children's contributions include references to home experiences but on this particular morning children are eagerly awaiting the school photographer to take their photos. Not surprisingly, this day's responses to Ms. Sakamoto's question regarding important information to include in the Morning Message focus on the events at school:

> We will have our pictures taken today.
> Then we will go to the science
> circus at the Boys and Girls Club.
> It will be a busy day.

Ms. Sakamoto asks for children's assistance as she writes the message on the board. For example, on the second iteration of "day," children are asked to find it on the board and spell it. The class reads the message aloud as Ms. Sakamoto tracks the print. When Ms. Sakamoto asks students to comment on what they observed about the day's message, one child points to the word, *will,* which appears three times. This leads to children identifying other words appearing more than once (i.e., *we, day,* and *the*).

Ms. Sakamoto then directs children's attention to capitals and periods. Children go up to the board to point to the capital letters at the beginning of sentences and the beginning of proper names (i.e., Boys and Girls Club) and to the periods at the end of sentences. A discussion follows about how this information might be helpful in children's own writing.

Many teachers at the kindergarten through second-grade levels have integrated this event into their school days. An example of the integration of a

Morning Message where the connection is made more directly to children's home experiences comes from Dawn Harris Martine's classroom in New York City (Martine, 1991):

> Today is Thursday. It is raining. It's also very muggy.
> We will have share time. Chantee will share "Cherries and the Cherry Pie" by Vera Williams.
> Nerfettiti's aunt is having a baby.

Ms. Martine leads a discussion with students throughout the Morning Message, asking children if a summary statement captures the gist of their message and requesting opinions from others about their views on issues. On this particular day, she asks about preferences for different kinds of weather and for explanations on chosen preferences of weather. Everything that is said does not go into the Morning Message but the discussion that surrounds its creation invites class members to share and explain their views.

Integrating Content and Strategies throughout the School Day.   The content of the message, as well as the literacy processes that are highlighted in the event, become part of the shared body of experiences and knowledge of the class. Throughout the day—and even on future days—references are made to the content and processes of these events. For example, as children wonder about conventional spellings of words, the words on the Morning Message become a resource for checking one's work. In Ms. Martine's classroom, the scribe for the day copies the Morning Message from the board into the classroom journal. This journal becomes a permanent record of classroom life across the year and is available for children and visitors. Extensions also can be made beyond the classroom. The record made by the scribe of the day can be photocopied and sent home as a record of the school day to share with family members.

Extensions to Other Literacy Events

The same principles of identifying literacy potential in an event, highlighting literacy strategies and content during the event, and integrating the shared understandings from the literacy event across the class day apply to other events such as daily classroom routines of attendance-taking, read-alouds, and literacy across the curriculum.

Many common occasions in classrooms can become literacy events when teachers begin to explore ways of increasing literacy uses for their students. Attendance-taking is frequently teachers' responsibility, but as the kindergarten classrooms described in Vignette 7.1 revealed, it was rich in opportunity for students to develop and use their letter and word knowledge. Similarly, occasions such as singing the national anthem and reciting the pledge of allegiance can become literacy-rich classroom events. Posters with the text of the song and the pledge, supported by the teacher pointing to the print as the song is sung and the pledge chanted, give young children daily opportunities to understand the relationship between speech and print.

Even an event such as the read-aloud that is literary in nature can benefit from teachers' consideration of how literacy opportunities can be enhanced (Hoffman, Roser, & Battle, 1993). When Gury (1994) observed kindergarten teachers reading aloud to their students, it became apparent that the teachers rarely focused children's attention on the role that the print had in reading. Teachers asked children to predict the book content, pointing to the pictures on the cover but rarely drawing children's attention to the words on the cover. Such behaviors were common in read-alouds with enlarged or big books as well, even though the words were visible for all children to see. Teachers' reflections on this tried-and-true literacy event in their classrooms may reveal additional ways in which their students can learn about and apply their literacy knowledge and strategies.

Finally, knowledge and strategies from literacy events can become a thread that runs throughout the school day. That is, literacy events can create transitions from one period to another or the means for regrouping after a particularly hectic recess or lunch hour. In particular, the content of books that have been read aloud can become the shared knowledge of the classroom community. In Dawn Martine's second-grade classroom, *Hattie and the Fox* (Fox, 1988) was used as a means of transition when the excitement level had reached an unproductive level. As the year progressed, all the teacher had to do was to begin a chant from the book, "Oh dear," and children immediately joined in to finish the refrain. Then, with their attention focused, they could return to other productive activity in the classroom.

Framing the Classroom Contexts: Literacy Lessons

Lessons are frequently viewed as the context in which "teaching" occurs. Within our elaborated emergent literacy perspective, we define teaching to encompass modeling and interaction, rather than simply lecturing or telling. In our earlier discussion of classroom events, we described teaching that occurred in event mini-lessons. Similarly, in our upcoming section on activities, we describe the teaching that occurs within classroom activities.

In small-group lessons, teachers guide children in acquiring facility with the strategies for independent reading and writing. In this section, we discuss the unique role of lessons over a period of one or two months within the context of teacher-led, small groups of children at similar developmental literacy levels. Using the case of repeated reading in small groups, we focus on aligning instructional goals with the participants, the content, and the materials used; then we describe ways to focus on goals during the lesson, ending with comments on assessing student's progress within the lesson. In the Extensions to Other Literacy Lessons section, we extend the planning, implementing, and summarizing phases to other lesson contexts, such as a whole class, and small groups that are formed according to criteria such as interest in an author, illustrator, or topic.

Exemplar of a Literary Lesson: Repeated Reading in Small Groups

Children may participate daily in whole-class lessons where an enlarged book is read together and in self-selected reading of library books but still not become independent readers and writers. In Chapter 3, we discussed the strategies and knowledge that distinguish movement into independent reading and writing—fluent recognition of high-frequency words and of words with common and consistent rimes or word patterns. For those children with few prior literacy experiences, teacher-led lessons will need to be frequent and well planned. Sometimes such lessons can occur through one-to-one tutoring (e.g., Lyons, Pinnell, & DeFord, 1993), but in many schools, especially those with a high proportion of students who struggle to learn literacy, a more realistic scenario is to provide such instruction in small groups.

The following description of small-group lessons comes from a collaborative project—Right Start in Reading—in which one of us, Hiebert, has been involved with a group of teachers since 1990 (see Hiebert et al., 1992). Right Start in Reading is representative of projects that have helped struggling emergent literacy students become successful readers and writers in ways that have not happened in schools without such projects (see Hiebert & Taylor, 1994). Successful projects such as Success for All (Slavin, Madden, Karweit, Dolan, & Wasik, 1994) and Early Intervention in Reading (Taylor et al., 1994) vary in features, including, among others, types of books that are used in lessons, the number of books to which children are introduced, and the focuses of the curriculum. However, they do share important features that include: (a) goals and plans for achieving those goals, (b) tasks that make up the regular schedule of lessons, and (c) techniques for evaluating children's progress. In the discussion that follows, we trace ways in which a lesson from a Right Start in Reading classroom provides insights into planning, implementing, and evaluating literacy lessons.

Aligning Goals with Participants, Content, and Materials. The lesson that we will describe can best be viewed within the larger structure of the Right Start in Reading project, the name by which teachers in this particular district refer to the small-group instruction in first and second grades. Teachers view their daily lessons in relation to the larger goal that children will be fluent readers and writers by the end of the primary grades. While teachers make numerous decisions as they respond to students during lessons, they make choices about materials, tasks, strategies, and skills during periodic planning sessions that occur weekly.

To illustrate the manner in which teachers create a lesson requires an understanding of the profile of children within a group. The four children— Dustin, Jeremy, Yolanda, and Katrina—who are the focus of this particular set of lessons are first graders who were identified as having low levels of emergent literacy at the beginning of grade one. Their Title 1 teacher, Pam Chrisman, designs her lessons using information on these children's strategies on the critical goals of literacy that were identified in Chapter 3. While these children are beginning to consistently recognize a core group of words, the words are idiosyncratic to each child. Children are able to recognize their own names and those of one another in the group. Each child has a word bank of special words with Jeremy's words, for example, including Rockies, Broncos, and dirt bike. They can name lowercase letters with accuracy and have a solid sense of one-to-one correspondence between spoken and written words. They are also quite attentive to the initial consonants of words and are becoming aware of the word patterns or rimes with the short /a/ as in *at* and *an*.

Teachers such as Pam Chrisman make decisions about what to teach and what books to use on a *weekly* basis as they reflect on children's progress over the previous week and identify emphases and books for the subsequent week. They use children's journal entries and running records as a basis for their decision making. Running records, described in greater depth in Chapter 8, summarize children's reading of a text. As teachers reflect on what children are able to do and what they are still unable to do, they use the framework of strategies and knowledge that was presented in the first section of the book— the central, necessary, and interim processes of reading and writing described in Table 3.1. The conclusions from these reflections become the basis for the small-group lessons for the next week. For this particular group, Pam Chrisman observes that, overall, children are beginning to attend to rimes with short *a* and to high-frequency words such as *and, you, me,* and *I.* The running records also reveal a pattern of overreliance on illustrations for words. Dustin is the only member of the group who does not seem to be overusing picture clues. An example of the heavy reliance on pictures and the failure to confirm the hypothesis from the contextual clue with the print is Yolanda's substitution of *bread* for sandwich in a book the group read the past week. Coordinating the use of picture clues with the beginnings and patterns of words will be a focus for the next week's lessons.

The running records are also examined to determine the match between children's developing reading and the books' characteristics. While the teachers in the Right Start in Reading project make book selections on a daily or weekly basis, they draw on work that teachers in the project have done over an extended period of time in correlating available books with the project's curriculum. In Table 7.2, we provide a list similar to ones developed by teachers in the Right Start in Reading project. This list is similar in all but one way to those that teachers have created: It is confined to trade books. Our reason for confining the list in Table 7.2 to trade books rather than to titles from the little book programs used by the Right Start teachers is that the trade books are familiar to most teachers. We also wished to include in this volume a list of trade books that are accessible for children at the very earliest stages of reading. As was evident in the analysis of text accessibility (see Table 5.6), many trade books have features that make them difficult for young children at the earliest stages of reading. Even in books where the total number of words may be small, the number of unique words may be high. For example, *Rosie's Walk* (Hutchins, 1968) is similar to the books that were identified as level two books in Table 5.6 in having a fairly small number

TABLE 7.2 Examples of Library Books: Possible Patterns and High-Frequency Words for Instruction

Trade Book	Common Rimes	High-Frequency Words	Number of Distinct Words	Distinct to Total Words	Size of Predictable Unit and Its Percentage of Text
Dog In, Cat Out (G. Rubinstein, 1993; Illus. A. James)	og, at, in	in, out	4	1:14	• small (4 words) • 100% of text
Have You Seen My Cat? (E. Carle, 1987)	at, is, ot	have, you, my, this, is, not	9	1:9	• sizable (8 words) • 99% of text
Have You Seen My Duckling? (N. Tafuri, 1984)	[none]	have, you, my	8	1:4	• small (5 words) • 89% of text
Cat on the Mat (Wildsmith, 1982)	at	the	10	1:4	• small (4 words) • 73% of text
What Do You Like? (Grejniec, 1992)	at, ike	I, the, too	17	1:4	• small (4 words) • 58% of text
Whose Footprints? (M. Coxe, 1990)	at, og	the, a, and	13	1:2	• small (3 words) • 63% of text
All I Am (E. Roe, Illus. H. Cogancherry, 1990)	am	I, a	23	1:3	• small (3 words) • 56% of text

of words. But when only two of the 32 words are repeated as is the case with *Rosie's Walk* and these two words, *the* and *for,* are not part of a predictable unit, the word recognition strategies needed to be successful with this book will be beyond those of most beginning readers.

Like the Right Start in Reading lists, the books in Table 7.2 represent teachers' judgments about the accessibility of the book for readers with particular strategies. All of the books in Table 7.2 have at least some of the characteristics of the first-level books of the little book and Reading Recovery trade book exemplar programs in Table 5.6: *Jack-in-the-Box* (Butler, 1989) and *Cat on the Mat* (Wildsmith, 1982). Some books vary in one or more characteristics, as should be the case when teachers view books in relation to students rather than apply guidelines rigidly. For example, some books such as *All I Am* (Roe, 1990) have a higher number of unique words because the predictable pattern of the book involves a new noun in each sentence as the child describes his different roles (e.g., "I am a friend." "I am a neighbor."). Most of these roles will be familiar to young children and can be recognized through the illustrations, making this book an appropriate one for beginning readers. As we discussed in Chapter 5, teachers in the Right Start in Reading project use guidelines such as the size of the predictable unit and the number of distinct words not as absolute but relative to the needs and strengths of the particular children who will be using the books.

Also like the Right Start in Reading lists, the list in Table 7.2 presents common rimes that can be found in key words in the books as well as high-frequency words. Teachers' decisions drive the selection of books, not vice versa. A teacher who is working with a group of children on rimes with the vowel *o* followed by a consonant would look for books that give children opportunities to apply that pattern. This teacher also might choose to use books from other sources. For example, a teacher might decide that *Whose Footprints?* (Coxe, 1990) is an excellent context in which to work on using syntactic and semantic cues. Whatever the content of the books, teachers attend carefully at this point in the instruction to the density of new to unknown words and the total number of words. Because they wish for children to extend their repertoire of word recognition strategies beyond the use of illustrations, teachers are intent on selecting books that will encourage children to attend to the words in the texts and not to overrely on memorizing the patterns because the volume of new words overwhelms children.

Pam Chrisman uses her observations of children's responses on running records to confirm that the length and density level of books is appropriate. To help children to generalize their understandings of word patterns, she chooses books containing words with rimes containing the short i (-it, -in, -ip) as the focus for the following week. She continues to ask students to work with books at the same difficulty stage but Ms. Chrisman is eager for children to focus on word patterns with vowels other than *a*. When children spend too much time with the rimes for a single vowel such as those that are formed with the short *a*, they fail to grasp the idea that the same principle applies with the five primary vowels. That is, they are no closer to understanding that a vowel followed by a consonant is associated with the short sound of the vowel when they have experience only with short *a* rimes.

Another set of decisions relating to group composition is made on a quarterly basis. Quarterly reading and writing assessments (see Chapter 8 for a complete description of the assessment tools) provide the basis for determining which children require small-group instruction, which children have compatible profiles, and how many children will be in a group. The decisions depend on the overall profiles of the entire class and the available resources. Children who are progressing well through whole class lessons, events, and independent and peer activities do not need to receive this particular form of small-group instruction. In the schools with the Right Start in Reading project, all available support teachers work with classroom teachers to pool resources. Because the resources for programs such as special education and Title I have been allocated as a function of need, those schools with the most resources tend to have the greatest needs. Speech and language, special education, bilingual, and Title I teachers have combined forces to work with children on similar strategies and goals. In those schools where such resources are not available, classroom teachers provide the instruction.

Focusing on Purposes and Goals during the Lesson.   Within classrooms in the Right Start in Reading project, lessons are viewed as a primary vehicle in which those children who are not yet conventional readers and writers receive guided experiences in developing interim and necessary processes while engaged in the central processes. That is, instruction of phonetically regular and common patterns and high-frequency words is embedded within reading and writing tasks.

Each lesson has a basic structure of three tasks: reading daily, writing daily, and guidance about high-frequency words and rimes that are consistent in many common words. While teachers vary among one another as well as across the school year in the way they employ each of these tasks, the three tasks provide an important structure and reminder of those processes critical to young children's literacy development. Teachers noted that prior to the project, some first graders did not read a book or write even a handful of words for several days. Instead they spent time listening to stories or creating artwork related to stories. Within this project structure, students read and write daily, as well as engage in daily lessons designed to push their word knowledge. Each lesson includes exposure to a new book with compelling illustrations and interesting stories, which contribute to students' high interest levels.

The lesson cycles through the three tasks, beginning with reading, moving to writing, and then returning to reading. Talk about words and strategies for figuring out unknown words is interspersed throughout the book reading and the writing tasks. In the week of lessons for the group of Dustin, Jeremy, Katrina, and Yolanda, a midweek lesson such as the following was typical.

The lesson begins with a brief discussion about the children's readings with family members the previous evening. As each child receives a copy of the book, *That Fly!* (Riley, 1996), which was the focus of the group's lesson the previous Friday, Pam Chrisman asks children to describe the strategies that they have been studying such as looking for word patterns in unknown words. For example, the teacher and children note the presence of the word *that* in the title since it contained the target pattern, at. Children then describe the way in which they correlate information from pictures with the print to figure out new words.

After the book has been reread—some pages silently and some aloud by individuals, a new book, *Fix It, Fox* (Lynch, 1996) is introduced. Ms. Chrisman previews the book's content with the children by asking them to describe what content and words they expect to find in the book based on its illustrations. Words that will aid children's reading but that cannot be figured out with children's current strategies are introduced (e.g., *said*).

During the first reading of the book, Ms. Chrisman reads along with the children but, over time, she decreases her support and encourages children to take the lead. The first reading is then followed by a discussion of how children's predictions matched the book. The teacher also asks children to describe the ways in which they used the strategy of matching clues from pictures and words and the strategy of using patterns inside words. The book is reread several times until children are reading with expression and fluency.

Activities designed to enhance students' word knowledge follow. First, books are closed and Ms. Chrisman engages children in a phonemic awareness activity, identifying words that have the same rime or pattern as the target words, *fix* and *six, it* and *sit*. Acetate slates (pieces of paper that have been covered with acetate) are then distributed and children are asked to write the word *it*. Requests follow such as changing *it* to *sit*, then back to *it*. Ms. Chrisman encourages children to generalize their understandings of rimes by asking them to change *it* to *at* and then back to *it*, followed by *sit*. Children consistently read what they have written and orally compose phrases and sentences with their words. At the beginning of the year, when children were gaining fluency with letters, magnetic letters were used for this word-writing activity. Ms. Chrisman writes the words *fix* and *fat* on the board, leading children in a conversation that makes explicit the commonalities between these words as well as the differences.

Teachers cycle through a number of writing activities, including free writing and writing sentences or phrases with one or more of the rhyming words over several days. Because of an interest in fostering children's generalization of V-C rimes, Ms. Chrisman dictates a sentence stem that contains instances of rimes with vowels that have been the focus for the lesson: "I will fix the _____ ." When the dictation concludes, children add their description to finish the sentence. Children are encouraged to spell these words as best they can with the teacher providing guidance as needed. To end the lesson, the group rereads *Fix It, Fox* and children choose a book to take home. The cycle of the lesson is complete, focusing on engagement in literacy tasks for both reading and writing, as well as participation in specific instructional lessons designed to help students develop knowledge of words, decoding strategies, and comprehension strategies.

Assessing Content and Composition of Group Relative to Goals.   Assessment and evaluation are integral to the planning and implementation phases of lessons and take the form of both ongoing, in-situ assessments of students' progress within lessons as well as more formal quarterly assessments. Ongoing assessment occurs in the midst of lessons as teachers take brief but important notes on children's reading and writing progress. Information gained from these assessments within the lesson serves as the source for teachers' decisions as to which strategies to introduce or reinforce during subsequent lessons and which books to select. The lessons of a project such as this one illustrate the cyclic nature of instruction that builds on children's strengths and meets their needs.

The information that comes from quarterly assessments is integral to teachers' decisions about group formation. These more extensive assessments conducted during periodic evaluations provide teachers with essential information for determining who would benefit from intensive instruction and whose profiles would be compatible within a single group. The periodic re-assessment prevents the small-group intensive instruction from becoming a form of tracking (Allington, 1983). In tracking, also called ability grouping, children's reading status is viewed generically in terms of "good," "average," or "poor" readers. Goals tend to be global and hence rather ambiguous, in contrast to the definable strategies illustrated above. Ongoing assessments in which children's participation and group assignments are evaluated give the small-group lessons we have described here a different foundation from that of the ability groups in which generations of children were tracked. In contexts such as the Right Start in Reading program, teachers' lessons are viewed as a source of support and growth for children rather than a source of stigma and perpetuation of literacy problems.

Extensions to Other Types of Lessons

The context of the lesson is defined in terms of the presence of instructional goals, plans for reaching those goals, and means for implementing and evaluating the plans. The first-grade lesson described above, focusing on the instructional needs of first-grade students who were struggling with their literacy development, illustrated these features. However, there are many other forms that lesson contexts can take in an emergent literacy classroom. We chose to illustrate the small-group lessons for children with similar literacy profiles to underscore the need for such lessons for some students in emergent literacy classrooms. Without consistent participation in such lessons at least several times weekly, a sizable number of children may not become highly proficient independent readers and writers.

However, not all young children will require small-group lessons of this sort. At least a handful of children in most classes may have acquired conventional literacy by the time they enter first grade, while another significant group of children are on the verge of being conventionally literate at the beginning of first grade. The children with the latter characteristics may pick up literacy with a minimum of lessons in small groups during the first or second quarters of grade one. Lessons may vary in terms of size and structure, as well as focus. For example, students for whom literacy acquisition is moving along well may participate in groups that are somewhat larger than those in which children with initially lower levels of emergent literacy meet with the teacher. Further, these groups may meet several times a week with the teacher rather than daily as the strategy groups do. The focus of these groups may be more like the book clubs of the middle grades (Grattan, in press; McMahon & Raphael, in press) where children study particular books and focus on literary elements and higher-level vocabulary strategies.

There may be variations in lesson structure even within the same general programs. For example, in the Right Start in Reading project from which the first-grade, teacher-led lesson was drawn, kindergarten teachers created lessons with small groups that differed in composition and content from the small-group instruction in grades one and two (Gury, 1994). The kindergarten teachers divided their classes into three groups, each including a range of proficiencies in book-reading stages (Sulzby, 1985), writing forms (DeFord, 1980), phonemic awareness, and letter naming. These groups met with the teacher in two weekly sessions that began with the repeated reading of a big book. Children then read with partners in little versions of the book and shared their favorite parts with the larger group with responses that ranged from pretend to conventional readings. Such lessons were then followed by games that encouraged phonemic awareness, such as listening for words that began alike or that rhymed from the book and writing with magnetic letters and chalk and chalkboards. These types of lessons benefited the kindergartners. By midyear, when teachers studied their students' literacy knowledge, they were delighted to learn that with the support of the project lessons, their current students knew as much about literacy as their students the previous year knew at the end of the year.

Lessons occur across a range of contexts, from the small-group lesson in which Dustin and his peers participated to formal lessons with larger groups of students or in whole-class settings. We end this section on lessons by considering issues related to grouping for instruction. For a time, whole-class lessons were seen as an alternative to any small-group lessons. Some believed that whole-class instruction could serve as an antidote for the negative outcomes of ability grouping that was the primary context for reading instruction for generations. We have also heard anecdotes from teachers who described district mandates for whole-class instruction on the mistaken assumption that the "whole" in whole-class and whole language were equivalent. Educators have become increasingly aware that whole-class lessons are not a substitute for small-group lessons (see Pardo & Raphael, 1991; Raphael & Hiebert, 1996).

For students whose literacy experiences have been few, the whole-class format may contain too many distractions and too many opportunities to be passive, to serve as the sole instructional format. However, when whole-class instruction is in the form of mini-lessons (Atwell, 1987), there are numerous aspects of literacy that can be modeled and highlighted such as ways to select books in a library (Mervar & Hiebert, 1989). Mini-lessons are short, focused instructional sessions that teachers conduct as extensions of events or as a prelude to activities, but not as a substitute for small-group strategy instruction (Reutzel & Cotter, 1991). For example, Hemmeter (1991) conducted a brief—less than five minutes—whole-class mini-lesson where she intro-duced children to the variety of ways in which her name could be written, including with a picture, with the initial consonant of her surname, and with the words "Mrs. Hemmeter."

Flexible grouping is a second alternative to ability grouping on the basis of similar literacy needs. In flexible groups, children receive small-group experiences but in groups whose compositions change frequently and where the literacy proficiencies within a group cover the range of the classroom (Radencich, McKay, & Paratore, 1995). While numerous anecdotal accounts for flexible groups have been described (e.g., Berghoff & Egawa, 1991; Keegan & Shrake, 1991; Radencich & McKay, 1995), little evidence has been provided on children's literacy acquisition when these are the only contexts for instruction. However, reports over several decades have found that, at least for part of their literacy instruction, children who are reading well need to have challenging reading material and that children who are learning to read need to be guided in the text that they receive (Allington, 1984; Anderson, Evertson, & Brophy, 1979; Barr, 1973-74; Juel, 1990). In a heterogeneous group of emergent literacy students, where struggling readers are looking at books with few recognizable words and where proficient readers are looking at books that present no challenge, none is served well.

If small-group lessons such as the one described in this section are to work, goals must be clear, assessments ongoing, and groups reformed and reconstituted regularly. Further, all children within the classroom, regardless of literacy proficiency, should have the opportunity to interact within the same range of literacy events and around the same literacy content. This provides a common thread that runs throughout the school day. The activities we describe next are a third literacy context in which all children interact and learn with one another. The mechanisms of learning that underlie an emergent literacy classroom make it imperative that children are not segregated to particular literacy activities because of literacy proficiency. Rather, children can learn from each other, assuming a range of roles as literacy users within the activities.

Framing the Classroom Contexts: Literacy Activities

Occasions for reading and writing by one's self and with other children assume as critical a role in an emergent literacy perspective as the teacher-led events and lessons. Activities—as we refer to the classroom contexts where children work independently or with one another—require children to apply their constructions about reading and writing. Communicating understandings and accomplishments of literacy with peers of equivalent social power gives children compelling reasons to revise, clarify, and explain their interpretations. While activities involve children working independently or collaboratively, the existence of successful activities in an emergent literacy classroom reflects the design and planning of a skillful teacher. This planning need not occur on a daily basis; a set of activities for independent and peer participation can be in place for a week or more. The materials and tasks of a particular center change but the basic structure of activities remains intact for extended time periods. The most common of these activities in emergent literacy classrooms include reading self-selected library books, writing, and play.

Often activities are organized in a "center" format, which means that all of the materials for an activity are in one location. In some classrooms, children participate at a center at a designated time; in others, children choose from among centers within particular guidelines. While we refer to activities as centers throughout this discussion, we do not wish to suggest that children need to cycle through all of these activities, nor do we think they can occur only when small groups of students or individual students are at work. In some classrooms and with some activities, all children may participate at designated times, such as when reading with a partner or a book buddy. Further, not all students must participate in all centers.

We have opted to highlight the library center as our exemplar activity because the creation of a successful library center is more involved than may be apparent on the surface. The library center's focus is on reading self-selected books. Reading in library books has several subcategories, including listening to audio-taped versions of books and buddy reading (i.e., reading with a peer). Thus, for children to be productive at a library center, more is involved on the part of teachers than making books available. The actions of (a) planning, (b) communicating and monitoring, and (c) summarizing are particularly evident in the creation of a successful library center.

Exemplar of a Literacy Activity: A Library Center

Throughout the primary years, children require many classroom occasions for interacting with books independently and with peers. Initially, children engage in pretend or memorized reading that characterizes early literacy development. Increasingly, they read and explain the text to one another in more conventional ways. These occasions have many benefits for young children but the efficacy of these occasions can vary considerably, depending on their teachers' attention to the physical and social dimensions of these activities.

Planning.   The books that make up the library center need to be chosen with care and, once selected, their physical arrangement in a library center requires thought (Fractor, Woodruff, Martinez, & Teale, 1993). Insight into the books that children choose at a library center and the kinds of processes in which young children engage with the books while at the center comes from a study by Martinez and Teale (1988). The kindergartners who were observed in this project gravitated to books that their teachers had read aloud several times. While books that the teacher had read only once were less popular at the library centers than highly familiar books, a one-time reading by the teacher generated more interest for children than books that had not been introduced previously. Further, when the enlarged versions of books were available at the center, children chose those more frequently than regular-sized books. Kindergartners also were more likely to choose books with predictable structure such as *My Friends* (Gomi, 1989), *What Do You Like?* (Grejniec, 1992), or *Polar Bear, Polar Bear* (Martin, 1991) as compared to books without a predictable structure.

Martinez and Teale (1988) also described the kindergartners' three most prominent ways of interacting with books at the library centers and one less frequent but important pattern that would be expected to emerge in first- and second-grade library centers. The first most prominent pattern was what was described as browsing or "rapid flipping" through part or all of a book. Browsing tended to occur most often with unfamiliar books.

The second frequent form of interaction was to silently "study" a book. Because most of these kindergartners were not reading conventionally, this response pattern involved the most sustained attention of any of the patterns that Martinez and Teale observed. The silent studying of books occurred most frequently with books that had an unpredictable structure. For example, *Make Way for Ducklings* (McCloskey, 1941) or *Dandelion* (Freeman, 1964) are representative of such books. They have considerable detail in their illustrations to sustain the attention of young children.

The third way of interacting occurred with books that had predictable structures, such as *Quick as a Cricket* (Wood, 1982), *Cookie's Week* (Ward, 1988), and other titles in Table 5.5, after they had been part of shared reading in the class. The activity that these books elicited was pretend reading, often produced chorally as several children did a read-along that modeled the activities that had occurred in teacher-led classroom events.

The fourth type of interaction pattern that occurred least frequently involved conventional reading, or listening to a peer read a book aloud. Martinez and Teale did not extend their project to first and second grades but it would be assumed that this fourth category would increase as the majority of children become conventional readers. Yet, browsing behaviors may remain prominent as children select books to read, because these behaviors also characterize second graders who are proficient readers (Mervar & Hiebert, 1989).

Patterns at library centers can also be expected to be a function of the tasks that are part of the library center. If participation at a library center requires documentation on a book log, fewer browsing behaviors might be expected than in a center where such documentation was not required. If tasks at a library center call for a range of responses to literature such as acting out stories or writing a summary of favorite books, children will interact differently than they will in a library center where the responses are completely open-ended.

What has been documented consistently is that children are more likely to select books with which they have had some prior involvement, particularly through book talks or read-alouds by their teacher, than with unfamiliar books (Morrow & Weinstein, 1982). Further, the physical presentation of books also influences children's choices and their subsequent engagement with books. When teacher-featured or familiar books are visible in library centers, children spend more time with books. When the display of books is disheveled and disorganized, children's attention is likely to diminish.

Communicating and Interacting with Children.   While centers are intended for independent or peer collaboration, teachers continue to serve an important role during the activity. First, teachers create expectations for appropriate processes and potential products for an activity. In a project that considered the ways in which second graders interacted with books in libraries, the classroom demonstrations and modeling of book selections influenced children's actions. Those children who had been exposed consistently to discussions about authors, illustrators, and topics, as well as processes for selecting books of interest and appropriate difficulty, behaved quite differently in a library from those children who had not been part of such discussions (Mervar & Hiebert, 1989). Classroom discussions about books and processes of book selection were evident in an array of strategies for selecting books, while those second graders who had not been involved in such discussions typically chose books in much the same way that Martinez and Teale (1988) described as characteristic of kindergartners. Consistent discussions about selecting books of appropriate interest and difficulty levels prior to involvement in library centers will reap benefits in the behaviors that children show at library centers.

In the midst of children's participation at the library center, an interaction with the teacher of a minute or two can also contribute to a productive atmosphere. Even if the teacher is interacting with another group of children in a lesson or at another center activity, the teacher's attention at a center can improve the quality of children's involvement significantly. For example, a timely question posed to a group in the middle of a center activity might be: "What have you and your partner chosen to do about your book share? Jeremy and Trina have chosen to write a play about one of the events in their book. What other responses might be possible with the books that you've chosen? Andrew and Greg?"

Sharing Processes and Products.   The final phase of an activity period is often given short shrift: sharing and reflecting on the activity. Observations by Fisher and Hiebert (1990) showed that activities usually ended with an announcement by the teacher that the time had come to change to another subject area or with the ringing of a school bell that signaled lunchtime or recess. An evaluation phase completed the activities in some cases but this phase occurred with children as silent partners when the teacher graded products after school.

In some classrooms, however, teachers paused before moving on to another subject or another phase of the school day to acknowledge what children had accomplished in activities. In observing these interactions, Fisher and Hiebert saw at least three benefits to these summaries of activities. First, children's actions during the activity period were identified as legitimate and valued within the classroom learning community. Second, sharing or summarizing highlights from the activity period required children to present their knowledge to another audience. In this way, they were engaged in the reconceptualization and reformulation that was described in Chapter 2 as fundamental in children's literacy learning. Finally, children's comments became part of the shared knowledge of the entire community. When a teacher reinforces the strategy that Pablo used in locating a book on a new topic, this strategy becomes recognized within the community of readers in that classroom. On most occasions, these times for summing up and sharing with the community after the activity period were short—rarely more than a handful of minutes. Teachers posed questions such as, "Who has something to tell us about what you learned during activities today?" Children were advised to summarize what they had learned, a difficult albeit critical skill in learning. In some classrooms, sharing with a peer before the community share gave children a chance to be succinct.

Extensions to Other Activities

Successful implementation of other emergent literacy classroom activities that foreground writing, reading with a partner, or play with literacy reflect a similar three-pronged set of actions by teachers: (a) planning the activity, (b) communicating and monitoring during the activity, and (c) summarizing processes and products after the activity.

In the case of writing, the activity results in a more concrete outcome than is likely with library activities. Even beginning kindergartners can be engaged in a writing center for an extended period of time as they draw and scribble. Examples of the assistance that children give one another at writing centers have been interspersed throughout this book. For example, in Vignette 4.3, James receives advice from his peers during their interactions in the writing center. Writing activities are illustrative of centers that, once established, vary little in terms of their structure. Variations in a writing center relate to the content and forms of children's writing.

An activity where children listen to books read aloud will be relatively stable in expectations and outcomes. As they progress through the primary grades, the center may transform from one in which they listen to books to one in which they make recordings of their compositions or of their favorite books.

Play centers tend to vary more than do listening or writing centers. For example, the play center designed to represent a veterinary clinic, described in Vignette 7.3, will need revision to encourage continued imaginative play and a wide range of literacy uses. The expectations of what happens at the center will stay the same but the materials will change as the center moves from a veterinarian's office to a restaurant or kitchen. Without more frequent adaptations, the engagement of children such as Preston in Vignette 7.3

will wane, causing significant consequences for children's learning and attentiveness.

Summary

The three contexts described in this chapter—events, lessons, and activities—form the basis for an interesting, engaging, and effective emergent literacy program, one based on the learning principles that emphasize meaningful engagement in reading and writing, with extensive connections to and building upon students' oral language. The three contexts encourage and support formal instruction as well as students' application of learned strategies, skills, and knowledge. The different contexts provide opportunity for the social and public discourse described in Chapter 2 that is the basis for students' literacy acquisition. Further, together, these contexts provide ample opportunity for students to appropriate and transform what they have learned as well as make public their literacy learning. Within this variety of contexts, teachers have ample opportunity to teach and to evaluate the outcomes of their instruction. They can work with small groups of students who have special needs, with larger groups of students as they journey toward conventional literacy, and with the entire class as they build a literacy-rich community of learners.

chapter 8

Assessment in Early Literacy Classrooms

A second-grade teacher entered the following observations into her anecdotal record during a reading period where many of the students were reading in pairs:

> Brooke & Larry reading a Nate the Great Story together—
> switching off at each paragraph. Brooke jumps in to correct
> Larry or give him a word at the slightest hesitation.
> Aaron & Stewart reading—switching off after every 2 pgs.
> Stewart loves the story—keeps telling Aaron the next part
> will be funny & chuckling as he reads aloud. Stewart is the
> leader in this situation. He interrupts with immediate help
> when Aaron hesitates with a word.

> (Rhodes and Nathenson-Mejia, 1992, p. 504)

At the same point in the year, these were the daily journal entries of two first graders:

> I wis I had a hamsdr his name is cdls. I wd pl wt hma—Kristin
> (I wish I had a hamster. His name is Cuddles. I would play with
> him.)
> IWTOM—Bobby (I went to Madison.)

> (Pils, 1991, pp. 47–48)

After the child had drawn a rainbow, she copied her label for a rainbow on a previous page of her journal: "RNO." The exclusion of a letter associated with /b/ perplexed the teacher who was observing the child. Was the child not aware of it? This teacher decided to conduct an impromptu interview. She crouched down beside the child's desk and asked the child to tell about her picture and to read the words that she had written. When the child said "rainbow" for each of her representations of this word, the teacher asked whether the child could hear any other sounds in the word. She followed her question by modeling a very slow and extended pronunciation of the word "rainbow," prompting the child to do the same. The child breathed a sigh of recognition, took a red crayon, and scribbled over the O in her first rainbow. She then wrote B and finished the word with another O—RNΘBO.

(Taylor, 1991)

These examples show how assessment is embedded in the literacy contexts in emergent literacy classrooms. When the second-grade teacher in Vignette 8.1 examined her anecdotal notes, she saw a consistent pattern across the dyads: one child in each pair had assumed responsibility for figuring out unknown words, instead of both children making efforts to do so. In response, she conducted a whole-class lesson about strategies for figuring out unknown words, encouraging all students to try these strategies when they read with partners.

Kristin's and Bobby's journal entries in Vignette 8.2 proved to be rich sources of information about their word identification skills for Linda Pils, their teacher. Pils concluded that Kristin was aware of beginning and ending sounds and some medial vowels and consonants, while Bobby relied on beginning consonants to figure out words. Based on her observations, Pils stressed word families when she worked with Kristin. When she worked with Bobby, she emphasized how to include all of the letters he hears in a word. To highlight these letters, she asked him to name the initial sound (which he usually did with accuracy). Then, she made boxes to designate additional letters in the word and worked with him to identify remaining letters.

Vignette 8.3 shows the value of evidence gained from informal interviews with students. Through interviews, teachers establish children's underlying ideas and their metacognitive knowledge (i.e., their knowledge about how they think language works). They also can determine a child's potential level of learning. Children's potential learning is reflected in the degree to which they are able to respond to small prompts or scaffolds. In this vignette, we saw how the child was able to identify a major syllable in the word "rainbow" with prompting from the teacher (see our discussion of the zone of proximal development in Chapter 2).

This chapter elaborates on assessment that is indistinguishable from learning, embedded within the ongoing literacy events of existing classroom contexts. These learning events, the core of the emergent literacy program, are the basis for determining children's progress toward critical literacy goals. This view of assessment emanates from the principles of learning that have provided the foundation for our conceptualization of emergent literacy.

Literacy Assessment within an Emergent Literacy Perspective

Just as the principles of learning have transformed views of instruction, so, too, have these principles transformed our views of assessment. Assessment and testing are not synonymous. Quite the contrary. Within assessment, the dynamic, diverse, and daily literacy occurrences of the emergent literacy classroom are the source for information on children's literacy learning. This view contrasts sharply with testing, wherein tests are isolated and static events that occur outside young children's normal language and literacy practices.

Literacy Learning Occurs through Meaningful Use of Reading and Writing

Literacy, as with all language processes, is purposeful for young children. The pairs of readers described in Vignette 8.1 illustrate peer reading as a meaningful act. Bobby and Kristin, in Vignette 8.2, demonstrate the meaningful use of literacy to document favorite possessions like a pet hamster or favorite events such as a trip to Madison.

Because the essence of literacy use involves communicating meaning, assessments should capture children's literacy development within their *daily* acts of using literacy to accomplish meaningful functions. Knowledge about the strategies that children use to spell words is gained best from examining their messages. Each type of message described in Chapter 6 can be a source of information on how students apply the central and necessary strategies of composing. A personal narrative such as Kristin's in Vignette 8.2 provides insight into her ability to structure a message as well as her understandings of spelling-sound correspondences.

A long-held assumption among experts in testing is that children should be assessed using tasks that can control for factors that they believe mask pure measures of children's literacy proficiency. Consequently, tasks are designed to eliminate the effect of factors such as children's interest and background knowledge. Unfortunately, these paper-and-pencil tests, thought to provide pure measures of literacy, actually eliminate the meaningfulness that is basic to literacy use. The initial tests of literacy acquisition—reading readiness tests and early levels of norm-referenced reading tests—usually do not include text for children to read. The tasks of these tests concentrate on the interim skills of letter-sound matching and letter naming (Stallman & Pearson, 1990). When texts become part of tests, they are based on the high-frequency criterion that we illustrated in Chapter 5 with the passage from *Tiny* (Rider, 1986).

In short, requiring children to independently mark multiple-choice responses about a short passage based on high-frequency words eliminates the various features that make literacy interesting and meaningful to young children. By stripping the literacy act of its meaningfulness to young children, these assessments become less meaningful to teachers. First, teachers cannot be sure that young children's performances represent their "actual" level within their zone of proximal development because their difficulty in attending to tasks often results in hit-or-miss responses. Second, because the texts do not involve illustrations or predictable structures, these assessments fail to provide insight into critical literacy related to use of contextual support and text structures.

For teachers to understand their students' comprehending and composing development, they need to observe comprehending and composing strategies as children use literacy for meaningful functions.

Literacy Learning Is Embedded in Oral Language

One of the most problematic shortcomings within the testing tradition is its elimination of oral language opportunities. Both writing and reading are constructed through talk as we discussed in Chapter 4. For a true picture of children's literacy learning, teachers must listen as literacy is used and shared—as in the peer reading described in Vignette 8.1. Teachers must also talk with children in the midst of literacy events to establish what they are thinking, as illustrated in Vignette 8.3. In doing so, teachers can understand the range of children's knowledge or, to use Vygotsky's (1978) term, the proximal or potential level of development. Teacher-student talk after the literacy act also is informative, as illustrated by Linda Pils's interactions with her students about their journal entries. Through interviews, teachers can establish what children know and thus can identify directions for future instruction.

Assessments where teachers and students talk about the products and processes of literacy have been described as *dynamic* or interactive (Lidz, 1987). Conclusions about children's literacy are no longer made in solitary contexts where children are forbidden to talk with one another as they mark Xs on a page. When Bobby—in Vignette 8.2—was given the chance to talk about what he had written, he could share the meanings he associates with the symbols he has written. When literacy assessment is dynamic, literacy instruction, too, can be dynamic. Teachers design instructional lessons and activities that build on children's knowledge and that engage children's interest and capabilities.

Literacy Learning Occurs in Multiple Contexts with Teachers and Peers

The assessments of children's facility with literacy need to be *diverse* to capture the multifaceted character of literacy. The testing stance could be likened to a photo album where every child in a class is represented by a single photo of the same event—the posed portrait. In contrast, a metaphor for the assessments in an emergent literacy classroom is an extensive library of videotapes and photographs of the diverse set of literacy acts.

In an increasing number of today's classrooms, videotapes and photographs are more than simply metaphors for assessment. Teachers collect tape recordings, artwork, and the artifacts from projects and use them to understand children's learning. Teachers who effectively use such an approach for evaluating their students are cautious not to simply gather materials without regard to the purposes each of the materials might serve, or the various literacy accomplishments they are able to represent. The multiple and rich goals of an emergent literacy curriculum mean that assessments should include journal entries, compositions, reports, running records of children's oral readings, observational notes on children's activities, and so forth. When mapped against the teacher's, the school's, the district's, and other related curriculum goals, these multiple sources provide teachers with a rich database from which they can evaluate their students' progress, design ongoing instructional lessons, and create relevant literacy contexts. Initiating new assessments such as portfolios, a term used to describe this method for gathering children's work, without a clear sense of the underlying goals of the curriculum may simply lead to thick folders and bulging file boxes that serve little purpose. Used effectively, they provide a view of children's literacy development that is dynamic, meaningful, and comparable to the use of literacy both in and out of school.

Assessments need to be diverse to represent children's varying use of strategies when working independently, with peers, and with the teacher. These different contexts of strategy use provide a window into students' current and potential strategy use. It reflects a view of literacy competence as being a continuum from complete understanding and independence to being able to succeed with a range of support or scaffolding. An example of assessment of a literacy element that extends across multiple contexts is reflected in Vignette 8.2. When Bobby worked independently, he was able to identify only the initial consonant in the word "Madison." When his teacher provided the scaffold of boxes for subsequent letter-sound correspondences, Bobby could extend his knowledge of consonants to the ending of the word. Linda Pils, the teacher, was able to use this insight to help establish Bobby's zone of proximal development.

For the remainder of this chapter, we describe the processes that guide teachers in creating dynamic and diverse assessments as part of daily literacy acts in their classrooms. The processes are interwoven and overlap but, at one point or another, teachers need to attend to three aspects of assessment as part of learning and instruction: identifying goals and benchmarks; gathering portfolio and performance assessments through observing, sampling, and interviewing; and reflecting and using information in instructional decision making.

Identifying Literacy Goals and Their Manifestations

Identifying Literacy Goals

We began this book by grounding the creation of emergent literacy classrooms in a comprehensive set of goals. These goals become the foundation for assessments. In the framework of goals that we presented in Table 3.1, comprehending and composing are central. We also identified several subprocesses as being *necessary* for young students' independence. These include identifying and spelling words and awareness of literary elements. We also described *interim* processes such as phonemic awareness and letter naming. These processes are important during the initial stages of literacy learning but are no longer a focus of literacy instruction once children move into independent reading and writing.

Because becoming literate involves a general progression, we expect that most emergent literacy programs will include this core set of goals. However, for individual teachers and classrooms, the emphasis given to a particular goal, the meaning ascribed to it, and the language used to define and describe it will vary. The discussion around the United States' national goals in literacy stands as evidence that, as individuals and as groups, professional educators need to engage in numerous conversations with one another about the form that goals take at particular points in children's development (see Pearson, 1993). One forum for such interactions is around identifying benchmarks of literacy goals for students at particular points in their reading and writing development.

Defining Benchmarks

Just as educators must define their goals, they must be able to describe what attainment of particular goals would look like for the students in their classrooms. What does the goal that "children read appropriate books fluently" mean for first graders? Does this goal manifest itself with second graders in the same forms? *Benchmarks* are the manifestations of goals (Au, 1994). Benchmarks can be thought of as points along the way to developing competency. The dictionary definition of *benchmark* is a "marked point of known or assumed elevation" (American Heritage Dictionary, 1992). Marking or describing the critical characteristics of "particular elevations" in a goal is an important part of the process because the descriptions can be thought of as guideposts. The benchmarks are the reference points for determining progress and plotting direction as teachers plan their instruction, select materials, and interact with parents and fellow teachers about their students' reading and writing development.

While there will be commonalities in goals and benchmarks for beginning readers and writers across settings, each group of teachers will define their goals and describe benchmarks in appropriate ways for their students and teaching contexts. Just as children learn by interacting with one another and with teachers around meaningful tasks, conversations among teachers about benchmarks are fundamental to planning curriculum and assessment practices. As teachers create their own benchmarks in study groups, collaborative projects, or school/district teams, they can consult sources such as the National English/Language Standards (NCTE/IRA, 1996), their own state and district English/language arts frameworks, as well as those of other school systems (see Au, 1994).

To illustrate the nature of benchmarks, we generated a set that is congruent with the goals and instructional program that have been described throughout this volume. Consequently, the benchmarks that appear in Table 8.1 are derived from the critical processes of literacy acquisition that we described in the first section of this volume (see Table 3.1). Further, the tasks used to establish these critical processes are precisely the same as the literacy acts and materials we have consistently described as forming the literacy acts and materials of an emergent literacy classroom. When assessments capture the critical goals of an emergent literacy program, the tasks will be no different from the meaningful use of literacy that comprises the daily lives of children in their classrooms.

We direct attention to three features of our sample benchmarks in Table 8.1: (a) designating developmental phases, not ages, (b) grounding benchmarks within tasks, not in generic proficiencies or traits, and (c) focusing on central and necessary, not interim processes. All three features are congruent with the emergent literacy perspective.

First, notice that the progression is marked in terms of phases (one through three). We did this to avoid the problem faced by young children who have few literacy experiences prior to entering school. For such children, age expectations not "lived up to" become the basis for ongoing school failure. They are seen as students to remediate, rather than 25 students on a journey toward literacy. By using phases to lay out our expectations, we instead convey that particular behaviors are to be encouraged and form the basis for continued development, regardless of a child's age.

Second, we choose to view children's proficiencies relative to particular tasks to underscore how children can perform quite differently as a function of the text and the context. When children's literacy is viewed in relation to the task rather than to ability, the dimensions of the task can be scaffolded to determine what it is that children can do and what it is that they are still learning. In effect, by labeling the task, not the child, we make visible the nature of support a child might need to learn and become independent.

Third, we view interim processes as temporary supports to avoid any expectations that children would need to perform these processes isolated from meaningful literacy uses. Isolated performances on interim processes have often been used as hurdles that children must scale before they are involved in meaningful literacy use. By embedding the interim processes within meaningful literacy use, instruction and assessment support their role as interim processes—that is, as temporary supports, not as ends in themselves.

Gathering Information

We noted earlier that assessment from an emergent literacy perspective was dynamic, diverse, and part of daily classroom events. These assessments take quite different forms from the single-event tests characteristic of earlier perspectives on children's learning. To better represent dynamic and diverse literacy use in daily events, portfolios and performance assessments have replaced tests as the primary forms of assessment.

TABLE 8.1   Benchmarks for Comprehending and Composing over the Early Literacy Period

Process	Early Literacy Period		
	Phase One	**Phase Two**	**Phase Three**
Comprehending	With an unfamiliar, Level 1 book (e.g., *Cat on the Mat,* Table 5.6), a reader is able to: • give a meaningful reading, using all text systems including written message, illustrations, and text pattern, • self-correct nonmeaningful miscues, • provide personal response to book, • retell the gist of book.	With an unfamiliar, Level 3 book (e.g., *Across the Stream,* Table 5.6), a reader is able to: • give a meaningful, fluent reading, using all text systems, • self-correct nonmeaningful miscues, • provide a personal response to text, • retell gist of message and respond to questions about potential inferences.	With an unfamiliar, Level 5 book (e.g., *Morning Star,* Table 5.6), a reader is able to: • give a meaningful, fluent reading, • self-correct nonmeaningful miscues, • provide a personal, written response, • provide a written summary of important parts of book.
Composing	A student's portfolio of writing includes: • Samples of messages of interest/ importance to child, • Messages include descriptions of ideas, • Samples indicate movement toward early spelling and conventions such as spacing, left to right.	A student's portfolio of writing includes: • Samples of messages with elaborated ideas as well as simple descriptions, • Spelling and conventions are sufficient for readers to comprehend gist of message.	A student's portfolio of writing includes: • Samples with genres such as stories and simple reports as well as personal narratives, • Spelling and conventions support communication of message.

Teachers who have, in the past, collected samples of students' work over time may find it helpful to begin with these collections, refining them to become portfolios. Similarly, teachers whose students are engaged in meaningful use of literacy within a variety of contexts could build their performance assessments into these contexts. Teachers obtain relevant information on students' competencies and progress by observing them, sampling their work from a range of literacy contexts, and interviewing them during classroom literacy contexts. We begin this section with an overview of portfolio and performance assessments, followed by descriptions of the information on emergent literacy learning that can be gained through observing, sampling students' work, and interviewing.

Portfolio and Performance Assessments

When assessments are true portfolio and performance assessments, they take forms quite different from generically published paper-and-pencil tests. In portfolios, illustrations of work have been systematically collected and, perhaps, annotated so that someone examining the portfolio would have insights into the competence of the person whose work is represented. Portfolios have been used historically for evaluating professionals, such as artists and photographers. Because the best work of the professional is included in the portfolio, it can be shared with clients, the professional's ultimate judge. Similarly, in today's emergent literacy classrooms, many teachers have begun helping students develop portfolios of their literacy use, systematically collecting evidence of students' literacy use, and annotating the items to explain what they represent. For example, students' writing portfolios would contain representative compositions produced across a school year. Like the photographer's client, the students' teacher can evaluate students' competency in literacy, and, important to an educational setting, areas that reflect growth as well as areas that would benefit from additional instruction. Further, teachers can interact with children, family members, and colleagues about students' strengths and areas that require attention.

Some teachers have found it useful to have both "showcase" portfolios and "working" portfolios (Valencia, 1991). Children and teachers may identify those selections that go into the showcase portfolio, which follows children across the primary grades as evidence of their best work. A working portfolio is a place for keeping work in progress. The samples maintained in a working portfolio can serve as important sources for discussion. For example, in a working writing portfolio, students may use partially completed illustrations to develop a related story with their peers. A work in progress may be used to interact about growth toward conventional spelling in a teacher-student conference.

Teachers play critical roles in developing both showcase and working portfolios. Teachers are critical in determining how entries in the working portfolio may be used in instruction and in classroom literacy use. They are critical in guiding students' selection of entries for their showcase portfolio.

By separating the working from the showcase portfolio, teachers can help students differentiate between concepts such as "final text" and "work in progress" and can help them begin to develop their own standards and criteria for what constitutes their "best" piece of work. By virtue of their flexibility and open-endedness, portfolios permit teachers and children to add and delete selections. In this way, evidence of children's learning can be studied over time. Parents, teachers in subsequent grades, and even school board members can share in this reflection, using evidence of students' work as the basis for their analysis.

A second form of assessment in today's emergent literacy classrooms, the performance assessment, is consistent with the portfolio. The key difference is that performance assessments come from specific, meaningful literacy acts within particular time periods in contrast to the more open-ended formats of portfolio assessments. In fact, it is the design of the literacy act that defines the performance assessment. This might involve defining the following context: Children listen to a narrative read aloud by their teacher, create a journal entry that includes their personal response to the narrative, then join in talking about the books with their peers, first in partners, then in a whole-class setting. Such an event could yield a range of literacy products such as the students' written response and transcripts of the students' contributions to a partner discussion and to the whole-class discussion. A contrasting performance assessment context might involve asking children to read orally from a relatively familiar text and a relatively unfamiliar one, recording their oral renditions using running records, then interviewing the students individually about their views of themselves as readers.

The performance assessment tasks may occur within a short session (e.g., 30 minutes) or may be extended across several days. For example, some schools create an annual book fair, where students contribute individually authored books to the school library. In this way, the school has an ongoing record of its students' writing. The book writing in which students engage could form a meaningful context for a performance assessment on writing, since students would be engaged in all aspects of creating their books. With performance assessments, particular events are designated for taking stock and summarizing children's performances. These events are no different from the events that happen regularly—children read, children write, children perform a play based on a favorite book, and children talk with their teacher about their reading and writing. Note that in all the examples of the performance assessment, the products (e.g., written response, interview responses, running records, student drafts) could become part of the students' portfolio(s).

In summary, portfolios and performance assessments complement one another and both rely on the processes of *observing, sampling,* and *interviewing.* The information that is gained from these three processes may be gathered from ongoing classroom events or from performance assessment events. The resulting artifacts can be maintained in portfolios. Through *observing,* teachers learn about the literacy processes in which students engage. Through *sampling* students' work, teachers learn their students' grasp of strategies and knowledge across different tasks and contexts. Through *interviews,* teachers hear students talk about the processes they use and the growth they see in their literacy development.

Information from Observations

Throughout this book, we have illustrated the understanding about young children's literacy learning that teachers gain through observation or "kid-watching" (Goodman, 1985). The composition in Vignette 6.2 shows Eugenie's connections between reading and writing as she draws from *The Cat in the Hat* to create her statement, "Cat, don't sit on the hat!" A teacher observing the peer interaction in Vignette 4.2 would note James's unfamiliarity with letter names as he repeatedly asks his peers about forming letters.

This role of teachers as child observers is fundamental to who teachers are within an emergent literacy perspective. Through their actions, statements, and choices, children reveal valuable information about what they know and what they have yet to learn. There are opportunities for teachers to observe their students' learning processes and knowledge in any classroom context. Teachers constantly observe their students but often do not document these observations, storing information in "the mental file cabinet" as a teacher in one project described it (Hiebert, Hutchinson, & Raines, 1991, p. 100). Storing information inside one's head makes retrieval and reflection more challenging than need be. The impression that stays in mind after an interaction may not necessarily be the most important or relevant. In Vignette 4.2, a teacher might leave the interaction believing simply that Kevin and Monica are doing James's work for him, rather than recognizing their scaffolding as evidence of their literacy learning since the beginning of the year. As an event recedes in memory, information may become difficult to extract. Robert Wortman, an emergent literacy teacher, describes the benefits of keeping notes as part of his daily routines as follows (cited in Matlin & Wortman, 1989, pp. 53–54):

> Although it was not easy for me, I began to carry a clipboard to make notes to myself during the day and to keep samples of children's work. There were at least three ways this form of record keeping helped. First, I had a record of children's strengths; I knew which children needed to continue working independently and which needed individual or group attention. Second, it encouraged me when I felt that a child was not making progress. I could look at the notes or samples and see that progress might be slow, but it was being made. Third, I had concrete examples to show parents when we had conferences.

Wortman's description of carrying a clipboard as he worked with his students illustrates one way in which teachers can record their observations. Other teachers keep handy a stack of sticky notes on which they jot down notes. Another strategy is to focus on students' strategy use during a particular part of the day or within a particular activity (e.g., pair reading), as the second-grade teacher in Vignette 8.1 did. Because the students described in Vignette 8.1 spent a substantial amount of literacy time each day in reading with one another, it makes good sense that their teacher wants to understand their strategy use during this time.

Observations can be particularly revealing in ways not available from analyses of students' written work. We present three examples to show how observations embedded in classroom events help teachers understand their children's learning of central, necessary, and interim literacy processes. The first example, choosing books, illustrates insights into students' *central* literacy process of comprehending. The second, oral reading strategies, illustrates how informative observations can be about the *necessary* processes of word recognition. The third example, observations of children's conversations while writing, illustrates how observations provide an important source for insights into the *interim* processes of letter naming and phonemic awareness.

Choosing Books.   Observations of children's strategies for selecting books can provide insights into their purposes for reading, what they think makes a book worth reading, and what they think it means to "understand" a book. An illustration of the information that can be gained from such observations comes from Mervar and Hiebert (1989) who observed the weekly school library visit of second-grade students from a literature-based classroom. They observed both the number of minutes each student spent in making selections and strategies a child used to make his or her selections. They noticed that all the children used a sampling strategy, looking at a number of books before making their final choice. Sometimes the students read a part of the books to themselves, sometimes they read aloud to a peer. Sometimes they used a card catalog to find books on a specific topic or a favorite author or illustrator. Such observations helped the researchers recognize the literate basis for students' book choices and the importance students seemed to place on the book's content (e.g., reading from the book, finding specific topics) or on their histories as literacy users (e.g., favorite authors and illustrators). Relying on such factors reflects a focus on comprehension and meaning for these young children.

Mervar and Hiebert (1989) also conducted similar observations of a classroom of students who did not have literature as the basis for their instruction, but instead read textbook selections, such as *Tiny* which we described in Chapter 5. They found that many of these children, during the library visit, were less focused on strategic book selection. For example, some children simply chose a book from the shelf without examining it. Others waited for their teacher to select a book for them. Such observed behaviors reflect that students had less understanding of how readers choose books, and less knowledge of book features that may contribute to their comprehension and enjoyment, than did the other group of second graders. This example contrasted students in two different types of classrooms, but similar observations within a single classroom have the potential to reveal individual differences among the children.

Oral Reading Strategies.   A second area where observational methods of assessment can be especially useful is in understanding students' word recognition strategies. There are numerous occasions for such observations in emergent literacy classrooms. In Vignette 8.1, a second-grade teacher's observational notes were useful in establishing that one child often took over the work of figuring out new words when reading with a buddy. This helping behavior by some children means that others do not have the chance to apply strategies themselves. Further, the prominent readers in the dyads were not making visible the strategies they used to figure out the unknown words.

In addition to observations of oral reading during regular classroom events, opportunities for observation may be developed as a planned part of the performance assessments that are conducted periodically to determine children's reading of a particular set of passages. Observations of children's physical actions and comments as they read aloud add information not captured by running records of children's reading. What is observed is likely to vary as a function of children's reading development. For example, at the very beginning stages of reading development, teachers may wish to focus their observations during a performance assessment on the match between children's oral reading and the words on the page. Children who have memorized a book may be saying a phrase that belongs in the book but doesn't match what is on the page.

Observations of children's behaviors during oral reading will focus on one or more of the following elements at different points during the emergent literacy years:

- speed of reading, including the manner in which children chunk the text,
- tracking of print,
- glancing at illustrations and at subsequent parts of the text,
- requests for assistance,
- self-correcting miscues that distort meaningfulness or syntax, and
- comments about the topic, the task, or the text.

As teachers observe such behaviors, they can gain insights into students' developing knowledge of necessary processes used during reading.

Writing Center Activities.   Illustrations throughout this book have highlighted how, through observations, teachers can gather rich information on *interim* processes such as letter naming and phonemic awareness. Such observations often occur in the classroom writing center. In Chapter 7, we described the Right Start in Reading project. Teachers participating in that project have found that observations during the daily activities of writing on acetate slates and in journals can be invaluable. For example, one teacher observed how long it took Miguel to write anything in his journal. She watched closely over a few days and was surprised to find that Miguel sang the alphabet song to locate every letter as he tracked the letters on the alphabet chart that went around the blackboard. If he were writing "dog," for example, he would mouth and track the letters through "d." Then he would write the letter "d" on his page. Next he would mouth the song and track the letters until he got to "o," at which point he wrote the letter down. Then he did the same thing with "g." Such information convinced her, early in the project, that observations were critical to understanding students' interim literacy processes.

Sampling.   Sampling refers to collecting examples of children's work from a variety of literacy acts to provide insights into students' grasp of literacy knowledge in general, and the strategies they use in different tasks and with different materials. These work samples come from typical classroom literacy acts (e.g., summaries of children's oral reading during a pair-reading activity), as well as activities they may have engaged in outside the classroom (e.g., writing they have completed at home, lists of books read outside the classroom). The journal entries in Vignette 8.2 illustrate samples of children's writing from a typical literacy act in Linda Pils's classroom. Brooke and Larry's interactions, described in Vignette 8.1, provide an opportunity for sampling. Their teacher could have taken notes about the miscues they had made; that is, record the students' responses that differed from the words in the text. Sometimes, teachers may wish to create specific tasks from which to sample students' literacy performances. For example, a teacher may use a set of increasingly complex books that students read from throughout the school year. The teacher records the students' strategy use each time they read from one of the books in the set, providing both insights into their ability to apply learned strategies in increasingly complex situations and a record of their progress over time. Such occasions allow teachers and children to step back from everyday classroom interactions and to study children's strategies and accomplishments from the vantage of the benchmarks, without initiating testlike tasks that are unfamiliar to the students or isolated from meaningful literacy activities.

In the Right Start in Reading project that we described in Chapter 7, Hiebert and her colleagues used sampling methods to gather information about the participating students' progress over the school year. They created a series of contexts that were virtually indistinguishable from the daily classroom literacy events, forming performance assessments that students participated in at the beginning, middle, and end of the year. By creating these performance assessments, the teachers were able to gather the samples of students' literacy performances that they drew on to make instructional decisions, to satisfy the accountability mandates of Title I, and to respond to parents', teachers', students' and researchers' needs for information about individual students as well as overall group progress. To illustrate the collection of compositions, running records, and writing and reading of words, we focus on two children, Yolanda and Matthew (both pseudonyms) who were taught by, respectively, Pam Chrisman and Brenda Fifer (again, pseudonyms), Title I teachers in the Right Start in Reading project (Hiebert et al., 1992).

Compositions.   Compositions represent messages that children wish to share with others and, relative to other types of data sources, are relatively easy to gather during a performance assessment or within everyday classroom literacy events. As we discussed in Chapter 6, students value their compositions, which makes this writing an important candidate for including in their portfolios.

In Figures 8.1 and 8.2, we present samples of Yolanda's and Matthew's fall, winter, and spring writing samples. First, there is the information about a child's growth over the academic year. In Yolanda's writing, we see growth as she moves from using a picture to represent her story to writing a short story about the cat and the dog playing. In this story, she demonstrates her beginning writing vocabulary (e.g., conventionally spelling several words such as "the," "dog," "cat"). Notice that by the end of the year, she is writing a personal narrative about things that matter to her: her dolls. In her writing, she shows greater flexibility of word choices, continued success in conventionally spelling words (e.g., "because"), while she also shows more risk-taking as she applies sound-symbol knowledge to approximate "other dollies" in the last line of her text.

Matthew begins the year by refusing to produce a message, even when encouraged to use whatever means he would want for communicating, including drawing a picture. By winter, Matthew was willing to produce a text but chose to copy from an enlarged book that was in his line of vision, *Splosh* (Cowley, 1981). Unlike the fall assessment, he is intent on putting something down on paper; however, since he was not particularly concerned about the content, he ended up simply copying random words from the book he could see from his desk. By the spring, like Yolanda, Matthew writes a paragraph of sentences on a topic that is personally meaningful to him—his dog. He elaborates on why he likes his dog, including an anecdote of how he plays with his dog after the lawn is mowed.

Yolanda's and Matthew's writing samples represent important teacher choices about time (i.e., When do I sample students' writing?), texts (i.e., What kind of product should I include?), and tasks (What kind of assignment should I initiate to produce the texts?). In short, each teacher chose particular writing contexts to sample. They had access to many more samples of children's writing and they had rich information on the contexts in which the writing was done. For example, Yolanda and Matthew wrote almost daily in their journals as part of small-group lessons. However, for the purpose of getting an overall sense of the writing proficiency of the many students in a classroom, asking their children to respond to the same task at different times in the school year was useful in establishing fundamental patterns in writing. Sampling reflects the importance of choices because,

---

FIGURE 8.1 **Samples of Yolanda's Composing During Grade One**

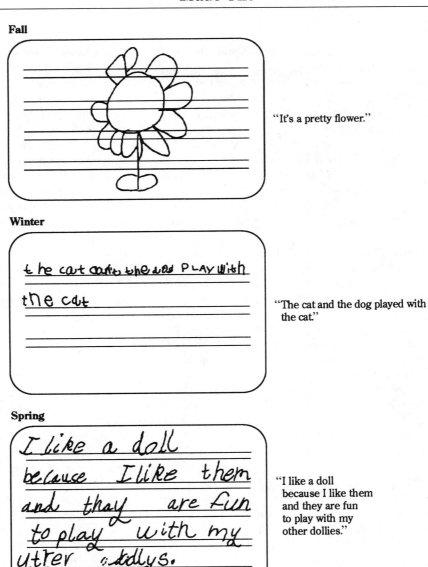

Fall

"It's a pretty flower."

Winter

the cat and the dog PLAY with the cat

"The cat and the dog played with the cat."

Spring

I like a doll because I like them and thay are fun to play with my utrer dollys.

"I like a doll because I like them and they are fun to play with my other dollies."

Reprinted by permission of Jacalyn M. Colt, Instructional Coordinator, Title I, St. Vrain Valley School District, Longmont, CO.

FIGURE 8.2   **Samples of Matthew's Composing During Grade One**

Fall

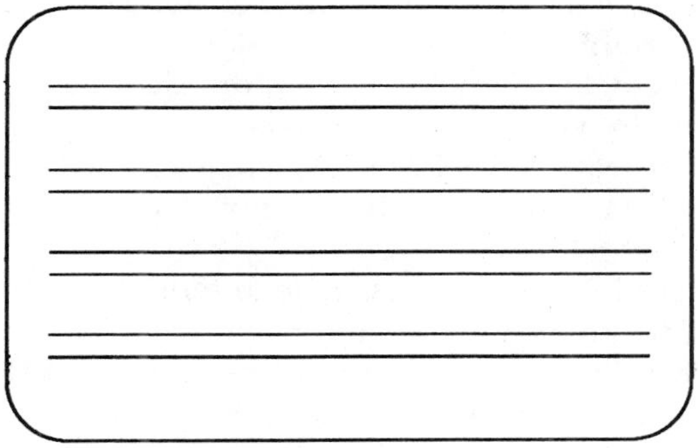

"I don't want to write."

Winter

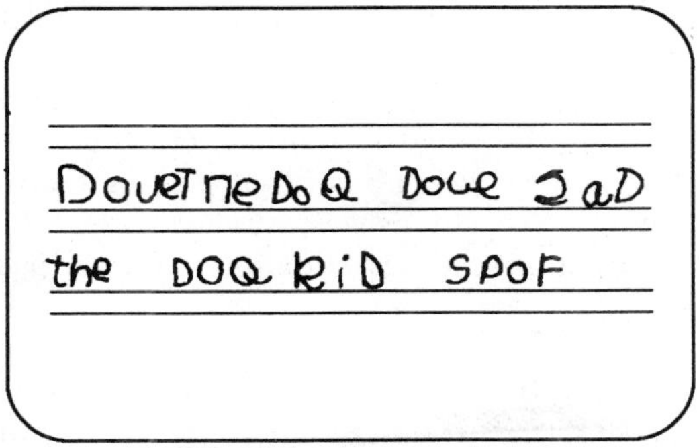

Dover ne Do Q Dowe Ja D
the DOQ RiD SPOF

"Donkey the dog Donkey said the dog rid splosh."

Spring

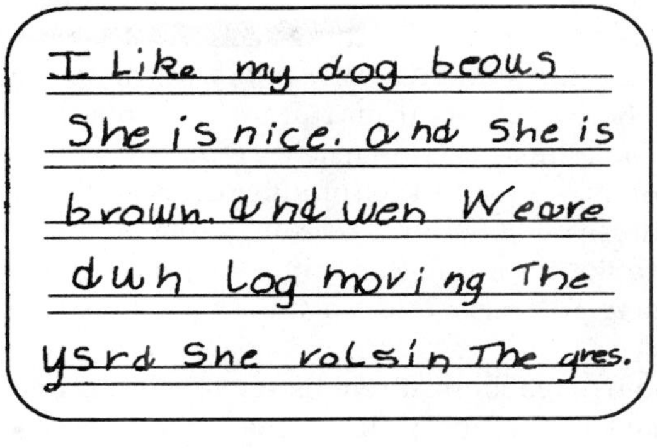

I Like my dog beous
She is nice. a nd She is
brown. a nd wen We are
d u h Log movi ng The
ysrd She rolsin The gres.

"I like my dog because she is nice. And she is brown. And when we are done lawn mowing the yard she rolls in the grass."

Reprinted by permission of Jacalyn M. Colt, Instructional Coordinator, Title I, St. Vrain Valley School District, Longmont, CO.

by definition, the sample will be only a small set of children's overall literacy productions.

Like the other teachers in the Right Start project, Matthew's and Yolanda's teachers draw on their knowledge of the contexts in which their students write to describe movement along the continuum of benchmarks. Matthew's refusal to write in the performance assessment task was interpreted in relation to his struggles in the daily journal writing in the classroom. He also struggled in other contexts in which he needed to spell words. These different sources of information led his teacher to consider one plausible explanation for Matthew's stance toward writing: He was not able to produce all of the letters.

Matthew's teacher encouraged him to use magnetic letters in the daily journal writing tasks. He then wrote his message in his journal, saying the letters aloud as he wrote them. His response in the winter indicated that copying messages had begun to dominate his perception of what counted as writing. After a spelling assessment revealed that he had grown considerably in his fluency in producing letters, he was encouraged to write his messages without the support of the magnetic letters. By spring, Matthew was able to identify important ideas and communicate them.

In addition to providing insights into an individual child's growth, such samples also help teachers understand the range of competencies among the students in their classrooms. This knowledge is helpful in making instructional decisions about the content to be taught, as well as management decisions such as identifying buddies for paired readings or identifying participants for small, short-term groups.

Running Records.   In addition to drawing on samples of students' writing, teachers will also want to sample students' reading competencies. Because reading silently provides little to no information about students' strategy use or letter-sound knowledge, one important method for sampling students' reading competencies is to create a "running record" of their oral reading. Running records are the notes that teachers take while listening to children read orally (Clay, 1985). Excerpts from running records that we have shared throughout the book illustrate the insights teachers gain from running records. In this section, we describe the running record and related teachers' decisions for sampling students' oral reading using running records. Then we describe how teachers in the Right Start in Reading project gathered running records, using Yolanda's and Matthew's participation to illustrate the process.

In primary-level classrooms, teachers often listen to children read aloud—as part of lessons, share times, and visits to the library center. As students read, teachers can gain insights into the ways in which students are applying what they have learned by attending to the nature of the mistakes students make. Goodman (1973) introduced the concept of miscues, rather than errors, opening the door for a more interpretative analysis of oral reading. In earlier forms of records of children's oral reading called informal reading inventories, children's deviations from or changes of the text were uniformly regarded as errors. Each error was counted the same and used to establish children's reading levels. Goodman proposed that responses that differ from the words in the text or "miscues" be viewed as the most concrete evidence that teachers have of beginning readers' underlying strategies and constructions of the purposes and forms of text. From this perspective, the first step in making sense of children's reading samples is to examine what it is they can do. Readers make basically four types of miscues during oral reading: omission, insertion, substitution, and repetition (Allington, 1984). Noting both when such miscues occur and how students may attempt to correct their miscues is the primary focus of a running record.

[handwritten margin note: Running Records w/out copy of text]

Clay (1985) illustrated how documenting children's oral reading could be made easier than was typically the case during more formalized testing situations such as the informal reading inventories introduced decades earlier. In a "running record," marks are placed on a regular piece of paper (a photocopied form of the text is not necessary). Checks are used when children read a word correctly. Dashes are used when children omit a word. For substitutions, the substituted word is placed over the word in the text. Words that are repeated are written out with an R over them, and a superscript with the letters "sc" (self-correction) are noted when the student responds with a match to the text after several attempts.

Sampling Yolanda's and Matthew's reading competence through a running record involves a series of teacher choices similar to those made about collecting compositions: Choices about time, texts, and tasks. Additionally, one set of decisions is unique to running records. To study patterns in children's oral reading, teachers need to jot down notes either *during* the event or—if the oral reading is recorded on audio- or videotape—after it. Thus, teachers need to make choices about the kinds of notes they will take *before* children's oral reading.

Samples of children's oral reading can be gained in the course of daily lessons and activities. Pils, the teacher in Vignette 8.3, describes a technique that is quite doable in a classroom setting: listening to "one-minute reads" by children. The teacher moves around the classroom (or, the teacher can ask the children to move to a place where she is sitting). The teacher has a notebook or clipboard, making a running record of students' reading from the text they have in front of them. Another means for sampling children's oral reading through running records is to ask children to audiotape short selections, including the episodes of reading with peers such as those illustrated in Vignette 8.1. Teachers then can listen to the audiotapes at a later time, developing a running record from the tape. These two methods share common approaches to decisions about texts (i.e., the child's current book), but vary in time (i.e., real time versus delayed) and task (i.e., individual face-to-face reading aloud to the teacher versus paired or individual reading while being recorded).

At some points throughout the school year, teachers will want to gather samples of children's oral reading with texts and tasks that have some of the parameters of informal reading inventories. Specifically, teachers may want to ask students to respond to short passages reflecting different degrees of difficulty, rather than simply reading aloud from a student-selected book or from a single text at one level of difficulty. If, for example, trade book exemplars are used as the basis for the reading program, one or two exemplars for each level would be selected for assessment purposes. The books are drawn from the instructional program, the classroom, and the school library. Teachers then define the task in terms of the amount of text from each book that students will be asked to read (e.g., a section from a book, a specific number of words or sentences from each book). Children begin with the easiest passage, then are asked to read through the ordered passages until that time when they provide nonmeaningful miscues on more than approximately one out of ten words, when they begin to read in a slow, halting fashion, or both.

The running records for Yolanda and Matthew that resulted through a series of choices by Pam Chrisman, Brenda Fifer, and the other teachers in the Right Start project appear in Tables 8.2 and 8.3. Except for the first level,

TABLE 8.2 Excerpts from Running Records for Yolanda: Fall, Winter, Spring of First Grade

Point in Time	Passage Level	Text	Yolanda's Rendition
Fall	Illustrated Predictable[1]	The big hill. We climb up.	Climbing people. Once the big boy tried to get the little boy.
Winter	Illustrated Predictable[2]	We climb up. . . . Then we climb up again.	We climb up. . . . There we come up again.
	Primer[3]	Pat sat by the tree. "Mom wants me to work," Pat said.	Pat sat by the tree. "Mom went me to walk," Pat said.
Spring	Grade 1[4]	He had something for Show and Tell in a big paper bag.	He had so—something for Showing and Tell in a big paper bag.
	Grade 2[5]	Whiz! The baseball went right by me, and I struck at the air! "Strike one," called the man. I could feel my legs begin to shake!	Iz! The baseball went right by me, and I struck at the air! "Strike on," called the man. I could feel my legs being to shake!

[1]From J. Cowley (1983), *The Big Hill.* Auckland, New Zealand: Shortland Publications, Ltd., pp. 1–2.
[2]From Cowley (1983), pp. 2, 8.
[3]From M.L. Woods and A.J. Moe (1989), *Analytical Reading Inventory* (4th ed.). Columbus, OH: Merrill Publishing Co., p. 45.
[4]From Woods and Moe (1989), p. 46.
[5]From Woods and Moe (1989), p. 47.

TABLE 8.3   Excerpts from Running Records for Matthew: Fall, Winter, Spring of First Grade

Point in Time	Passage Level	Text	Matthew's Rendition
Fall	Illustrated Predictable[1]	The big hill. We climb up.	They're running. He fell.
Winter	Illustrated Predictable[2]	We run down. . . . Then we climb up again.	We ran down. . . . Then we climb up it.
	Primer[3]	Pat sat by the tree. "Mom wants me to work," Pat said.	Pat sat Pat the it/the. mom yes me to walk Pat said.
Spring	Grade 2[4]	Whiz! The baseball went right by me, and I struck at the air.	Waz/Whiz! The baseball wen/went right by me, and I struck at the air.
	Grade 3[5]	"Boxer!" he shouted, "Now I recognize those green eyes of yours! Let's get out of here!"	"Boxer!" he shouted, "Now I recoddentalize those green eyes of yours! Let's go out of here!"

[1]From J. Cowley (1983), *The Big Hill*. Auckland, New Zealand: Shortland Publications, Ltd., pp. 1–2.
[2]From Cowley (1983), pp. 3, 8.
[3]From M. L. Woods and A. J. Moe (1989), *Analytical Reading Inventory* (4th ed.). Columbus, OH: Merrill Publishing Co., p. 45.
[4]From Woods and Moe (1989), p. 47.
[5]From Woods and Moe (1989), p. 48.

which used an illustrated, predictable book, the passages on which these running records were based came from a graded series of passages or an informal reading inventory (IRI) (Woods & Moe, 1989). The excerpts of the running records in Tables 8.2 and 8.3 indicate a rich and extensive database on Yolanda's and Matthew's reading over the course of first grade. We will discuss ways to reflect on this information and plot instructional directions as we proceed with the chapter. But a survey of the information in Tables 8.2 and 8.3 indicates that Yolanda and Matthew have made a substantial amount of progress as first graders. They both began at the early stages of book-reading responses according to Sulzby's (1985) levels (see Table 3.2). Both were commenting on the action of the characters in the illustrations. By winter, both children were attending to the words in the illustrated predictable book. Each child made miscues but these miscues showed that each was using syntactic and semantic knowledge to create meaning. By the end of first grade, both children could read a passage designated for the grade in which they will be in September.

Writing and Reading Words.   In Chapter 3, we described children's literacy acquisition as an interaction between text-level strategies and word-level strategies. The samples of composing and comprehending that we described earlier provide evidence of children's text-level strategies. Their word-level strategies can be studied with these text-level samples once children have some conventional reading and writing skills. However, until children have some conventional reading and writing proficiency, the tasks of reading and writing texts do not provide any indication of children's understanding about words. For example, in the fall, Matthew is stymied when confronted with the task of writing a text; in the winter, he copies a text within his line of vision. From these tasks, we do not know whether he still would be stymied if able to focus on a single word rather than on a message as a whole. That is, is he able to try out hypotheses about the associations between sounds and letters in writing or in reading individual words?

Just as there are interim strategies that disappear in importance as children progress in a literacy program, so, too, there are interim assessment tasks that yield critical information about beginning readers and writers. We illustrate such assessments through word-level tasks that assess children's knowledge of word patterns and ability to recognize and to spell written words.

Yolanda's and Matthew's fall, winter, and spring responses to reading a list of words with common word patterns are noted in Table 8.4; their responses when asked to write the words are in Table 8.5. Each of the lists from which these words came had been developed to emphasize a particular set of patterns (Hiebert, Burton, & Goudvis, 1989). Words with more advanced patterns which children had not yet been taught were included in these lists in order to determine whether children had generalized their word pattern knowledge (Juel, 1991). Thus, the last several words in each list have patterns from the next developmental stage. For example, List 1 emphasizes words with simple letter-sound correspondences, but ends with words that have complex vowel associations: (e.g., "hide," "seat").

By comparing the children's reading and writing responses in the fall and winter, we can see one of the reasons for using common patterns across the two tasks. While Yolanda names letters in the reading task, her responses to writing show that she has a good sense of the letters associated with most initial consonants. That is, when her teacher presented the word "mat," Yolanda did not say the word, but rather said the individual letters: m-a-t. However, when asked to write the word "hat," she wrote "hjt," indicating her awareness of both the initial and final consonant.

A similar type of word list could be created for examining students' responses to high-frequency words. Most published informal reading inventories include such lists of high-frequency words (see, for example, Silvaroli, 1990; Woods & Moe, 1989). Teachers could easily devise their own assessments by taking a group of 10 or 15 words from the 50 most-frequent words listed in Table 3.4.

Other tasks have also been proposed as measures of children's application of strategies in reading and writing words. In Clay's (1985) battery of literacy tasks, children are asked to write as many words as they can in a short time period. Depending on the nature of instruction and the goals of

TABLE 8.4 Reading Words[1]

	Yolanda			Matthew		
	Fall	**Winter**	**Spring**	**Fall**	**Winter**	**Spring**
List 1						
mat	m-a-t	✓		m	✓	
pig	p-i-h	✓		i	/p	
sun	s-u-r	✓		s	/s/	
jet	j-e-t	✓		e	/j//e//t/	
top	t-o-p	✓		o	toop/tube	
go	q-o	✓		o	Is that a q?	
hide	n-i-b-e	hid		e	NR	
seat	s-e-o-t	sit		s	/s//e/ sand sun	
car	c-a-r	✓		c	cat/cowr	
List 2						
wish			✓			✓
cry			✓			✓
plane			plan			✓
green			✓			✓
barn			bârn			burn[sc]
brown			✓			✓
boy			✓			✓
cupcake			✓			✓
puppy			✓			✓
List 3						
why			✓			way
choke			chook			✓
throat			throught			✓
tire			✓			✓
found			✓			✓
shook			✓			show[sc]
railroad			✓			✓
circus			cercis			cercos
clover			✓			✓

[1]These are selected words from lists developed by Hiebert et al. (1989).

the curriculum, teachers can create or select from a range of tasks that capture children's beginning literacy development.

Information from Interviewing

Unlike a typical teacher-student interaction where the teacher is the source of knowledge, in an interview, the student provides information. Interviews

TABLE 8.5		Writing Words[1]			
	Yolanda			Matthew	
	Fall	**Winter**	**Spring**	**Fall**	**Winter**	**Spring**
List 1						
hat	hjt	√	√	I	nat	√
dig	DA	√	√	D	ll	√
fun	FL	√	√	[NR]	fo	√
net	iN	√	√	A	NoT	√
mop	MI	√	√	[NR]	√	√
so	ST	soj	√	C	√	√
ride	MOT	rid	rid	A	rid	√
meat	NOLT	MeI	meet	K	met	√
far	FAOM	fr	√	A	rr	for
List 2						
dish			√			√
fly			√			√
came			√			√
tree			√			√
farm						form
down			√			√
toy			√			√
inside			insiad			√
funny			√			funy
List 3						
shy			shi			√
while			whil			wile
queen			quen			quean
fire			fir			fier
round			rand			√
crook			crok			crowk
pinecone			pincon			√
napkin			√			√
tiger			√			√

[1]These are selected words from lists developed by Hiebert et al. (1989).

can occur as part of daily classroom events, as did the impromptu interview in Vignette 8.3, though, even with informal interviews, teachers need to have clear goals as well as ways of documenting the information. This on-the-spot interview takes the form of asking children to elaborate or explain what the teacher has noted in his or her observations.

More extended opportunities to interview children about their work also need to be built into the schedule of the emergent literacy classroom. Regularly scheduled conferences when individual students meet with the teacher have become part of the routine of many classrooms. When such conferences are used as a time for reflecting on progress and identifying goals, their value can be immeasurable. Questions that clarify students' understandings and strategies and ones that probe children's knowledge, such as the kindergartner's awareness of additional sounds in "rainbow," can be part of these conferences. In addition, conferences can be a time when teachers and students reflect on students' growth over a span of time and identify future goals. Interviews are, in effect, purposeful questioning that yields records of children's responses.

While an interview between teacher and student may have the appearance of spontaneity, interviews that generate useful information result from careful design. Interviews serve two purposes: (1) to establish students' proficiencies under different conditions (scaffolding) and (2) to establish students' knowledge about specific tasks or questions (responding to specific tasks). A single interview may accomplish one or both of these functions, with a teacher's strategies differing depending on the type of information of interest.

Scaffolding Tasks. Interviews, or segments of interviews, that focus on scaffolding attempt to determine students' proficiencies under different conditions. This relates closely to establishing students' zone of proximal development, which we described in Chapter 2. This zone represents the actual level at which children function independently and the potential level at which they operate when supported by an adult or more capable peer. Recall Ben's response, described in Vignette 3.3, to the task of reading *Would You Like to Fly?* Essentially, he refused to read. If Ben had been engaged in an interview to determine his proficiency under different conditions, various scaffolds would be provided, helping Ben identify what he is able to read. For example, his teacher could ask him to locate a favorite book in the classroom library and tell about it. This might have revealed his ability to remember particular words in a frequently heard book.

Alternatively, his teacher might have tried to determine Ben's ability to associate the words on a page with the related illustrations. She could ask Ben to identify the helicopter among the illustrations in *Would You Like to Fly?* If Ben is unable to identify the name of the vehicle, the interviewer could share the name with him and follow up by asking him what letter he would expect to find at the beginning of the word "helicopter." Ben's ability or lack of ability to name the letter would be revealing about his knowledge of letter-sound associations. Following this exchange with a request for Ben to point to the word that he thinks might be "helicopter" would provide further information about his knowledge of letter-sound correspondences. If Ben were reluctant or unable to directly point to the word, the interviewer might point to two different words, one being the word "helicopter" and the other word being one substantially different in length and letters (e.g., "is"). By asking Ben to point to the word that would likely be "helicopter" and to tell why he chose that word, the teacher would further probe for information about Ben's associations between spoken and written words and the relationship between multisyllabic words in speech and in print.

A third set of questions could tap into other understandings Ben might have related to print. The teacher could read the book *Would You Like to Fly?* to Ben several times. By interviewing Ben the following day about the content of the book, she would have an indication of Ben's memory for text. Such an interview provides a much richer picture of Ben's literacy progress than simply recording his reluctance to attempt to read.

Responding to Specific Tasks.   Examples throughout the chapter have shown how teachers can obtain information about children's phonics strategies through observations and follow-up conversations. But, as we discussed in Chapter 3, there are processes related to phonemic awareness or letter naming that underlie successful use of the cues from the graphophonic system. Because phonemic awareness or letter naming are part of phonics use and not a strategy in and of themselves, children's facility with the interim processes may be difficult to determine through observations or studying work samples. While interim processes should take a back seat to the necessary and central processes of literacy use, insight into children's grasp of these processes can be helpful when children are first learning to read and write or are struggling to move beyond the initial stages of literacy. An interview that focuses specifically on these processes is useful to understand children's facility with these processes.

Teachers in the Right Start in Reading project (Hiebert et al., 1992) assess students' phonemic awareness and letter naming as part of interviews they conduct with their students several times a year. Abbreviated forms of the phonemic awareness tasks appear in Table 8.6. The three dimensions of phonemic awareness assessed by these tasks were described in Chapter 3 as predicting young children's reading acquisition (Stanovich, Cunningham, & Cramer, 1984) and were used by Cunningham (1986) in a study of kindergartners' literacy acquisition.

In Table 8.6, we have included the beginning-of-the-year performances of Yolanda and Matthew on this set of tasks. Both were experiencing considerable difficulty in segmenting phonemes. Observers of young children, such as Adams (1990), have suggested that young children may not understand the requirements of the phoneme segmentation task such as the one described in Table 8.6. For example, children may be distracted by the need to physically move the markers to correlate with the sounds that they hear in a word. The phoneme deletion task, however, involves a skill that is critical to using an analogy strategy. While their teacher has given them several examples where real words are created by dropping the initial phoneme of a word, neither Yolanda nor Matthew produces responses similar to this modeling. Both children employ a rhyming strategy, focusing on the ending or the rime of the word rather than on deleting the initial consonant. Further, they are not concerned that they are creating nonsense words rather than meaningful words as has been modeled in all of the tasks by their teacher. Their inability

TABLE 8.6		Interim Processes Tasks			
Process	**Task[1]**	**Example**	**Target Word**	**Yolanda's Response**	**Matthew's Response**
Phoneme Segmentation	Using a card with 4 boxes and 4 markers, teacher demonstrates how to move a marker for each sound heard in a word. Child is asked to do the same with target words.	• me: 2 • bug: 3	• it • sand • red • pigs • cup	√ 3 √ 3 √	1 2 1 1 1
Phoneme Deletion	After hearing a spoken target word, the child's task is to produce a new word by taking away the first sound of the word.	• ball: all • pink: ink • meat: eat	• man/an • nice/ice • win/in • bus/us • hit/it	√ nice win bus her	girl mean win car [NR]
Phonological Oddity	Of a group of four words that teacher says, child is to pick the one word that has a different beginning sound.	• ball, note, bath, bite • me, vet, mice, move	• not, no, nice, son • ball, bite, dog, beat • girl, pat, give, go • yes, run, rose, round • cap, jar, coat, come	√ beat go √ come	√ beat give round come

[1]From A.E. Cunningham (1986). *Phonemic awareness: The development of early reading competency.* Unpublished dissertation, University of Michigan.

to consistently detect the word with distinct initial phonemes is a further indication of the need for Yolanda and Matthew to participate in additional activities in which they play with the sounds of language.

Reflecting on Children's Learning

In presenting the assessments of Yolanda and Matthew, we have included observations of their accomplishments and prominent strategies. Similarly, as they gather information, teachers identify patterns and choose particular paths to follow in guiding children to the next set of literacy strategies. For some instructional decisions and at particular times in children's literacy development, teachers will want to study their information in great depth. For example, when making decisions about increasing the difficulty of the books for literacy instruction or identifying children who would benefit from sessions with a Title I teacher, additional reflection on information can be useful.

In this section, we examine ways in which teachers can reflect in depth on children's literacy development. Schemes for studying children's learning, often called rubrics, can be helpful in this process. A rubric describes a particular set of literacy processes or strategies. Typically, rubrics include descriptions of early forms of a strategy as well as the strategies that characterize facile readers or writers. The best way to view a rubric is as a compass pointing the direction in which children's strategies can grow.

While the benchmarks in Table 8.1 are not themselves rubrics, the primary dimensions of literacy can be established from these benchmarks. Once the primary dimensions are identified, rubrics can be developed to assist teachers in viewing children's current development and in plotting the course for their continued development.

We will describe possible rubrics that guide teachers in establishing children's strengths and needs on the two dimensions of literacy highlighted in our guiding benchmarks: comprehending and composing. In presenting these rubrics, we emphasize as we have throughout this chapter that these rubrics are intended to be examples—grist for the mill as teams of teachers develop their own assessment systems—rather than prescriptive or comprehensive. The frameworks or rubrics that are presented here pertain to only a small fraction of an emergent literacy program. Our purpose is to demonstrate particular concepts about assessment, not to claim a complete or definitive assessment scheme for the emergent literacy period.

Reflecting on Development in Comprehending

When the benchmarks on comprehending in Table 8.1 are examined, four dimensions can be identified. Two—personal responses to increasingly more difficult texts and critical responses to the same—pertain to the central goal of comprehending. The other two dimensions—growth in word recognition strategies as evident in ability to read increasingly more difficult texts and integration of these strategies in making meaning—relate to the necessary processes of word recognition. We will examine the information on Yolanda and Matthew to illustrate how teachers can reflect on children's proficiency with the benchmarks.

Critical Responses.   The descriptions of the oral reading assessment earlier did not include the assessments of Yolanda's and Matthew's growth in responding critically to text. Two of the four benchmarks for comprehending in Table 8.1 pertain to responses to text: provide personal response to book and retell the gist of book. The passages from an informal reading inventory that Yolanda and Matthew read orally were brief and, after the predictable level, unillustrated. Because of these characteristics, personal responses were not requested for these passages. Children's growth in responding with personal connections and insights to texts was established through other tasks, such as comments in discussions and journal entries.

The meanings that children constructed of the passages were analyzed, particularly in the spring assessment when the content of passages grew in complexity. There are at least two ways in which children's comprehension of a text after reading silently or orally can be assessed: (1) answering questions or (2) retelling or summarizing the gist of the passage. This particular assessment used a combination of retelling and answers to questions. The specific question for a particular passage focused on an inference or understanding that was critical to the resolution or dilemma of the story. A summary with the key components of the story, the specific question for each passage, and the responses of Yolanda and Matthew are given in Table 8.7.

One way of studying the quality of children's responses to a text is to establish the components of a complete retelling. What are critical elements? What are the trivial aspects of the passage that are descriptive or interesting but not essential? One response is for teachers to generate a retelling of the passage themselves, identifying the elements that are central and distinct. Such model summaries for the three passages that either Yolanda or Matthew read in the spring assessment are given in Table 8.7. The model summary can be kept at hand while a teacher is listening to children read, allowing the teacher to check off the elements as children describe them in their retellings.

A checklist such as those in the "Model Retelling" column of Table 8.7 can also be used to probe children's understandings of the stories. Once children have given an unassisted or "free" retelling or summary of the story, teachers can question or probe children about specific elements that are crucial to the meaning of the selection but which were not apparent in the retelling. Take, for instance, the responses of Yolanda and Matthew to the second-grade selection. Yolanda has not included the point that the batter scores a run, allowing the team to win and making the batter a hero. While Matthew uses the vocabulary for a football score, his summary indicates that he understands the significance of the batter's accomplishment. By asking Yolanda to describe what happened because the batter hit the ball the last time, her teacher might have gained insight into whether she understood the implications of the hit. The inference question that was used as a follow-up serves this function. When given another opportunity to reflect on the meaning of the batter's intent to hit the ball hard, Yolanda repeats her idea that the batter simply hit the ball. When probes for specific critical elements,

TABLE 8.7 **Critical Responses of Yolanda and Matthew to Text: Spring of Grade One**

Text Level	Model Retelling	Inference Question	Yolanda's Responses	Matthew's Responses
First Grade	• Each of four children in a car pool brings a large bag with something to share for Show and Tell. • When all the children and their bags are in the car, the car is very crowded.	What did Terry mean when he said that he thought the little car was getting fat? *It was getting very crowded or full.*	*Summary:* One boy and one girl with paper bags got into the car. The car got full and fat. *Inference Response:* There were big paper bags and kids.	[Not given]
Second Grade	• After striking at the first two pitches, the batter is scared but determined to hit a home run on the third pitch. • The batter hits the home run and is a star.	In this story, what was meant when the batter said, "I would kill the ball"? *Hit the ball hard; hit a home run.*	*Summary:* He was playing a game and he kept missing and missing. But he hit it the last time. *Inference Response:* He hit it.	*Summary:* The boy was playing baseball. He hit the ball and made a touchdown. *Inference Response:* Hit it hard.
Third Grade	• After Mark and Boxer, his dog, go into a cave, the dog runs off. As the light in the cave fades, Mark gets frightened and lights his candle. • As the light goes out, Mark hears a growl near him and sees eyes glowing in the dark. • He finally gets the candle lit and sees that the eyes are those of Boxer.	Why might Mark have been frightened when he heard the growl and saw the eyes in the dark? *It could have been a wild animal, not his dog, Boxer.*	[Not given]	*Summary:* This boy was in a cave by himself and it got dark. He got scared. *Inference Response:* The dog. I forgot his name.

such as the inference question, are included, two levels of responses can be established: (1) a free response and (2) an assisted response. This form of probing illustrates the use of scaffolding or establishing the upper limits of the child's zone of proximal development within an assessment.

A rubric can be developed from the model summary, providing teachers with a means for studying what children can do and what requires continued work. For example, the elements of the model retelling in Table 8.7 might be used to establish a rubric with the following four categories:

- **Elaborated:** All of the crucial elements of the passage are included in the retelling. There is a particular focus or elaboration on the problem and its resolution.
- **Complete:** The primary elements are included in the student's unassisted response. Some aspects that are ambiguous in the unassisted response become clear with teacher probing.
- **On Track but Incomplete:** Some but not all of the primary elements are given in the student's unassisted response. Even with teacher probing, student's response remains incomplete.
- **Inaccurate:** Even after probing, student's response indicates a misinterpretation of one or more critical aspects of the passage. Often, an inaccurate response is dominated by a focus on trivial aspects of the passage.

While this rubric or set of categories is applied to children's oral retellings in this context, such rubrics can also be used with children's written summaries of texts (Mullis, Campbell, & Farstrup, 1993). Until the middle or end of second grade, however, the same amount of information will likely not be forthcoming from a written summary as from an oral summary.

Several aspects of a rubric such as this one are worth noting. First, the use of an even rather than an odd number of categories is preferable because raters tend to use the middle category (Herman, Morris, & Fitz-Gibbon, 1987). For example, on a five-point scheme, there might be a clustering in the middle, with those that are clearly differentiated as complete or incomplete placed in the first or last categories. By using an even number of categories such as the four that are listed above, raters focus on distinctions of particular categories rather than global characteristics.

Second, the categories are distinguished by descriptors that pertain to the quality of the retelling rather than numbers or letters. When numbers or letter grades are used, global attributions of children's abilities often result. When a descriptor such as "elaborated" is used rather than a "1" or a "4," attention is directed to the content of a specific retelling. If Yolanda's retelling of the second-grade passage is described as "on track but incomplete," another teacher, Yolanda's parents, or Yolanda herself knows that she is understanding some of the ideas of a passage designated as second grade, but that there is some aspect of this passage that Yolanda is misunderstanding. A likely explanation is that Yolanda is unfamiliar with baseball or perhaps team sports. Perhaps, on a passage of similar difficulty level but with a different topic, Yolanda might give a complete response. Support for this possibility comes from Yolanda's response to the first-grade passage that deals with a familiar topic—the trip to school. With a familiar topic, she is able to give a concise and logically ordered response: "One boy and one girl with paper bags got into the car. The car got full and fat." While she does not elaborate on this description to include the arrival of each of the four children, she communicates the cause-and-effect nature of the passage. She goes so far as to use the same language in her summary as in the passage when she describes the car as "fat." She also indicates that she understands the meaning of that metaphor by giving a synonym, "full."

Matthew begins at a higher level than Yolanda on the passages from the informal reading inventory during the spring assessment, skipping the first-grade passage. Matthew draws on his knowledge of sports in conveying an essential aspect of the passage that Yolanda misses. While Matthew confuses baseball and football, he indicates his awareness that the individual in the passage has been successful in scoring a "touchdown." On a second-grade passage with a topic for which Matthew has at least some prior knowledge, Matthew is able to provide a complete retelling. When a passage includes more complex vocabulary and syntax as with the subsequent passage on Mark and Boxer, Matthew gives an incomplete response. He is on track in identifying the setting and the boy's fear. He fails to mention the specific event that exacerbated the boy's fear—seeing eyes glowing in the dark. Matthew is aware that there was a dog in the story, as indicated by the follow-up inference question. In his retelling, however, he does not include this critical element nor does he elaborate on the dog's role when asked the inference question. Matthew appears to have some grasp of this passage but, as indicated by his response of *recoddentalize* for *recognize* when reading this passage orally (given on Table 8.3), the strategies needed to be successful in making meaning of this level of text are still developing.

Word Recognition Strategies.   Two of the benchmarks for comprehending pertain to the necessary processes of word recognition: gives a meaningful, fluent reading, using all text systems, and self-corrects nonmeaningful miscues. Progress in each of these dimensions involves coordination of all of the word recognition strategies that were discussed in Chapter 3: contextual supports, meaningful chunks of words, high-frequency words, and consistent letter-sound patterns in words. There are at least two forms of information that running records provide on children's growth in word recognition strategies: (1) application of strategies to more complex texts are read fluently and (2) the acceptability of miscues.

Fluent Reading of Increasingly More Complex Texts.   Evidence of children's success in coordinating word recognition strategies comes from their success with increasingly harder books. One of the distinctions of the benchmarks across the three phases in Table 8.1 is the level of books with which children are applying their strategies. For example, to achieve the benchmarks for Phase 2 involves a fluent or smooth reading of books that are more difficult than the books that are read for Phase 1. We suggest that the levels of text that are used within a program should also form the basis for assessment. Assessments of Yolanda and Matthew consisted of passages from an informal reading inventory—texts that were derived from the high-frequency criterion that was described in Chapter 5. In the years subsequent to Yolanda's and Matthew's participation in the project, the Right Start in Reading teachers have moved to a set of books that typify the books that are used in instruction (see Table 7.2). The target books for the assessment have been pulled out of the instructional program so that teachers can study children's proficiency in applying their strategies in unassisted as well as scaffolded contexts.

As we showed in Table 5.6, publishers present materials such as little book programs and the trade books in literature-based programs in levels or stages. The rationales for these levels or stages are not always spelled out or obvious after studying books from these different levels or stages. In creating our benchmarks in Table 8.1, we used the Reading Recovery exemplar trade books to illustrate change in complexity of text. As our discussion in Chapter 5 indicated, efforts such as the Reading Recovery exemplars are beginning to clarify the features that make books accessible or inaccessible to readers at particular points in their development. In one project, same-grade-level teachers in a school ranked the books that they typically used in their classrooms. This ranking was used to establish what elements of text were emphasized at one level or another in children's growth as readers (Borko, Davinroy, Flory, & Hiebert, 1994). Whatever the scheme that teachers use to establish the difficulty of books, a similar method should be applied to select the books for instruction and assessment.

In order to discuss Yolanda's progress on the benchmarks, we correlated the selections on the informal reading inventory and the illustrated, predictable book with the Reading Recovery levels that underlie the benchmarks in Table 8.1. The illustrated predictable book is roughly equivalent to a Level 1 book, the first-grade passage to a Level 3 book, and the second-grade passage to a Level 5 book. In consulting the running records for Yolanda in Table 8.2, we can see that she had nearly attained the benchmark of fluent reading of books such as *Cat on the Mat* (Wildsmith, 1982) by the middle of grade one. Yolanda's reading of the predictable text indicated that she was using illustrations, she knew some high-frequency words (e.g., "we"), and she was attending to the graphophonic characteristics of words, at least initial consonants (e.g., *there* for *then* and *come* for *climb*). By the end of grade one, we would hope that Yolanda had developed strategies such as use of letter-sound patterns in words. We would also hope that Yolanda's use of these strategies would be expressed with text that had words with complex letter-sound patterns and that did not allow a text to be read entirely on knowledge of a predictable pattern and labeling of illustrations.

Yolanda does just that, as indicated by the samples of her reading in the spring of first grade. The running records in Table 8.2 indicate that Yolanda has an extensive repertoire of knowledge about word patterns and high-frequency words. When the number of unique words in the text that require her to draw on her strategies (e.g., reading words such as "strike" and "shake") increases, she begins to make substitutions.

In reflecting on Yolanda's development of word recognition strategies, her teacher—Ms. Chrisman—would draw the following conclusions from the complete running records that are excerpted in Table 8.2. In the fall, Yolanda was using illustrations exclusively. Word recognition strategies related to meaningful chunks of words, high-frequency words, and consistent letter-sound patterns were not yet in evidence.

By winter, Yolanda could coordinate the use of various word recognition strategies so that she could read a predictable text fluently. When given a text with no illustrations, Yolanda relies on the graphophonic information, attending to the beginnings and endings of words. She also recognizes a number of high-frequency words. While not able to fluently read a text designated on the informal reading inventory as primer level, Yolanda is reading simple predictable texts fluently.

By the end of grade one, we would conclude that Yolanda has attained the phase-two benchmark of reading a level-three text (approximately a grade-one passage on the informal reading inventory). Her reading at this level is fluent and automatic. When she encounters text with concepts that are unfamiliar (i.e., the grade-two text), she becomes less fluent. When the text becomes dense with words that require her to apply knowledge about meaningful chunks of words and consistent letter-sound patterns such as *baseball, struck, air, strike,* and *whiz,* Yolanda becomes less fluent with words, such as *begin* and *one,* that she would read automatically in a text with less dense vocabulary. But Yolanda has made substantial progress over grade one, from the beginning where she relied solely on the illustrations to make sense of a text to the end where she is able to apply all of the word recognition strategies to texts that are dense with unfamiliar words.

We will concentrate on Matthew's reading as we discuss reflection on a reader's self-correction of nonmeaningful miscues as another form of evidence on word recognition strategies. Prior to that discussion, however, we will summarize the conclusions that can be drawn on Matthew's fluency in using word recognition strategies with increasingly more complex text. According to the information in Table 8.3, Matthew relied solely on the illustrations in a book to make meaning of the text in the fall of first grade. By winter, he was attending to the graphic symbols on the page when the text had illustrations. With unillustrated texts (as in the primer passage from the informal reading inventory), Matthew attempted to apply his knowledge of consistent letter-sound patterns and high-frequency words, but his strategies were inadequate for the task at hand. By the end of grade one, however, Matthew has attained the benchmark for phase three of an emergent literacy program in that he can read fluently a level-five passage (grade two on the informal reading inventory). To be a fluent and meaningful reader of more difficult passages such as the grade-three passage, Matthew needs to apply knowledge of meaningful chunks of words with increasingly complex, multisyllabic words such as *recognize.* The task that confronts Matthew is developmentally appropriate for a soon-to-be second grader, as he is. Matthew has an extensive and reliable repertoire of word recognition strategies on which to build.

The Characteristics of Miscues and Recognized Words.   To be a facile reader requires the coordination of all of the word recognition strategies that we discussed in Chapter 3. One of the benchmarks of reading is children's facility in applying their word recognition strategies to make meaning of texts. Running records provide an ideal context in which to glean information on this benchmark. Running records yield at least three forms of information about children's word recognition strategies: (1) the types of words that children can read accurately and quickly, (2) the types of words that challenge children's word recognition strategies (i.e., miscues), and (3) children's monitoring of the semantic and syntactic acceptability of the words they read (i.e., self-corrections).

What can we learn about Matthew's use of word recognition strategies over his first-grade year by reflecting on these three aspects of his running records in Table 8.3? In the fall, Matthew recognizes the text as a whole rather than as a function of the individual words. But by winter, his running records indicate that his word recognition strategies have moved beyond this earlier, sole reliance on contextual supports. When he has the contextual supports of illustrations and of a predictable text, Matthew is able to give a meaningful and almost accurate rendition of the text. The miscue of *ran* for *run,* whereby he changes the tense of the verb, was duplicated for other pages of the text. This change is entirely acceptable in the context of the sentence and the illustrations and indicates attention to the initial and final consonants of the word. With the miscue of *it* for *again* in the sentence *"Then we climb up again,"* the substitution indicates attention to meaning but not to the graphophonic characteristics.

When Matthew is asked to read a text where he can no longer rely on illustrations, his responses indicate a use of at least one consistent letter-sound pattern—*at.* In fact, Matthew overuses this pattern as indicated by the response *Pat* for *by.* Matthew has made substantial growth from the beginning of first grade in recognizing high-frequency words, as evident in his identification of *said, the, me,* and *to.* While Matthew has made substantial progress from the beginning to the middle of first grade in his facility with different word recognition strategies, his repertoire is not yet sufficiently extensive to allow his application of these strategies to give a meaningful rendition of a text without illustrations.

Reflections on miscues, recognized words, and monitoring of meaningfulness while reading indicate that Matthew's growth has been phenomenal from the middle to the end of grade one. He has a vast repertoire of words that he reads accurately. He monitors the meaning of what he reads as indicated by his correction of a miscue on a word that he has likely never seen before: *Waz* for *Whiz.* A miscue that he fails to self-correct is a word that may not be in his speaking vocabulary—*recoddentalize* for *recognize*. This miscue would lead to the recommendation to Matthew's second-grade teacher that he is ready for instruction on morphemes in multisyllabic words. When the number of multisyllabic words with Latin and Greek roots increases, as they do in the third-grade text Matthew was reading, he is sufficiently challenged that his attention to acceptability of the words he reads begins to waver. While we can be confident that Matthew knew the word *get* for which he substitutes *go* in the third-grade passage, the presence of challenging vocabulary such as *recognize* has made the text less meaningful to him. While the phrase *"Let's go out of here!"* contains a viable syntactic and meaningful substitution, the expression is not what a typical English speaker would say.

By the end of first grade, the three sources of information—his miscues, words recognized accurately and quickly, and monitoring of miscues—indicate that Matthew has a well-developed and effective repertoire of word recognition strategies. A source for insight into his ability to generalize knowledge of patterns comes from the word-reading task. As we described in presenting the word-reading task, the primary reason for including this task in the assessment is to establish students' generalizations of letter-sound and morphemic patterns. A typical text does not include all of the patterns, leaving teachers to wonder about children's ability to generalize. On the winter assessment, for example, Brenda Fifer—Matthew's teacher—could not determine how well Matthew understood the overall pattern of V-C rimes. As can be seen in Table 8.3, Matthew applied the *at* rime. In fact, Matthew overgeneralized this pattern in that he gave the miscue of *Pat* for *by*. While the strategies that children use in a word-reading task are not synonymous with those they use in reading text, these strategies are indicative of their sense of word patterns and their ability to apply this knowledge to a range of words. The ability to correctly identify words is especially informative of children's facility in applying their knowledge of word patterns quickly. Their miscues give a glimpse of their expectations about the patterns of words. When Hiebert et al. (1995) studied the word-reading responses of 100 first graders, they found that students' responses could be categorized into six types:

- refusal/no response
- guessing with no clear relationship to the word
- naming letters of word
- real word substitution based primarily on the beginning consonants or, at a more advanced level, the middle and/or end of word as well as beginning
- nonsense word substitution with attention to: (a) consonants of word, (b) simple vowel patterns, or (c) complex vowel patterns
- correct response

When we interpret Matthew's word reading in fall (Table 8.4, List 1) relative to this scheme, we note that he consistently uses a letter-naming strategy, but only after considerable prompting by his teacher. He uses only a handful of letters, almost all in his name (which differs from the pseudonym by which he is referred to here). While Matthew took longer than Yolanda in grasping word patterns, his performance on the word-reading task in the spring indicates that he does not approach unknown words with the expectation that there is a one-to-one correspondence between letters and sounds. Matthew expects a multiple set of relationships and he is facile in drawing on a range of strategies. With this understanding, his ability to recognize a wide range of words has grown rapidly.

Reflecting on Development of Composing

When we examine the benchmarks in Table 8.1, we can see two dimensions that relate to the central and necessary processes of composing: (1) communicative intent or the meaningfulness of the message and (2) conventions and spelling. Categories for each of these dimensions appear in Table 8.8.

Message Quality.   In Chapter 3, we described young children's writing development in terms of DeFord's (1980) nine categories. These categories form four clusters: writing-like responses such as scribbling and drawing, attempts to apply sound-letter correspondences, focus on messages, and conventional messages. As these labels suggest, the forms of children's messages and the content—or communicative intent—are intermingled. While helpful for describing emergent writing, they do not capture the responses of children such as Yolanda and Matthew (see Figures 8.1 and 8.2). While preschoolers often pretend to write a message and, when asked to read it, will respond that they cannot read (Hiebert, 1979), by fall of first grade, Yolanda and Matthew were not content to scribble and pretend to write a message. Among the first graders, the focus was on the message. Children told stories about their drawings, such as Yolanda's comment, "This is a pretty flower." Or, children refused to write, as Matthew did, stating that they were unable to write.

The "message quality" dimension relates to the message source, its structure, and its elaboration. Message source refers to understanding where the message content originated, whether from other readers or from one's own experiences. Matthew copies words from a book in the winter of first grade (see Figure 8.2), which indicates his uncertainty about the message source. He copies a random assortment of phrases and words, not a focused or strategic set of words or ideas.

An element of organization also contributes to the quality of a message. Children's use of a listing structure for their messages usually is meaningful. Some children will list objects that they see around a classroom or things that they like. Some draw on adult models of list production, usually around a specific category (e.g., grocery lists, items to pack). The child's list of things to take on a vacation (i.e., books, crayons, etc.), described in Chapter 6, is an example of such a category-based list. Writing the key words of a category such as names of family members or favorite toys allows children to

---

TABLE 8.8   Summaries of Children's Compositions: Message Quality and Conventions

Category	Subcategory	Description
Message Quality	Refuses to write	
	Copying	Production of one's given/surname name(s) or copying from another text or message
	Labeling and/or Listing	Description of a drawing or a list of words on a topic (e.g., names of family members)
	Description of an Event/Idea	Presentation of a single, simple idea
	Elaboration of an Event/Idea	Several sentences organized around a central theme or pattern
	Story or Report	Story or informational structure presents, respectively, a simple narrative or report of information
Conventions (Spelling and Usage)	Drawing	Main theme/topic of the composition may be evident from the drawing but verbal description is oral
	Scribbling	Letter-like forms and some features of writing such as linearity, top to bottom but content of message comes from the child's description/reading of text
	Early Spelling and Conventions	Invented spelling at early phonemic and phonetic stages, most of which can be deciphered by a perceptive reader; spacing may not be provided between words but left-to-right conventions are typically applied
	Comprehensible Spelling and Conventions	Spelling and usage (spacing and punctuation) are adequate so that the gist of the message can be grasped easily
	Facile Spelling and Conventions	Facility with most conventions of spelling and usage

communicate important messages without concern for the conventions of sentence and paragraph writing that they have seen modeled in Morning Messages and in more formal literacy lessons.

Examining students' elaborations provides further insight into their message quality. Yolanda's and Matthew's messages illustrate their writing development as they elaborate on their ideas. Although neither child moves to the point of composing a true narrative or informational text, Matthew's writing in the spring illustrates an elaboration of an event or idea. He includes reasons why he likes his dog and illustrates the enjoyment his dog gives him by telling about the way that they roll in the grass together after the lawn is mowed. The content of Yolanda's messages remains fairly constant across the year. While her message in the spring contains many more words than her description of her drawing in the fall, the structure and elaboration of her message stays relatively the same from fall to spring. Unlike Matthew, she does not elaborate on her reason for liking a new doll.

Conventions and Spelling. The second dimension of children's composing, conventions used to convey the message, refers to the physical production of the message. While message meaning can be described by a writer, regardless of the comprehensibility of the message to others, the conventions impact their readers' ability to comprehend their message. While peers may be able to construct the meaning of a drawing, messages that appear in scribbling and those that use early spelling and conventions depend on an accompanying retelling of the message by the author. As children's conventions move to comprehensible and facile use of spelling, grammar, and language conventions such as punctuation, the audience for children's writing expands considerably.

If there is not a sufficient body of information on children's spelling provided in the compositions in their portfolios, another useful source of information can be the spelling of individual words, such as the lists for Yolanda and Matthew that appear in Table 8.5. We described a useful framework for studying children's development of spelling strategies in Chapter 3. As we summarized in Table 3.7, the strategies of relying on prephonemic, early phonemic, phonetic, simple patterns, and strategic extensions capture the nature of children's spellings comprehensively. Children move from prephonemic and early phonemic strategies—where they represent sounds with unrelated or only some letters—to increasing facility with the patterns of English spelling.

This scheme has proven quite robust in its ability to account for children's strategies. From the vantage point of this scheme, Yolanda's and Matthew's spellings in Table 8.5 show two contrasting patterns of development. Yolanda is on the cusp of early phonemic and phonetic strategies in the fall. She knows that multiple sounds need to be represented by multiple letters but, except for the first sound, her choices in representing the initial or final sounds in her spellings are mostly prephonemic. By winter, she is using a simple association strategy consistently, including cases with complex patterns. She continues to rely on this pattern in spring at times, as shown by her spelling of "rid" for "ride" and "quen" for "queen."

Matthew is slower in coming to the representations of sounds. In the fall, he gives a random assortment of letters. He begins by drawing a handful of letters from his real name. Other times, he gives one of the first letters of the alphabet—A, B, C, or D. By winter, he has progressed, using a simple association strategy (as in "met" for "meat") for some words and a phonetic strategy for others, as in "fo" for "fun." By spring, Matthew shows a strong understanding of letter-sound patterns in English, although not always the ones that represent the choices of orthographers and dictionary writers over the ages. His efforts are outstanding, however, particularly in light of the prognosis at the beginning of the school year that he would experience difficulty with literacy.

Summary

In this chapter, we developed a perspective in which assessment is indistinguishable from learning and is embedded within the ongoing literacy events of existing classroom contexts. These learning events, the core of the emergent literacy program, are the basis for determining children's progress toward critical literacy goals. This view of assessment emanates from the principles of learning that have provided the foundation for our conceptualization of emergent literacy. Because the essence of literacy use involves communicating meaning, assessments should capture children's literacy development within their *daily* acts of using literacy to accomplish meaningful functions. Because both writing and reading are constructed through talk, a true representation of literacy learning is *dynamic,* as teachers listen to children as they use literacy. Finally, assessments need to be *diverse* to represent children's varying use of strategies when working independently, with peers, and with the teacher. To engage in assessments of this type, teachers need to attend to three aspects of assessment as part of learning and instruction: identifying goals and benchmarks; gathering portfolio and performance assessments through observing, sampling, and interviewing; and reflecting and using information in instructional decision making.

The component of assessment, together with oral language patterns, the texts that children read and write, and instructional contexts, are all critical to the creation of an emergent literacy classroom. All of these elements that teachers put in place contribute to the success of young children in becoming readers and writers. The classroom program, however, does not stand alone. The broader communities in which classrooms exist—schools, homes, neighborhoods, volunteer organizations, and professional networks for teachers—influence children's literacy learning. It is to the roles of these communities outside the classroom that we turn our attention in the last section of this book.

Connecting Early Literacy Classrooms to Other Literacy Communities

chapter *9*

Connecting Early Literacy Classrooms to Literacy Communities in and beyond the School

In a tutoring project where university athletes in a reading skills course worked with first and second graders in high-poverty schools, the following interaction occurred after a child had misread a word:

Tutor: That doesn't make sense. Could "him" run?
Child: (laughs)
Tutor: Does that make sense?
Child: (laughs)
Tutor: Okay, what sounds better? The boy "him" run, or The boy "can" run?
Child: The boy can run.
Tutor: There you go. You see you gotta listen to yourself as you read and see if it sounds right.

(Juel, 1994, p. 51)

Keith Baker, author and illustrator of books such as *Who Is the Beast?*, shares some of the letters that young children have sent him after he has visited their school:

Dear Keith Baker,
　　You are a good illustrator. And you have really improved on your books.
　　　　Sincerely, Brenna

Dear Keith Baker,
　　I really enjoyed you coming to our school. I hope you can come again. It was fun having you here. Because we got longer recess.
　　　　Your friend, Alicia

(Baker, 1993, p. 373)

Children's literacy learning can benefit greatly when other communities are brought into contact in meaningful ways with the emergent literacy classroom. These two vignettes illustrate two kinds of connections between the emergent literacy classroom and other literacy communities: *integration* and *extension*. *Integration* activities invite members of other communities into the emergent literacy classroom. In the first vignette, the *integration* of the university athletes as tutors brought the college students into direct contact with emergent readers and writers who had been having difficulties with literacy acquisition. It allowed for these first- and second-grade students to have extended guidance and to see literacy modeled by individuals whom they admired.

Extension activities create contacts such as that illustrated by the letters in Vignette 9.2—letters from the young students to an author of children's literature they had met. Letters such as these move the emergent literacy learners into contact with members of communities outside their classroom environment, extending the literacy community of the classroom.

In this chapter, we begin by examining how connections between emergent literacy classrooms and external communities relate to and are grounded within the assumptions underlying emergent literacy. We then explore the characteristics of and opportunities for integration activities, followed by a similar analysis of extension activities. Thus the purpose of this chapter is to detail the ways in which emergent literacy classrooms may be linked to other communities in interesting and meaningful ways to promote students' literacy learning. Because of the critically important connections between emergent literacy classrooms and the students' homes, we continue this discussion in Chapter 10, focusing specifically on home↔school connections.

The Role of Other Literacy Communities within the Emergent Literacy Perspective

Literacy Learning Occurs through Meaningful Use

Reading and writing, as with oral forms of language, are means for communication. Meaningful purpose for reading and writing is provided when literacy is used as part of social interactions with significant others. When meaningful activities involve broader communities in which children are interested, considerable negotiation and involvement with literacy occurs. The emphasis is on the concerted participation in literacy, rather than a school task where literacy may be viewed simply as a "performance." Such extensions encourage students to express their knowledge in more sophisticated forms as they communicate with adults and children beyond their classroom walls. As children share their interpretations and creations of written language in the public, social domain, they interact with others whose perspectives matter. Through extensions to other communities, children are able to make public their learning.

Literacy Learning Is Embedded in Oral Language

Because oral language provides the vehicle by which children's attention is drawn to literacy, enlarging the literacy community of the emergent literacy classroom means that children's opportunities for interaction can be increased many times over what is possible when the ratio between adults and children is 1:25 or more, as it is in many primary-level classrooms. These interactions can require children to clarify their understandings, as they explain and respond to the inquiries of adults who are not as familiar as their classroom teacher or parents with their idiosyncratic interpretations of literacy.

Further, as children prepare to share their literacy with members of new communities, they are involved in negotiations among one another. For example, the task of creating a play or a choral reading from a favorite book can be the source of considerable debate among children as they select dialogue and the stances of different characters. Or, preparing compositions for publication in a school newspaper can lead children to examine the content and mechanics of their writing in new ways. As children prepare to make their literacy public in a variety of social contexts, the talk that surrounds these tasks in the emergent literacy classroom spurs children's use of higher-level literacy.

Becoming literate depends upon having many and frequent occasions for using language in meaningful ways. While the emergent literacy classroom can be structured to provide multiple opportunities for using language to promote literacy learning and knowledge acquisition, there are important opportunities that lie in the potential of communities external to the classroom, from the school library to volunteers who work within the classroom.

Literacy Learning Occurs in Multiple Contexts

The integration of and extension to other communities by members of an emergent literacy classroom serves to increase the interactions that children have with a range of participants. By integrating other literacy communities into emergent literacy classrooms, opportunities are created within the classroom for children to interact with more knowledgeable others in addition to their classroom teacher. Teachers cannot be the sole members of a culture who are the source for information about or modeling of literacy. Interactions with readers and writers with ranges of expertise—peers, volunteer adults, librarians, and special teachers and their aides—help bring children to high levels of literacy.

Not all of these more knowledgeable others assume the role of "teacher," introducing new skills and genres to children. Adult volunteers in the classroom and older children can facilitate many other important literacy interactions, including: (1) reading with or listening to emergent readers and providing immediate feedback and support, (2) working with emergent writers as they prepare a composition for publication (being careful not to take over the voice and style of the composition), and (3) providing models of ways to engage in and to value literacy.

Integrating Other Communities into the Classroom

In this section, we describe the integration of four different communities into the emergent literacy classroom: (a) older students, (b) librarians, (c) volunteers, and (d) funded program personnel. Two of these communities—older students and librarians—are available in most schools. The third group—volunteers—usually are recruited from various local communities such as high schools, universities, children's families, neighborhoods, and philanthropic organizations and thus depend on the energies of the classroom teachers or school personnel. The fourth group varies across schools as a function of local, state, and federal funding initiatives, often in the form of special resource rooms (e.g., special reading support programs) or federally funded Title I programs.

Cross-Age Peers

Cross-age peer interactions have received attention for decades, with evidence of renewed interest in recent years (Topping, 1988). Such interactions take many different forms. At one end of the continuum of activities is formal tutoring in which the older student is expected to teach the younger student skills he or she may lack or provide support to the younger child in his or her attempts to apply particular strategies and knowledge in reading and writing. At the other end are more collaborative activities such as writing letters to each other or sharing favorite books. Such activities may occur within formal structures such as multi-age classrooms or more informal structures such as cross-grade reading "buddies."

Across the continuum are a range of activities that older and younger students can engage in for mutual benefit. For young children, the experience of working with older students directly provides important models of literacy engagement as well as occasions to receive support and feedback on their reading and writing. Further, cross-age interactions have proven to be as beneficial—if not more so—for the achievement and attitudes of students who assume the role of teacher or tutor as for those who assume the role of student or tutee (Cohen, Kulik, & Kulik, 1982).

Whatever the form of the cross-age programs, preparation by both older and younger participants is necessary for collaborations to be effective. Labbo and Teale (1990) describe a program where fifth graders, who were struggling readers themselves, read books for kindergartners. The fifth graders prepared extensively for the sessions with the younger children, selecting books and repeatedly reading those books to build fluency and expression in their renditions for the kindergartners. While the details are not provided, kindergarten teachers presumably also prepared their students for these sessions by selecting compositions or books to share with older students and modeling and discussing ways of interacting with older peers and with books. The activities were central to the literacy programs of both grade levels, and time to prepare for and participate in the sessions was built into the school day.

In a second example of a cross-age collaboration, Morrice and Simmons (1991) designed a program in which Morrice's middle-grade students and Simmons's primary-grade students worked together to create Big Books. The middle-grade peers were responsible for applying their knowledge of the writing process as they guided the younger children in writing and publishing the Big Books. But the primary-grade children were part of the decision-making process in selecting predictable patterns to emulate from the books that they read with their cross-age buddies. One of the middle-grade students described how hard they had worked to involve the emergent readers and writers:

> In the Big Book Buddy system you sometimes lose patience because you are working with people an awful lot younger than you, but usually it is very much fun letting your buddy ask questions, give ideas and answering. Sometimes it has suspense, when your buddy gets stuck and you are waiting for your buddy to get an idea that you know . . . but don't tell them.   (p. 575)

We found this student's description of the attribute of "suspense" as the stance that a teacher takes toward the learner to be particularly interesting. It seems to capture the essence of good teaching. With buddies such as these, emergent readers and writers have many more occasions for using and learning about written language.

Librarians and Libraries

Close links between the school library and the emergent literacy classroom are essential if children are to become full participants in the broad world of literacy. When the term *fluency* is used with literacy, the first thought may be of children's ability to decode unknown words. But to use literacy in all of its forms, readers need to develop fluency with library resources that help in choosing books of interest, identifying sources for information, researching a topic, and evaluating which newspapers and magazines provide reputable reports. *Classroom* libraries are one important context where children learn to negotiate the search for favorite titles, authors, and genres, but it is in the *school* and the *public* libraries that children need to apply their strategies to be lifelong readers. In schools where children read extensively, Hughes (1993) found that school libraries were busy and central places: "Children were coming to the library to get another book, to write when the classroom was too noisy, to find answers to their questions, or just to read in a different setting" (p. 393). Making such links results from action on the part of both teachers and librarians.

The teacher's role involves first collaborating with the librarian by providing critical information about topics and themes as well as about the students who will pursue questions related to these themes so that the librarian can be more involved in identifying related texts and appropriate tasks. Teachers also work with students in integrating their library experience with ongoing activities within the classroom.

The librarian also has a critical role in this reconceptualization of the school library. In addition to observing the use of libraries in schools where students are avid readers, Hughes (1993) interviewed teachers about their relationships with the librarian. A composite of the school librarian emerged from these interviews: "She is sort of a liaison between what's going on in the classroom and what's available in the library. She helps kids learn their way around the library. She matches kids with books" (Hughes, 1993, p. 397).

With trade books now at the center of the literacy instructional program as we discussed in Chapter 5, there are needs and gaps in school programs such as guidelines about the books that are used for units and read-aloud events in classrooms. Lamme and Ledbetter (1990) describe a school where the librarian stepped in to provide leadership for this aspect of the literacy program. As the school librarian, Ledbetter surveyed teachers for lists of their favorite books to read aloud and used the books recommended by Jim Trelease in the *Read-Aloud Handbook* (1989) to create annotated lists of titles for each grade level. Teachers supplemented the program by reading favorites that were not on the list (as long as the extra titles were not on another grade's list) and by using books related to theme, genre, and author studies. By the end of fifth grade when children left the school, they had had exposure to a wide variety of books through this read-aloud curriculum.

Volunteers

Volunteers include individuals who are recruited from off-campus sites to be integrated into the emergent literacy classroom events. Like the cross-age peers, volunteers can serve multiple roles in their work with young students (e.g., reading to a student, listening to a student read aloud, helping students who are experiencing difficulties with specific tasks), but the most prominent role of the volunteer is as a tutor—with small groups and one-to-one during class sessions or after school, weekends or summers (Leto, 1995). Tutors are recruited from various sources: sororities and fraternities at local universities, organizations for retired persons, corporations with community outreach programs, members of children's families and neighborhoods, university preservice teachers, and, as illustrated in Vignette 9.1, tutoring programs for athletes within universities.

Serving as tutors so that young children become better readers and writers requires preparation. In Vignette 9.1 at the beginning of this chapter, the tutor's comment, "You see you gotta listen to yourself as you read and see if it sounds right," summarizes for the child an important strategy that, when applied, will make him or her a better reader. Quality interactions such as this one do not happen serendipitously. The tutors in Juel's (1994) project participated in weekly sessions of two-and-a-half hours that dealt with the content of the tutoring sessions (which were 45 minutes twice a week). For example, the tutors learned about assisting children in making connections between sounds and letters when they were writing. One of the contexts for developing the tutors' awareness of features of text involved their writing of stories for their tutors. Guidelines for the tutoring sessions themselves were deliberately kept flexible rather than lock-step. But the discussions of literacy (including attention to the tutors' own reading) led to supportive and knowledgeable actions on the part of the tutors, as illustrated in Vignette 9.1.

Analyses of video- and audiotapes of the sessions between the athlete tutors and the emergent readers and writers indicated that there were nine dimensions of the tutoring sessions (Juel, 1994); (1) a warm, supportive, caring atmosphere; (2) teaching the system (e.g., "You can't read a word without looking at it"); (3) an attitude of "we're in this together and I know how you feel;" (4) personalizing stories by playing and teasing each other while reading them (e.g., changing Curious George to Curious Eddie, the name of the tutee); (5) a lot of visual and auditory support while the child is reading (e.g., tutor points with the eraser end of a pencil while the child is reading); (6) breaking down word recognition and spelling into small steps ("So whenever you see those two letters together, it sounds like aaaaattt, aaaaaattttt"); (7) routines ("How do we always start?"); (8) verbal reinforcement ("You're gonna be a famous writer someday, you got all the pages"); and (9) nonverbal reinforcement (e.g., holding hands).

Programs such as these may not be possible in all contexts but volunteers do need to be given guidelines and supervision. The READ-WRITE-NOW program, a national initiative by the Department of Education, illustrates the kinds of materials that can be helpful for volunteers in community organizations (U.S. Department of Education, 1995). A booklet with descriptions of activities for children at different developmental levels and ways of responding to children's risk-taking efforts is provided for volunteers. A hands-on booklet for kindergartners is also included with suggestions for how volunteers can support and extend the activities.

There are other important roles for adults who cannot be in the classroom on a regular basis. For example, parents or members of the business community whose schedules do not permit regular interactions in the classroom can tape-record passages so that children can have additional models for read-along events. The voice of a high school athlete on an audiotape, a firefighter from the local fire station, or a foster grandparent from a senior citizen facility shows students that everyone reads—not just their teacher.

The contributions of some volunteers may also be very task-specific, such as that of individuals who come to the classroom to read a book or experts who talk about their specialty. For example, during a unit on tornadoes that a grade-level team shared, a weatherperson from one of the local television stations visited to demonstrate the workings of a tornado "in a jar" (Borko et al., 1994). This was a case where a practical demonstration is worth a thousand words. Children's knowledge and interest in the topic, including their collection of a small library of books on weather, was noticeable.

Even a simple volunteer program provides an important context for helping integrate other communities into the emergent literacy classroom. Whether volunteers attempt to formally teach students, or whether they simply share their love of literacy, students can see the value that others place on literacy in their own lives and benefit from the additional attention to their own literacy development.

Support Teachers

Nowhere is integration of a community with the emergent literacy classroom more important than in the case of support teachers and their instruction. Support teachers are found in many, if not most, of the schools that are of focus in this book—schools with a high population of students from homes with incomes at the poverty level. These specialists serve a range of populations that have been categorized according to needs. Such efforts include programs for students with special learning needs (i.e., special education, Title I), programs designed to support students for whom English is a second language (ESL) or who come from non-mainstream cultures (e.g., ESL, bilingual education, children of migrant workers), and programs for students who have specific needs ranging from speech and language therapy to sociopsychological issues stemming from situations such as homelessness. The range of needs of students from high-poverty areas is great, and the specialists concerned with and trained in addressing these problems often focus on basic needs in language and literacy.

The instructional practices of teachers with these special assignments, or support teachers as we will call them here, have been described throughout this volume. The need for integration of support teachers into the regular education classroom is great, because much research has documented the lack of congruence between these communities (Allington, 1991a). This incongruence reduces the benefits to the participating students and, in fact, may even impede their learning. Throughout this section, we draw on examples from support teachers associated with the federally funded Title I program. We do so for three reasons. First, the new Title I legislation calls for school-wide efforts rather than the traditional pull-out approach that has characterized it in the past. The new legislature has targeted the integration of classroom and support programs in Title I specifically because of the problems created by a lack of coordination in the past (National Assessment of Chapter 1 Review Panel, 1993). Second, Title I is the only sustaining federally funded program that provides additional resources for the instruction in reading and mathematics of poor children (National Assessment of Chapter 1 Review Panel, 1993). Third, a primary focus of Title I programs has been and continues to be language and literacy education. However, the principles that we will describe to promote the integration of support teachers into emergent literacy programs are the same whether the expertise of support teachers is the literacy learning of at-risk children through Title I programs or the learning of children with unique speech patterns or different languages.

Unlike previous legislation where Title I funds were spread across numerous schools (schools with as few as 10 families receiving free or reduced lunch services were eligible for Title I resources), Title I programs now will be concentrated in those schools that have the highest numbers of low-income children. Whereas services to ESL children were up to the discretion of individual school agencies, support for the literacy instruction of ESL children has now been included in the Title I legislation. Further, while Title I services were frequently provided through pull-out programs taught by specialists or aides, the move to school-wide Title I programs requires that the resources be used in concert with the school program. For example, schools could choose to have smaller class sizes rather than use the funds for a literacy specialist, or could use support teachers as resources for teachers, teaching particular lessons or providing model lessons across classrooms in several schools (Winfield, 1995). These changes in federal policy are aimed at integrating Title I resources into classroom programs.

A consistent set of features has been found to characterize the literacy programs of schools that are particularly successful in bringing low-income students to high levels of literacy (Hoffman, 1991; Purkey & Smith, 1983): (1) clarity of goals, (2) clarity of instructional focus and implementation, and (3) shared assessment practices. Reports of the choices in goals, instructional strategies, and assessment made by particular teams of teachers in schools can be found in numerous sources (e.g., Allington & Walmsley, 1995; Hiebert & Taylor, 1994; Pikulski, 1994; Richek & Glick, 1991). Choices made by the teachers in the Right Start in Reading project (Hiebert et al., 1992) are described throughout this volume. Initially a collaboration between Title I teachers, school teams now include classroom teachers and specialists for bilingual, speech, special education, and Title I. This project was based on identifying critical literacy goals (see Chapter 3), establishing a repertoire of common instructional practices (see Chapter 7), and creating a shared set of assessments (see Chapter 8). We have also referred to efforts such as the Early Literacy Project (Englert et al., 1994) and Early Intervention in Reading (Taylor et al., 1994), describing all of these as "projects." None of these efforts, however, is a prepackaged program. In all of these collaborative efforts, the goals, instructional activities, and assessment practices are clarified from year to year by the participating teachers, who include classroom and support teachers with specialties in literacy learning, special education, speech and language learning, and bilingual education. The particular combinations and manifestations of these components will—and should—vary as a function of contexts of schools and communities. But, in programs that support low-income children over time, classroom and support teachers work together and have ways of continuing to sustain their efforts.

Clear and common goals, instructional focus, and assessment practices— these three features have been the focus of this book. Rather than reiterating the contents of the goal-instruction-assessment framework, we raise underlying issues related to these three choices that face teams of teachers.

Clarity of Goals.   Clarity of goals is critical for helping young readers and writers who struggle to acquire literacy. As we noted in Chapter 1, the literacy field has seen a range of definitions of what counts as literacy and experienced debates about the content of literacy education programs. Often, supplementary programs designed to support students' classroom literacy acquisition are faced with situations in which their goals are in conflict with those of the regular classroom, where their goals are orthogonal (i.e., do not conflict or support but, rather, are disconnected) to the regular classroom, or where their goals are so underspecified that there is a lack of consistency within the program as well as between the support program and the classroom (National Assessment of Chapter 1 Review Panel, 1993). Yet, the message is consistent in any report of high-poverty schools where students have high patterns of success: In high-poverty schools in which children learn to read and write, goals are clear and expectations are high (Hoffman, 1991; Purkey & Smith, 1983). Because of the range of relationships between support programs and regular classrooms, frequently students' progress in the support program (e.g., Title I) has not been shared or discussed with the school staff (Allington, Stuetzel, Shake, & Lamarche, 1986). Not surprisingly, such lack of connections between the support services and the classroom has created situations in which children remain in Title I programs throughout elementary school but are still struggling to read.

Even when Title I teachers' instruction occurs in the regular classroom, a coordinated program is not ensured (Bean, Cooley, Eichelberger, Lazar, & Zigmond, 1991; Rowan & Guthrie, 1989). Whatever the shape or form of the Title I or special education program, discussions and instructional planning are necessary to ensure that goals for a school year are clear among all those who work with students. In the Right Start in Reading project (Hiebert et al., 1992) in which Title I teachers' instructional time is spent on bringing children to independent reading and writing, goals are shared with everyone in the school. Prior to the initiation of the project, goals had been diffuse. While the district had a curriculum guide for classroom teachers, the role of Title I in relation to the district objectives had not been specified. Some of the Title I teachers did extended activities, such as making puppets or cooking, in conjunction with favorite children's books. Their view was that children who were not successful in classroom activities needed experiences in which they could be successful. Creating contexts in which young children are successful is at the heart of an emergent literacy perspective. However, in this case, little time was spent on gaining the literacy strategies that were needed to be successful in reading books independently or in writing compositions for an audience. Consequently, few children became more successful in their classroom literacy contexts. After classroom, Title I, and other resource (special education, speech and language, bilingual) teachers shared the goals and benchmarks for focused instruction, the levels of literacy in schools rose remarkably.

Clarity of Instructional Focus and Implementation.   Clarity of instructional focus and means of implementing instruction is a second feature of successful support programs. Allington et al. (1986) found that children who went to Title I programs in some schools had to cope with quite discrepant instructional materials in their classrooms and in Title I. In successful programs, similar materials, instructional strategies and activities, and assessments are shared by support and classroom teachers.

The Right Start in Reading project began with Title I teachers asking questions about how their meetings with children could be used to develop strategies that were needed to be successful in the tasks of the predominantly whole language instruction in their schools' classrooms. Title I teachers agreed that activities should be similar to those of the classroom but should permit Title I teachers to guide children in particular processes such as those described in Chapter 3. A core set of instructional activities was identified that met these criteria. For instance, one of the instructional activities fostered children's spelling strategies. In many of the schools' classrooms, children were encouraged to use invented spelling as they wrote stories and in journals. The children who were identified as "at risk" and in need of Title I guidance often failed to move to the conventional spelling that can be read by a wider audience. Title I teachers included activities such as journal writing—common in children's classrooms—where children were encouraged to make predictions about spellings of words. But they extended children's spelling strategies by showing them how to verify predictions through slowly "stretching" the sounds of the words and determining whether and how particular sounds were represented in their spellings. Further, they initiated an instructional strand that was aimed at children's facility in spelling and reading words with common rimes such as those that appear in many tradebooks, the material children saw in their classrooms (see Table 3.6). If the word *like* appeared in a book such as *What Do You Like?* (Grenjiec, 1992), children would study that word and write words with the same rime, such as *bike, Mike,* and *hike.* We will not elaborate on other elements of the instruction here because part of Chapter 7 was devoted to a description of a typical lesson by teachers within this project. Our reason for returning to this example is to emphasize the manner in which Title I teachers met children's literacy needs by creating activities and selecting materials that had connections to the classroom program.

We are not suggesting that Title I teachers should implement a regimen of worksheets, if that is the content of the classroom program. Title I teachers worked from their vision of literacy, first and foremost. However, as classroom teachers and other support teachers saw the new levels of literacy among the Title I students, they began to make refinements and changes in their programs as well. By ensuring that children were developing the central and necessary processes of literacy, the Title I teachers served as catalysts in their schools.

Other case studies point to the increased literacy learning for children who would otherwise struggle in school when classroom and support teachers provide congruent instruction. For example, Goatley (1995) has presented a case study of the first- and second-grade students in Mrs. Casey's resource room. By grades one and two, these students had been identified by classroom teachers as learning disabled in literacy. Among the features that characterized Mrs. Casey's program were clear goals for her students that were attainable with the instructional support she provided. Goatley noted that Mrs. Casey's collaboration with the regular education first-grade teacher was critical for these students' success. The two teachers shared their instructional practices, using overlapping activities to support vocabulary development and reading of easy-to-read books. Because of similarities across the two contexts in terms of the content taught and some of the methods of instruction, students from the resource classroom were able to participate with their regular education peers, often taking leadership roles that would not have been likely or possible without such commonalities across the two classrooms.

Similarly, the Early Literacy Project or ELP (Englert et al., 1994) which we have discussed previously (Chapter 6) illustrates what can happen when children identified as learning disabled are taught by special education teachers who make connections to children's regular education classrooms. In the ELP classrooms, specific instructional contexts such as Morning Message, author's chair, and a writing center provided environments that were similar to those in the regular education classroom. The ELP classrooms also provided children with opportunities to work within thematic units, to identify questions they wished to study, to read literature from the school and public libraries, to listen to guest speakers who had expertise in specific subjects they studied, and so forth. These experiences prepared the young readers who had previously struggled in their regular education classroom to participate in the same activities as their regular education peers. By embedding skill and strategy instruction within these holistic activities, children also developed the proficiencies to participate fully in their regular classroom contexts.

Unlike the programs characterized by lack of congruence between support and regular education classrooms (Allington, 1991a), students in these classrooms experienced successes in their regular education contexts because of the congruence between support and classroom programs. However, clarity of goals and congruence of instruction will mean nothing if the assessments on which teachers and students are held accountable are not similarly modified.

Shared Assessments. A common vision of literacy among teachers working with the same group of children leads to shared assessments. Shared assessments imply an exchange among teachers in assessment tasks, although every teacher may not use an identical set of tasks. Whatever assessments are gathered on children's literacy learning, shared assessments mean that all of the teachers who work with particular children give one another information and interpretations of children's learning. To illustrate the manner in which assessments are shared among a group of teachers, we return to the assessment tasks of the Right Start in Reading project that were the focus of Chapter 8.

When assessments are shared, teachers who work with the same students inform one another of the content of assessments. When teachers know about all of the tasks on which children are assessed, they can determine if particular tasks can be extended or modified to provide the information that they need. In this manner, superfluous assessments are eliminated and the time of children and teachers is spent profitably in learning rather than testing or evaluating. Before the Right Start in Reading project began, the only assessments which classroom and support teachers shared were the norm-referenced tests that were given in Title I schools at the beginning and end of each school year. While important decisions were made about which children would receive services based on these tests, neither classroom nor support teachers believed that the information pertained to the important goals of their literacy instruction. For children who were at the very earliest stages of reading and writing, the subtests of these standardized tests provided information on interim processes, especially auditory discrimination (Stallman & Pearson, 1990)—and even these interim processes were not necessarily the ones that teachers viewed as important in literacy acquisition such as phonemic blending. Because the norm-referenced tests did not pertain to the goals that classroom and support teachers valued, children were given additional assessments by various teachers. Classroom teachers had individually devised their own assessments of reading books or words. Sometimes the same assessments were used by all of the teachers within a grade level but rarely were the same assessments used by teachers across the primary grades of a school. Each type of support program administered another set of assessments, often to the same children. Title I teachers asked children to write stories because they emphasized writers' workshop. Speech specialists gave language production and perception tasks to children. Bilingual teachers tested children on their language comprehension and production.

As classroom and support teachers began to clarify their vision of literacy through collaboration in the Right Start in Reading project, they also identified assessment tasks that represented the most critical aspects of literacy and language. As the core tasks that were described in the previous chapter (Chapter 8)—running records, compositions, word-level reading and writing—were identified, support teachers with particular needs extended particular tasks. For example, speech teachers recognized that children's personal and critical responses to the texts that they have read could be tape recorded so that language production could be studied in a meaningful context. For speech teachers, this dimension of the assessment was more prominent in their interpretations of children's learning than for classroom or support teachers with other specialties. Classroom teachers across grade levels came to see the benefits of common tasks such as reading from a set of books that served as benchmarks for the primary grades in a school. These books were identified by groups of teachers and removed from the instructional program so that their use as benchmarks could be guaranteed.

Shared assessments also mean that assessment information obtained by individual teachers is available to other teachers who work with those children. This sharing of information applies to the teachers who work with the same children at any given point in time such as classroom teacher, Title I teacher, and speech specialist. Teachers in the Right Start in Reading schools also have a set of assessments that are shared with teachers from year to year. The full array of children's learning as represented through observing, interviewing, and work samples can be established when different teachers are contributing perspectives on the same children. The lenses provided by different teachers from different contexts and with different tools make it possible to establish children's typical strategies when unaided or working independently as well as their potential strategies when tasks are scaffolded. Thus the pooling of information by classroom and support teachers produces a complete view of children as readers and writers rather than the piecemeal views that teachers had before they began collaborating with one another on goals, instruction, and assessment.

Extending the Emergent Literacy Classroom to Other Communities

An underlying theme of this volume has been the role of meaningful literacy acts in children's development as readers and writers. Many meaningful literacy acts are part of the daily life of emergent literacy classrooms. A community read-along of *Millions of Cats* (Gag, 1928), creation of the Morning Message, or record keeping of the feeding schedule of the classroom gerbil are examples of meaningful literacy acts that make up the emergent literacy program. But there need to be many reasons for children to use literacy, which extend beyond the walls of the classroom or even the school. The read-along of *Millions of Cats* can be rehearsed and presented by first graders to a class of kindergartners. The events of the school day—including the weather—can be compared via e-mail with the events and weather of an emergent literacy classroom in another state or even another country (Songer, 1996). Literacy activities such as these give children many more reasons to write and read and to see the role that literacy serves in a variety of worlds.

Identifying relevant communities with which to share children's products is an important part of making an event or activity meaningful. Teachers choose these communities based on different purposes. For example, students' homes are a critical community into which teachers extend school literacy practices, both to share information and to draw upon students' home literacy activities and experiences (see Chapter 10 for extensive discussion on home↔school connections). Teachers may integrate future students by creating extensions to Head Start programs with first-grade students reading aloud to preschoolers. To demonstrate what children are learning in the primary grades to middle-grade teachers, primary-grade teachers may extend their students' literacy activities to work with a "buddy" class of older students in the school. To inform school board members of literacy acquisition activities within the early grades, this community may be invited to particular events as a learning experience for the board members. Thus, extension to other communities involves taking students' literacy learning beyond the walls of the classroom. We examine four means of extending the school literacy activities to external communities: (1) through publishing students' written pieces, (2) through oral productions such as choral reading and Readers' Theatre, (3) through cross-age activities such as buddy reading, and (4) through letter writing.

Publishing

The richness of children's writing was evident in the examples in Chapter 6—poems, stories, persuasive arguments, and reports. By no means are all compositions in an emergent literacy classroom published in the public, social domain but occasions for publication can be valuable in showing children that their views and imaginations are valued. When the occasion is an appropriate one, most children are eager to share their compositions.

We begin with the use of classroom and school hall walls as the venue for publishing because this context is accessible and allows children to proudly display their work, while serving another purpose—informing members of the broader community of the capabilities and interests of young children in writing. In a school in Colorado, kindergartners combined their imaginations, art projects, and initial awareness of letter-sound correspondence and shared these with the school community through a display in the entryway of the school. The labels on their paintings (which involved blotting the paint to create a mirror image) that follow were displayed under the caption "I see a . . .":

WRM	*(worm)*
BAR	*(bear)*
BRNKO HLmts	*(Bronco helmets)*
Snta Klas	*(Santa Claus)*
calrs	*(colors)*
2 people	
TrTL	*(turtle)*
PRATE CLOWD	*(pretty cloud)*
CMLS WITH GLASES	*(camels with glasses)*
A EGL	*(a eagle)*
BRNCO KLRS	*(Bronco colors)*
SUM BUBLZ	*(some bubbles)*
GOSST	*(ghost)*

These examples show the capabilities of these kindergarten students to convey their ideas to an audience. Publishing these drawings and writing communicated an important message to those who entered the school: From their initiation into this school, children were involved as writers.

Some schools have moved publications beyond the walls of the classroom and school to the walls of local businesses such as banks, which display
the artwork and compositions on the walls of their establishments. Some
local newspapers have supplements that publish an annual compendium of
children's compositions and artwork, while others have weekly columns with
children's work. There are magazines that accept children's writing and art
such as *Stone Soup: The Magazine by Children* (aimed at children 6 to 12
years), *Ranger Rick's Nature Magazine,* which is published by the National
Wildlife Federation (aimed at children 5 to 11 years), and *Highlights for
Children* (ages 3 to 12 years).

Many schools have purchased equipment so that children's books can be
bound. In University Hill School in Boulder, Colorado, the Rainbow Press
(the internal school publisher) has published children's books for several
decades—with copies of the books placed in the school library. Children can
check out the books written by their parents and neighbors when they were
children at the school.

A summer workshop series entitled Young Writers Workshop, held in
Jefferson County (Colorado) School District, has produced a series of books
that involve collaborations of children. Available through John Muir Press,
the most current is entitled *Kids Explore America's Japanese American
Heritage* (Lobach, 1995). The participants in these workshops have been as
young as eight but the books illustrate the important contributions that child
authors have to make. Other books in the series, dealing with the cultures of
Hispanic-American, African-American, and Western Native-American families, have been described by teachers as well received by children because of
the authenticity of the voices of their peers (Lobach, 1995).

In some schools, children's reviews of books have become part of some
school libraries. Jenks and Roberts (1990) describe the components of a
book review as a brief summary of the story, comment about the writing,
and recommendations for reading. While the first grader who wrote the following review did not include all of the components, this child's comments
do convey the gist of the book as well as provide a hook to interest other
children:

> giant oF BarLetta by Tomie DePaola
> it reminds me oF When I saw the Stachew of Liberty becouse BarLetta
> has a big Stachew to and they bothe have bin here a long time.
>
> *[It reminds me of when I saw the Statue of Liberty because Barletta has a big
> statue too and they both have been here a long time.]*

Publishing students' products can range from informal extensions such
as displays on school walls and bulletin boards to formal extensions that
parallel the publishing industry such as through Rainbow Books and the
John Muir Press. Extensions outside the school walls are both possible and
beneficial to students and should be an integral part of the early literacy
curriculum. When students see their work published as part of the literacy

community, they are well on their way to seeing themselves as members of the literate community, a basis for becoming a lifelong literacy participant.

Choral Reading and Readers' Theatre

Literacy comes alive as children add their own voices to literature in the form of plays, choral readings, and recitations of favorite poems. Sharing these literacy creations with a broader community, such as children from other classes in the school and family members, can be the source of sustained interest for young children. The comments of a second-grade student, Nathan, whose composition had been the basis for a play in his class, attest to the interest as well as the higher thinking processes that are enhanced when literacy is shared with a broader community: "Sometimes you hear it a different way when they read it than when acting it out because the actors add more to it. I like it better when they act it. It's fun to watch and I can pay attention better and think of other things" (Knipping, 1993, p. 45).

We have visited classrooms where we have been the audience for an impromptu presentation from the class's repertoire of poems and rhymes. The voices of a class of second graders reciting part of Eloise Greenfield's (1978) "Honey, I love" in Dawn Harris Martine's classroom in Harlem, New York, still echo in memory. In Dawn's classroom, children's repertoire of poems and rhymes changes over the school year with new poems, chants, and rhymes added, some forgotten, and a set of favorites revisited time and time again (Martine, 1991).

Other events involve choral readings of rhymes or poems, or readers' theatre, where two or more readers read a play, poem, or story from scripts based on written texts (McCaslin, 1990). Readers' theatre is characterized by the transformation of a story into a play. Writing the script involves many literacy processes and negotiations among children about their interpretations of the text. The transformation occurs in social interactions among children as they read various texts and discuss the merits of one or another for presentation, negotiate as to what should be transformed or deleted, determine and refine their interpretations, and develop presentable performances (Shanklin & Rhodes, 1989).

These activities appear to be particularly appropriate contexts for students who are acquiring a second language. In a project with children who represented a range of Pacific cultures in Guam, McCauley and McCauley (1992) found that the repeated reading of text through choral reading allowed ESL students to use English in a no-risk environment (mispronunciations could be absorbed by the overriding voices of the group). The repeated readings and the expressiveness that was added to the reading as children became more adept with a piece allowed them to make clearer associations between concepts and words in their native language and English.

A project in which many of the children were ESL learners illustrates the manner in which the opportunity to share one's reading through readers' theatre serves as a context for beginning readers (although in the middle grades) to become immersed in a text (Wolf, 1993). In preparing for a performance of *Tikki Tikki Tembo* (Mosel, 1968), the following discussion among a group of children illustrates the nature of discussion and involvement that can be part of readers' theatre:

> **Maia:**   No, we have to look in the book. . . . We have to find out the scene that we're gonna do.
>
> **Henry:**   It's right here. [turning to the book and reading] Chang ran as fast as his little legs could carry him to his mother.
>
> **Bobby:**   No, that's not the scene. . . .
>
> **Henry:**   and said, "Oh, most honorable Mother, Tikki tikki tembo—"
>
> **Bobby:**   No, I've already told . . . the scene. The scene is Maia tells us never to play by the well.
>
> **Maia:**   No, Bobby, you don't know if we agree on that scene!
>
> (Wolf, 1993, p. 542)

These negotiations around treatment of scenes in the book and development of characters eventually led to a production that was shared with students from other classrooms. Henry, Bobby, Maia, and their peers who were members of a resource classroom shone in this production. Members of one of the classes that watched the performance wrote a thank-you note in which they declared, "You are all stars!" (Wolf, 1993, p. 545).

Buddy Reading with Kindergartners and Preschoolers

Just as fourth and fifth graders plan sessions with emergent readers, first and second graders can select favorite books, practice reading these with expression and with appropriate questions, and read to kindergartners and preschoolers. Writing is also shared as Lamme and Ledbetter (1990) describe in an anecdote about a group of second graders who shared their compositions with their kindergarten book buddies. The kindergartners responded to the second graders' sharing by bringing books that they had memorized or written to sessions.

The accessibility of audio and video recorders in many schools lends support for another form of collaboration as first and second graders tape books for kindergartners and preschoolers. Real reasons for children to tape record their favorite books are many—creating a library of tapes from which families can draw when children are absent from school because of illness; the sharing of tapes with children who are learning English in another country (or a neighboring school); or establishing a set of audiotapes for a local Head Start.

The choice of book and the preparation of the book for taping or for interactive sessions involve children in many metacognitive discussions about appropriate topics and genres for children who are younger than they are. When first graders were asked to select books that were appropriate for kindergartners, few first graders were at a loss for words (Hiebert et al.,

1995). Many were quick to identify features of texts that would be appropriate for children younger than themselves.

Letter Writing

Letter writing is a means whereby children can get information and can interact with others. While these interactions can occur with same-age peers for emergent readers and writers, a correspondent who is somewhat older can respond to the emergent writer's sometimes cryptic phrases and "nudge" the younger writer to higher levels of expression. Exchanges have been reported between young readers and adults who are learning to read and write English (Dorotik & Betzold, 1992) and between children and adults in convalescent homes (Ashe, 1987). One group of correspondents for whom such extensions can benefit their learning as well as that of children consists of university students in teacher education programs. Overwhelmingly, exchanges between preservice teachers and emergent or struggling readers and writers are declared successful from the perspective of all participants—preservice teachers, young children, university instructors, and classroom teachers (Crowhurst, 1992; Rankin, 1992). For example, Greenlee, Hiebert, Bridge, and Winograd (1986) reported on the quality and quantity of second graders' writing when preservice teachers responded to their letters. Those students who wrote letters to an imaginary audience and received the conventional comments of the teacher did not write as well or as much as their peers who received letters in response. The notion of audience becomes quite real and can make students' writing, even that of first or second graders, discernibly different.

Exchanges between university students and children can focus on particular stories, as was the case in Bromley, Winters, and Schlimmer's (1994) project. Students in a master's-level literacy course at a university and a group of children exchanged webs (graphic organizers that represent categories of information and relationships between the categories) of stories and letters based on those webs. The exchange began with the creation by each graduate student of a web on personal information, such as interests, pets, family members, and similar topics, and an introductory letter based on the information in the web. The children received both the web and the letter and used these as models for creating their own webs and letters of introduction. After this initial exchange of letters, each graduate student chose a folk tale and created a partial web of it which, with a letter, was sent to the "book buddy." In response, the child read the graduate student's folk tale and completed the web, chose another folk tale and made a partial web of it, and wrote a letter requesting the graduate student to finish the web. The graduate students used knowledge of their book buddies to make the webbing of the stories meaningful, as this excerpt from a letter from Jan (the graduate student) to Brent (the book buddy and an aspiring football player) shows:

> So, my defensive football player, let's tackle the story Tricky Tortoise and fill in
> the game plan (web). I filled in the players (characters) in the story. You have to

list the plays (the events) that took place in the story, the problem, and the strategy to turn the story around (the solution). You also have to report on the web what the overall game plan of the story was (the theme). I already wrote my theme on the web. Just like two sportscasters reporting on a football game, each sportscaster will have his/her own theme (moral or main idea) about why the game went the way it did. So, write away, Brent!

These exchanges are also occurring through electronic mail, even though the children in reported projects to date have been in the middle grades. Moore (1991) used electronic mail for conferencing between graduate education students and struggling fifth graders. Campione, Brown, and Jay (1992) have set up electronic exchanges between graduate students who are specializing in aspects of the sciences (e.g., botany, ecology) and elementary students. This form of exchange increasingly will be part of emergent literacy classrooms.

Summary

Children's literacy learning can benefit greatly when other communities are brought into contact in meaningful ways with the emergent literacy classroom. *Integration* activities invite members of other communities into the emergent literacy classroom. *Extension* activities create contact with members of communities outside the classroom environment, extending the literacy community of the classroom. Integrating the resources of other communities and extending the learning of emergent readers and writers to other communities increase children's opportunities to use reading and writing meaningfully.

For members of available literacy communities—including but not limited to older students, librarians, and volunteers—to be full participants in emergent literacy classrooms, their roles and responsibilities need to be clear. For the resources of teachers from specially funded programs to be used to the full benefit of children, support and classroom teachers need to share goals, instructional focus and implementation, and assessment techniques.

The ways in which young children's literacy learning can be extended beyond the walls of the classroom are many and reflect the interests of children and teachers. Extensions that can be adapted in numerous ways include publishing students' written pieces, oral productions such as choral reading and readers' theatre, buddy reading with kindergartners and preschoolers, and writing letters to pen pals.

Because of the critically important connections between emergent literacy classrooms and the students' homes, we continue this discussion in Chapter 10, focusing specifically on home↔school connections.

chapter 10

Connecting to Children's Homes and Communities

———————————— V I G N E T T E 1 0 . 1 : ————————————

With a classroom of first graders all designated as "potential failures" because of their reading readiness scores, Mrs. Gardner began by scouting the
children's neighborhoods to identify shapes in the environment that resem-
bled letters. For example, a T could be seen in a telephone pole. As homework, children looked for letters in their environment. A next step was to
identify the print on cars and license plates. As the year wore on, children
made advertisements for school events and created birthday cards by past-
ing together parts of commercial advertisements and photographs from
magazines.

(Heath, 1983)

———————————— V I G N E T T E 1 0 . 2 : ————————————

In an all-Spanish-speaking school in Lenox (California) School District,
kindergarten teachers have been using a series of simple booklets called
Libros to initiate children into reading. These booklets begin with captions
and become progressively more challenging. An early book about a bear
includes statements such as: El oso se levanta. El oso come. (The bear gets
up. The bear eats.) Once children have learned to read a booklet, they take
a copy home to share with family members and to include in their home
libraries.

(Goldenberg, 1990)

These vignettes illustrate the two primary aspects of home-school connections that we examine in this chapter. The example from Mrs. Gardner's
classroom demonstrates the *integration* of literacies from children's homes
and communities into the classroom. The example of children's sharing of
their literacy accomplishments with family members as they read the Libros
in the school in Lenox School District illustrates *extensions* of school literacy
events and accomplishments to children's home communities.

As these two examples show, the connections between home and school
involve the same two processes as those described in Chapter 9 between the

emergent literacy classroom and other literacy communities in general. Because children's homes and neighborhoods are the most important literacy communities for students' literacy development, the nature of these connections merits in-depth treatment. Too often, the connection between school and home has been one-sided; messages and advice flow from the school to the home, informing parents and guardians about specific literacy practices that should happen in the home or about problems that their children are experiencing in school. Movement in the opposite direction is rare, exploring those existing literacy expectations and events in children's homes that could be integrated into school contexts to facilitate their literacy development. From an emergent literacy perspective, the literacies of children's homes and communities are central to the multiple literacies that they are to develop in school, while the literacies of school are enhanced by extensions from school to home contexts.

There are many misconceptions around home-school connections especially in high-poverty schools (Lightfoot, 1978). The underlying assumptions of an emergent literacy perspective challenge us as teachers to carefully study and understand the existing literacies and support for literacy in children's homes. We first examine these assumptions in relation to home-school connections and then elaborate on the processes of integrating home literacies into classrooms and extending school literacies into children's homes.

Home-School Connections within an Emergent Literacy Perspective

The principles of learning that are part of the emergent literacy perspective not only underscore the importance of home-school connections, but they also guide teachers' interactions with parents, integration of children's home literacies into the classroom, and extensions of school literacies into the home.

Literacy Learning Occurs through Meaningful Use

Throughout this volume, we have described the essence of literacy as communicating meanings—either interpreting the meanings of other authors or expressing one's own meanings as an author. Many children have discovered the meaningfulness of books, as adults have read to them in homes and preschools. These known and familiar uses of literacy form the foundation of the emergent literacy program in a school. Parents join the class for storytime and read favorite family books. Children bring their favorite books and drawings that they have done as preschoolers to the classroom. They bring examples of print from their homes and communities—words from cereal boxes and toys. Teachers take photos of the signs in children's neighborhoods. They create play centers of familiar literacy events such as the veterinarian center that was described in Vignette 7.3. By integrating children's existing literacy knowledge and experiences into the emergent literacy classroom, children approach literacy learning in a new situation with confidence and knowledge.

Similarly, children's growing knowledge about literacy as a result of their school experiences needs to be shared and used in meaningful ways with members of their families and communities. Without such extensions, it is doubtful that literacy will become an integral part of their lives. When teachers guide children in using their developing literacy at home, children become aware of the purposes and power of literacy. As children identify television programs in a newspaper, read about the sugar content on the cereal box, or share a new book with a family member, they develop lifelong literacy habits.

Literacy Learning Is Embedded in Oral Language

The mediating role of language in knowledge acquisition draws attention to the integration of children's home language patterns as the foundation for the classroom literacy program (see Chapter 4 for an extended discussion of the role of students' home language patterns). Briefly, when children's language facility in home and community organizations such as the church and extended families is acknowledged and integrated into classroom literacy events, children can bring their experiences and linguistic knowledge to learning to read and write. When existing language patterns are dismissed or deemed inappropriate as was the case with some of the kindergartners in the Show and Tell event that Michaels (1981) observed, children's access to literacy events in the classroom is limited. When children's ways of reasoning and manipulating language are recognized as Mrs. Gardner did in the first vignette, the familiar becomes the basis for acquiring new strategies and skills.

Literacy Learning Occurs in Multiple Contexts

The third principle that describes the need for children to interact with participants who range in their roles and literacy proficiencies draws teachers' attention to the scaffolding of tasks for children and their family members. Without considerable scaffolding, many young children may not share the literacy materials and events with which they are proficient in home and preschool environments. Similarly, without appropriate and well-designed tasks, children may not share their growing literacy proficiencies developed in school with family members. For example, family members may not be aware that young children can be capable and interested writers. Extending children's literacies to the home environment may be a function of the scaffolding of tasks for children in their homes.

It has been through interactions with family members, from older siblings to adults, that children have gained the literacy and language that they bring to school. Understanding how parents interpret the role of guide or teacher in literacy interactions with their children is central to the design of any literacy program that extends from school to home. Effective school-home literacy programs build on what parents do well. Parents' existing views of their roles and their interaction styles must be understood if parents are to be asked to engage in activities that are new to the home. We will illustrate these principles in action as the literacies of home are *integrated* into the classroom and as the literacies of the classroom are *extended* to the home.

Integrating the Literacies of Home into the Emergent Literacy Classroom

There are literacy events in the homes of all children, regardless of educational level or socioeconomic status of the family (Anderson & Stokes, 1984; Taylor & Dorsey, 1988). While some of these uses of print may not be directly articulated to children, they have seen people around them use print. Children are frequently present when an adult scans the shelves of a grocery store, looking for the label on a particular product. An announcer clearly articulates the name of a product as it is flashed onto the television screen. The name of a store is highly visible, as is the claim of "sale" on its windows.

Further, parents of all socioeconomic levels want their children to do well in school, express interest in supporting their children's literacy learning, and attempt to engage their children in literacy events. Existing events and parents' expectations are important to integrate into classrooms. We begin by describing the visions and hopes that parents have for their children and then describe how books and print in children's home environments can be integrated into classrooms.

Interacting around Shared Goals

Understanding that parents share the goal of bringing children to high levels of literacy is important. While parents' actions aimed at fostering these goals will not necessarily take identical forms to those of classrooms, teachers need to understand the visions of success in school and literacy that parents hold for their children. Evidence of the misperceptions that educators hold of parents' aspirations for their children and the activities that parents believe contribute to literacy can be found in several interview studies.

Before Goldenberg and his colleagues began the project in the Lenox School District from which Vignette 10.2 was taken, teachers based their assumptions about parents' interest and involvement in their children's literacy on parents' linguistic proficiency in English (80% of the district's students were limited English proficient) and on socioeconomic status (95% of them receive free or reduced lunch). Goldenberg (1994) describes the assumptions of teachers as follows: "Parents needed a great deal of training before they could help their children, parents were largely illiterate and de-emphasized academic achievement in favor of family or survival values, families were under such economic stress they could not play a meaningful role in children's academic development, or literacy in the home was not a part of the families' culture" (Goldenberg, 1994, p. 188). Teachers took the view that "You have to take the kids from where they are and get them as far as possible" (Goldenberg, 1994, p. 190). This seemingly reasonable educational goal was translated into passivity in the face of students' initial low performances. That is, because children had started school with low levels of literacy knowledge, they could not be expected to attain very high levels of literacy.

When Goldenberg and his colleagues talked with parents in their homes, they found that, while some parents' educational levels were low, all had minimum reading skills and many were performing at much higher levels. School-like literacy activities were not prominent but literacy events such as the exchange of letters with relatives in other countries were quite common in almost all homes. Also, most parents described themselves as discussing print on advertisements and flyers with their children. Parents valued educational achievement highly and its role in social and economic mobility. A comment by a mother confirms the status of education:[1] "If you've studied a lot, you can open up opportunities for yourself. Otherwise, you have to clean houses or ask for handouts because you don't know how to do anything else" (Goldenberg & Gallimore, 1991, p. 9).

Parents' interpretations of what was important to do with their children differed, however, from the views of teachers. Goldenberg and his colleagues (Goldenberg, Reese, & Gallimore, 1992) sent the Libros (see Vignette 10.2) home to one group of children as a home intervention (rather than taught in the classrooms) and, for another group of students, sent worksheets extending the Libros. The researchers found that use of the worksheets at home, but *not* use of the Libros, seemed to help the students' literacy development in kindergarten. The researchers had expected the opposite—that the more enjoyable activities associated with the Libros would foster students' kindergarten literacy successes. In follow-up interviews, parents stated their beliefs that children learn to read by progressing through a sequence beginning with letters and continuing through sounds, syllables, words, and finally extended texts with each step requiring systematic repetition until accuracy is achieved. In short, they may have valued and spent more time on worksheets than on those literacy activities that seemed to be simply "for fun." Goldenberg et al. reasoned that this view of learning to read may derive from the experiences that many parents had had in Mexico or Central America, but similar perceptions of the appropriateness of organized rather than playful literacy activities have been confirmed among Head Start mothers (McLane & McNamee, 1990).

Fitzgerald et al. (1991) studied parents' perceptions of appropriate literacy activities for young children as a function of parents' literacy levels. While both groups of parents who read extensively and those who did not

---

[1] In the articles in which these quotes appear, the statement appeared in Spanish as well as the English translation which we provide here.

thought that simple materials such as paper, pens, and books were most important, the top-ranked items by parents who read less frequently were instructional materials such as alphabet blocks and flash cards and instructional events such as viewing educational television. By contrast, parents who frequently read ranked these as least important. For example, a parent who infrequently read, when asked "Do you think there is anything parents of two- to four-year-olds might do to help their children learn to read and write better when they start school? If yes, what?" responded with "Learn names, practice with letters and writing, maybe read with them." Parents who frequently read embraced natural artifacts and activities and were outspoken in their disavowal of skill-oriented materials and activities: "I just don't believe in pushing any of this stuff. I think it can do more harm than good" (Fitzgerald et al., 1991, p. 205).

From these projects, we can conclude that parents place high value on their children's literacy learning but that, for some, success in the early stages of literacy translates into the acquisition of rudimentary skills. What does this information mean for classroom teachers? Should their time be devoted to changing parents' minds? Or is there a way in which parents' value of literacy can be used as a resource? From work on projects such as the one described in Vignette 10.2, Goldenberg (1994) has concluded that the first step is for educators to recognize parents' values and contributions. Delpit (1988) also argues that the "skill-oriented" view of literacy held by some groups of parents should not be discounted by educators. Many low-income children have been shortchanged, Delpit points out, when schools have moved to instruction that is modeled after the parent-child interaction in middle-class homes. A review of the literature on parent-child literacy interactions in middle-income homes verifies that considerable teaching of skills occurs even when nurturing is the espoused philosophy of parents (Hiebert, 1993). Much of this teaching of skills occurs as parents and children participate in everyday events such as a rhyming game in the car (Tobin & Pikulski, 1983). In a subsequent section, we explore discussions and brochures that give parents ideas for involving their children in book reading, including attention to letters and sounds. These extension activities are successful only insofar as they are based on educators' respect of their students and their families.

Without such respect, communication between school and home flows one way, with many messages traveling from school to home. In a study of school-home communication, Fraatz (1987) observed in four types of schools that she characterized by prominent context (Factory City, Trade City, Blue Collar Suburb, White Collar Suburb). She reported that most information went from school to home. Children's behavior was the primary focus of the communication, including requests for help from the family to bring children's behaviors in line with classroom routines. When teachers sought information from parents, questions pertained to possible home circumstances that teachers believed could be contributing to problems with the child's school performance. For example, teachers probed parents about possible sources (e.g., a domestic crisis) behind a child's changed behavior pattern.

When teachers talk with parents, however, they often discover eager partners. Shockley (1994), a teacher in a school within a low-income community, received 100% participation from families when she asked parents to "Tell me about your child" (in conversation as well as through a survey). In addition, Shockley instituted a home-school dialogue journal in which adult family members and the teacher corresponded with one another about accomplishments and events that were significant to children. Families also compiled stories—records of special stories in a family's history—for a classroom book. These activities emanated from a teacher's belief in parents' interest in their children's literacy learning and in the critical contributions of existing literacy and language events in children's home lives to learning in school.

Together, these studies make clear how important it is for teachers and parents to understand each other, and through this understanding come to share goals for children's literacy development. With such shared goals, events from students' homes are more fluidly brought into and integrated with classroom literacy events.

Integrating Children's Home Literacy Events and Artifacts into the Classroom

As we noted in Chapter 4, children's access to literacy is integrally tied to the language patterns that are used in the classroom (Michaels, 1981). Emergent literacy classrooms are contexts where the focus is on facilitating children's expression of *ideas,* not simply the *form* of their oral language. We consider two aspects of integration of the home literacy events into classroom learning: bringing environmental print into the classroom and discovering what students already know about written language.

Bringing Environmental Print into the Classroom.   An emphasis on ideas opens the possibilities of drawing on the range of environmental print—the print that students likely encounter in their day-to-day activities within their families—rather than being limited to the sight-word lists dictated by district guidelines or commercial materials. Making connections to environmental print helps students begin to recognize the extensive literacy background they already have to draw upon as they learn to read the language of children's literature and textbooks.

An aspect of environmental print that is present in the physical environment—labels on T-shirts and containers, phrases on billboards, words on shoes, hats, and placards—is familiar to young children, even if they cannot read the print when it is transposed to another context. Hiebert (1978) found that low-income children responded with enthusiasm and delight when presented with environmental print. Researchers such as Masonheimer et al. (1984) assumed that this interest should mean that children could accurately read these words even in other contexts. However, because children used the context to give meaning to the print (a fundamental process in beginning the road to literacy), they gave the name for the cola even though the word on the bottle was *Stop.* Consequently, these researchers concluded that environmental print recognition was not highly useful in becoming literate.

What these researchers missed was the role of the adult in scaffolding children's attention to the graphic rather than contextual features of the environmental print. Mrs. Gardner's lessons in Vignette 10.1 demonstrate well the manner in which children's interest in environmental print and their familiarity with their environments can be used to focus attention on the features of written language. In addition to the use of environmental print to learn about letter names, Mrs. Gardner used photographs of the children to illustrate concepts like "over" and "under," and these became part of books that students made.

Heath (1983) also provides a case study of a second-grade teacher who participated in the same project as Mrs. Gardner. The teacher, too, built on what children knew by using signs from advertisements, traffic and road signs, political posters, announcements of meetings, and notices of sales. This teacher emphasized that reading and writing were things that children already did—at home, riding their bikes, at the barbershop. She likened reading and writing to sports, reminding students that when they play in a league they have a coach. They read price tags, names and instructions for toys, and notices of upcoming events in school and the neighborhoods. There was a specified time each day when students told about information they had acquired from these types of reading.

Children's reading of familiar materials—from newspaper advertisements about toys to comic books—as part of recognized literacy events in the classroom conveys to them that this process called "reading" is one about which they are knowledgeable. Anne Hemmeter (1991), a teacher whose classroom we have referred to previously (see Chapter 2), takes her kindergarten class on a visit to a local grocery store during the first month or so of a school year, thus making concrete the link between common events in children's lives beyond school and the literacy events of the classroom. The purpose of the grocery store visit is to purchase the ingredients for "stone soup," following their reading of the big book with that title. Opening children's eyes to the treasure chest of print in a grocery store has extended children's literacy learning, while also guiding parents in extending events such as this one on a regular basis. The letter the children have written to the store manager to request a "personal shopping tour" is posted prominently on a large piece of posterboard in the local store where many of the children and their parents shop, and their thank-you letter, which follows the visit, is posted there, too. Prior to the visit, the store manager (with guidance from Anne) sends a bag of groceries with items that begin with the letters that children are studying. These activities serve to scaffold children's attention to the letters on grocery items before the class visit (and after the visit as well). The class visit to the store is full of discussions about the words on packages that need verification so that strange items do not get into the soup by mistake, such as *rice,* not *rinse.*

Discovering What Children Know about Written Language.   Much can be gained by learning early what it is that students already know about how our language works, recognizing that parents have different priorities for what they emphasize during preschool years. For example, some parents have given a priority to letter naming through a range of home games and activities, and such dimensions of children's knowledge should be recognized. Reading Recovery (Clay, 1985), an early literacy intervention, devotes the first ten lessons of instruction to establishing what children already know in a process that is called "roaming the known." Activities are created around what children know. A child's knowledge of letters and an interest in animals might be employed by making an alphabet book with illustrations of animals for each letter.

Part of this process of establishing what children know is to understand the nature of their literacy experiences in preschool settings. A study of the match between literacy in preschool and kindergarten classrooms showed that kindergarten teachers conducted no surveys and asked no questions about the types of literacy experiences their students had had in day-care centers or preschools (Papierz, Hiebert, & DiStefano, 1990). Kindergarten teachers initiated no communication with the preschool teachers, unless a child had severe behavioral problems or unless their own family had a child in the preschool or day-care center. This lack of connection did not deter the preschools from pursuing literacy programs. One of them conducted such a program quite aggressively. But it was quite a different version of literacy than was common in the kindergarten classroom—copying letters rather than scribbling and looking at books. Little wonder that Clay (1991) describes the transition for children between preschools and public schools as harsh.

Edwards (1995) has worked with first-grade teachers to collect their students' "literacy histories." Edwards notes that when a child sees a physician for the first time, extensive family histories are gathered to help interpret subsequent events in the child's medical life. She argues that students' literacy development is just as contextually based upon their family history as is their physical and emotional development. She has found parents to be willing and eager participants in helping their child's teachers understand his or her preschool history with literacy events in the home and community.

In summary, it is critically important to create opportunities for integrating students' early experiences in literacy and with print into their formal instruction in literacy acquisition. There are a range of opportunities for teachers to involve parents, some designed simply to gather information, others designed to help integrate the students' activities with their parents into the classroom literacy instructional program. In the next section, we explore the connections in the other direction: how the school can interact with parents to involve them in extending their children's school literacy acquisition into the home in meaningful ways.

Extending Literacy Learning from School to Home

The call for enhancing children's literacy experiences is pervasive. Professional organizations have brochures, booklets, and videotapes that carry the message to parents that they should read to their children. Local branches of professional organizations go to hospitals with the message to parents of infants that they should read to their children. The new legislation for Title I (formerly Chapter 1) mandates home liaison components which are typically interpreted to mean that literacy experiences need to be increased within the home. Businesses sponsor home reading programs, with major grocery chains, newspapers, and television stations reinforcing the message that parents should read to their children. There is an obvious perception that literacy should become a more important part of the experiences of children at home.

There can be no doubt that children whose parents read to them benefit from this experience, and there should be no doubt that parents should be supported to read to their children. However, the manner in which schools deliver and support this message is critical. Simply disseminating the message "Read to your child" without additional support may be as ineffectual as public service messages to "eat well." We will describe three ways in which classroom teachers can support students and their family members in engaging in productive literacy events: (1) sharing information about already existing home literacy events, (2) providing families with books, book lists, information, and other materials, and (3) providing scaffolds for home reading programs.

As background for these three forms of extensions, we discuss an underlying issue—the language of communication. In talking with adult family members or in sending home materials with children, the diversity of language and educational experiences of children's families needs to be continually recognized by educators. Individuals who will translate conversations and written messages are available in most school communities. In addition, the messages that educators write need to be informative, clear, and succinct. When messages from school to home communicate the content of the classroom literacy programs, links will be forged between children's literacy learning at school and at home.

Sharing Information about Already Existing Home Literacy Events

There are many instances of literacy in everyday lives of all families. While all of the potential literacy events may not occur in every family, Anderson and Stokes (1984) identified nine literacy events that can occur in homes:

(1) daily living routines, such as reading recipes and writing shopping lists; (2) entertainment, such as reading a novel, the *TV Guide,* or labels and information on a videotape; (3) school-related activities, such as doing homework and reading messages from school; (4) interpersonal communication, such as reading or writing personal letters and messages on greeting cards; (5) religion, such as reading brochures and documents in the place of worship and at home; (6) the exchange or reporting of information, such as reading baseball scores; (7) work, such as reading a list of new products; (8) literacy techniques and skills aimed at teaching young children to read, such as providing a workbook bought at a supermarket; and (9) storybook time, when a book is read to the child. Examining the occurrence of the nine literacy events in lower-income and middle-income homes, Anderson and Stokes (1984) concluded that homes of lower-income families would be described as providing fewer opportunities with literacy when the definition was limited to book reading. But when literacy was viewed more broadly, all families had contact with print (particularly across the daily living, entertainment, and religion categories).

Purcell-Gates, L'Allier, and Smith (1995) used these same categories of literacy events in observations and interviews with families well over a decade after Anderson and Stokes (1984) had conducted their observations. Their findings were similar to Anderson and Stokes's in substantiating the variety of literacy events in homes of the same socioeconomic level. Purcell-Gates et al. also verified a pattern that we have discussed in describing the results of Fitzgerald et al.'s (1991) surveys of parents' perceptions about appropriate literacy experiences: Some parents may be unaware of the benefits to children's emergent literacy in pointing out and talking about environmental print. For them, literacy acquisition may equate with learning to name letters and, as advertised by some companies on television, phonics.

Sharing with adult family members the potential of the many literacy events and artifacts that already exist in their homes and communities can be eye-opening and productive. Hiebert and Coffey (1983) produced a simple brochure with the names of popular fast-food franchises and products such as soft drinks on the cover. Inside was a description of the importance of pointing out this print to children and identifying letters within these words. Many parents of kindergartners were eager and glad to be supported in an activity that had seemed so ordinary and commonplace to them. The kindergartners' letter-naming proficiency increased as a result.

As well as brochures and discussions with parents, assigning tasks to children is another means of communicating to families the importance of the everyday literacy events in homes. Mrs. Gardner's activities in Vignette 10.1 illustrate ways in which homework tasks can draw children's attention to the print in their environments. We recommend that the nature of the task be communicated clearly to children and their families. Written notes in which children describe to their parents the homework task, outcomes, and time lines are effective and give children another opportunity to communicate.

Another area for connections with already existing home events has to do with television viewing. From every indication, many American schoolchildren spend a sizable portion of their after-school time watching television. While data are not available on the 1992 National Assessment of Educational Progress for children younger than fourth grade, self-reports by fourth graders indicate that they watch an average of three and a half hours of television daily (Mullis et al., 1993, Table 6.5). For those children who watch television, teachers can assign activities that encourage children to reflect on their television viewing. The strongest results for children's literacy learning as a function of viewing *Sesame Street* came when adults in the home discussed the contents of the show with children and made extensions of information from the show to other contexts (Ball & Bogatz, 1971).

A literacy initiative entitled READ-WRITE-NOW (U.S. Department of Education, 1995) suggests activities that extend children's television viewing in ways that promote literacy: (1) have children identify their favorite television shows, categorize them (e.g., family show, cartoon, situation comedy, sports, news and information), rate their interest in the shows, and explain why the rating was given; and (2) have children keep weekly TV logs in which they record at least five unfamiliar words that they have heard or seen. These unfamiliar words can become the basis for discussion. Purcell-Gates et al. (1995) also recommend that the value of television programs aimed specifically at literacy development such as *Sesame Street* and *Reading Rainbow* be communicated to children and their parents. Other programs such as *Storytime* on PBS, where celebrities read books together with young children, are also aimed at modeling family literacy. An example of another form of scaffolding that teachers provide is a viewing schedule on which shows such as these are marked.

Providing Books, Book Lists, Information, and Other Materials

In response to research that shows the value of home reading programs (Teale, 1986, 1987), many schools have enacted programs to encourage children's book reading at home. For such programs truly to assist children in establishing consistent patterns of book reading, they require thoughtful design. First, programs need to be designed to use materials that already exist in the home as a primary basis for home reading and discussion. As Purcell-Gates et al. (1995) have emphasized, the availability of books for children varies substantially from home to home, regardless of socioeconomic status. A study by Pellegrini et al. (1990) suggests that one criterion for successful interaction around home literacy materials is familiarity. Existing materials such as toy advertisements and comics from the local newspaper that were familiar to low-income parents and their preschool children were the source of more lively discussions than were unfamiliar picturebooks.

In addition to encouraging reading of familiar materials, there are other features, many reflected in Vignette 10.2 describing the Libros program, that are likely to increase the children's involvement with books in the home.

First, children were well versed with the books that were sent home and the related activities. In developing the home aspect of the Libros program, Goldenberg was influenced by the findings of other researchers (e.g., McCormick & Mason, 1989) who recognized that there were times when adults are not available to read along with the students at home. Thus Goldenberg and his colleagues modeled for students how they could engage in home reading and the activities. When parents, guardians, or siblings were available, the students were able to teach them how to be effective supporters in the home reading program. When children read by themselves, they were still able to have experiences with books, albeit without the support of a more experienced reader.

A second feature of the Libros project was the provision of materials. The Libros consisted of a special set of materials that could be used in both the classroom and the home (Goldenberg, 1990). In the Right Start in Reading project that was described in Chapter 7 (Hiebert et al., 1992), the little books that children had read during their school reading program were sent home nightly. Because collections of books were critical to the teachers' instruction, teachers were initially reluctant to send books home from these collections. Teachers who were willing to send books home, however, quickly saw the benefits of children's sharing with family members their increasing literacy proficiency with books that they had successfully completed. Those teachers who participated fully in the school-home book reading program sent home numerous books on extended vacations such as the winter break. Also critical was students' reading over the more extended summer vacation. A district grant of several hundred dollars made it possible for teachers to send children an installment of three books in the middle of the summer. Such a reminder of reading has been found to be successful in previous efforts (McCormick & Mason, 1989) and may be one reason that children in this program did not experience drops in reading levels that often occur over the summer months (Catto, 1993).

One form of material that is often forgotten involves paper and pens or pencils so that children can write at home (Baghban, 1989; Clay, 1987). The central place of writing in an emergent literacy classroom means that this dimension of children's growth in literacy needs to be shared with family members. Writing activities and materials can be modeled through writing packets that originate in the classroom, packets that are relatively inexpensive. Reutzel and Fawson (1990) created a Traveling Tales backpack for use by students and their teacher in a first-grade classroom. The backpack had several plastic zippered pouches for storing the range of supplies that were included (e.g., water-base markers, colored pencils, scissors, small stapler, staples). Guidelines to parents that contained ideas and directions for working with their children to create a composition were included. Each child kept the backback for several days, the number of days divided so that each child in the first-grade classroom had the opportunity to take the backpack home at least one time over a several-month period. The backpack served at least two purposes: (1) illustrating the kinds of materials the parents might provide and activities they could engage in with their children, even without the backpack, and (2) providing parents with the materials and guidance so they could help their students produce compositions.

Ideas and guidelines that accompany materials are the third component of an effective school-home book reading program such as the Libros and Traveling Tales backpack. In the school-home program that Goldenberg and his colleagues initiated in Lenox, students kept a list of words gained from their reading of books at home and a homework assignment list. At the fall parent-teacher conference parents agreed to support their children's participation in the home reading program, though follow-up notes and phone calls from the teachers were found to help sustain parents' involvement.

The use of books with young children can also be demonstrated to adult family members. In the intervention project described earlier (Hiebert et al., 1992), the benefits of early success were discussed with parents early on in the school year. Parents' support in two arenas was also elicited: children's regular attendance at school and a daily read-along of a book at home. By modeling a read-along of a book, teachers demonstrated to parents how they could guide their child in tracking print. This occasion also afforded an opportunity for teachers to advise parents that initially children would not be able to remember all of the words in books that they brought home.

The READ-WRITE-NOW initiative (U.S. Department of Education, 1995) provides guidelines for adults' interaction with beginning readers in community and home settings, suggesting that adults listen to children read as well as read to them. A turn-taking strategy is described where an adult family member and the child take turns, beginning with a small unit (e.g., a paragraph) and moving to longer units (such as a half page and then a page). When children have trouble reading words, adults are advised to:

- Ask the child to skip over the word, read the rest of the sentence, and then say what would make sense in the story for the missing word.
- Guide the child to use what he or she knows about letter sounds.
- Supply the correct word.
- Tell your child how proud you are of his or her efforts and skills.

Inasmuch as many American homes have videotape players, this medium offers possibilities for informing families about interactions around books. Videotapes of adult-child book reading are available through professional organizations—such as the International Reading Association (IRA) which distributes *Read to me,* a production of the Idaho Literacy Project (1991). Organizations such as IRA also have printed materials to distribute to parents, including versions in languages other than English. A booklet such as Baghban's (1989) "You can help your child to write" can be useful in explaining to parents an emergent literacy perspective on writing.

Ideas and guidelines about activities can assist parents in supporting their children and in understanding children's learning, in and out of school. Also important are explanations that accompany the literacy artifacts that children take home—stories that they have written, little books to which they have added their own text. Because families may not understand the nature of young children's writing, short descriptions written by the teacher about the purposes of the activity can be helpful accompaniments when sending home children's early compositions. A photocopied note sent with students' journals might state: "A goal of first grade is to learn to express ideas and to spell. Like learning to talk, learning to spell begins with efforts that don't necessarily look like adult spelling. But you'll see over the year how spelling grows when children write and write." As we have observed previously, notes such as this one need to be short but informative. Such notes also need to be translated, when necessary, to accommodate parents who speak other languages.

Scaffolding Home Book Reading Experiences

The goal of teachers' activities is to *scaffold* home book reading experiences so that families select their own books, rather than to direct these experiences by mandating materials and activities. Providing children and their parents with book lists is one step along the way to family involvement in selecting books. Table 10.1 gives the portions of the book lists that are intended for young children from the READ-WRITE-NOW material (U.S. Department of Education, 1995). Because these lists are heavily loaded with "old favorites," lists that include literature representing various cultural groups (see Table 5.2) are important additional sources for many children and their families.

A second means for teachers to scaffold school-home book reading extensions for children is to take children on tours of the local public library. Tours of the local library give children a comfort level with the library and also a sense of excitement about visiting the library. Introducing children to librarians and asking librarians to feature the books on the book list that has been shared with parents are other ways of ensuring that children can serve as "family guides" at the local public library. Providing information on summer literacy and language arts programs at the public library, the city or county's department of recreation, and the school district is another way in which teachers can scaffold extension experiences for families.

A third form of scaffolding home reading is to identify support services within the community. There are many community centers, corporations, and volunteer organizations, such as university sororities and fraternities, that provide tutoring and services associated with literacy and language arts. Putting families in touch with these services is a two-step process: (1) familiarizing children with the services and representatives of the services and (2) providing information to families. A letter exchange with members of a sorority or fraternity may make children comfortable and eager to continue interactions. This familiarity on the part of children may provide the initiative for adult family members to enroll children in after-school and summer programs that these groups offer.

TABLE 10.1   Book Lists for Families
Favorite Books of RIF Kids

(Provided by Reading Is Fundamental, Inc.)

For Preschool to Kindergarten-Age Children
  Allard, Harry. *Miss Nelson Is Missing!*
  Ames, Lee J. *Draw Draw Draw*
  Anonymous. Fairy tales, folk tales, and nursery rhymes, including: "Cinderella,"
      "The Gingerbread Man," "Little Red Riding Hood," "The Three Little Pigs,"
      "The Three Billy Goats Gruff," "Goldilocks and the Three Bears," and Mother
      Goose rhymes
  Bemelmans, Ludwig. *Madeline*
  Berenstain, Stan and Jan. *The Berenstain Bears*
  Bridwell, Norman. *Clifford, the Big Red Dog*
  Brown, Margaret W. *Goodnight, Moon*
  Carle, Eric. *The Very Hungry Caterpillar*
  Mayer, Mercer. *There's a Nightmare in My Closet*
  McCloskey, Robert. *Make Way for Ducklings*
  Piper, Watty. *The Little Engine That Could*
  Potter, Beatrix. *The Tale of Peter Rabbit*
  Rey, H. A. *Curious George*
  Sendak, Maurice. *Where the Wild Things Are*
  Seuss, Dr. *The Cat in the Hat*
  Solbodkina, Esphyr. *Caps for Sale*
  Waber, Bernard. *Ira Sleeps Over*
  Zion, Gene. *Harry the Dirty Dog*

Grades 1 through 3
  Allard, Harry. *Miss Nelson Is Missing!*
  Berenstain, Stan and Jan. *The Berenstain Bears Nursery Tales*
  Blume, Judy. *Freckle Juice*
  Bridwell, Norman. *Clifford, the Big Red Dog*
  Cleary, Beverly. *Ramona Quimby, Age Eight*
  Dahl, Roald. *Charlie and the Chocolate Factory*
  Hoban, Russell. *Bedtime for Frances*
  Lobel, Arnold. *Frog and Toad Are Friends*
  McCloskey, Robert. *Make Way for Ducklings*
  Mosel, Arlene. *Tikki Tikki Tembo*
  Parish, Peggy. *Amelia Bedelia*
  Rey, H. A. *Curious George*
  Sendak, Maurice. *Where the Wild Things Are*
  Seuss, Dr. *The Cat in the Hat*
  Sharmat, Marjorie W. *Nate the Great*
  Silverstein, Shel. *Where the Sidewalk Ends*
  Sobol, Donald J. *Encyclopedia Brown, Boy Detective*
  Viorst, Judith. *Alexander and the Terrible, Horrible, No Good, Very Bad Day*
  Warner, Gertrude. *Boxcar Children*
  White, E. B. *Charlotte's Web*
  Wilder, Laura. *Little House on the Prairie*
  William, Margery. *The Velveteen Rabbit*

TABLE 10.1 *continued*
American Library Association Reading List
(Provided by the American Library Association)

Preschool

    Brown, Margaret Wise. *Goodnight Moon*

    Carle, Eric. *The Very Hungry Caterpillar*

    Freeman, Don. *Corduroy*

    Hughes, Shirley. *Alfie Gives a Hand*

    Martin, Bill Jr. *Brown Bear, Brown Bear, What Do You See?*

    Potter, Beatrix. *The Tale of Peter Rabbit*

Ages 5–7

    Keats, Ezra Jack. *The Snowy Day*

    Lobel, Arnold. *Frog and Toad Are Friends*

    McCloskey, Robert. *Make Way for Ducklings*

    Sendak, Maurice. *Where the Wild Things Are*

    Steptoe, John. *Mufaro's Beautiful Daughters: An African Tale*

    Viorst, Judith. *Alexander and the Terrible, Horrible, No Good, Very Bad Day*

Organizations that Offer Book Lists Free or at Little Cost

American Library Association Publications Order Department 50 East Huron St. Chicago, IL 60611	Reading Is Fundamental, Inc. Publications Department Smithsonian Institution 600 Maryland Ave. SW, Suite 600 Washington, DC 20024-2520
The Children's Book Council Attn: Publication List 568 Broadway Suite 404 New York, NY 10012 (enclose stamped, self-addressed envelope)	International Reading Association 800 Barksdale Rd. P.O. Box 8139 Newark, DE 19714-8139

A Pitfall to Avoid in Designing School-Home Literacy Connections

Tasks that extend children's literacy accomplishments from school to home, that permit children to see how literacy functions in their environments, and that encourage family members to go to public libraries with children are important *positive* school-home reading extensions. They are distinguished from another set of tasks that can make the school-home literacy connection a negative one—completing unfinished tasks from school, specifically worksheets that children may not have understood or have found too tedious to complete.

    Delgado-Gaitan (1992) observed interaction around such homework assignments in homes in which children's parents had immigrated to the United States from Mexico. In visiting the homes of three second graders whom the school viewed as "novice readers," Delgado-Gaitan found that the children, Norma, Jorge, and Jose, spent between half an hour and two hours nightly working on their homework. Despite the faithfulness of the children and their parents in attending to the homework, the children frequently did not complete the assignments in the "right way." The interaction that follows between Norma and her mother illustrates one of the fundamental difficulties with the homework assignments, which consistently were workbook pages and ditto sheets.

Norma's mother interrupted her dinner preparations to assist Norma.[2]

> **Mother:**   Yes, dear, I'll help you right now. [Mother sat down with Norma at the kitchen table and began to work with her.]
>
> **Mother:**   Let's see what you have to do.
>
> **Norma:**   What's a character? [The mother looked at the book cover.]
>
> **Mother:**   Let's see what the character is . . . [The mother continued to look at the book cover and pointed to the illustrator's name.]
>
> **Mother:**   I think this is the person you need. Wait, that isn't it. [Norma watched as her mother continued to search for the author of the book. Her mother looked at the book cover and found the book title with the name *Zorro* written in small letters at the bottom.]
>
> **Mother:**   This is it. Here is the one who wrote the book. [She pointed to the book title. Norma proceeded to write the book title in the space that called for the name of the author.]
>
> (Delgado-Gaitan, 1992, p. 510)

Although Norma and her mother worked hard on the assignment, neither understood the task. Similar to the other parents of the novice readers, Norma's mother expressed frustration because she often could not understand the tasks. Tasks were drill and practice and depended on information that had been covered in the classroom. As this example shows only too poignantly, worksheets that were not done in school because of disinterest or a lack of understanding can create misinterpretations on the part of teachers, parents, and children. They do not begin to parallel the home book reading experiences that contribute to students' literacy acquisition.

The observations of Delgado-Gaitan (1992), Delpit (1988), and Goldenberg and Gallimore (1991) direct our attention to the potential for misunderstanding between educators and families, particularly when cultures, oral languages, and educational experiences are not shared. Over the past decade, numerous projects that aim to improve the links between families from diverse cultural groups and the school have been initiated. Most of these projects include the resources of researchers from interdisciplinary backgrounds such as anthropology, social work, and educational specialties. Initiation of such projects requires involvement from community leaders as

---

[2]The following is a translation of a Spanish conversation.

well as educators (see Morrow, 1995; Morrow & Neuman, 1995). These efforts embody the principles of the collaborative projects in which many school- and university-based educators have directed their energies. Such collaborative projects provide one of the focuses of Chapter 11. In the next section, we highlight several of these projects where extensive interventions have been conducted in communities and homes.

Extensive School-Home Interventions

The school-home interventions that are described in this section have occurred in precisely the types of situations that have been the focus of this book—communities where high percentages of children live in low-income homes. The individuals who participate in the interventions, however, are the adults in children's communities. In some cases, children are involved in the intervention. But in other cases, the intervention is aimed entirely at adults with the belief that children's literacy experiences will be influenced when the adults in their homes engage in literate activity. The principles that characterize appropriate home-school and school-home connections can be seen in these projects, but they involve considerable additional resources. Included in these resources are leaders who know the communities in which these interventions are implemented. These projects are built on a solid understanding of the interaction styles and the beliefs and aspirations of communities.

The first project aimed to extend the interaction styles of parents around books. Edwards (1991), similar to several other research teams (e.g., Heath with Thomas, 1984), has worked with low-income mothers on how to question and respond to children while reading books. The project, Parents as Partners in Reading, has been tied to the school reading program in that it was situated in the school library and had as its aim the support of children's school success. After initial phases of demonstration and application of book-sharing and discussion techniques, children were integrated into sessions as their parents read with them.

In the original site of the project, parents have assumed leadership for training other parents (Edwards, 1995). When Edwards moved, she collaborated with four of the parents in taking over leadership of the training sessions with a new group of parents. While the basic activities and aims of the project stayed intact, the parent leaders made adaptations as they saw fit. For example, children were part of the interactions from the outset rather than after several training sessions. The intent of these earlier phases had been to develop fluency and confidence with the techniques prior to implementing them with children. But the parent leaders did not believe that parents were overly embarrassed to read or attempt to read to their children or to receive feedback from their peers. Edwards (1995) describes these adaptations that reflected the participants' cultures as creating a book-reading style that fit with the interaction styles of the community. Parents had assimilated the school context and the book reading event into their lives as evident in this parent's description:

> "The book reading program to me is another way of sharing what you know with your neighbor or friend. It's like meeting at the grocery store, circle meeting at church, sharing a cooking idea or recipe. There is a format to reading to your children and that is what I learned."   (Edwards, 1995, p. 562)

Project FLAME—<u>F</u>amily <u>L</u>iteracy: <u>A</u>prendiendo, <u>M</u>ejorando, <u>E</u>ducando (Learning, Bettering, Educating)—is a family literacy program in Chicago's Hispanic neighborhoods (Shanahan, Mulhern, & Rodriguez-Brown, 1995). Any adult who lives in a household with children over age three is eligible to participate. FLAME participants are involved in two types of classes: (1) ESL/ basic skills classes that occur twice weekly and (2) Parents as Teachers classes that occur twice monthly. In the second strand, sessions are conducted in Spanish to encourage parents to foster their children's learning in their native language.

In the Parents as Teachers sessions, parents learn to select appropriate books and magazines for their children; to use the library; to share books with their children; to draw children's attention to parents' uses of literacy during cooking, marketing, and other activities; to teach the ABCs and letter sounds; to use language games, songs, and stories with children; and to interact with school personnel. As the program moves to other sites, parents from the program have been hired as the facilitators of the Parents as Teachers sessions in other neighborhoods.

There is no direct intervention by the project staff with children but, in addition to improving English proficiency on the part of parents, significant improvements have been found in children's basic concepts, letter names, and print awareness. Further, parents visit their children's schools more often, volunteer more, and implement teachers' suggestions more readily. The comments of a mother—Isabel—at the end of her second year of participation in FLAME give further evidence of the interest and involvement in literacy that the project has spawned:

> We read every day in the living room, in the afternoon. I read short children's stories from the library, our own (over and over) . . . and even though my son doesn't read, he reads from pictures and from memory and imagination. My husband reads, too.   (Shanahan et al., 1995, p. 592)

These illustrations show that family literacy projects derive from the principles of learning that we have discussed throughout this book. A goal is to increase the language interactions in homes, especially around literacy materials and uses. Parents are guided in scaffolding literacy use for their children. Further, events that increase children's involvement in using literacy meaningfully are created with parents. Whether the effort involves an extended support team as in projects such as FLAME or a team of kindergarten and first-grade teachers in a school, home-school and school-home connections require solid groundwork.

Summary

We began this chapter by establishing the critical need for classrooms to be places that use children's home literacies as the foundation for learning. When the uses of language and literacy in families are recognized and these familiar events and materials are integrated into classroom events and activities, children can make links between what they know about literacy and language and what they are learning. Further, extensions of literacy use to children's homes and communities need to be regarded as essential for development and ownership of literacy. In scaffolding events for children and their families, the differences between home and classroom contexts are important to keep in mind. The aim is for children and their families to enjoy and use literacy for interesting and productive reasons in the home environment—not for parents to be responsible for teaching children things that did not get done in school. If children are to become avid and active readers and writers, the literacies of the home need to be integrated into the literacies of the classroom. Similarly, the literacy uses of the classroom need extensions that mesh with the contexts of home if children are to acquire fully these different uses of literacy.

chapter 11

Connecting to Communities of Early Literacy Teachers

─────────────── VIGNETTE 11.1: ───────────────

Carol Avery, a teacher-researcher, tells this story about her students' perceptions of her as a learner as a result of her work as a teacher-researcher. "Walking back from getting paper in the writing center, he [Michael, the first-grade student] noticed me writing. "Hmmm, I see you're writing, too, Mrs. Avery." I looked up and nodded an acknowledgment. "I bet I know why," he continued, "'Cause you're learning, too. Just like us."

(Avery, 1990, p. 44)

─────────────── VIGNETTE 11.2: ───────────────

In a teacher support group, Laura, a first-grade teacher, shares this story: "Do you remember Jeff? The child I told you about who wouldn't put pen to paper at the beginning of the year? Today he wrote a wonderful two-page story about a dog that had magical powers (MJKL PRS). I was so excited with this story that I showed it to the other first-grade teacher. Her reaction was, "For gosh sakes, why do we want kids to write when we can't even read what they've written?" In the spirited discussion of ways in which other teachers had responded to similar comments, teachers in the group offered Laura encouragement as well as substantive ideas for interacting with her colleague.

(Watson & Stevenson, 1989, pp. 118–119)

Michael's comment to his teacher, Carol Avery, "'Cause you're learning, too. Just like us," succinctly conveys the theme of this chapter: mechanisms and sources for emergent literacy teachers' ongoing professional growth. The three principles of learning we have applied to children's literacy acquisition throughout this book apply just as appropriately to adults' learning. In this chapter, we begin by exploring the ways in which the three principles extend to teachers' and teacher educators' learning. We then turn to a discussion of contexts in which professionals can interact around concepts and ideas, whether from traditional sources such as books or from the experiences that arise through collaborative projects. We make the case that, just as we want

256

to create contexts for our students that encourage their meaningful use of literacy, embedded within oral language activities, and across multiple sources and contexts, we want to provide such opportunities for ourselves. In doing so, we embody the principles of a social constructivist perspective on learning, literacy learning, and learning to teach literacy.

Applying the Principles of the Emergent Literacy Perspective to Learning to Teach Literacy

To make ideas their own, teachers need to be engaged in goal-directed activity as they reflect on their classrooms and design new structures and events. To do this, teachers benefit greatly from interaction with other professionals. Interactions are enhanced when a range of participants is included: other teachers who are at similar points in their practice as emergent literacy teachers, knowledgeable teachers with greater experience with the newer ideas, within a variety of classrooms and other contexts, or both.

The interactions may be face to face as in teacher book clubs, collaborative research projects, in-service opportunities, and university courses and related projects. Alternatively, they may reflect a written dialogue among distant colleagues, reading what others have published through professional writings, participating in video conferences, and exchanging ideas on electronic mail networks. The interactions may occur among individuals at similar levels of professional development, such as the autobiography book club for teacher candidates described by Florio-Ruane (1994). They may occur among individuals who participate in different professional contexts such as the Inquiry Group—first grade through high school teachers and teacher educators—described by Goatley, Highfield, Bentley, Pardo, Folkert, Scherer, Raphael, and Grattan (1994). They may be focused groups that meet together to address a specific issue: improving literacy instruction in special education settings or in Title I settings, described by Englert et al. (1994) and Hiebert et al. (1992), respectively.

Across these settings, the interactions provide support for teachers of emergent literacy students to learn about, question, extend, and modify new ways of thinking about literacy learning and teaching. They provide the reasons for examining literacy instruction through meaningful applications of the instructional practices. They provide the settings for embedding these applications within the context of peer dialogue. They provide the sources for considering literacy instructional practices across contexts and in terms of multiple sources of information.

Learning about Literacy Instruction Occurs through Meaningful Use of Related Practices

At the most basic level, just as children learn to read and write in the context of meaningfully using these skills or tools, literacy teachers learn to engage in new methods from new perspectives by reading about and applying the ideas within meaningful contexts, especially their own classrooms. We have found this to be true in our roles as teacher educators at our respective universities. For example, during the past decade, we have read widely about the importance of writing for enhancing learning, and about the range of journals to encourage deeper thinking about the texts our students—future and practicing teachers—read in our classes. Barone (1990) wrote one of these articles, describing double entry journals. These journals are created when students divide their journal pages into two columns, using the first to note a quote from a book or a classroom discussion and the second to respond with their thinking about the idea. By applying Barone's notions within our own classrooms, we were applying the principle that learning occurs through meaningful use of the to-be-learned activities. We *used* literacy for meaningful ends, and we applied what we had learned through our literacy use within meaningful contexts.

Information becomes meaningful as individuals grapple with the implications of new ideas within their own contexts. As teachers experience the impact of particular practices within their own teaching, they are armed with important knowledge about literacy instruction that can then serve as a basis as they interact with other professionals. However, opportunities to discuss experiences and explore different interpretations of the teachers' and students' experiences are critical. When we began to use the double entry journals, we found that we talked with each other, and with other professionals, about the roles of journals within our classrooms. These discussions illustrate the importance of the second principle, that learning is embedded within oral language.

Learning to Teach Literacy Is Embedded in Oral Language

Knowledge does not exist in a text or an individual but rather reflects the meanings that have been agreed upon and negotiated by a group of people. Language is the tool for this construction process. Teachers as groups—within a school, a district, or a more extended educational community—interpret topics or ideas in particular ways as a result of the interactions that have occurred in that social setting. Technological developments (e.g., electronic mail, video conferences) have made new venues for teacher interaction possible, blurring the boundaries of what constitutes the "oral language" so important to literacy learning or learning about literacy instruction. Developments in learning perspectives, particularly the social-constructivist view, have encouraged new opportunities through collaborative projects in which a group of educators work on implementing particular activities in their classrooms. In short, just as literacy learning within an emergent literacy classroom is embedded within oral language (i.e., the immediate language exchanges among participants), so, too, is the development of practices in literacy instruction embedded in the person-to-person exchange of ideas, from traditional face-to-face interactions to the more distant exchanges made possible through technological advances.

The meanings that a group of teachers construct typically are the product of many conversations. While there are few accounts of the development of conversations that build schools' beliefs and practices, such conversations are beginning to be studied. For example, within the Reading Recovery program—an early intervention program to which we have referred periodically in this book (e.g., Chapter 5)—researchers have examined the manner in which oral language is used to construct, or to reconstruct, teachers' perceptions about students' literacy learning. In the following conversation, the focus is on defining what "counts" as appropriate reading among potentially at-risk first graders (Gaffney & Anderson, 1991):

Teacher Leader:	We are observing familiar reading, the first component of a lesson. What are some of the purposes of familiar reading?
Teacher 4:	To let the child practice what he knows.
Teacher 1:	So that the child can read fluently books he's had before.
Teacher Leader:	Is this child reading fluently?
Teacher 1:	Yes, I think so.
Teacher 6:	I do, too (two other teachers nod in agreement).
Teacher Leader:	Think of the children you're working with in Reading Recovery. How does his reading fluency compare to theirs?
Teacher 3:	Mine read like him.
Teacher 2:	Mine, too (all other teachers nod in agreement).
Teacher Leader:	You're all experienced teachers of Grade 1 children. Think of the average and above-average readers in first grade. Does this child read this book as fluently as they would?
All:	NO! (emphatically with head-shaking)
Teacher Leader:	Is this child reading fluently?
All:	NO! (in unison)
Teacher Leader:	It is important for you to keep in mind your purpose. Your goal is to have this child read as well as average readers in his class . . . that's your standard. Now, is fluency the only thing that's important . . . that he goes fast?

(Gaffney & Anderson, 1991, pp. 192–193)

Note that such conversations reflect a more experienced "teacher leader" using questions and participating teachers' experiences with their students to help frame a standard for thinking about fluency in reading. Such conversations underscore the importance of opportunity for teachers to draw on

their own experiences, to have shared information about students' performance levels, and to have an opportunity to bring these together for examining
their own instructional expectations and standards.

Programs such as Reading Recovery are intended to serve as a catalyst
for conversations among colleagues within the school sites, not simply for
those who are part of the Reading Recovery training group. These efforts are
based on the third principle of learning within a social-constructivist perspective, emphasizing the importance of multiple contexts and sources. In
the next section we highlight efforts to engage teachers in conversations to
examine classroom practices through dialogues with colleagues.

Learning to Teach Literacy Occurs in Multiple Contexts

Just as children benefit from interactions with a variety of others, so, too,
is adults' learning enhanced through interactions with others who vary in
their roles and expertise. Projects that identify "schools of thought" (Brown,
1991) and that create communities of practice (Magnusson & Palincsar,
1995) or inquiring schools (Calfee, 1992) consistently demonstrate the importance of teachers interacting with colleagues and more knowledgeable
others (e.g., teacher leaders in Reading Recovery, language arts coordinators
within schools or school districts, professors from nearby and not-so-nearby
schools of education). The projects also reveal three aspects important to consider when first venturing into one's own professional development: (a) time
for reflection, (b) opportunity for scaffolding from more experienced others,
and (c) opportunity to engage in reflective conversations with other colleagues.

First and foremost, teachers need to have time when they can reflect,
analyze, and evaluate new or revised practices. For most teachers, this means
finding time in an already overly filled day. For teachers of young children,
finding time for reflection is particularly difficult, because the entire class is
rarely involved in independent activity. Some early literacy teachers such as
Pam Scherer and Kristin Grattan who are part of the Book Club teacher-
researcher network maintain informal reflective journals (McMahon & Raphael,
in press). Their journal entries, sometimes written while their students are
engaged in writing in their journals, sometimes during lunch or after school,
form a basis for them to explore trends in their classroom or with individual
students. As we noted in Chapter 8 in discussing observation or "kid-watching"
(Goodman, 1985), children's strategies also need to be studied in action.
Vivian Paley (1986), similarly, emphasizes that it is only through listening
and watching that teachers can truly understand their students' social interactions, the use of literacy within various school settings, and students'
use of language to achieve various goals. When listening and kid-watching
are built into a teacher's day, the issue of time changes—from finding
"extra" time to reflect on practice to making such reflection integral to
teaching.

As teachers reflect more on their own literacy instruction and their students' literacy use, they often identify questions or concerns that they wish

to examine more closely or begin to change in systematic ways. Hubbard and Power (1993) describe how "all teachers have wonderings worth pursuing" (p. 2). There are many ways that teachers can pursue these wonderings, from engaging in their own teacher research to interacting with more knowledgeable others in the field. To identify the wonderings is a first step in beginning a focused process of professional development.

In early literacy instruction, one area of wonderings that many teachers note is concern for students who are not achieving competence in their early literacy development, and because of this, are likely to be at a disadvantage throughout their school careers. Programs such as Reading Recovery provide an example of how the second aspect of professional development can work. With time for reflection and identification of a concern, such as problems with early reading development, teachers may turn to others who have expertise in the area of change. For example, in Reading Recovery, teachers are guided as they tutor struggling, beginning readers. They observe one another and identify similarities or uniquenesses with their tutees. A teacher leader who is both an experienced tutor and who has had additional staff development in scaffolding the learning of teachers leads these observations and follow-up discussions. Gaffney and Anderson (1991, pp. 192–193) provide an excerpt of a session that illustrates the exchange between teachers and the manner in which the teacher leader asks questions that scaffold participating teachers' knowledge of early literacy acquisition:

Teacher Leader:	The teacher just praised the child for getting the 'ch' down in 'chair.' Why did she praise her?
Teacher 9:	Because that's a hard one to learn.
Teacher 5:	It's important.
Teacher Leader:	And she isn't doing it in pieces . . .
Teacher 7:	Chunks.
Teacher Leader:	Is getting chunks down important at this level? The teacher said she wanted to work for transfer. Why would chunks be helpful for that?
Teacher 1:	They might start . . . they might start to see patterns.
Teacher Leader:	Why is it more important to see patterns than to talk about individual letters?
Teacher 4:	She's got a way to get to unknown words. When she goes to another word that contains the same sound cluster she's able to write more of the word.
Teacher 1:	Another suggestion I have is that I don't think she needs to look back at the practice page. She did just look back up at 'chair' but I would fold the book under and have her write, or cover it or something.
Teacher Leader:	Why would you choose to do that?
Teacher 1:	Because if she can write that many words, she ought to be able to do it from memory without an example.
Teacher 6:	Seeing and retaining visual patterns.

Teacher Leader:	And how does that help her? Why would it be beneficial for her to be doing it from memory rather than just copying it?
Teacher 7:	It indicates a certain knowledge of what she's working on and also the idea of being able to not only hear, but how to utilize the chunks—the clusters—of letters. I think the book talks about the more fluent readers are those that are able to use those chunks, at specific times and transfer them to other areas in that particular practice time.

(Gaffney & Anderson, 1991, pp. 192–193)

The questions asked by the teacher leader in this dialogue illustrate her knowledge of how to ask questions that encourage professional development. She rarely provides answers, but rather, raises possibilities for the participating teachers to consider. She helps to direct the flow of the discussion, highlighting important aspects of literacy acquisition within the context of a particular child's learning experience. Reading Recovery teacher leaders' skills have been developed through extensive staff development in scaffolding learning experiences for teachers at different stages in their learning about reading processes. Other projects, but with the same scaffolding strategies, have focused on guiding colleagues with similar expertise and experience to coach one another (e.g., Costa & Garmston, 1994).

In the next section, we focus on teachers' activities that reflect the three aspects important to professional development: time for reflection, interactions with more experienced others, and reflective conversations among peers.

Contexts and Sources for Emergent Literacy Professionals' Learning

The contexts for interacting with other emergent literacy professionals are many and varied, as are the sources of information that undergird these contexts. We divide professional interactions into two broad categories: (a) interactions around texts and related topics, and (b) interactions within collaborative projects and teams. We chose these two contexts primarily because they represent relatively recent additions to the plethora of experiences that allow teachers to become part of a wider (i.e., beyond their own classroom and schools) professional community.

Interactions around Texts and Related Topics

Interactions for the purpose of professional development usually involve some form of dialogue that leads to what Dewey (1938) termed "educative experiences." Such dialogue is necessary for creating new understandings (Burbules, 1993) among teachers, just as the dialogues that we described in Chapter 4 form the basis for children's learning. Dewey identified two criteria that are necessary for educative experiences: (a) continuity and (b) interaction. From face-to-face contexts such as book clubs to distant, but relatively immediate, interactions made possible through electronic mail, new contexts for teachers' professional development show a great deal of promise.

Book Clubs.   One exciting context that has received increased attention nationally, as well as within the field of education, is that of book clubs. Book clubs have existed for a long time in the general public, often providing a reason for women to come together on a regular basis to meet and discuss intellectual issues and to share camaraderie (see, for example, Santmyer's [1982] *And Ladies of the Club*). Other book clubs focus on specific issues, such as *The Beardstown Ladies' Common-sense Investment Guide* (Beardstown Ladies Club, 1994). Participating in such focused book clubs has become one context for professional development among literacy educators.

Some book clubs have focused on reading children's and adolescent literature, a way of heightening teachers' enthusiasm for and knowledge about literature as our field has moved toward literature-based instruction. Others have identified a particular type of literature that might yield insights into how culture influences our life experiences as well as literacy learning (Flood & Lapp, 1994; Florio-Ruane, 1994). For example, Florio-Ruane (1994) has explored how reading autobiographies written by ethnic minorities could enhance preservice teachers' understanding of people who come from cultures quite different from their own, and how these preservice teachers came to understand the role of culture in their own lives. Participants met over a six-month period, reading one book per month. Books were authored by immigrants and the children of immigrants who had left their homelands for economic opportunities (e.g., Conway's [1989] *Road from Coorain* and Hoffman's [1989] *Lost in Translation*), as well as books by immigrants or those whose ancestors had been forced to leave their homeland, through slavery or economic hardship (e.g., Angelou's [1969] *I Know Why the Caged Bird Sings* and Rodriguez's [1981] *Hunger of Memory*). Participants wrote individual responses in their sketchbooks, and used their written notes as food for conversation during the monthly book club sessions. The participants found the readings and the experience of talking about the readings to be powerful. They learned about how different each was from one another, despite similarities such as gender or race. They also learned about the very subtle ways in which culture dominates each of their own and others' lives. Such insights will be useful for them as they embark on a teaching career where they will encounter students from diverse linguistic, cultural, and economic backgrounds.

Flood and Lapp (1994) have initiated book clubs where teachers read literature written by members of, and written about the range of, cultures represented by the students in the participants' classrooms. Similar to Florio-Ruane's findings, they describe the insights that teachers gained about their students' cultures and worldviews through reading literature from the various cultures represented in the local school system.

Other teachers have formed groups to discuss professional literature. These groups draw on various media related to literacy instruction and focus their conversation on how they can draw from this media in ways that can impact their own literacy instructional practice. Rex Brown (1991), a literacy educator, captures this principle well in the concluding paragraph of his book on school restructuring, *Schools of Thought:*

> To the inevitable question 'What should I do differently tomorrow, now that I have read this book?' I have no better answer than this: Get three friends, and ask them three questions raised by the case studies. Follow your answers with tougher and tougher questions, until you all start seeing things differently. You will know what to do.   (p. 251)

We use "media" to capture the various means whereby information about teaching, learning, and literacy is communicated. Books, journals, newsletters, audiotapes of sessions from conferences, videotapes, and web sites on the Internet are each instances of media. Selecting texts for such book clubs can be challenging, because of both the sheer amount of media from which to choose and the fact that the availability of specific titles varies considerably each year. We thought it helpful to provide broad guidelines, rather than specific titles, to help our readers navigate the ever-changing and multiplying body of resources.

We begin our description by turning to the professional organizations in literacy as an initial reference point in the search for resources. Two principal professional organizations in literacy, the International Reading Association (IRA) and the National Council of Teachers of English (NCTE), provide a starting point. They can also direct readers to other related organizations that focus on specific issues—developmental, linguistic, cultural—that influence literacy learning. For example, the National Association for the Education of Young Children addresses aspects of young children's development and the National Association for Bilingual Education emphasizes the learning and teaching of children for whom English is a second or third language.

Both IRA and NCTE have at least one journal dedicated to elementary literacy instruction: *The Reading Teacher* published by IRA and *Language Arts* and *Primary Voices,* published by NCTE. Both organizations also have monthly newspapers that are part of basic membership. These newspapers have columns on current issues and resources. Further, these organizations have local chapters as well as state groups. Conferences offered by the national, regional, state, and local affiliates are either advertised in the newspapers or can be obtained by contacting the organizations.

Both organizations have been involved in publishing important reference books. IRA and NCTE have collaborated with publishers and numerous educators in publishing handbooks and an encyclopedia on literacy issues: *Handbook of Reading Research* (Barr, Kamil, Mosenthal, & Pearson, 1991);

Handbook of English/Language Arts (Flood, Jensen, Lapp, & Squire, 1991); the *Encyclopedia of English/Language Arts* (Purves, 1994). These references can often provide good overviews of current perspectives on particular topics. These two professional organizations also publish journals that report on current research: *Reading Research Quarterly* and *Research in the Teaching of English,* published by IRA and NCTE, respectively.

Another source for current research information is the newsletters of the national research centers in literacy. Since the late 1970s, the U.S. Office of Education has awarded grants for national centers in education. At present, there are centers that specialize in reading, writing, literature, and second language acquisition. The locations of these centers (and even the focuses of the centers) change with federal policies and grant competitions. Interested readers can find these centers on the Internet. As well as providing reports on ongoing research, these centers publish documents that are intended for practitioners. These centers also have electronic mail sites where individuals can interact with colleagues.

Certain publishing houses specialize in books about education and literacy education more specifically. For example, publishers such as Heinemann Educational Books, Richard Owens Publishing Company, and Christopher Gordon Publishers offer books about teaching, teacher research, literacy curriculum, and literacy learning, by teachers and teacher educators. Each company provides teachers with current book catalogs as well as announcements of new publications.

From our experience in identifying books and resources on a variety of topics, colleagues remain our best source of recommendations. Whether our interest is in reading to be informed on general or specific topics related to literacy, we have been introduced to stimulating and challenging resources by asking two simple questions of educators whom we respect: "If you could recommend one resource on this topic, what would it be?" and "What have you read recently that has made you understand children, literacy, and learning differently?" As teachers meet with other professionals in informal and formal contexts, these two questions arise quite naturally out of the interactions and serve as the basis for continued ongoing identification of new and interesting sources.

Electronic Networks.   New technologies such as electronic mail (e-mail) allow for forms of interaction that have not been accessible to professionals in the past. Electronic networks vary considerably. Some may have members from a single school district, opening lines of communication among administrators and teachers and between teachers from different schools within the district. Some may be associated with a particular community, such as those teachers who are members of a master's degree program. Still others may have a broader membership, such as the XTAR network with an international membership of teachers, teacher educators, and teacher researchers working in a variety of educational settings (Blanton & Wells, 1995).

Discussion topics on electronic mail sometimes focus on books. For example, within the context of an e-mail conversation on XTAR about parent-teacher conferences and how to make connections with parents, a network member described the book, *Engaging Families* (Shockley, Michaelove, & Allen, 1995), as a source for information. She summarized the focus of the book, leading other network members to respond with questions or comments. Although it is a brief exchange, it highlights the potential power of such networks for giving visibility to new books related to topics under discussion, because this short set of exchanges potentially was read by several hundred network members.

Electronic mail also facilitates interactions with distant colleagues around specific instructional issues. For example, one XTAR exchange beginning in early December 1994, and continuing for several days, focused on how teachers around the country use journals to help them reflect on and enhance their teaching. Contributors shared how they used their teaching journals, including suggestions for finding the time to write in their journals, forms the journals took, and how they organized their entries for later reflection. There were also questions from other network members, such as one regarding opinions about or experiences in sharing entries with students or with student teachers.

E-mail among individuals also provides important opportunities for professional development. For example, MacGillivray and King (1995) describe their experience as two teacher educators at opposite ends of the country—California and Florida. They had each been reading extensively on the topic of feminist pedagogy. Both were grappling with the manner in which these ideas translated into their teaching of literacy pedagogy courses. They had difficulty in locating groups in their own teaching situations in which they could share the issues with which they were struggling. They became aware of their mutual interest in a conversation at a national conference and, subsequently, began an e-mail conversation on a fairly regular basis that they augmented with phone calls. Their aim was to interact with one another so that they could better support their students' learning as well as their own learning. MacGillivray and King cite three benefits that they gained from their e-mail dialogue.

The first was that the medium allowed for both intrapersonal and interpersonal reflection. While both responded to one another's comments and shared questions that had arisen in their teaching, the e-mail context also allowed them to reflect individually. That is, one can reflect on one's response before sending it off. Also, one can choose to respond to the comments of others. Intrapersonal reflection is also fostered by the opportunity for lag time between a message that another has sent and the response that one returns.

A second benefit that supported the learning of these teachers was the "provisional" nature of the interactions. Because these interactions are relatively new, neither teacher felt pigeonholed into particular kinds of responses.

Third, the medium created a sense of community, while maintaining a sense of uniqueness. When one teacher wrote a message, she or he knew that a colleague would respond. There was also the awareness that each was not teaching "alone." At the same time, the physical distance meant that each was able to maintain his or her voice. According to MacGillivray and King (1995), "We have wondered aloud if we would have shared as freely as we did if we had been in closer proximity" (p. 413).

There are numerous e-mail exchanges that teachers can access through the Internet. For teachers who are initiating change in their classrooms, contexts such as these promise opportunities for exploration and learning that may extend and enhance their interactions with colleagues face-to-face, or may provide a source of professional interaction that they may currently not have in place.

The contexts we described in this section include meeting in book clubs to discuss children's literature, adult literature, or professional reading and meeting across distance through available technology. They share the common features of providing a site for dialogue around educational issues, dialogue that stems from a range of media and supports the individual learning of the participants. In the next section we describe interactions that grow out of identifying a common question and participating in collaborations to examine or address the question.

Collaborative Projects

The collaborative projects of the past decade have been characterized by extended interactions among a group of teachers, both school- and university-based; by focuses around particular problems in children's learning; by solutions that derive from the principles of learning that have been part of this volume; and by active roles by teachers in reflecting, experimenting, analyzing, and evaluating their classroom practices. Collaborative projects represent a new form of inquiry for school- and university-based educators alike, leading teachers to refer to themselves as teacher-researchers as Carol Avery did in Vignette 11.1.

This teacher inquiry can take many forms. Richardson (1994) describes four different types of teacher research. The first form of research grows out of the belief that, by its very nature, *teaching is research*. Effective teachers constantly identify problems, test different ways of solving the problems, and evaluate students' progress. A second form of teacher research involves *reflective practice*. This form suggests that teacher research occurs only when there is conscious reflection on one's practice. Teacher-researchers might maintain a teaching journal or tape their classroom interactions so they can study them more closely at a later time (see, for example, Evans, 1995).

A third form has been referred to as *action research*. This work is characterized by attempts to change or reform practices beyond one's own classroom. For example, many teachers have engaged in efforts to transform school assessment practices, studying practices within their own classrooms or working collaboratively within a single classroom. Action research can be seen in the writings of teacher research teams such as Au, Scheu, Kawakami, and Herman (1990) and Paradis, Chatton, Smith, and Yovich (1991).

The fourth form of research is the most formal, and closely parallels the *traditional research* models found within universities and professional journals. This teacher research is defined by teachers studying their own practices, then "going public" with the results through a variety of means. These include publications in professional journals, presentations at state through international conferences, as well as presentations within local schools and districts (e.g., Au et al., 1990; Paradis et al., 1991). The public sharing of the research to contribute to the knowledge base for teaching is what characterizes this form of teacher research. A new journal entitled *Teacher Researcher* encourages teachers to share their solutions to problems as well as the means whereby they conducted their collaboration. Many of the vignettes that have introduced the chapters in this volume have come from reports of these groups of teacher-researchers.

Cochran-Smith and Lytle (1993) have described teacher research in their book, *Inside/Outside,* sharing examples of teachers' reflections, providing recommendations for how such inquiry might be conducted, and making visible the challenges faced by teachers who research their own practices. What is clear from the range of teacher narratives is that engaging in reflections about their own practices, then sharing their experiences with other professionals, helped teachers to continually expand their own thinking about their teaching.

Goatley et al. (1994) describe their experiences as members of a teacher research group. They note that they had three reasons for coming together as a research group: (1) discussing goals and classroom instruction, (2) responding to each other's writings, and (3) discussing professional readings. They felt that these three focus areas would contribute to their ability to reflect on their own practice and to design teacher research studies they would be interested in conducting in their respective settings. The eight-member group met monthly at each other's homes, beginning in 1992. In their article, based on their first year's experience, they describe two important benefits. First, their participation helped them maintain a strong sense of themselves as professionals, especially in the current political environment that places much of the blame for school failure on the quality of teaching. Second, they also found it important, given the isolation they felt when in their own classrooms, to have a community to share with, to nurture each other's ideas, and to promote one another's learning.

The variation in the focuses of collaborative projects is substantial but all involve partnerships between educators in solving particular problems in literacy learning. These partnerships may involve individual teachers from different schools who meet regularly to discuss the inquiry they are conducting (e.g., Allen, Cary, & Delgado, 1996; Goatley et al., 1994; Laird, Crawford, Ferguson, Kauffman, Schroeder, & Short, 1994). Others, such as the Book Club project, begin with the involvement of a few teachers within a single school (Raphael, McMahon, Goatley, Bentley, Boyd, Pardo, & Woodman,

1991) and expand to include teachers from a range of grades, schools, and districts (McMahon & Raphael, in press). Collaborative projects share the following features:

- a common goal (e.g., enhancing the curriculum in the Title I setting for at-risk first-grade students; creating a whole-literacy curriculum for students receiving literacy instructional support in a resource room setting; initiating student-led discussion groups as the center of a literacy instruction program)
- a collaborative research team (e.g., teachers and researchers from both university and school settings; classroom teachers and district curriculum leaders; teachers across grade levels)
- an emphasis on the learning principles underlying a social-constructivist perspective (i.e., learning embedded within meaningful contexts, within oral language, and through interactions within multiple contexts and with a range of peers)

Because collaborative projects vary so greatly, we illustrate through examples the range of forms they may take, drawing on the Right Start in Reading project, codirected by Hiebert, and the Early Literacy Project, co-directed by Englert and Raphael.

The Right Start in Reading Project.   In the Right Start project, several teachers from a school district that was part of a partnership with Hiebert's university asked if she would participate with them in a study group. The aim of the study group was to examine ways to clarify and substantiate the emergent literacy experiences of first and second graders who had been identified as potentially at risk when beginning first grade. The Title I teachers who served these children believed in holistic activities but they were uncertain how to integrate instruction about word-level strategies into these activities, such as shared reading of big books and journal writing. After a year of reading and discussing the existing literature on emergent literacy instruction for at-risk children, the group identified a set of instructional strategies. Members of this group, as well as several other Title I teachers who expressed interest, began implementing these strategies over a school year with a group of first graders.

Hiebert et al. (1992) studied the results of this effort to determine areas of modification. As a result of this evaluation, it became apparent that many more children could benefit if classroom teachers, as well as Title I teachers, implemented the strategy; if the procedures were extended to second-grade students; and if supportive activities were initiated in the kindergarten curriculum. Different groups of individuals in the district have extended the instructional strategies and made them specific to their own areas, such as adapting the program for children in the monolingual Spanish program and examining the needs of children in the middle grades.

Visits by teachers from other districts have proven to be highly valuable as a learning experience. When teachers are put in the role of docents who guide visitors through the daily lessons and ways of interacting with colleagues, they find themselves articulating and clarifying concepts in new ways.

The Early Literacy Project.   The Early Literacy Project, or ELP, in which Raphael has been a collaborator, was designed to apply emergent literacy principles to special education students (see Englert et al., 1994; Englert, Gavelek, Mariage, & Raphael, 1995). While the students were chronologically in grades one through three, their cognitive processing levels varied from one another as well as from their non–special education peers. Some students, like Tess—whose advice on caring for dogs was presented in Vignette 6.2—were classified as educable mentally retarded; others had learning disabilities that made processing of literacy and mathematical content challenging.

For both the school and the university educators, this project presented challenges. There had been few reports of extensions of emergent literacy principles to special education students. As Poplin (1988) concluded in her review of special education practice, a skill-and-drill mentality has dominated this area of schooling. The response has been to "slow it down" and make the elements of literacy as discrete as possible (Allington, 1991b). As a result, children with any kind of difference in learning—whether linguistic, cognitive, or social—rarely get to participate in the whole acts of literacy but rather spend their school careers attempting to master little bits of literacy (Rueda, 1991). With a strong emphasis on skills and rote learning, special learners understandably lost the focus on the central processes of literacy— comprehending and composing. Literacy became a set of disparate skills that they found to be of little use. Changing this pattern required the team of ELP participants to engage in extended conversations about possible solutions and the responses of students to these solutions.

The school and university educators met weekly to design literacy experiences for special education students that allowed them to engage in whole acts of literacy. The focus was on embedding the instruction of necessary literacy strategies within these whole acts of literacy—not in foregrounding the skills at the expense of comprehending and composing. The teachers returned for a second year of weekly meetings, adding new colleagues whose interest was piqued by the reports of ELP teachers.

An issue that initially challenged the group in their efforts to create a community had to do with phonics instruction. For a number of years, Title I and special education teachers in the district had used a particular phonics program for struggling readers. A typical reading period in this program consisted of instruction of particular letter-sound correspondences. Children applied their knowledge in exercises on worksheets. The perspective that emergent readers could be involved in the "whole acts" of literacy before they had been taught letter-sound correspondences ran counter to teachers' existing practices and beliefs.

Solutions were considered that allowed children to participate in the whole acts of literacy while they acquired strategies that would move them to independent reading and writing in the long run. One of these solutions was immediate and extensive involvement in writing. Teachers observed their students as they wrote, coming to see that the act of writing requires children to attend to letter-sound correspondences more closely than recognizing phonic elements in worksheet exercises requires. To write the composition in Vignette 6.2, Tess had to continually apply her knowledge about letter-sound correspondences. An exercise on "vowel digraphs" (rimes such as "ee" in see) might have required Tess to underline or cross out words with the pattern. The task of writing a paragraph of advice on the care of dogs required Tess to use her knowledge of this pattern to write several words ("feed," "tree") and to produce words such as "good"—which have two vowels but in which the pattern takes another form. After years of teaching letter-sound correspondences through demonstration followed by worksheet practice, teachers came to see that writing messages on topics of interest and importance fostered their students' learning of phonics patterns in a way that workbook exercises had never done.

This change in perspective required many conversations as the team of school and university educators struggled to apply ideas with special education students. Julia, one of the ELP teachers, described the process: "First year, I remember trying things and doing things the way they were kind of prescribed to do. And really trying to keep to the letter, and then, either it wasn't working for me or I wasn't doing it right. I've changed in that I kind of try to use my own style now. Before I would listen to other people and try to use their style and that wasn't necessarily working out. (Now) I feel more comfortable in using my own style, using the ideas, and the principles and so forth, but maybe using my own style of doing it" (Englert et al., 1995).

One teacher shared her perspective on the crucial aspect of this community in her professional development: "I see my role as trying stuff and bringing it to the group. That's the object of the group is to try the stuff that (might) bring benefit to everybody's classroom. Then come back. That's how we really started feeling more comfortable is in having everybody do it (share). It's because people would come back and they would take that risk and then share. You have an obligation to share with others (too) not in the group. As long as we're learning this, we need to be sharing this with other specialists" (Englert et al., 1995).

Collaborative projects foster the principles of learning. The need to solve problems that are immediate in teachers' classrooms means that the experiences are meaningful for teachers. The use of oral language to clarify and interpret ideas is central. Further, there are numerous interactions with a range of participants—teachers new to the project, colleagues who have had more extended experiences, university-based educators who teach and observe. In these collaborative projects, efforts are ongoing as the collaborators identify new topics on which to focus.

Summary

In this chapter, we have focused on the importance of ongoing professional development for all teachers, but specifically for those who are teaching young children to read. We have argued that teachers' learning can be thought of within the same principles as we would approach literacy acquisition, from the importance of the learning being meaningful to the valuing of oral interactions across a range of contexts. We have presented a number of different contexts that can support teachers' professional development and provide them with access to the broader professional community.

These contexts should not be viewed as competing but as complementary. Some contexts serve particular needs better than others. Some contexts are accessible to a particular group of teachers while others are available to another group. Further, particular contexts may foster specific goals for a group of teachers at a particular point in their professional development. What is critical is that teachers are members of a community of learners. The forms that these communities can take vary considerably—for different individuals and at different points in a teacher's development.

We end our book as we began, with a vignette. This vignette is illustrative of our goal for writing the book, conveying the gist of this chapter as well as our reason for writing this volume.

——————————————— VIGNETTE 11.3: ———————————————

In a classroom in which a university-based educator (Elfrieda Hiebert) was collaborating with the children's teacher, children asked whether the university-based educator could be the focus of a sharing session. Numerous questions were asked, such as, "What's your favorite football team?" As the session came to a close, a child at the edge of the circle on the floor timidly raised her hand. Her question, quietly raised, was: "When you're a teacher of teachers like you are, who teaches you?"

This child's question gets at the core of the view of learning and literacy that underlies this book. As learners, we observe children and teachers and we interact with children, teachers, and other teachers of teachers. And when we finish books like this one, we know that it is only an opening—the start of a conversation.

Children's Books

Ackerman, K. (1988). *Song and dance man.* Illus. S. Gammel. New York: Knopf.

Ahlberg, J. (1991). *The jolly postman.* Boston, MA: Little, Brown.

Anderson, D. (1991). *The origin of life on earth: An African creation myth.* Illus. K. A. Wilson. Mount Airy, MD: Sights Productions.

Angelou, M. (1993). *Soul looks back in wonder.* New York: Dial.

Appelt, K. (1994). *Elephants aloft.* Illus. J. Yardley. New York: Harcourt Brace.

Arnold, T. (1994). *Green Wilma.* New York: Dial.

Auch, M. J. (1994). *Peeping beauty.* New York: Holiday House.

Bash, B. (1989). *Desert giant: The world of saguaro cactus.* Boston: Little, Brown.

Bauer, C. F. (1981). *My mom travels a lot.* Illus. N. W. Parker. New York: Frederick Warne.

Bemelmans, L. (1939). *Madeline.* New York: Simon & Schuster.

Bennett, R. (1960). *The secret hiding place.* Cleveland, OH: World.

Berlan, K. (1994). *Andrew's amazing monsters.* Illus. M. Chambliss. New York: Atheneum.

Bonne, R. (1931). *I know an old lady.* New York: Scholastic.

Brown, M. W. (1942). *The runaway bunny.* New York: Harper.

Brown, M. W. (1947). *Goodnight moon.* New York: Harper & Row.

Brown, M. (1993). *Arthur's family vacation.* Boston, MA: Little, Brown.

Brown, R. (1994). *What rhymes with snake?* New York: Tambourine Books.

Buehner, C. (1994). *A job for Wattilda.* Illus. M. Buehner. New York: Dial.

Bunting, E. (1994). *Smoky night.* San Diego, CA: Harcourt Brace.

Butler, A. (1989). *Jack-in-the-box.* Crystal Lake, IL: Rigby.

Butterworth, N., & Inkpen, M. (1993). *Jasper's beanstalk.* New York: Bradbury Press.

Cameron, P. (1934). *"I can't," said the ant.* New York: Coward-McCann.

Camp, L. (1994). *Dinosaurs at the supermarket.* Illus. C. Skilbeck. New York: Viking.

Campbell, R. (1982). *Dear zoo.* New York: Four Winds Press.

Carle, E. (1973). *Have you seen my cat?* New York: F. Watts.

Carle, E. (1983). *The very hungry caterpillar.* New York: Philomel.

Carle, E. (1994). *Today is Monday.* New York: Philomel.

Charlip, R. (1964). *Fortunately.* New York: Four Winds Press.

Clayton, G. (1987). *Foal.* New York: Dorling Kindersley, Inc.

Coerr, E. (1993). *Sadako.* New York: Putnam.

Compton, K. & J. (1994). *Granny Greenteeth and the noise in the night.* Illus. K. Compton. New York: Holiday House.

Connery, R. (1989). *We make music.* Crystal Lake, IL: Rigby.

Cowley, J. (1981). *Splosh.* Auckland, NZ: Shortland Publications Ltd.

Cowley, J. (1983). *The big hill.* Auckland, NZ: Shortland Publications Ltd.

Coxe, M. (1990). *Whose footprints?* New York: Thomas Y. Crowell.

Crews, D. (1980). *Truck.* New York: Puffin Books.

Crews, D. (1984). *School bus.* New York: Greenwillow Books.

Cummings, P. (1985). *Jimmy Lee did it.* New York: Lothrop, Lee & Shepard Books.

Curtis, J. L. (1994). *When I was little: A four-year-old's memoir of her youth.* New York: HarperCollins.

Cuyler, M. (1991). *That's good! That's bad!* Illus. D. Catrow. New York: Henry Holt.

de Paola, T. (1975). *Strega Nona.* New York: Simon & Schuster.

Deming, A. G. (1988). *Who is tapping at my window?* Illus. M. Wellington. New York: Dutton.

Dobeck, M. (1996). *Stop that!* Parsippany, NJ: Modern Curriculum Press.

Dobeck, M. (1996). *Six go by.* Needham Heights, MA: Silver Burdett Ginn.

Doubilet, A. (1991). *Under the sea from A to Z.* New York: Crown.

Dragonwagon, C. (1986). *Half a moon and one whole star.* Illus. J. Pinkney. New York: Macmillan.

Dunphy, M. (1994). *Here is the arctic winter.* Illus. A. J. Robinson. New York: Hyperion.

Eastman, P. D. (1960). *Are you my mother?* New York: Beginner Books, Random House.

Ehlert, L. (1990). *Feathers for lunch.* New York: Greenwillow Books.

Ehlert, L. (1991). *Red leaf, yellow leaf.* San Diego: Harcourt, Brace, Jovanovich.

Emberley, E. (1974). *Klippity klop.* Dubuque, IA: Little, Brown.

Emberley, E. (1994). *Go away, big green monster!* Boston, MA: Little, Brown.

Ericsson, J. (1994). *No milk!* Illus. O. Eitan. New York: Tambourine Books.

Florian, D. (1989). *Nature walk.* New York: Greenwillow Books.

Flournoy, V. (1985). *The patchwork quilt.* New York: Dial Books for Young Readers.

Fox, M. (1988). *Hattie and the fox.* Illus. P. Mullins. New York: Bradbury.

Freeman, D. (1964). *Dandelion.* New York: Viking.

Gackenbach, D. (1977). *Harry and the terrible whatzit.* New York: Houghton Mifflin/Clarion Books.

Gag, W. (1928). *Millions of cats.* New York: Coward McCann, Putnam.

Ginsburg, M. (1982). *Across the stream.* Illus. N. Tafuri. New York: Greenwillow Books.

Gomi, T. (1979). *Coco can't wait!* New York: Puffin Books.

Gomi, T. (1989). *My friends.* San Francisco: Chronicle Books.

Greenblat, R. (1994). *Slombo the gross.* New York: HarperCollins.

Greenfield, E. (1978). *Honey, I love and other love poems.* New York: Harper Trophy.

Greenfield, E. (1988). *Nathaniel talking.* Illus. J. S. Gilchrist. New York: Writers & Readers.

Grejniec, M. (1992). *What do you like?* New York: North-South Books.

Grenner, B., & Chardiet, B. (1994). *Where's that fish?* Illus. C. Schwartz. New York: Scholastic.

Grifalconi, A. (1987). *Darkness and the butterfly.* Boston: Little, Brown.

Gwyne, F. (1994). *Easy to see why.* New York: Hyperion.

Harrison, T. (1977). *Children of the Yukon.* Montreal: Tundra Books.

Hartman, G. (1991). *As the crow flies: A first book of maps.* New York: Aladdin Books.

Hausherr, R. (1994). *What food is this?* New York: Scholastic.

Hayes, S. (1988). *Eat up, Gemma.* New York: Mulberry Paperback Book.

Hearn, D. D. (1994). *Dad's dinosaur day.* New York: Macmillan.

Heller, R. (1983). *The reason for a flower.* New York: Scholastic Inc.

Hennessy, B. G. (1990). *Jake baked the cake.* Illus. M. Morgan. New York: Puffin.

Hennessy, B. G. (1990). *School days.* New York: Viking.

Hewett, J. (1994). *Tiger, tiger, growing up.* Photo. R. Hewett. New York: Clarion.

Hill, D. (1976). *This is the house.* New York: New American Library.

Hirschi, R. (1991). *Summer.* New York: Cobblehill Books.

Hoban, T. (1972). *Count and see.* New York: Macmillan.

Hoban, T. (1972). *Push pull empty full.* New York: Macmillan.

Hoguet, S. (1983). *I unpacked my grandmother's trunk.* New York: E. P. Dutton.

Holleyman, S. (1994). *Mona the brilliant.* New York: Doubleday/Bantam Doubleday Dell.

Hutchins, P. (1968). *Rosie's walk.* New York: Aladdin Paperbacks.

Inkpen, M. (1988). *If I had a pig.* New York: Macmillan Children's Books.

Isadora, R. (1979). *Ben's trumpet.* New York: Greenwillow Books.

Jennings, L. (1994). *The dog who found Christmas.* Illus. C. Walters. New York: Dutton.

Jeunesse, G., Delafosse, C., Fuhr, U., & Sautai, R. (1994). *Whales: A first discovery book.* Illus. U. Fuhr & R. Sautai. New York: Scholastic.

Jeunesse, G., Delafosse, C., Millet, C., & Millet, D. (1994). *Castles: A first discovery book.* Illus. C. & D. Millet. New York: Scholastic.

Johnson, P. (1990). *Morning star.* Crystal Lake, IL: Rigby.

Johnson, J. W. (1994). *The creation.* New York: Holiday House.

Kafka, S. (1971). *I need a friend.* Boston: Silver Burdett Ginn.

Kalan, R. (1978). *Rain.* New York: Greenwillow Books.

Keats, E. J. (1972). *Pet show.* New York: Collier Books.

Kinsey-Warnock, N., & Kinsey, H. (1994). *The bear that heard crying.* Illus. T. Rand. New York: Cobblehill Books.

Kirk, D. (1996). *Three little pigs and one big pig.* Parsippany, NJ: Modern Curriculum Press.

Kitchen, B. (1994). *When hunger calls.* Cambridge, MA: Candlewick Press.

Kline, S. (1994). *Song Lee in Room 3B.* Illus. F. Remkiewicz. New York: Viking.

Koss, A. (1996). *You can ride.* Parsippany, NJ: Modern Curriculum Press.

Kramer, S. (1992). *Avalanche.* Photo. P. Cone. Minneapolis: Carolrhoda.

Kramer, S. (1992). *Lightning*. Photo. W. Faidley. Minneapolis: Carolrhoda.

Kraus, R. (1970). *Whose mouse are you?* New York: Scholastic Book Services.

Krauss, R. (1945). *The carrot seed*. New York: Harper.

Krauss, R. (1948). *Bears*. Illus. P. Rowand. New York: Harper & Row.

Kuklin, S. (1992). *How my family lives in America*. New York: Bradbury Press.

Langley, J. (1994). *Goldilocks and the three bears*. New York: HarperCollins.

Leemis, R. (1994). *Smart dog*. Illus. C. Demarest. Honesdale, PA: Boyds Mills Press.

Lewin, H. (1983). *Jafta*. Minneapolis: Carolrhoda Books, Inc.

Lindbergh, R. (1994). *What is the sun?* Illus. S. Lambert. Cambridge, MA: Candlewick Press.

Lionni, L. (1969). *Alexander and the wind-up mouse*. New York: Random House.

Lobel, A. (1972). *Frog and toad together*. New York: HarperCollins.

Lobel, A. (1976). *Frog and toad all year long*. New York: Harper & Row.

Lund, J. (1994). *Way out west lives a coyote named Frank*. New York: Dutton.

Lynch, P. A. (1996). *Fix it, Fox*. Parsippany, NJ: Modern Curriculum Press.

Macaulay, D. (1990). *Black and white*. Boston: Houghton Mifflin.

MacDonald, S. (1992). *Alphabetics*. New York: Aladdin Books.

Machotka, H. (1993). *Outstanding outsides*. New York: Morrow Junior Books.

Mahy, M. (1994). *The three-legged cat*. Illus. J. Allen. New York: Viking.

Maris, R. (1986). *I wish I could fly*. New York: Greenwillow Books.

Markle, S. (1991). *Outside and inside you*. New York: Bradbury.

Marshall, J. (1994). *Rats on the range and other stories*. New York: Dial.

Martin, B. (1967). *Brown bear, brown bear, what do you see?* New York: Henry Holt.

Martin, B. (1991). *Polar bear, polar bear, what do you hear?* Illus. Eric Carle. New York: Henry Holt.

Martin, J. R., & Marx, P. (1994). *Now everybody really hates me*. Illus. R. Chast. New York: HarperCollins.

Maurer, D. (1993). *Annie, Bea, and Chi Chi Dolores: A school day alphabet*. New York: Orchard Books.

Mayer, M. (1975). *Just for you*. Racine, WI: Western Publications.

Mazer, A. (1990). *Yellow button*. New York: Alfred Knopf.

McCloskey, R. (1941). *Make way for ducklings*. New York: Viking.

McConkey, L. (1990). *Sea and cedar: How the Northwest Coast Indians lived*. Illus. D. Tait. Vancouver: Douglas & McIntyre.

McCully, E. A. (1992). *Mirette on the high wire*. New York: Putnam.

McGovern, A. (1968). *Stone soup*. New York: Scholastic.

McKissack, P. (1988). *Mirandy and Brother Wind*. Illus. J. Pinkney. New York: Knopf.

McMillan, B. (1993). *What the class pet saw*. New York: Holiday House.

McPhail, D. (1993). *Pigs aplenty, pigs galore!* New York: Dutton Children's Books.

Michel, F. (1994). *Water*. Illus. Y. Larvor. New York: Lothrop, Lee & Shepard.

Miles, B. (1995). *Hey! I'm reading!* New York: Alfred A. Knopf.

Miller, M. (1991). *Whose shoe?* New York: Greenwillow Books.

Miller, M. (1994). *My five senses*. New York: Simon & Schuster Books for Young Readers.

Minarik, E. H. (1957). *Little bear*. New York: Harper.

Minarik, E. H. (1960). *Little bear's friend*. New York: HarperTrophy.

Morris, A. (1989). *Bread, bread, bread*. New York: Lothrop, Lee & Shepard Books.

Morris, A. (1990). *On the go*. New York: Lothrop, Lee & Shepard Books.

Mosel, A. (1968). *Tikki, Tikki, Tembo*. Illus. B. Lent. New York: Holt, Rinehart & Winston.

Moss, L. (1995). *Zin! zin! zin!: A violin*. New York: Simon & Schuster.

Mueller, V. (1985). *Monster and the baby*. Illus. L. Munsinger. Niles, IL: A. Whitman.

Myers, L. (1994). *Earthquake in the third grade*. Illus. K. Ritz. New York: Clarion.

Naden, N. (1989). *Dad didn't mind at all*. Crystal Lake, IL: Rigby.

Naylor, P. R. (1991). *Shiloh*. New York: Atheneum.

Nicholas, M. (1996). *Who made that?* Parsippany, NJ: Modern Curriculum Press.

Nodset, J. (1963). *Who took the farmer's hat?* New York: HarperCollins.

Numeroff, L. (1994). *Dogs don't wear sneakers*. Illus. J. Mathieu. New York: Simon & Schuster.

Pascoe, G. (1989). *The grump*. Crystal Lake, IL: Rigby.

Patent, D. H. (1994). *What good is a tail?* Illus. W. Munoz. New York: Cobblehill.

Peppe, R. (1970). *The house that Jack built*. New York: Delacourt Press.

Perlman, J. (1994). *Cinderella penguin*. New York: Viking.

Peters, S. (1983). *Animals at night*. Mahwah, NJ: Troll Associates.

Peters, L. W. (1988). *The sun, the wind and the rain*. Illus. T. Rand. New York: Henry Holt.

Peterson, P. J. (1994). *The sub.* Illus. M. Johnson. New York: Dutton.

Pinczes, E. (1994). *One hundred hungry ants.* Illus. B. MacKain. Boston: Houghton Mifflin.

Potter, K. (1994). *My mother the cat.* New York: Simon & Schuster.

Price, L. (1990). *Aida.* Illus. L. & D. Dillon. San Diego: Harcourt.

Riddell, C. (1988). *The trouble with elephants.* New York: HarperCollins.

Riley, K. (1996). *That fly.* Parsippany, NJ: Modern Curriculum Press.

Ringgold, F. (1991). *Tar beach.* New York: Crown.

Robart, R. (1986). *The cake that Mack ate.* Illus. M. Kovalski. Boston: Atlantic Monthly Press.

Robinson, F. (1992). *Real bears and alligators.* Chicago: Children's Press.

Roddie, S. (1994). *Mrs. Wolf.* Illus. K. Paul. New York: Dial.

Roe, E. (1990). *All I am.* New York: Bradbury Press.

Rosen, M. (1993). *How giraffe got such a long neck . . . and why rhino is so grumpy.* New York: Dial Books for Young Readers.

Rosetti, C. G. (1971). *What is pink?* New York: Macmillan.

Rounds, G. (1994). *Three billy goats gruff.* New York: Holiday House.

Rubinstein, G. (1993). *Dog in, cat out.* New York: Ticknor & Fields.

Russo, M. (1994). *Trade-in mother.* New York: Greenwillow Books.

Say, A. (1993). *Grandfather's journey.* Boston, MA: Houghton Mifflin.

Schanzer, R. (1994). *Ezra in pursuit: The great maze chase.* New York: Doubleday/Bantam Doubleday Dell.

Serfozo, M. (1990). *Rain talk.* New York: Margaret K. McElderry Books.

Serfozo, M. (1994). *Benjamin bigfoot.* Illus. J. Smith. New York: Margaret K. McElderry Books.

Seuss, D. (1957). *The cat in the hat.* New York: Random House.

Seuss, D. (1960). *Green eggs and ham.* New York: Beginner Books, Random House.

Seuss, D. (1963). *Hop on pop.* New York: Beginner Books.

Seuss, D. (1963). *Dr. Seuss' ABC book.* New York: Beginner Books.

Shannon, M. (1994). *Elvira.* New York: Ticknor & Fields.

Sharmat, M. W. (1972). *Nate the great.* Illus. M. Simont. New York: Coward, McCann & Geoghega.

Shaw, C. G. (1947). *It looked like spilt milk.* New York: Harper & Row.

Shaw, N. (1991). *Sheep in a shop.* Boston, MA: Houghton Mifflin.

Siebert, D. (1994). *Plane song.* Illus. V. Nasta. New York: HarperCollins.

Simon, S. (1993). *Autumn across America.* New York: Hyperion Books for Children.

Siracusa, C. (1994). *The giant zucchini.* New York: Hyperion.

Slater, T. (1994). *Walt Disney's Mickey and the beanstalk.* Illus. P. Wilson. New York: Disney Press.

Slobodkina, E. (1940). *Caps for sale.* New York: W. R. Scott, Inc.

Society, C. (1992). *Dolphins.* New York: Little Simon.

Soto, G. (1993). *Too many tamales.* New York: Putnam.

Stadler, J. (1984). *Hooray for snail.* New York: Crowell.

Steptoe, J. (1987). *Mufaro's beautiful daughters: An African tale.* New York: Lathrop.

Stock, C. (1993). *Where are you going, Manyoni?* New York: Marion Junior Books.

Suteyev, V. (1972). *Chick and the duckling.* Trans. M. Ginsburg. New York: Macmillan.

Tafuri, N. (1984). *Have you seen my duckling?* New York: Greenwillow Books.

Tafuri, N. (1987). *My friends.* New York: Greenwillow Books.

Tafuri, N. (1988). *Spots, feathers, and curly tails.* New York: Greenwillow Books.

Trelease, J. (1982). *The read-aloud handbook.* New York: Penguin Books.

Trivizas, E. (1994). *The three little wolves and the big bad pig.* Illus. H. Oxenbury. New York: Margaret K. McElderry Books.

Uchida, Y. (1993). *The bracelet.* New York: Philomel Books.

Underhill, L. (1987). *This is the house that Jack built.* New York: Holt.

Van Allsburg, C. (1983). *The wreck of the Zephyr.* Boston, MA: Houghton Mifflin.

Van Allsburg, C. (1985). *The polar express.* Boston: Houghton Mifflin.

Vesey, A. (1994). *Hector's new sneakers.* New York: Viking.

Voake, C. (1986). *Tom's cat.* New York: Walker Books.

Vozar, D. (1994). *Yo, hungry wolf!* Illus. B. Lewin. New York: Doubleday/Bantam Doubleday Dell.

Waber, B. (1972). *Ira sleeps over.* Boston: Houghton Mifflin.

Waddle, M. (1991). *Squeak-a-lot.* Illus. V. Miller. New York: Greenwillow Books.

Wandelmaier, R. (1985). *Stars.* Mahwah, NJ: Troll Associates.

Ward, C. (1988). *Cookie's week.* New York: G. P. Putnam's Sons.

Wesler, J. (1987). *Flowers fruits seeds.* New York: Simon & Schuster Books for Young Readers.

West, C. (1986). *Have you seen the crocodile?* New York: Lippincott.

Westcott, N. B. (1987). *Peanut butter and jelly.* Boston: Houghton Mifflin.

Wiesner, D. (1991). *Tuesday.* New York: Clarion.

Wildsmith, B. (1982). *Cat on the mat.* Oxford: Oxford University Press.

Williams, R. (1990). *Would you like to fly?* Haskell, WA: The Wright Group.

Wolff, A. (1984). *A year of birds.* New York: Dodd, Mead.

Wood, A. (1982). *Quick as a cricket.* New York: Child's Play.

Wood, A. (1984). *The napping house.* Illus. D. Wood. New York: Harcourt Brace Jovanovich.

Yabuuchi, M. (1981). *Whose baby?* New York: Philomel Books.

Yolen, J. (1987). *Owl moon.* New York: Philomel Books.

Yorinks, A. (1986). *Hey, Al.* Illus. J. Schoenherr. New York: Farrar, Straus, & Giroux.

York, C. B. (1994). *Pudmuddles.* Illus. L. Thiesing. New York: HarperCollins.

Young, E. (1989). *Lon Po Po: A Red Riding Hood story from China.* New York: Philomel Books.

Zoehfeld, K. W. (1994). *What lives in a shell?* New York: HarperCollins.

References

Adams, M. (1990). *Beginning to read: Thinking and learning about print.* Cambridge, MA: MIT Press.

Allen, J., & Carr, E. (1989). Collaborative learning among kindergarten writers: James learns how to write at school. In J. B. Allen & J. M. Madson (Eds.), *Risk makers, risk takers, risk breakers: Reducing the risks for young literacy learners* (pp. 30–47). Portsmouth, NH: Heinemann.

Allen, J., Cary, M., & Delgado, L. (1996). *Exploring blue highways: Literacy reform, school change, and the creation of learning communities.* New York: Teachers College Press.

Allington, R. L. (1983a). The reading instruction provided readers of different reading abilities. *Elementary School Journal, 83,* 549–559.

Allington, R. L. (1983b). Fluency: The neglected reading goal. *The Reading Teacher, 36,* 556–561.

Allington, R. L. (1984). Oral reading. In P. D. Pearson, R. Barr, M. L. Kamil, & P. Mosenthal (Eds.), *Handbook of reading research* (pp. 829–864). New York: Longman.

Allington, R. L., Stuetzel, H., Shake, M. C., & Lamarche, S. (1986). What is remedial reading? A descriptive study. *Reading Research and Instruction, 26,* 15–30.

Allington, R. L. (1991a). Children who find learning to read difficult: School responses to diversity. In E. H. Hiebert (Ed.), *Literacy for a diverse society: Perspectives, practices, and policies* (pp. 237–252). New York: Teachers College Press.

Allington, R. L. (1991b). The legacy of "Slow it down and make it more concrete." In J. Z. McCormick & S. McCormick (Eds.), *Learning factors/teacher factors: Issues in literacy research and instruction* (40th Yearbook of the National Reading Conference). Chicago: National Reading Conference.

Allington, R. L., & Walmsley, S. A. (Eds.). (1995). *No quick fix: Rethinking literacy programs in America's elementary schools.* New York: Teachers College Press.

American Heritage Dictionary of the English Language (1992). (3rd Ed.). Boston: Houghton Mifflin.

Anderson, L., Evertson, C., & Brophy, J. (1979). An experimental study of effective teaching in first grade reading groups. *Elementary School Journal, 79,* 183–223.

Anderson, A. A., & Stokes, S. J. (1984). Social and institutional influences on the development and practice of literacy. In H. Goelman, A. Oberg, & F. Smith (Eds.), *Awakening to literacy* (pp. 24–37). Portsmouth, NH: Heinemann Educational Books.

Anderson, R. C., & Pearson, P. D. (1984). A schema-theoretic view of basic processes in reading comprehension. In P. D. Pearson, R. Barr, M. L. Kamil, & P. Mosenthal (Eds.), *Handbook of reading research* (pp. 255–292). New York: Longman.

Angelou, M. (1969). *I know why the caged bird sings.* New York: Random House.

Applebee, A. N. (1991). Environments for language teaching and learning: Contemporary issues and future directions. In J. Flood, J. M. Jensen, D. Lapp, & J. R. Squire (Eds.), *Handbook of research on teaching the English language arts.* New York: Macmillan.

Armbruster, B. B., & Anderson, T. H. (1985). Frames: Structures for informative text. In D. H. Jonassen (Ed.), *The technology of text* (Vol. 2, pp. 90–104). Englewood Cliffs, NJ: Educational Technology Publications.

Ashe, P. M. (1987). *Letters to pen pals at a convalescent center: A school project that rewards warmth and understanding.* Paper presented at the annual spring conference of the National Council of Teachers of English, Louisville, KY.

Ashman, A. F., & Elkins, J. (1990). Cooperative learning among special students. In H. C. Foot, M. J. Morgan, & R. H. Shute (Eds.), *Children helping children* (pp. 207–233). New York: John Wiley & Sons.

Ashton-Warner
Bantam Boo963). *Teacher.* New York:

Atwell, N. (1987,
NH: Heinemate *middle.* Portsmouth,

Au, K. H. (1979).
relationship mdhe experience-text-
dren. *The Readvith* minority chil-
679. *:her, 32(7),* 677–

Au, K. H., & Mason, J.
nizational factors in1). Social orga-
balance of rights hyg to read: The
search Quarterly, 17, Reading Re-

Au, K. H., Scheu, J. A., ,
Herman, P. A. (1990). ni, A. J., &
countability in a whole t and ac-
lum. *The Reading Teach* curricu-
74–578.

Au, K. (1993). *Literacy insti*
cultural settings. Fort W multi-
court Brace. Har-

Au, K. H. (1994). Portfolio asse
riences at the Kamehameha
Education Program. In S. Ve-
E. H. Hiebert, & P. Afflerbach y
thentic reading assessment: Pra
possibilities (pp. 103–126). Nev
International Reading Association

Aukerman, R. C. (1984). *Approaches t*
ning reading (2d ed.). New York:

Avery, C. S. (1990). Learning rese
Researching to learn. In M. W.
(Ed.), *Opening the door to classroom*
search. Newark, DE: International Read
Association.

Baghban, M. (1989). *You can help your chil*
with writing. Newark, DE: International
Reading Association.

Baker, K. (1993). "Have you been dead?" Questions and letters from children. *The Read-*
ing Teacher, 46, 372–374.

Bakhtin, M. (1986). *Speech genres and other*
late essays. Austin, TX: University of Texas
Press.

Bakhtin, M. (1990). Art and answerability. In
M. Holquist & V. Liapunov (Eds.), *Art and*
answerability: Early philosophical essays
by M. Bakhtin (pp. 1–3). Austin, TX: University of Texas Press.

Barnes, D. (1976). *From communication to*
curriculum. New York: Penguin Books.

Barnes, D. (1995). Talking and learning in
classrooms. *Primary Voices K-6, 3(1),* 2–7.

Barone, D. (1990). The written responses of
young children: Beyond comprehension to
story understanding. *The New Advocate,*
3, 49–56.

Barr, R. C. (1973–74). Instructional pace differences and their effect on reading acquisition. *Reading Research Quarterly, 9,*
526–554.

Barr, R., Kamil, M., Mosenthal, P., & Pearson,
P. D. (Eds.). (1991). *Handbook of reading*

research. New York: Longman Publishing
Group.

Bean, R. M., Cooley, W. W., Eichelberger, R. T.,
Lazar, M. K., & Zigmond, N. (1991). Inclass
or pullout: Effects of setting on the remedial reading program. *Journal of Reading*
Behavior, 23, 445–464.

Beardsley, L., & Marecek-Zeman, M. (1987).
Making connections: Facilitating literacy
in young children. *Childhood Education,*
63, 159–166.

Beardstown Ladies Club (1994). *The Beards-*
town ladies' common-sense investment
guide. New York: Hyperion.

Bennett, W. J. (Ed.). (1993). *The book of vir-*
tues: A treasury of great moral stories.
New York: Simon & Schuster.

Bereiter, C., & Scardamalia, M. (1984). Learning to write from reading. *Written Com-*
munication, 1, 163–188.

Berghoff, B., & Egawa, K. (1991). No more
"rocks": Grouping to give students control
of their learning. *The Reading Teacher, 44,*
536–540.

Blanton, W. E., & Wells, G. (1995). *XTAR: A*
network for teacher researchers. In
listserv@lester.appstate.edu.

Catz, G. A., & Ball, S. (1971). *The second*
year of "Sesame Street": A continuing evalu-
ation. Princeton, NJ: Educational Testing
ice.

& Dykstra, R. (1967). The Coopera-
search program in first-grade reading
ion. *Reading Research Quarterly,*

avinroy, K. H., Flory, M. D., &
H. (1994). Teachers' knowledge
bout summary as a component
R. Garner & P. Alexander
about text and instruc-
p. 155–182). Hillsdale, NJ:
n Associates.

Bredek P. E. (1983). Categoriz-
app ning to read: A causal
gram 01, 419–421.

age 8. 7). *Developmentally*
tion for *arly childhood pro-*

Bredekamp om birth through
Reaching ational Associa-
ulum and oung Children.
Washington (Ed.). (1992).
the Educati *iate curric-*

Bromley, K., W *g children.*
(1994). Book iation for
for literacy lear
47, 392–400. mer, K.

Brown, A. L., & Sm usiasm
the importance of cher,

ing
e

passages: A problem of metacognitive development. *Child Development, 48,* 1–8.

Brown, A. L., & Palincsar, A. S. (1989). Guided, cooperative learning and individual knowledge acquisition. In L. B. Resnick (Ed.), *Knowing, learning, and instruction: Essays in honor of Robert Glaser* (pp. 392–451). Hillsdale, NJ: Erlbaum.

Brown, R. G. (1991). *Schools of thought.* San Francisco, CA: Jossey-Bass Publishers.

Bruner, J. (1991). Introduction. In S. R. Graubard (Ed.), *Literacy: An overview by fourteen experts* (pp. vii–xi). New York: The Noonday Press.

Burbules, N. (1993). *Dialogue in teaching: Theory and practice.* New York: Teachers College Press.

Calfee, R. C. (1992). The Inquiring School: Literacy for the year 2000. In C. Collins & J. N. Mangieri (Eds.), *Teaching thinking: An agenda for the twenty-first century.* Hillsdale, NJ: Erlbaum.

California Language Arts/English Framework Committee (1987). *English-language arts framework for California public schools: Kindergarten through grade 12.* Sacramento, CA: California Department of Education.

Campione, J. C., Brown, A. L., & Jay, M. (1992). Computers in a community of learners. In E. DeCorte, M. Linn, H. Mandle, & L. Verschaffel (Eds.), *Computer-based learning environments and problem solving* (NATO ASI Series F: Computer and Systems, Vol. 84, pp. 163–192). Springer-Verlag.

Carroll, J. B., Davies, P., & Richman, B. (1971). *Word frequency book.* Boston: Houghton Mifflin.

Catto, S. L. (1993). *An examination of first-grade literacy intervention: Pupil student performance and the relationship of selected factors.* Unpublished dissertation, University of Colorado.

Cazden, C. B. (1988). *Classroom discourse: The language of teaching and learning.* Portsmouth, NH: Heinemann.

Cazden, C. B. (1991). Contemporary issues and future directions: Active learners and active teachers. In J. Flood, J. M. Jensen, D. Lapp, & J. R. Squire (Eds.), *Handbook of research on teaching the English language arts* (pp. 248–260). New York: Macmillan.

Chall, J. S. (1982). *The great debate* (2nd ed.). New York: McGraw-Hill. (Original work published 1967).

Chall, J. S., & Squire, J. R. (1991). The publishing industry and textbooks. In R. Barr, M. Kamil, P. Mosenthal, & P. D. Pearson (Eds.), *Handbook of reading research* (pp. 120–146).

Children's Book Council (1989). *Children's books: Awards and prizes.* New York: Children's Book Council.

Children's Choices (1993). Children's Choices for 1993. *The Reading Teacher, 46,* 155.

Chomsky, C. (1972). Stages in language development and reading exposure. *Harvard Educational Review, 42,* 1–33.

Chomsky, N. (1965). *Aspects of the theory of syntax.* Cambridge: The MIT Press.

Christie, J. F. (Ed.) (1991). *Play and early literacy development.* Albany, New York: State University of New York Press.

Clarke, L. K. (1988). Invented versus traditional spelling in first graders' writings: Effects on learning to spell and read. *Research in the Teaching of English, 22,* 281–309.

Clay, M. M. (1982). Emergent reading behavior. Unpublished doctoral dissertation, University of Auckland, New Zealand.

Clay, M. M. (1975). *What did I write? The patterning of complex behavior.* Auckland, New Zealand: Heinemann Educational Books.

Clay, M. M. (1985). *The early detection of reading difficulties* (3rd ed.). Hong Kong: Heinemann.

Clay, M. M. (1987). *Writing begins at home.* Portsmouth, NH: Heinemann.

Clay, M. M. (1991). *Becoming literate: The construction of inner control.* Portsmouth, NH: Heinemann.

Cochran-Smith, M. (1984). *The making of a reader.* Norwood, NJ: Ablex Publishing Corp.

Cochran-Smith, M., & Lytle, S. (1993). *Inside/outside: Teacher research and knowledge.* New York: Teachers College Press.

Cohen, P., Kulik, J. A., & Kulik, C. (1982). Educational outcomes of tutoring: A meta-analysis of findings. *American Educational Research Journal, 19,* 237–248.

Commire, A. (Ed.). (1982). *Something about the author.* Detroit, MI: Gale Research Company.

Conway, J. K. (1989). *The road from Coorain.* New York: Alfred A. Knopf.

Costa, A. J., & Garmston, R. J. (1994). *Cognitive coaching: A foundation for Renaissance schools.* Norwood, MA: Christopher-Gordon Publishers.

Coulthard, M. (1977). *An introduction to discourse analysis.* Essex, England: Longman Group.

Crowell, D. C., Kawakami, A. J., & Wong, J. L. (1986). Emerging literacy: Reading-writing experiences in a kindergarten classroom. *The Reading Teacher, 40,* 144–149.

Crowhurst, M. (1992). Some effects of corresponding with an older audience. *Language Arts, 69,* 268–273.

Cullinan, B. E., & Galda, L. (1994). *Literature and the child* (3rd ed.). Fort Worth: Harcourt Brace College Publishers.

Cunningham, P. M. (1979). A compare/contrast theory of mediated word identification. *The Reading Teacher, 33,* 774–778.

Cunningham, E. (1986). *Phonemic awareness: The development of early reading competency.* Unpublished dissertation, University of Michigan.

Cunningham, P. M. (1995). *Phonics they use: Words for reading and writing* (2d ed.). New York: HarperCollins.

Daiute, C. (1993). ...th genres and literacy: Links between sociocultural and developmental theorists. *Language Arts, 70,* 402–416.

Davison, A., & Kantor, N. (1982). On the failure of readability formulas to define readable texts: A case study from adaptations. *Reading Research Quarterly, 17,* 187–209.

DeFord, D. E. (1980). Young children and their writing. *Theory into Practice, 19,* 157–162.

Delgado-Gaitan, C. (1992). School matters in the Mexican-American home: Socializing children to education. *American Educational Research Journal, 29,* ...–513.

Delpit, L. D. (1988). The silenced dialogue: Power and pedagogy in educating other people's children. *Harvard Educational Review, 58(3),* 280–298.

Dewey, J. (1938). *Experience and education.* New York: Macmillan.

Dickinson, D. K. (1986). Effects of a reading program on one Head Start language and literacy environment. In J. ... & J. M. Mason (Eds.), *Risk Makers, risk takers: Reducing the ... for young literacy learners* (pp. 125–...). Portsmouth, NH: Heinemann.

Doiron, R. (1994). Using nonfiction in a read-aloud program: Letting the facts speak for themselves. *The Reading Teacher, 47(8),* 616–624.

Dorotik, M., & Betzold, M. R. (1992). Expanding literacy for all. *The Reading Teacher, 45,* 574–579.

Durkin, D. (1966). *Children who read early.* New York: Teachers College Press.

Durkin, D. (1987). A classroom-observation study of reading instruction in kindergarten. *Early Childhood Research Quarterly, 2,* 275–300.

Durkin, D. (1993). *Teaching them to read* (6th ed.). Boston: Allyn & Bacon.

Dyson, A. H. (1993). *Social worlds of children learning to write in an urban primary school.* New York: Teachers College Press.

Edelsky, C., Altwerger, B., & Flores, B. (1990). *Whole language: What's the difference?* Portsmouth, NH: Heinemann.

Edwards, P. (1991). Fostering early literacy through parent coaching. In E. H. Hiebert (Ed.), *Literacy for a diverse society: Perspectives, practices and policies* (pp. 199–213). New York: Teachers College Press.

Edwards, P. (1995). Empowering low-income mothers and fathers to share books with young children. *The Reading Teacher, 48,* 558–564.

Eeds, M., & Wells, D. (1989). Grand conversations: An explanation of meaning construction in literature study groups. *Research in the Teaching of English, 23,* 4–29.

Eller, W., Hester, K. B., et al. (1980). *The Laidlaw reading program (Level 6, Reader 1).* River Forest, IL: Laidlaw Brothers.

Ellwein, M. C., Walsh, D. J., Eads, G. M. I., & Miller, A. (1991). Using readiness tests to route kindergartner students: The snarled intersection of psychometrics, policy, and practice. *Educational Evaluation and Policy Analysis, 13,* 159–175.

Elson, W. H., & Gray, W. S. (1930). *Elson Basic Readers.* Chicago, IL: Scott, Foresman & Company.

Englert, C. S., Raphael, T. E., & Mariage, T. V. (1994). Developing a school-based discourse for literacy learning: A principled search for understanding. *Learning Disability Quarterly, 17(1),* 2–32.

Englert, C. S., Gavelek, J. E., Mariage, T. V., & Raphael, T. E. (April 1995). *A multi-year literacy intervention: Transformation and personal change in the community of the Early Literacy Project.* Paper presented at the annual meeting of the American Educational Research Association, San Francisco, CA.

Evans, K. S. (1995). Teacher reflection as a cure for tunnel vision. *Language Arts, 72,* 266–271.

...rreiro, E., & Teberosky, A. (1982). *Literacy before schooling.* Portsmouth, NH: Heinemann Educational Books.

...iro, E. (1986). The interplay between information and assimilation in beginning literacy. In W. H. Teale & E. Sulzby (Eds.), *Emergent literacy: Writing and reading* (pp. ...–49). Norwood, NJ: Ablex.

...y of school. (1987, August 26). *The Fish Daily Camera,* p. 1.

...P..., & Berliner, D. C. (Eds.). (1985). Fisher... *...es on instructional time.* New man.

...acte... Hiebert, E. H. (1990). Characteristics...litera...tasks in two approaches to *Journ...*ction. *Elementary School...*

Fitzgerald...8.
(1991). ...l, D., & Cunningham, W. literacy... ...nship between parental literacy. J...erceptions of emergent 191–213. *Reading Behavior, 23,*

Flavell, J. H. (1970). Developmental studies of mediated memory. In H. W. Reese & L. P. Lipsitt (Eds.), *Advances in child development and behavior* (pp. 181–211). New York: Academic Press.

Flavell, J. H. (1979). Metacognition and cognitive monitoring: A new area of cognitive-developmental inquiry. *American Psychologist, 34,* 906–911.

Flesch, R. (1957). *Why Johnny can't read.* New York: Random House.

Flood, J. (1977). Parental styles in reading episodes with young children. *The Reading Teacher, 31,* 864–867.

Flood, J., Jensen, J., Lapp, D., & Squire, J. (1991). *Handbook of research on teaching the English language arts.* New York: Macmillan.

Flood, J., & Lapp, D. (1994). Teacher book clubs: Establishing literature discussion groups for teachers. *The Reading Teacher, 47,* 574–576.

Florio-Ruane, S. (1994). The future teachers' autobiography Club: Preparing educators to support literacy learning in culturally diverse classrooms. *English Education, 26,* 52–66.

Fraatz, J. M. B. (1987). *The politics of reading: Power, opportunity, and prospects for change in America's public schools.* New York: Teachers College Press.

Fractor, J. S., Woodruff, M. C., Martinez, M. G., & Teale, W. H. (1993). Let's not miss opportunities to promote voluntary reading: Classroom libraries in the elementary school. *The Reading Teacher, 46,* 476–484.

Freeman, D., & Freeman, Y. (1994). *Between worlds: Access to second language acquisition.* Portsmouth, NH: Heinemann.

Fried, C., Hershey, P., Koblitz, D., Stiles, B., Stotts, N., Unanue, M., Woodman, M., & Pierce, K. (1995). Children's books: Mysteries of a child's world. *The Reading Teacher, 48,* 508–516.

Fries, C. C. (1963). *Linguistics and reading.* New York: Holt, Rinehart & Winston,

Fromkin, V., & Rodman, R. (1974). *An introduction to language.* New York: Holt, hart, & Winston, Inc.

Gaffney, J. S., & Anderson, R. C. (1991). tiered scaffolding: Congruent pro teaching and learning. In E. H. Hie *Literacy for a diverse society* tives, practices, and policies (p New York: Teachers College P

Gallagher, J. M., & Sigel, I. E. (19 tion to special issue: Hothou children. *Early Childhood* terly, 2, 201–202.

Gates, A. I. (1937). The neces beginning reading. *The Journal, 37,* 497–508.

Gavelek, J. R., & Raphael, T. E. (1996). Changing talk about text: New roles for teachers and students. *Language Arts, 73*(3), 182–192.

Gentry, J. R. (1982). An analysis of developmental spelling in GNYS AT WRK. *The Reading Teacher, 36,* 192–99.

Gentry, J. R., & Gillet, J. W. (1992). *Teaching kids to spell.* Portsmouth NH: Heinemann.

Gesell, A. L. (1925). *The mental growth of the preschool child.* New York: Macmillan.

Goatley, V., Highfield, K., Bentley, J., Pardo, L. S., Folkert, J., Scherer, Raphael, T. E., & Grattan, K. (1994). Empowering teachers to be researchers: A collaborative approach. *Teacher Research: The Journal of Classroom Inquiry, 1,* –144.

Goatley, V. J. (1995). *The literacy communities of emergent readers and writers: A sociocultural perspective.* Unpublished doctoral dissertation, Michigan State University, East Lansing, MI.

Goldenberg, C. (1990). Beginning literacy for Spanish-speaking children. *Language Arts, 67,* 590–5

Goldenberg, C., & Gallimore, R. (1991). Local knowledge, research knowledge, and educational change: A case study of first-grade Spanish reading improvement. *Educational Researcher, 20*(8), 2–14.

Goldenberg, C., Reese, L., & Gallimore, R. (1992). Effects of school literacy materials on children's home experiences and reading achievement. *American Journal of Education, 100,* 497–536.

Goldenberg, C. (1994). Promoting early literacy development among Spanish-speaking children: Lessons from two studies. In E. H. Hiebert & B. M. Taylor (Eds.), *Getting reading right from the start: Effective early literacy interventions* (pp. 171–199). Boston, MA: Allyn & Bacon.

Goodman, K. S. (1973). Miscues: Windows on the reading process. In K. Goodman (Ed.), *Miscue analysis: Applications to reading instruction* (pp. 3–14). Urbana, IL: National Council of Teachers of English/ERIC Clearinghouse on Reading & Communication Skills.

Goodman, K. S., & Goodman, Y. M. (1979). Learning to read is natural. In L. B. Resnick & P. A. Weaver (Eds.), *Theory and practice of early reading* (pp. 137–153). Hillsdale, NJ: Lawrence Erlbaum Associates, Publishers.

Goodman, Y. M. (1985). Kidwatching: Observing children in the classroom. In A. Jaggar & M. T. Smith-Burke (Eds.), *Observing the language learner* (pp. 9–18). Newark, DE: International Reading Association.

Goodman, K. (1986). *What's whole in whole language.* Portsmouth, NH: Heinemann.

Ashton-Warner, S. (1963). *Teacher.* New York: Bantam Books.

Atwell, N. (1987). *In the middle.* Portsmouth, NH: Heinemann.

Au, K. H. (1979). Using the experience-text-relationship method with minority children. *The Reading Teacher, 32(7),* 677–679.

Au, K. H., & Mason, J. M. (1981). Social organizational factors in learning to read: The balance of rights hypothesis. *Reading Research Quarterly, 17,* 115–152.

Au, K. H., Scheu, J. A., Kawakami, A. J., & Herman, P. A. (1990). Assessment and accountability in a whole literacy curriculum. *The Reading Teacher, 43,* 574–578.

Au, K. (1993). *Literacy instruction in multicultural settings.* Fort Worth, TX: Harcourt Brace.

Au, K. H. (1994). Portfolio assessment: Experiences at the Kamehameha Elementary Education Program. In S. W. Valencia, E. H. Hiebert, & P. Afflerbach (Eds.), *Authentic reading assessment: Practices and possibilities* (pp. 103–126). Newark, DE: International Reading Association.

Aukerman, R. C. (1984). *Approaches to beginning reading* (2d ed.). New York: Wiley.

Avery, C. S. (1990). Learning research/Researching to learn. In M. W. Olson (Ed.), *Opening the door to classroom research.* Newark, DE: International Reading Association.

Baghban, M. (1989). *You can help your child with writing.* Newark, DE: International Reading Association.

Baker, K. (1993). "Have you been dead?" Questions and letters from children. *The Reading Teacher, 46,* 372–374.

Bakhtin, M. (1986). *Speech genres and other late essays.* Austin, TX: University of Texas Press.

Bakhtin, M. (1990). Art and answerability. In M. Holquist & V. Liapunov (Eds.), *Art and answerability: Early philosophical essays by M. Bakhtin* (pp. 1–3). Austin, TX: University of Texas Press.

Barnes, D. (1976). *From communication to curriculum.* New York: Penguin Books.

Barnes, D. (1995). Talking and learning in classrooms. *Primary Voices K–6, 3(1),* 2–7.

Barone, D. (1990). The written responses of young children: Beyond comprehension to story understanding. *The New Advocate, 3,* 49–56.

Barr, R. C. (1973–74). Instructional pace differences and their effect on reading acquisition. *Reading Research Quarterly, 9,* 526–554.

Barr, R., Kamil, M., Mosenthal, P., & Pearson, P. D. (Eds.). (1991). *Handbook of reading research.* New York: Longman Publishing Group.

Bean, R. M., Cooley, W. W., Eichelberger, R. T., Lazar, M. K., & Zigmond, N. (1991). Inclass or pullout: Effects of setting on the remedial reading program. *Journal of Reading Behavior, 23,* 445–464.

Beardsley, L., & Marecek-Zeman, M. (1987). Making connections: Facilitating literacy in young children. *Childhood Education, 63,* 159–166.

Beardstown Ladies Club (1994). *The Beardstown ladies' common-sense investment guide.* New York: Hyperion.

Bennett, W. J. (Ed.). (1993). *The book of virtues: A treasury of great moral stories.* New York: Simon & Schuster.

Bereiter, C., & Scardamalia, M. (1984). Learning to write from reading. *Written Communication, 1,* 163–188.

Berghoff, B., & Egawa, K. (1991). No more "rocks": Grouping to give students control of their learning. *The Reading Teacher, 44,* 536–540.

Blanton, W. E., & Wells, G. (1995). *XTAR: A network for teacher researchers.* In listserv@lester.appstate.edu.

Bogatz, G. A., & Ball, S. (1971). *The second year of "Sesame Street": A continuing evaluation.* Princeton, NJ: Educational Testing Service.

Bond, G., & Dykstra, R. (1967). The Cooperative Research program in first-grade reading instruction. *Reading Research Quarterly, 2,* 5–141.

Borko, H., Davinroy, K. H., Flory, M. D., & Hiebert, E. H. (1994). Teachers' knowledge and beliefs about summary as a component of reading. In R. Garner & P. Alexander (Eds.), *Beliefs about text and instruction with text* (pp. 155–182). Hillsdale, NJ: Lawrence Erlbaum Associates.

Bradley, L., & Bryant, P. E. (1983). Categorizing sounds and learning to read: A causal connection. *Nature, 301,* 419–421.

Bredekamp, S. (Ed.). (1987). *Developmentally appropriate practice in early childhood programs serving children from birth through age 8.* Washington, DC: National Association for the Education of Young Children.

Bredekamp, S., & Rosegrant, T. (Ed.). (1992). *Reaching potentials: Appropriate curriculum and assessment for young children.* Washington, DC: National Association for the Education of Young Children.

Bromley, K., Winters, D., & Schlimmer, K. (1994). Book buddies: Creating enthusiasm for literacy learning. *The Reading Teacher, 47,* 392–400.

Brown, A. L., & Smiley, S. S. (1977). Rating the importance of structural units of prose passages: A problem of metacognitive development. *Child Development, 48,* 1–8.

Brown, A. L., & Palincsar, A. S. (1989). Guided, cooperative learning and individual knowledge acquisition. In L. B. Resnick (Ed.), *Knowing, learning, and instruction: Essays in honor of Robert Glaser* (pp. 392–451). Hillsdale, NJ: Erlbaum.

Brown, R. G. (1991). *Schools of thought.* San Francisco, CA: Jossey-Bass Publishers.

Bruner, J. (1991). Introduction. In S. R. Graubard (Ed.), *Literacy: An overview by fourteen experts* (pp. vii–xi). New York: The Noonday Press.

Burbules, N. (1993). *Dialogue in teaching: Theory and practice.* New York: Teachers College Press.

Calfee, R. C. (1992). The Inquiring School: Literacy for the year 2000. In C. Collins & J. N. Mangieri (Eds.), *Teaching thinking: An agenda for the twenty-first century.* Hillsdale, NJ: Erlbaum.

California Language Arts/English Framework Committee (1987). *English-language arts framework for California public schools: Kindergarten through grade 12.* Sacramento, CA: California Department of Education.

Campione, J. C., Brown, A. L., & Jay, M. (1992). Computers in a community of learners. In E. DeCorte, M. Linn, H. Mandle, & L. Verschaffel (Eds.), *Computer-based learning environments and problem solving* (NATO ASI Series F: Computer and Systems, Vol. 84, pp. 163–192). Berlin: Springer-Verlag.

Carroll, J. B., Davies, P., & Richman, B. (1971). *Word frequency book.* Boston: Houghton Mifflin.

Catto, S. L. (1993). *An examination of a second-grade literacy intervention: Patterns of student performance and the relationship of selected factors.* Unpublished doctoral dissertation, University of Colorado-Boulder.

Cazden, C. B. (1988). *Classroom discourse: The language of teaching and learning.* Portsmouth, NH: Heinemann.

Cazden, C. B. (1991). Contemporary issues and future directions: Active learners and active teachers. In J. Flood, J. M. Jensen, D. Lapp, & J. R. Squire (Eds.), *Handbook of research on teaching the English language arts* (pp. 418–422). New York: Macmillan.

Chall, J. S. (1982). *Learning to read: The great debate* (2d ed.). New York: McGraw-Hill. (Original work published 1967).

Chall, J. S., & Squire, J. R. (1991). The publishing industry and textbooks. In R. Barr, M. Kamil, P. Mosenthal, & P. D. Pearson (Eds.), *Handbook of reading research* (pp. 120–146). New York: Longman.

Children's Book Council (1992). *Children's books: Awards and prizes.* New York: Children's Book Council.

Children's Choices (1994). Beginning independent readers and younger readers. *The Reading Teacher, 48,* 147–155.

Chomsky, C. (1972). Stages in language development and reading exposure. *Harvard Educational Review, 42,* 1–33.

Chomsky, N. (1965). *Aspects of the theory of syntax.* Cambridge, MA: The MIT Press.

Christie, J. F. (Ed.). (1991). *Play and early literacy development.* Albany, New York: State University of New York Press.

Clarke, L. K. (1988). Invented versus traditional spelling in first graders' writings: Effects on learning to spell and read. *Research in the Teaching of English, 22,* 281–309.

Clay, M. M. (1966). *Emergent reading behavior.* Unpublished doctoral dissertation, University of Auckland, New Zealand.

Clay, M. M. (1972). *The patterning of complex behavior.* Auckland, New Zealand: Heinemann Educational Books.

Clay, M. (1985). *The early detection of reading difficulties.* (3rd ed.). Hong Kong: Heinemann.

Clay, M. (1987). *Writing begins at home.* Portsmouth, NH: Heinemann.

Clay, M. (1991). *Becoming literate: The construction of inner control.* Portsmouth, NH: Heinemann.

Cochran-Smith, M. (1984). *The making of a reader.* Norwood, NJ: Ablex Publishing Corp.

Cochran-Smith, M., & Lytle, S. (1993). *Inside/outside: Teacher research and knowledge.* New York: Teachers College Press.

Cohen, P., Kulik, J. A., & Kulik, C. (1982). Educational outcomes of tutoring: A meta-analysis of findings. *American Educational Research Journal, 19,* 237–248.

Commire, A. (Ed.). (1982). *Something about the author.* Detroit, MI: Gale Research Company.

Conway, J. K. (1989). *The road from Coorain.* New York: Alfred A. Knopf.

Costa, A. J., & Garmston, R. J. (1994). *Cognitive coaching: A foundation for Renaissance schools.* Norwood, MA: Christopher-Gordon Publishers.

Coulthard, M. (1977). *An introduction to discourse analysis.* Essex, England: Longman Group.

Crowell, D. C., Kawakami, A. J., & Wong, J. L. (1986). Emerging literacy: Reading-writing experiences in a kindergarten classroom. *The Reading Teacher, 40,* 144–149.

Crowhurst, M. (1992). Some effects of corresponding with an older audience. *Language Arts, 69,* 268–273.

Cullinan, B. E., & Galda, L. (1994). *Literature and the child* (3rd ed.). Fort Worth: Harcourt Brace College Publishers.

Cunningham, P. M. (1979). A compare/contrast theory of mediated word identification. *The Reading Teacher, 33,* 774–778.

Cunningham, A. E. (1986). *Phonemic awareness: The development of early reading competency.* Unpublished dissertation, University of Michigan.

Cunningham, P. M. (1995). *Phonics they use: Words for reading and writing* (2d ed.). New York: HarperCollins.

Daiute, C. (1993). Youth genres and literacy: Links between sociocultural and developmental theorists. *Language Arts, 70,* 402–416.

Davison, A., & Kantor, R. N. (1982). On the failure of readability formulas to define readable texts: A case study from adaptations. *Reading Research Quarterly, 17,* 187–209.

DeFord, D. E. (1980). Young children and their writing. *Theory into Practice, 19,* 157–162.

Delgado-Gaitan, C. (1992). School matters in the Mexican-American home: Socializing children to education. *American Educational Research Journal, 29,* 495–513.

Delpit, L. D. (1988). The silenced dialogue: Power and pedagogy in educating other people's children. *Harvard Educational Review, 58(3),* 280–298.

Dewey, J. (1938). *Experience and education.* New York: Macmillan.

Dickinson, D. K. (1986). Effects of a shared reading program on one Head Start language and literacy environment. In J. Allen & J. M. Mason (Eds.), *Risk Makers, risk takers, risk breakers: Reducing the risks for young literacy learners* (pp. 125–153). Portsmouth, NH: Heinemann.

Doiron, R. (1994). Using nonfiction in a read-aloud program: Letting the facts speak for themselves. *The Reading Teacher, 47(8),* 616–624.

Dorotik, M., & Betzold, M. R. (1992). Expanding literacy for all. *The Reading Teacher, 45,* 574–579.

Durkin, D. (1966). *Children who read early.* New York: Teachers College Press.

Durkin, D. (1987). A classroom-observation study of reading instruction in kindergarten. *Early Childhood Research Quarterly, 2,* 275–300.

Durkin, D. (1993). *Teaching them to read* (6th ed.). Boston: Allyn & Bacon.

Dyson, A. H. (1993). *Social worlds of children learning to write in an urban primary school.* New York: Teachers College Press.

Edelsky, C., Altwerger, B., & Flores, B. (1990). *Whole language: What's the difference?* Portsmouth, NH: Heinemann.

Edwards, P. (1991). Fostering early literacy through parent coaching. In E. H. Hiebert (Ed.), *Literacy for a diverse society: Perspectives, practices and policies* (pp. 199–213). New York: Teachers College Press.

Edwards, P. (1995). Empowering low-income mothers and fathers to share books with young children. *The Reading Teacher, 48,* 558–564.

Eeds, M., & Wells, D. (1989). Grand conversations: An explanation of meaning construction in literature study groups. *Research in the Teaching of English, 23,* 4–29.

Eller, W., Hester, K. B., et al. (1980). *The Laidlaw reading program (Level 6, Reader 1).* River Forest, IL: Laidlaw Brothers.

Ellwein, M. C., Walsh, D. J., Eads, G. M. I., & Miller, A. (1991). Using readiness tests to route kindergartner students: The snarled intersection of psychometrics, policy, and practice. *Educational Evaluation and Policy Analysis, 13,* 159–175.

Elson, W. H., & Gray, W. S. (1930). *Elson Basic Readers.* Chicago, IL: Scott, Foresman & Company.

Englert, C. S., Raphael, T. E., & Mariage, T. V. (1994). Developing a school-based discourse for literacy learning: A principled search for understanding. *Learning Disability Quarterly, 17(1),* 2–32.

Englert, C. S., Gavelek, J. E., Mariage, T. V., & Raphael, T. E. (April 1995). *A multi-year literacy intervention: Transformation and personal change in the community of the Early Literacy Project.* Paper presented at the annual meeting of the American Educational Research Association, San Francisco, CA.

Evans, K. S. (1995). Teacher reflection as a cure for tunnel vision. *Language Arts, 72,* 266–271.

Ferreiro, E., & Teberosky, A. (1982). *Literacy before schooling.* Portsmouth, NH: Heinemann Educational Books.

Ferreiro, E. (1986). The interplay between information and assimilation in beginning literacy. In W. H. Teale & E. Sulzby (Eds.), *Emergency literacy: Writing and reading* (pp. 15–49). Norwood, NJ: Ablex.

The first day of school. (1987, August 26). *The Boulder Daily Camera,* p. 1.

Fisher, C. W., & Berliner, D. C. (Eds.). (1985). *Perspectives on instructional time.* New York: Longman.

Fisher, C. W., & Hiebert, E. H. (1990). Characteristics of tasks in two approaches to literacy instruction. *Elementary School Journal, 91,* 3–18.

Fitzgerald, J., Spiegel, D., & Cunningham, W. (1991). The relationship between parental literacy level and perceptions of emergent literacy. *Journal of Reading Behavior, 23,* 191–213.

Flavell, J. H. (1970). Developmental studies of mediated memory. In H. W. Reese & L. P. Lipsitt (Eds.), *Advances in child development and behavior* (pp. 181–211). New York: Academic Press.

Flavell, J. H. (1979). Metacognition and cognitive monitoring: A new area of cognitive-developmental inquiry. *American Psychologist, 34,* 906–911.

Flesch, R. (1957). *Why Johnny can't read.* New York: Random House.

Flood, J. (1977). Parental styles in reading episodes with young children. *The Reading Teacher, 31,* 864–867.

Flood, J., Jensen, J., Lapp, D., & Squire, J. (1991). *Handbook of research on teaching the English language arts.* New York: Macmillan.

Flood, J., & Lapp, D. (1994). Teacher book clubs: Establishing literature discussion groups for teachers. *The Reading Teacher, 47,* 574–576.

Florio-Ruane, S. (1994). The future teachers' autobiography Club: Preparing educators to support literacy learning in culturally diverse classrooms. *English Education, 26,* 52–66.

Fraatz, J. M. B. (1987). *The politics of reading: Power, opportunity, and prospects for change in America's public schools.* New York: Teachers College Press.

Fractor, J. S., Woodruff, M. C., Martinez, M. G., & Teale, W. H. (1993). Let's not miss opportunities to promote voluntary reading: Classroom libraries in the elementary school. *The Reading Teacher, 46,* 476–484.

Freeman, D., & Freeman, Y. (1994). *Between worlds: Access to second language acquisition.* Portsmouth, NH: Heinemann.

Fried, C., Hershey, P., Koblitz, D., Stiles, B., Stotts, N., Unanue, M., Woodman, M., & Pierce, K. (1995). Children's books: Mysteries of a child's world. *The Reading Teacher, 48,* 508–516.

Fries, C. C. (1963). *Linguistics and reading.* New York: Holt, Rinehart & Winston, Inc.

Fromkin, V., & Rodman, R. (1974). *An introduction to language.* New York: Holt, Rinehart, & Winston, Inc.

Gaffney, J. S., & Anderson, R. C. (1991). Two-tiered scaffolding: Congruent processes of teaching and learning. In E. H. Hiebert (Ed.), *Literacy for a diverse society: Perspectives, practices, and policies* (pp. 184–198). New York: Teachers College Press.

Gallagher, J. M., & Sigel, I. E. (1987). Introduction to special issue: Hothousing for young children. *Early Childhood Research Quarterly, 2,* 201–202.

Gates, A. I. (1937). The necessary mental age for beginning reading. *The Elementary School Journal, 37,* 497–508.

Gavelek, J. R., & Raphael, T. E. (1996). Changing talk about text: New roles for teachers and students. *Language Arts, 73(3),* 182–192.

Gentry, J. R. (1982). An analysis of developmental spelling in GNYS AT WRK. *The Reading Teacher, 36,* 192–199.

Gentry, J. R., & Gillet, J. W. (1992). *Teaching kids to spell.* Portsmouth, NH: Heinemann.

Gesell, A. L. (1925). *The mental growth of the preschool child.* New York: Macmillan.

Goatley, V., Highfield, K., Bentley, J., Pardo, L. S., Folkert, J., Scherer, P., Raphael, T. E., & Grattan, K. (1994). Empowering teachers to be researchers: A collaborative approach. Teacher Research: *The Journal of Classroom Inquiry, 1,* 128–144.

Goatley, V. J. (1995). *The literacy communities of emergent readers and writers: A sociocultural perspective.* Unpublished doctoral dissertation, Michigan State University, East Lansing, MI.

Goldenberg, C. (1990). Beginning literacy for Spanish-speaking children. *Language Arts, 67,* 590–598.

Goldenberg, C., & Gallimore, R. (1991). Local knowledge, research knowledge, and educational change: A case study of first-grade Spanish reading improvement. *Educational Researcher, 20(8),* 2–14.

Goldenberg, C., Reese, L., & Gallimore, R. (1992). Effects of school literacy materials on Latino children's home experiences and early reading achievement. *American Journal of Education, 100,* 497–536.

Goldenberg, C. (1994). Promoting early literacy development among Spanish-speaking children: Lessons from two studies. In E. H. Hiebert & B. M. Taylor (Eds.), *Getting reading right from the start: Effective early literacy interventions* (pp. 171–199). Boston, MA: Allyn & Bacon.

Goodman, K. S. (1973). Miscues: Windows on the reading process. In K. Goodman (Ed.), *Miscue analysis: Applications to reading instruction* (pp. 3–14). Urbana, IL: National Council of Teachers of English/ERIC Clearinghouse on Reading & Communication Skills.

Goodman, K. S., & Goodman, Y. M. (1979). Learning to read is natural. In L. B. Resnick & P. A. Weaver (Eds.), *Theory and practice of early reading* (pp. 137–153). Hillsdale, NJ: Lawrence Erlbaum Associates, Publishers.

Goodman, Y. M. (1985). Kidwatching: Observing children in the classroom. In A. Jaggar & M. T. Smith-Burke (Eds.), *Observing the language learner* (pp. 9–18). Newark, DE: International Reading Association.

Goodman, K. (1986). *What's whole in whole language.* Portsmouth, NH: Heinemann.

Goodman, Y. M., Watson, D. J., & Burke, C. L. (1987). *Reading miscue inventory: Alternative procedures.* New York: Richard Owen Publishers.

Goodman, K. S. (1989). Whole-language research: Foundations and development. *Elementary School Journal, 90,* 207–222.

Goswami, U., & Mead, F. (1992). Onset and rime awareness and analogies in reading. *Reading Research Quarterly, 27,* 152–163.

Gough, P., & Hillinger, M. L. (1980). Learning to read: An unnatural act. *Bulletin of the Orton Society, 30,* 179–196.

Grattan, K. (in press). "They can do it too!" Using book club components with first and second graders. In S. I. McMahon & T. E. Raphael (Eds.), *The book club project: Exploring literature-based literacy instruction.* New York: Teachers College Press.

Graves, D. H., & Hansen, J. (1983). The author's chair. *Language Arts, 60,* 176–183.

Greene, J. (1985). Children's writing in an elementary school postal system. In M. Farr (Ed.), *Advances in writing research: Children's early writing development* (pp. 201–296). Norwood, NJ: Ablex.

Greenlee, M., Hiebert, E. H., Bridge, C. A., & Winograd, P. N. (1986). The effects of different audiences on young writers' letter writing. In J. Niles & R. Lalik (Eds.), *Solving problems in literacy: Learners, teachers, and researchers.* Rochester, NY: National Reading Conference.

Gury, E. C. (1994). *Interactive book reading events as the context for a kindergarten intervention.* Unpublished dissertation, University of Colorado at Boulder.

Hagerty, P., Hiebert, E. H., & Owens, M. K. (1989). Students' comprehension, writing, and perceptions in two approaches to literacy instruction. In S. McCormick & J. Zutell (Eds.), *Cognitive and social perspectives for literacy research and instruction* (pp. 453–460). Chicago, IL: National Reading Conference.

Hall, G. S. (1904). *The psychology of adolescence.* New York: Appleton.

Halliday, M. A. K. (1977). *Learning how to mean.* New York: Elsevier North-Holland, Inc.

Harre, R. (1986). The step to social constructionism. In M. P. M. Richards & P. Light (Eds.), *Children of social worlds.* Oxford, England: Polity Press.

Harste, J. C., Short, K. G., & Burke, C. (1988). *Creating classrooms for authors: The reading-writing connection.* Portsmouth, NH: Heinemann.

Harste, J. C., & Woodward, V. A. (1989). Fostering needed change in early literacy programs. In D. S. Strickland & L. M. Morrow (Eds.), *Emerging literacy: Young children learn to read and write* (pp. 147–159). Newark, DE: International Reading Association.

Harste, J. C., & Burke, C. L. (1993). Foreward: On gaining a literate identity. In J. P. Slaughter (Ed.), *Beyond storybooks: Young children and the shared book experience* (pp. v–vii). Newark, DE: International Reading Association.

Heath, S. B. (1982). What no bedtime story means: Narrative skills at home and school. *Language in Society, 11,* 49–76.

Heath, S. B. (1983). *Ways with words: Language, life, and work in communities and classrooms.* Cambridge, MA: Harvard University Press.

Heath, S. B., & Thomas, C. (1984). The achievement of preschool literacy for mother and child. In H. Goelman, A. Oberg, & F. Smith (Eds.), *Awakening to literacy.* Portsmouth, NH: Heinemann.

Heath, S. B. (1991). The sense of being literate: Historical and cross-cultural features. In R. Barr, M. L. Kamil, P. B. Mosenthal, & P. D. Pearson (Eds.), *Handbook of reading research* (pp. 3–25). New York: Longman.

Hemmeter, A. (1991). Emergent literacy. In R. C. Anderson & K. H. Au (Eds.), *Teaching reading: Strategies for successful classrooms* (six-part videotape series). Urbana-Champaign, IL: Center for the Study of Reading.

Herman, J. L., Morris, L. L., & Fitz-Gibbon, C. T. (1987). *Evaluator's Handbook.* Newbury Park, CA: Sage Publications.

Hiebert, E. H. (1978). Preschool children's understanding of written language. *Child Development, 49,* 1231–1248.

Hiebert, E. H. (1979). *The development of reading-related knowledge over the preschool years.* Unpublished doctoral dissertation, University of Wisconsin-Madison.

Hiebert, E. H. (1983). A comparison of young children's self-selected reading words and basal reading words. *Reading Improvement, 20,* 41–44.

Hiebert, E. H., & Papierz, J. (1990). The content of kindergarten and readiness books in four basal reading programs. *Early Childhood Research Quarterly, 5,* 317–334.

Hiebert, E. H., Hutchinson, T. A., & Raines, P. A. (1991). Alternative assessments of literacy: Teachers' actions and parents' reactions. In S. McCormick & J. Zutell (Eds.), *Learner factors/teacher factors: Issues in literacy research and instruction* (40th Yearbook of the National Reading Conference) (pp. 97–105). Chicago: National Reading Conference.

Hiebert, E. H., Colt, J. M., Catto, S., & Gury, E. (1991). [Text-level and word-level performances of students in restructured and regular Chapter I programs at fall, winter, and spring of their first-grade grade year]. Unpublished raw data.

Hiebert, E. H., Colt, J. M., Catto, S., & Gury, E. (1992). Reading and writing of first-grade students in a restructured Chapter 1 program. *American Educational Research Journal, 29,* 545–572.

Hiebert, E. H. (1993). Young children's literacy experiences in home and school. In S. R. Yussen & M. C. Smith (Eds.), *Reading across the life span* (pp. 33–55). New York: Springer-Verlag.

Hiebert, E. H., & Taylor, B. M. (1994). *Getting reading right from the start: Effective early literacy interventions.* Boston: Allyn & Bacon.

Hiebert, E. H., Burton, N., & Goudvis, A. (December 1989). *Knowing how to read and write: Strategies of students in whole language classrooms.* Paper presented at the annual meeting of the National Reading Conference, Austin, TX.

Hiebert, E. H., & Coffey, M. (November 1983). *Parents involving their children with environmental print.* Paper presented at the annual meeting of the National Reading Conference, Dallas, TX.

Hiebert, E. H., Liu, G., Levin, L., Huxley, A., & Chung, K. (November 1995). *First graders reading the new first-grade readers.* In National Reading Conference, New Orleans, LA.

Hoffman, E. (1989). *Lost in translation.* New York: E. P. Dutton.

Hoffman, J. V. (1991). Teacher and school effects in learning to read. In R. Barr, M. Kamil, P. Mosenthal, & P. D. Pearson (Eds.), *Handbook of reading research* (pp. 911–950). New York: Longman.

Hoffman, J. V. (1992). Critical reading/thinking across the curriculum: using I-Charts to support learning. *Language Arts, 69,* 121–127.

Hoffman, J. V., Roser, N. L., & Battle, J. (1993). Reading aloud in classrooms: From the model to a "model." *The Reading Teacher, 46,* 496–503.

Hoffman, J. V., McCarthey, S. J., Abbott, J., Christian, C., Corman, L., Dressman, M., Elliot, B., Matheme, D., & Stahle, D. (1994). So what's new in the "new" basals. *Journal of Reading Behavior, 26,* 47–73.

Holdaway, D. (1979). *The foundations of literacy.* Sydney, Australia: Ashton Scholastic.

Hubbard, R. (1989). Notes from underground: Unofficial literacy in one sixth grade. *Anthropology and Education, 20,* 291–307.

Hubbard, R., & Powell, B. (1993). *The art of classroom inquiry: A handbook for teacher-researchers.* Portsmouth, NH: Heinemann.

Hughes, S. M. (1993). The impact of whole language on four elementary school libraries. *Language Arts, 70,* 393–399.

Hymes, D. (1974). *Foundations in sociolinguistics: An ethnographic approach.* Philadelphia, PA: University of Pennsylvania Press.

Hyson, M., Hirsch-Pasek, K., & Rescorla, L. (1990). The classroom practices inventory: An observation instrument based on NAEYC's guidelines for developmentally appropriate practices for 4- and 5-year-old children. *Early Childhood Research Quarterly, 5,* 475–494.

Idaho Literacy Project (1991). *Read to me.* Newark, DE: International Reading Association.

Jenks, C., & Roberts, J. (1990). Reading, writing, and reviewing: Teacher, librarian, and young readers collaborate. *Language Arts, 67,* 742–745.

Johnson, F. (November 1995). *What words do children remember from predictable text?* Paper presented at the annual meeting of the National Reading Conference, New Orleans, LA.

Juel, C., & Roper-Schneider, D. (1985). The influence of basal readers on first-grade reading. *Reading Research Quarterly, 20,* 134–152.

Juel, C., Griffith, P. L., & Gough, P. B. (1986). The acquisition of literacy: A longitudinal study of children in first and second grade. *Journal of Educational Psychology, 78,* 243–255.

Juel, C. (1990). Effects of reading group assignment on reading development in first and second grade. *Journal of Reading Behavior, 22,* 233–254.

Juel, C. (1991). Beginning reading. In R. Barr, M. L. Kamil, P. B. Mosenthal, & P. D. Pearson (Eds.), *Handbook of reading research* (pp. 759–788). New York: Longman.

Juel, C. (1994). At-risk university students tutoring at-risk elementary school children: What factors make it effective? In E. H. Hiebert & B. M. Taylor (Eds.), *Getting reading right from the start: Effective early literacy interventions* (pp. 39–61). Boston, MA: Allyn & Bacon.

Juel, C. (1996). *Phonemic awareness: What is it?* Needham, MA: Silver Burdett Ginn.

Keegan, S., & Shrake, K. (1991). Literature study groups: An alternative to ability grouping. *The Reading Teacher, 44,* 542–546.

Klare, G. (1984). Readability. In P. D. Pearson, R. Barr, M. Kamil, & P. Mosenthal (Eds.), *Handbook of reading research* (pp. 681–744). New York: Longman.

Knapp, M. S., Shields, P. M., & Turnbull, B. J. (1992). *Academic challenge for the children of poverty: Summary report.* Menlo Park, CA: SRI International.

Knipping, N. Y. (1993). Let drama help young authors "re-see" their stories. *Language Arts, 70,* 45–50.

Labbo, L. D., & Teale, W. H. (1990). Cross-age reading: A strategy for helping poor readers. *The Reading Teacher, 43,* 362–369.

LaBerge, D., & Samuels, S. (1974). Toward a theory of automatic information processing in reading. *Cognitive Psychology, 6,* 293–323.

Ladson-Billings, G. (1994). *The dreamkeepers: Successful teachers of African-American children.* San Francisco, CA: Jossey-Bass Publishers.

Laird, J., Crawford, K. M., Ferguson, M., Kauffman, G., Schroeder, J., & Short, K. (1994). Teachers as collaborators for an inquiry-based curriculum: *Teacher Research. The Journal of Classroom Inquiry, 1,* 111–121.

Lamme, L. L., & Ledbetter, L. (1990). Libraries: The heart of whole language. *Language Arts, 67,* 735–740.

Lesgold, A. M., Resnick, L. B., & Hammond, L. (1985). Learning to read: A longitudinal study of word skill development in two curricula. In W. MacKinnon (Ed.), *Reading research advances in theory and practice* (pp. 107–137). Orlando, FL: Academic Press.

Leto, D. J. (1995). Focus on research: Creating community with an after-school tutoring program. *Language Arts, 72,* 128–136.

Lidz, C. (Ed.). (1987). *Dynamic assessment: An interactional approach to evaluating learning potential.* New York: Guilford.

Lightfoot, S. L. (1978). *Worlds apart: Relationships between families and schools.* New York: Basic Books.

Lindfors, J. W. (1980). *Children's language and learning.* Englewood Cliffs, NJ: Prentice-Hall.

Lipson, M. Y., & Wixson, K. (1991). *Assessment and instruction of reading disability: An interactive approach.* New York: HarperCollins Publishers.

Lipson, M. Y., Valencia, S. W., Wixson, K. K., & Peters, C. W. (1993). Integration and thematic teaching: Integration to improve teaching and learning. *Language Arts, 70,* 252–263.

Lobach, M. R. (1995). Kids explore heritage through writers workshops and professional publication. *The Reading Teacher, 48,* 522–524.

Lundberg, I., Frost, J., & Petersen, O. (1988). Effects of an extensive program for stimulating phonological awareness in preschool children. *Reading Research Quarterly, 23,* 263–283.

Lyons, C. A., Pinnell, G. S., & DeFord, D. E. (1993). *Partners in learning: Teachers and children in Reading Recovery.* New York: Teachers College Press.

MacGillivray, L., & King, J. R. (1995). Inside/Out: Talking and questioning our teaching selves through e-mail exchanges. In K. A. Hinchman, D. J. Leu, & C. Kinzer (Eds.), *Perspectives on literacy research and practice* (pp. 407–415). Chicago, IL: The National Reading Conference, Inc.

Magnusson, S., & Palincsar, A. S. (1995). Learning environments as a site of science education reform: An illustration using interdisciplinary guided inquiry. *Theory into Practice, 34,* 43–50.

Martin, B., & Brogan, P. (1971). *Teacher's guide to the instant readers.* New York: Holt, Rinehart, & Winston.

Martin, L. A. (1997). *Becoming literate in school: Examining the profiles of first-grade readers in Chapter 1.* Paper presented at the annual meeting of the American Educational Research Association, Chicago, IL.

Martine, D. H. (1991). Reading-writing connections. In R. C. Anderson & K. H. Au (Eds.), *Teaching reading: Strategies for successful classrooms* (six-part videotape series). Urbana-Champaign, IL: Center for the Study of Reading.

Martinez, M. G., & Teale, W. H. (1988). Reading in a kindergarten classroom library. *The Reading Teacher, 41,* 568–572.

Martinez, M., Cheyney, M., McBroom, C., Hemmeter, A., & Teale, W. (1989). No-risk kindergarten literacy environments for at-risk children. In J. Allen & J. Mason (Eds.), *Risk-makers, risk takers, risk breakers: Reducing the risks for young literacy learners* (pp. 93–124). Portsmouth, NH: Heinemann.

Martinez, M. G., & Teale, W. H. (1993). Teacher storybook reading style: A comparison of six teachers. *Research in the Teaching of English, 27,* 175–199.

Mason, J. M. (1980). When do children begin to read: An exploration of four-year-old children's letter and word reading competencies. *Reading Research Quarterly, 25,* 203–227.

Mason, J. M., Peterman, C. L., Powell, B. M., & Kerr, B. M. (1989). Reading and writing attempts by kindergarteners after book reading by teachers. In J. M. Mason (Ed.), *Reading and writing connections* (pp. 105–120). Needham Heights, MA: Allyn & Bacon.

Masonheimer, P. E., Drum, P. A., & Ehri, L. C. (1984). Does environmental print identification lead children into word reading? *Journal of Reading Behavior, 14,* 257–271.

Matlin, M. L., & Wortman, R. C. (1989). Observing readers and writers: A teacher and a researcher learn together. In G. S. Pinnell & M. L. Matlin (Eds.), *Teachers and research: Language learning in the classroom.* Newark, DE: International Reading Association.

McCaslin, N. (1990). *Creative drama in the classroom.* New York: Longman.

McCauley, J. K., & McCauley, D. S. (1992). Using choral reading to promote language learning for ESL students. *The Reading Teacher, 45,* 526–533.

McCormick, C. E., & Mason, J. M. (1989). Fostering reading for Head Start children with little books. In J. B. Allen & J. M. Mason (Eds.), *Risk makers, risk takers, risk breakers: Reducing the risks for young literacy learners* (pp. 154–177). Portsmouth, NH: Heinemann.

McGee, L. M. (1992). An exploration of meaning construction in first graders' grand conversations. In C. K. Kinzer & D. J. Leu (Eds.), *Literacy research, theory, and practice: Views from many perspectives* (pp. 177–186). Chicago, IL: National Reading Conference.

McGill-Frahzen, A., & Lanford, C. (1994). Exposing the edge of preschool curriculum: Teachers' talk about text and children's literary understandings. *Language Arts, 71,* 264–273.

McLane, J., & McNamee, G. (1990). *Early literacy.* Cambridge, MA: Harvard University Press.

McMahon, S., & Raphael, T. E. (Eds.). (in press). *The book club project: Exploring literature-based literacy instruction.* New York: Teachers College Press.

Mehan, H. (1979). *Learning lessons.* Cambridge: Harvard University Press.

Mehan, H. (1982). The structure of classroom events and their consequences for student's performance. In P. Gilmore & A. A. Glatthorn (Eds.), *Children in and out of school.* Washington, DC: Center for Applied Linguistics.

Mervar, K., & Hiebert, E. H. (1989). *Literature-selection strategies and amount of reading in two literacy approaches.* In S. McCormick & J. Zutell (Eds.), *Cognitive and Social Perspectives for Literacy Research and Instruction* (38th Yearbook of the National Reading Conference), pp. 529–535. Chicago, IL: NRC.

Meyer, B. J. F. (1975). *The organization of prose and its effects on memory.* Amsterdam: North Holland.

Michaels, S. (1981). "Sharing time": Children's narrative styles and differential access to literacy. *Language in Society, 10,* 423–442.

Mishler, E. G. (1972). Implications of teacher strategies for language and cognition: Observations in first-grade classrooms. In C. B. Cazden, V. P. John, & D. Hymes (Eds.), *Functions of language in the classroom.* New York: Teachers College Press.

Montessori, M. (1964). *The Montessori method.* New York: Schoken Books.

Moore, M. A. (1991). Electronic dialoguing: An avenue to literacy. *The Reading Teacher, 45,* 280–286.

Morphett, M. V., & Washburne, C. (1931). When should children begin to read? *Elementary School Journal, 31,* 496–503.

Morrice, C., & Simmons, M. (1991). Beyond reading buddies: A whole language cross-age program. *The Reading Teacher, 44,* 572–577.

Morrow, L. M., & Weinstein, C. S. (1982). Increasing the children's use of literature through program and physical design changes. *Elementary School Journal, 83,* 131–137.

Morrow, L. M., & Parse, R. (1990). Early literacy strategies: Activities represented in current basal readers. In J. Zutell & S. McCormick (Eds.), *Literacy theory and research: Analyses from multiple paradigms, 39* (pp. 381–393). The National Reading Conference, Inc.

Morrow, L. M., & Rand, M. K. (1991). Promoting literacy during play by designing early childhood classroom environments. *The Reading Teacher, 44,* 396–402.

Morrow, L. M., & Neuman, S. B. (1995). Themed issue: Family literacy. *The Reading Teacher, 48,* 550–551.

Morrow, L. M. (Ed.). (1995). *Family literacy connections in schools and communities.* Newark, DE: International Reading Association.

Mosenthal, P., & Na, T. J. (1980). Quality of children's recall under two classroom testing tasks: Towards a socio-psycholinguistic model of reading comprehension. *Reading Research Quarterly, 25,* 504–528.

Mullis, I. V. S., Campbell, J. R., & Farstrup, A. E. (1993). *NAEP 1992: Reading report card for the nation and the states.* Washington, DC: U.S. Government Printing Office.

National Assessment of Chapter 1 Review Panel (1993). *Reinventing Chapter 1: The current Chapter 1 program and new directions.* Washington, DC: U.S. Department of Education.

NCTE/IRA (1996). *Standards for the English Language Arts.* Urbana, IL & Newark, DE: NCTE & IRA.

Newkirk, T. (1989). *More than stories: The range of children's writing.* Portsmouth, NH: Heinemann.

O'Flahavan, J. F. (1989). *Second graders' social, intellectual, and affective development in varied group discussions about narrative texts: An exploration of participation structure.* Unpublished doctoral dissertation, University of Illinois at Urbana-Champaign.

Paley, V. G. (1986). On listening to what the children say. *Harvard Educational Review, 56,* 122–131.

Palincsar, A. S., & Brown, A. L. (1984). Reciprocal teaching of comprehension-fostering and comprehension-monitoring activities. *Cognition and Instruction, 1,* 117–175.

Palincsar, A., & David, Y. M. (1991). Promoting literacy through classroom dialogue. In E. H. Hiebert (Ed.), *Literacy for a diverse society* (pp. 122–140). New York: Teachers College Press.

Panofsky, C. P., John-Steiner, V., & Blackwell, P. J. (1990). The development of scientific concepts and discourse. In L. C. Moll (Ed.), *Vygotsky and education: Instructional implications and applications of sociohistorical psychology* (pp. 251–267). New York: Cambridge University Press.

Papierz, J. M., Hiebert, E. H., & DiStefano, D. D. (1990, December). *Literacy experiences of preschool children.* Paper presented at the annual meeting of the National Reading Conference, Miami, FL.

Pappas, C. C., Kiefer, B. Z., & Levstik, L. S. (1990). *An integrated language perspective in the elementary school.* White Plains, NY: Longman.

Paradis, E. E., Chatton, B., Smith, M., & Yovich, S. (1991). Accountability: Assessing comprehension during literature discussion. *The Reading Teacher, 45,* 8–17.

Pardo, L. S., & Raphael, T. E. (1991). Classroom organization for instruction in content areas. *The Reading Teacher, 44,* 556–564.

Paris, S. G., Lipson, M. Y., & Wixson, K. K. (1983). Becoming a strategic reader. *Contemporary Educational Psychology, 8,* 293–316.

Paris, S., Wasik, B., & Turner, J. (1991). The development of strategic readers. In R. Barr, M. Kamil, P. Mosenthal, & P. D. Pearson (Eds.), *Handbook of reading research.* New York: Longman.

Pearson, P. D. (1993). Standards for the English Language Arts: A policy perspective. *Journal of Reading Behavior, 25,* 457–475.

Pellegrini, A. D., Perlmutter, J. C., Galda, L., & Brophy, G. H. (1990). Joint book reading between black Head Start children and their mothers. *Child Development, 61,* 443–453.

Pellegrini, A. D., & Galda, L. (1993). Ten years after: A reexamination of symbolic play and literacy research. *Reading Research Quarterly, 28,* 163–175.

Peretti, C. A., Beck, I., Bell, L., & Hughes, C. (1987). Phonemic knowledge and learning to read are reciprocal: A longitudinal study of first grade children. *Merrill-Palmer Quarterly, 33,* 283–319.

Perkins, W. H. (1971). *Speech pathology: An applied science.* St. Louis: Mosby.

Peterson, B. (1991). Selecting books for beginning readers: Children's literature suitable for young readers: A bibliography. In D. E. DeFord, C. A. Lyons, & G. S. Pinnell (Eds.), *Bridges to literacy: Learning from Reading Recovery* (pp. 119–147). Portsmouth, NH: Heinemann.

Philips, S. U. (1972). Participant structures and communicative competence: Warm Springs children in community and classroom. In C. B. Cazden, V. John, & D. Hymes (Eds.), *Functions of language in the classroom.* New York: Teachers College Press.

Piaget, J. (1962). *Play, dreams, and imitation in childhood.* New York: W. W. Norton.

Piaget, J. (1977). *The development of thought: Equilibration of cognitive structures.* New York: Viking.

Pikulski, J. J. (1994). Preventing reading failure: A review of five effective programs. *The Reading Teacher, 48,* 30–39.

Pils, L. J. (1991). Soon anofe you tout me: Evaluation in a first-grade whole language classroom. *The Reading Teacher, 45,* 46–50.

Pinnell, G. S., & McCarrier, A. (1994). Interactive writing: A transition tool for assisting children in learning to read and write. In E. H. Hiebert & B. M. Taylor (Eds.), *Getting reading right from the start: Effective early literacy interventions* (pp. 149–170). Boston, MA: Allyn & Bacon.

Poplin, M. (1988). Holistic/constructivist principles: Implications for the field of learning disabilities. *Journal of Learning Disabilities, 21,* 401–416.

Purcell-Gates, V., L'Allier, S., & Smith, D. (1995). Literacy at the Harts' and the Larsons': Diversity among poor, inner-city families. *The Reading Teacher, 48,* 572–578.

Purkey, S. C., & Smith, M. S. (1983). Effective schools: A review. *The Elementary School Journal, 83,* 427–452.

Purves, A. C. (Ed.). (1994). *Encyclopedia of English Studies and Language Arts.* New York: Scholastic/National Council of Teachers of English.

Radencich, M., McKay, L. J., & Paratore, J. R. (1995). Keeping flexible groups flexible: Grouping options. In M. C. Radencich &

L. J. McKay (Eds.), *Flexible grouping for literacy in the elementary grades.* Boston: Allyn & Bacon.

Rankin, J. (1992). Connecting literacy learnings: A pen pal project. *The Reading Teacher, 46,* 204–214.

Raphael, T. E., McMahon, S. I., Goatley, V. J., Bentley, J. L., Boyd, F. B., Pardo, L. S., & Woodman, D. A. (1991). *Reading instruction reconsidered: Literature and discussion in the reading program.* In (Vol. Series No. 47) East Lansing, MI: Center for the Learning & Teaching of Elementary Subjects, Institute for Research on Teaching.

Raphael, T. E., & Goatley, V. J. (1994). The teacher as "more knowledgeable other": Changing roles for teaching in alternative reading instruction programs. In C. Kinzer & D. Leu (Eds.), *Multidimensional aspects of literacy research, theory and practice* (pp. 527–536). Chicago: National Reading Conference.

Raphael, T. E., & McMahon, S. I. (1994). 'Book Club': An alternative framework for reading instruction. *The Reading Teacher, 48(2),* 102–116.

Raphael, T. E., Goatley, V. J., McMahon, S. I., & Woodman, D. A. (1995). Promoting meaningful conversations in student book clubs. In N. Roser & M. Martinez (Eds.), *Book talk and beyond* (pp. 71–83). Newark, DE: International Reading Association.

Raphael, T., & Hiebert, E. H. (1996). *Creating an integrated approach to literacy instruction.* New York: Harcourt Brace College Publishers.

Rasmussen, D., & Goldberg, L. (1964). *The Bad Fan (Level A, Basic Reading Series).* Chicago: Science Research Associates.

Read, C. (1975). *Children's categorization of speech sounds in English.* Urbana, IL: National Council of Teachers of English.

Read, C. (1971). Preschool children's knowledge of English phonology. *Harvard Educational Review, 41,* 1–34.

Reutzel, D. R., & Fawson, P. C. (1990). Traveling tales: Connecting parents and children through writing. *The Reading Teacher, 44,* 222–227.

Reutzel, D. R., & Cotter, R. B., Jr. (1991). Organizing for effective instruction: The reading workshop. *The Reading Teacher, 44,* 548–554.

Reutzel, D. R., Hollingsworth, P. M., & Eldredge, J. L. (1994). Oral reading instruction: The impact on student reading development. *Reading Research Quarterly, 29,* 41–62.

Rhodes, L. K., & Nathenson-Mejia, S. (1992). Anecdotal records: A powerful tool for ongoing literacy assessment. *The Reading Teacher, 45,* 502–510.

Richardson, V. (1994). Conducting research on practice. *Educational Researcher, 23,* 5–10.

Richek, M. A., & Glick, L. C. (1991). Coordinating a literacy support program with classroom instruction. *The Reading Teacher, 44,* 474–479.

Richgels, D. J. (1995). A kindergarten sign-in procedure: A routine in support of written language learning. In K. A. Hinchman, D. J. Leu, & C. Kinzer (Eds.), *Perspectives on literacy research and practice.* Chicago, IL: National Reading Conference, Inc.

Rider, N. F. (1986). Tiny. In W. K. Durr, J. J. Pikulski, et al. (Eds.), *Bells.* Boston: Houghton Mifflin Co.

Rodríguez, R. (1981). *Hunger of memory.* New York: D. R. Godine.

Rowan, B., & Guthrie, L. F. (1989). The quality of Chapter 1 instruction: Results from a study of twenty-four schools. In R. E. Slavin, N. L. Karweit, & N. A. Madden (Eds.), *Effective programs for students at risk* (pp. 195–219). Boston, MA: Allyn & Bacon.

Rowe, D. W. (1989). Author/audience interaction in the preschool: The role of social interaction in literacy learning. *Journal of Reading Behavior, 21,* 311–347.

Rowe, M. B. (1986). Wait time: Slowing down may be a way of speeding up! *Journal of Teacher Education, 37,* 43–50.

Rueda, R. (1991). Characteristics of literacy programs for language-minority students. In E. H. Hiebert (Ed.), *Literacy for a diverse society: Perspectives, practices, and policies* (pp. 93–107). New York: Teachers College Press.

Samuels, S. J. (1972). The effect of letter-name knowledge on learning to read. *American Educational Research Journal, 9,* 65–86.

Santmyer, H. H. (1982). *And ladies of the club.* New York: Putnam's.

Schank, R. C. (1973). Identification of conceptualizations underlying natural language. In R. C. Shank & K. M. Colby (Eds.), *Computer models of thought and language* (pp. 187–248). San Francisco: Freeman.

Schickedanz, J. A. (1986). *More than the ABCs.* Washington, DC: National Association for the Education of Young Children.

School Readiness Task Force (1988). *Here they come: Ready or not!* Sacramento, CA: California Department of Education.

Searle, J. R. (1969). *Speech acts: An essay in the philosophy of language.* New York: Cambridge University Press.

Shanahan, T., Mulhern, M., & Rodríguez-Brown, F. (1995). Project FLAME: Lessons learned from a family learning program for linguistic minority families. *The Reading Teacher, 48,* 586–593.

Shanklin, N. L., & Rhodes, L. K. (1989). Comprehension instruction as sharing and extending. *The Reading Teacher, 42,* 496–500.

Sharan, S. (1990). Cooperative learning and helping behavior in multi-ethnic classrooms. In H. C. Foot, M. J. Morgan, & R. H. Shute (Eds.), *Children helping children* (pp. 151–176). New York: John Wiley & Sons.

Shepard, L. A., & Graue, M. E. (1992). The morass of school readiness screening: Research on test use and test validity. In B. Spodek (Ed.), *Handbook of research on the education of young children* (pp. 293–305). New York: Macmillan.

Shockley, B. (1994). Extending the literate community: Home-to-school and school-to-home. *The Reading Teacher, 47,* 500–502.

Shockley, B., Michaelove, B., & Allen, J. (1995). *Engaging families.* Portsmouth, NH: Heinemann.

Silvaroli, N. (1990). *Classroom reading inventory* (6th ed.). Dubuque, IA: Wm. C. Brown Publishers.

Sinclair, J. M., & Coulthard, R. M. (1975). *Towards an analysis of discourse: The English used by teachers and pupils.* London: Oxford University Press.

Slavin, R. E., Madden, N. A., Karweit, N. L., Donlan, L. J., & Wasik, B. A. (1994). Success for all: Getting reading right the first time. In E. H. Hiebert & B. M. Taylor (Eds.), *Getting reading right from the start: Effective early literacy interventions* (pp. 125–147). Boston: Allyn & Bacon.

Smith, N. B. (1934/1965). *American reading instruction.* Newark, DE: International Reading Association.

Snow, C. E. (1983). Language and literacy: Relationships during the preschool years. *Harvard Educational Review, 53,* 165–189.

Snow, C. E., & Ninio, A. (1986). The contracts of literacy: What children learn from learning to read books. In W. H. Teale & E. Sulzby (Eds.), *Emergent Literacy: Writing and reading* (pp. 116–138). Norwood, NJ: Ablex.

Songer, N. B. (1996). Exploring learning opportunities in coordinated network-enhanced classrooms: A case of kids as global scientists. *The Journal of Learning Sciences, 5,* 297–327.

Stallman, A. C., & Pearson, P. D. (1990). Formal measures of early literacy. In L. M. Morrow & J. K. Smith (Eds.), *Assessment for instruction in early literacy.* Englewood Cliffs, NJ: Prentice-Hall.

Stanovich, K. E., Cunningham, A. E., & Cramer, B. (1984). Assessing phonological awareness in kindergarten children: Issues of task comparability. *Journal of Experimental Child Psychology, 38,* 175–190.

Stanovich, K. E. (1986). Matthew effects in reading: Some consequences of individual differences in the acquisition of literacy. *Reading Research Quarterly, 21,* 360–406.

Stein, N. L., & Glenn, C. G. (1979). An analysis of story comprehension in elementary children. In R. Freedie (Ed.), *New directions in discourse processing* (pp. 53–120). Norwood, NJ: Ablex.

Stein, N. L., & Trabasso, T. (1982). What's in a story: An approach to comprehension and instruction. In R. Glaser (Ed.), *Advances in the psychology of instruction.* Hillsdale, NJ: Lawrence Erlbaum Associates.

Strickland, D. S. (1989). A model for change: Framework for an emergent literacy curriculum. In D. S. Strickland & L. M. Morrow (Eds.), *Emerging literacy: Young children learn to read and write* (pp. 135–146). Newark, DE: International Reading Association.

Sulzby, E. (1985). Children's emergent reading of favorite storybooks: A developmental study. *Reading Research Quarterly, 20,* 458–481.

Sulzby, E., Teale, W. H., & Kamberelis, G. (1989). Emergent writing in the classroom; Home and school connections. In D. S. Strickland & L. M. Morrow (Eds.), *Emerging literacy: Young children learn to read and write* (pp. 63–79). Newark, DE: International Reading Association.

Sulzby, E., & Teale, W. H. (1991). Emergent literacy. In R. Barr, M. L. Kamil, P. Mosenthal, & P. D. Pearson (Eds.), *Handbook of reading research* (pp. 727–757). New York: Longman.

Taylor, B. M., Strait, J., & Medo, M. A. (1994). Early intervention in reading: Supplemental instruction for groups of low-achieving students provided by first-grade teachers. In E. H. Hiebert & B. M. Taylor (Eds.), *Getting ready right from the start: Effective early literacy interventions* (pp. 107–121). Boston: Allyn & Bacon.

Taylor, D. (1991). From the child's point of view: Alternative approaches to assessment. In J. A. Roderick (Ed.), *Context-responsive approaches to assessing children's language.* Urbana, IL: NCRE.

Taylor, D., & Dorsey-Gaines, C. (1988). *Growing up literate.* Portsmouth, NH: Heinemann.

Taylor, N., Blum, I. H., & Logsdon, D. M. (1986). The development of written language awareness: Environmental aspects and program characteristics. *Reading Research Quarterly, 21,* 131–149.

Teachers' Choices (1994). Primary level. *The Reading Teacher, 48,* 239–241.

Teale, W. H. (1986). Home background and young children's literacy development. In W. H. Teale & E. Sulzby (Eds.), *Emergent literacy: Writing and reading* (pp. 173–206). Norwood, NJ: Ablex.

Teale, W. H. (1987). Emergent literacy: Reading and writing development in early childhood. In J. E. Readence & R. S. Baldwin (Eds.), *Research in literacy: Merging perspectives* (pp. 45–74). Rochester, NY: National Reading Conference.

Teale, W. H., & E. Sulzby (Eds.). (1986). *Emergent literacy: Writing and reading.* Norwood, NJ: Ablex.

Temple, C., Nathan, R., Burris, N., & Temple, F. (1988). *The beginnings of writing* (2nd ed.). Boston: Allyn & Bacon.

Texas Education Agency (1990). Proclamation of the State Board of Education advertising for bids on textbooks (Proclamation 68). Austin, TX: Texas Education Agency.

Tharp, R., & Gallimore, R. (1988). *Rousing minds to life: Teaching, learning and schooling in social context.* New York: Cambridge University Press.

Thorndike, E. L. (1903). *Educational psychology.* New York: Lemcke & Buechner.

Tierney, R. J., & Shanahan, T. (1991). Research on the reading-writing relationship: Interactions, transactions, and outcomes. In R. Barr, M. L. Kamil, P. Mosenthal, & P. D. Pearson (Eds.), *Handbook of reading research* (pp. 246–280). New York: Longman.

Tobin, A. W., & Pikulski, J. J. (April 1983). *Parent and teacher attitudes toward early reading instruction.* Paper presented at the annual meeting of the American Educational Research Association, Montreal.

Topping, K. (1988). *The peer tutoring handbook: Promoting co-operative learning.* Cambridge, MA: Brookline Books.

Trelease, J. (1989). *The read-aloud handbook.* New York: Penguin Books.

U.S. Department of Education (1995). *READ-WRITE-NOW: Activities for reading and writing fun.* Washington, DC: U.S. Government Printing Office.

Valencia, S. (1991). Portfolios: Panacea or Pandora's box? In F. Finch (Ed.), *Educational performance testing* (pp. 33–46). Chicago, IL: Riverside.

Valencia, S. (1995, April). *Thematic teaching in the reading program.* Paper presented at the annual meeting of the International Reading Association, Anaheim, CA.

Venezky, R. L. (1967). English ortography: Its graphical structure and its relation to sound. *Reading Research Quarterly, 2,* 75–106.

Venezky, R. L. (1984). The history of reading research. In P. D. Pearson, R. Barr, M. L.

Kamil, & P. Mosenthal (Eds.), *Handbook of reading research* (pp. 3–38). New York: Longman.

Villaume, S. K., Worden, T., Williams, S., Hopkins, L., & Rosenblatt, C. (1994). Five teachers in search of a discussion. *The Reading Teacher, 47(6),* 480–487.

Vogt, L. A., Jordan, C., & Tharp, R. G. (1987). Explaining school failure, producing school success: Two cases. *Anthropology & Education Quarterly, 18,* 276–286.

Vygotsky, L. S. (1962). *Thought and language.* Cambridge, MA: MIT Press.

Vygotsky, L. S. (1978). *Mind in society.* Cambridge, MA: Harvard University Press.

Vygotsky, L. S. (1981). The genesis of higher mental functions. In J. V. Wertsch (Ed.), *The concept of activity in psychology* (pp. 144–188). Armonk, NY: M. E. Sharpe.

Vygotsky, L. S. (1987). Speech and thinking (N. Minick, Trans.). In R. Rieber & A. Carton (Eds.), *The collected works of L. S. Vygotsky* (pp. 39–285). New York: Plenum Press.

Watson, D. J., & Stevenson, M. T. (1989). Teacher support groups: Why and how. In G. S. Pinnell & M. L. Matlin (Eds.), *Teachers and researchers: Language learning in the classroom* (pp. 118–129). Newark, DE: International Reading Association, Inc.

Weaver, C., Stephens, D., & Vance, J. (1990). *Understanding whole language: From principles to practice.* Portsmouth, NH: Heinemann.

Weaver, C., Chaston, J., & Peterson, S. (1993). *Theme exploration: A voyage of discovering.* Portsmouth, NH: Heinemann.

Wells, G. (1986). *The meaning makers: Children learning language and using language to learn.* Portsmouth, NH: Heinemann.

Wilde, S. (1992). *You kan red this! Spelling and punctuation for whole language classrooms, K-6.* Portsmouth, NH: Heinemann.

Wilkinson, L. C., & Dollaghan, C. (1981). Peer communication in first grade reading groups. *Theory into Practice, 18,* 267–274.

Winfield, L. F. (1995). Change in urban schools with high concentrations of low-income children: Chapter 1 schoolwide projects. In R. L. Allington & S. A. Walmsley (Eds.), *No quick fix: Rethinking literacy programs in America's elementary schools* (pp. 214–235). New York: Teachers College Press.

Wolf, S. A. (1993). What's in a name?: Labels and literacy in readers' theatre. *The Reading Teacher, 46,* 540–545.

Women on Words & Images (1975). *Dick and Jane as victims: Sex stereotyping in children's readers.* Princeton, NJ: Women on Words & Images.

Wood, D., Bruner, J., & Ross, S. (1976). The role of tutoring in problem-solving. *Journal of Child Psychology and Psychiatry, 17,* 89–100.

Woods, M. L., & Moe, A. J. (1989). *Analytical Reading Inventory* (4th ed.). Columbus, OH: Charles E. Merrill Publishing Co.

Wylie, R. E., & Durrell, D. D. (1970). Teaching vowels through phonograms. *Elementary English, 47,* 787–791.

Wynn, T. (1993). Instructed and cooperative learning in human evolution. *Behavioral and Brain Sciences, 16,* 539–540.

Yaden, D. B., Jr., Smokin, L. B., & Conlon, A. (1989). Preschoolers' questions about pictures, print convention, and story text during reading aloud at home. *Reading Research Quarterly, 24,* 188–214.

Yussen, S. R., & Santrock, J. W. (1978). *Child development: An introduction.* Dubuque, IA: Wm. C. Brown Co.

Credits

fig. 2.1

Figure 1 from "Changing Talk about Text: New Roles for Teachers and Students," by James Gavelek and Taffy Raphael, *Language Arts*, March 1996. Copyright 1996 by the National Council of Teachers of English. Reprinted with permission.

fig. 3.1

From *You Can Ride* by Amy Koss, illustrated by Darius Detwiler, © 1996 Silver Burdett Ginn Inc. Used with permission.

fig. 5.1

Six Go By by Maryann Dobeck, illustrated by Rosario Valderrama. Part of the *Ready Readers* Series. © 1995 by *Modern Curriculum Press,* Simon & Schuster Elementary. Used by permission.

fig. 6.1, 6.2, 6.3

Reprinted with permission of the Council for Learning Disabilities.

fig. 8.1, 8.2

Reprinted by permission of Jacalyn M. Colt, Instructional Coordinator, Title I, St. Vrain Valley School District, Longmont, CO.

Index

Abbott, J., 6
Accommodation, 10–11
Across the Stream (Ginsburg), 123, 124
Action research, 267–268
Activities
  description and examples of, 152
  library center, 168–171
  listening center, 171
  literacy activities, 167–172
  meaningfulness of, 153
  multiple contexts of, 154
  play center, 171–172
  vignettes on, 150, 151
  writing center, 171, 185–186
Adams, M., 52, 54, 60, 64, 127, 198
Ahlberg, J., 141
Alexander and the Wind-up Mouse (Lionni),
  86–87
All I Am (Roe), 161, 162
Allard, H., 250
Allen, J., 75, 152, 266, 268
Allington, R. L., 37, 69, 165, 167, 191, 222,
  223, 224, 225, 226, 270
Alphabet books, 53
Altwerger, B., 9
American Library Association, 98, 251
Ames, L. J., 250
And Ladies of the Club (Santmyer), 263
Anderson, A. A., 15, 238, 244–245
Anderson, L., 167
Anderson, R. C., 46, 54, 259, 261–262
Anderson, T. H., 61
Angelou, M., 101, 263
Appelt, K., 101
Applebee, A. N., 105
Are You My Mother? (Eastman), 136
Armbruster, B. B., 61
Arnold, T., 100
Arthur's Family Vacation (Brown), 102
Ashe, P. M., 233
Ashman, A. F., 89

Assessment
  book choices, 184–185
  characteristics of miscues and recognized
    words, 207–209
  compositions, 187–190, 209–212
  comprehension, 200–209
  critical responses, 201–204
  defining benchmarks, 178–179, 180, 204–
    206, 227
  dynamic or interactive assessment, 176
  in emergent literacy perspective, 174–177
  fluent reading of increasingly more complex
    texts, 204–207
  gathering information, 179, 181–199
  identifying literacy goals, 177–178
  interviewing, 195–199
  meaningfulness of, 175–176
  observations, 183–195
  oral language and, 176
  oral reading strategies, 185
  performance assessment, 181–183
  portfolios, 181–183
  reflecting on children's learning, 200–212
  responding to specific tasks, 198–199
  running records of reading competencies,
    190–193
  sampling, 186–187
  scaffolding tasks, 197–198
  shared assessments, 226–228
  spelling and usage, 211–212
  vignettes on, 173–174, 176, 177, 186, 191
  word recognition, 204, 207–209
  writing and reading words, 193–195
  writing center activities, 185–186
Assimilation, 10–11
Attendance-taking, 150, 151, 157
Atwell, N., 166
Au, K. H., 77, 78, 178, 268
Auch, M. J., 100
Aukerman, R. C., 4
Author's chair, 84